Creating
Meaning
Through Art

Teacher as
Choice Maker

May a child's story inspire you

love, Jan

Creating Meaning Through Art

Teacher as Choice Maker

Judith W. Simpson
Boston University

Jean M. Delaney
Southwest Missouri State University

Karen Lee Carroll
Maryland Institute, College of Art

Cheryl M. Hamilton
Wichita State University

Sandra I. Kay
Monroe-Woodbury Central Schools

Marianne S. Kerlavage
Millersville University of Pennsylvania

Janet L. Olson
Boston University

Merrill,
an imprint of Prentice Hall
Upper Saddle River, New Jersey   Columbus, Ohio

Library of Congress Cataloging-in-Publication Data

Creating meaning through art : teacher as choice maker / Judith W. Simpson . . . [et al.].
     p. cm.
    Includes bibliographical references and index.
    ISBN 0-13-351421-8 (alk. paper)
    1. Art teachers—Training of—United States. 2. Art—Study and teaching (K–12)—United States. 3.
Children—Psychology. I. Simpson, Judith, W.
   N88.3.C74   1998
   707′.1—dc21   97-7713
                                                     CIP

Cover art: Collection of Judith Simpson, Jean Delaney, Marianne Kerlavage
Editor: Bradley J. Potthoff
Production Editor: Alexandrina Benedicto Wolf
Design Coordinator: Karrie Converse
Text Designer: STELLARViSIONs
Cover Designer: Russ Maselli
Insert Designer: Rod Harris
Production Manager: Patricia A. Tonneman
Electronic Text Management: Marilyn Wilson Phelps, Matthew Williams, Karen L. Bretz, Tracey
    B. Ward
Director of Marketing: Kevin Flanagan
Marketing Manager: Suzanne Stanton
Advertising/Marketing Coordinator: Julie Shough

This book was set in ITC Souvenir and Mirage by Prentice Hall and was printed and bound by
Courier/Kendallville, Inc. The cover was printed by Phoenix Color Corp.

 © 1998 by Prentice-Hall, Inc.
Simon & Schuster/A Viacom Company
Upper Saddle River, New Jersey 07458

Printed in the United States of America

10 9 8 7 6 5 4 3 2

ISBN: 0-13-351421-8

Prentice-Hall International (UK) Limited, *London*
Prentice-Hall of Australia Pty. Limited, *Sydney*
Prentice-Hall of Canada, Inc., *Toronto*
Prentice-Hall Hispanoamericana, S. A., *Mexico*
Prentice-Hall of India Private Limited, *New Delhi*
Prentice-Hall of Japan, Inc., *Tokyo*
Simon & Schuster Asia Pte. Ltd., *Singapore*
Editora Prentice-Hall do Brasil, Ltda., *Rio de Janeiro*

To those who choose to
foster meaning through art

Preface

The major purpose of this book is to introduce preservice art educators to the power of art as a vehicle for creating meaning—the choices they make in their classrooms can provide the opportunity and context for this to occur. The authors of *Creating Meaning Through Art: Teacher as Choice Maker* understand the nature of practice from various perspectives and share over 100 years of experience at all levels of art education. This book is not an anthology but a collaborative effort involving much reflection, dialogue, and choice making.

 ## Philosophy and Intent

Reflective choice making can set the stage for a balanced approach to art education that considers the child, society, and the curriculum. In 1952, Viktor Lowenfeld spoke of art education as embracing "the understanding of social, intellectual, emotional, and psychological changes and the creative needs of the child" (p. 6). Strategies that are planned with developmental principles in mind, and that value the lived experiences each learner brings to the art class, make the kinds of connections that promote understanding, reach learners, and foster the creation of meaning.

We want to help preservice art teachers develop a personal philosophy and an artful approach to teaching. Together the chapters form a composite of issues, ideas, and strategies related to the teaching of art in grades K–12. Because the choices that teachers make influence learning, we present various choices that determine what and how students will learn.

 ## Form and Structure

A major feature of this book is that the reader is addressed directly. Each chapter focuses on a different aspect of art education, identifies important concepts and recent research, and outlines advantages and challenges of making the choices suggested. Since the authors each center on their area of expertise, research is backed up with specific examples of how to implement theories and ideas in the classroom to generate active, meaningful learning.

Part I, "Teacher as Choice Maker," includes two chapters. The first invites the reader to examine why he or she might choose to become a teacher of art; it includes insights from all the authors on why they made this choice. Chapter 2 examines the learner through a developmental perspective and asks readers to consider why it is so important to have a clear understanding of our students.

In Part II, "Choices for Creating Meaning," readers are introduced to a range of choices for creating meaning. Chapter 3 looks at ways to cultivate artistic behaviors and find meaning through making art. Chapter 4 encourages readers to engage learners with art images so they can create personal meaning through the experience. The importance of storytelling and creating a partnership between visual and verbal expression is the focus of Chapter 5. Choosing to use artistic strategies to make thoughts visible and accommodate a broader range of learning styles is discussed in Chapter 6. Chapter 7 introduces ways to shape elegant problems that promote meaningful visual thinking and creative thought. Chapter 8 offers readers insights on designing units that make conceptual connections across the curriculum through a thematic focus that fosters teaching for meaning.

Part III, "Artful Teaching," revisits ideas introduced in all chapters. Chapter 9 suggests the metaphor "teacher as artist," and each author shares her definition of teaching as an art form. The reader is guided to consider the choices presented in each chapter and form a personal agenda for meaningful teaching.

 ## Audience

Preservice K–12 art educators are the primary audience, but this book addresses all teachers of art. It provides valuable information for preservice elementary and secondary majors who may use art as a tool for learning when they teach academic content. It also could help experienced art teachers who want to reconsider practice, as well as graduate students in education or art education.

Using This Book

Creating Meaning Through Art: Teacher as Choice Maker can be used in a variety of ways. It would work well as the core text for an introduction to art education class. However, individual chapters might provide important auxiliary information for several classes. For example, Chapter 2 offers a perspective on developmental characteristics of K–12 learners, and Chapter 3 presents new ways of thinking about the artistic process. Both chapters could be used in elementary and secondary methods classes. Chapter 4 could work in either a methods class or a class focused specifically on critical studies. Chapters 5, 6, and 7 can help art teachers and elementary or high school classroom teachers by offering ways to design and use visual and verbal approaches and by illustrating the importance of story as a vehicle for teaching. Chapters 8 and 9 could be revisited throughout an art education program.

Choice making is a complex affair, and helping learners construct meaning is an important goal in education. Both preservice and practicing art teachers benefit from understanding the implications of choices they make. Art educators who have a clear rationale for the validity of what they do—and how their teaching benefits students—are in a position of strength. They can articulate the worth of their program. By understanding advantages and challenges implicit in their choices, teachers gain ownership of an approach that is right for them and their students.

Special Features

- The **National Visual Arts Standards** are included in an appendix and addressed throughout the book in the context of curricular examples.

- In each chapter, a list of **Guiding Questions** serves as an advance organizer and could be the focus for a review of chapter content.

- The **Theory into Practice** feature includes curriculum models that implement ideas presented in each chapter. Case studies and strategies provide approaches to specific classroom situations.

- The **Advantages and Challenges of Making This Choice** provide rationales for considering each author's ideas.

- The **Action Plan for Instructional Decision Making** lists specific steps toward implementing ideas in the chapter.

- **Discussion Questions** and **Suggested Activities** sections provide ideas for group dialogue about issues and ways to apply the information in the chapter through research, field experiences, and other approaches.

- A list of **Annotated Resources** at the end of each chapter describes books and other materials related to the chapter.

- **Key Terms** are in set **boldface** the first time they are mentioned in a chapter and are compiled in a list at the chapter's end.

- Works cited throughout the book are consolidated in a master list of **References** at the end of the book.

We hope the book provides you with insights about the importance of choice making in shaping an art education program focusing on the value of creating meaning through art.

Jean M. Delaney

Acknowledgments

The authors would like to acknowledge David Baker, with whom we all share a vision of meaningful art education that connects with the experiences of learners.

The authors would also like to acknowledge all the students they have taught. In addition, we acknowledge all students whose names we did not know with the promise that if they are identified they will be credited in the second edition of the book.

We would also like to thank the following reviewers for their helpful comments: Victoria J. Fergus, West Virginia University; Roberta W. Rice, University of North Carolina-Greensboro; and Mary A. Zahner, The University of Dayton.

Our appreciation for excellent coordination and editing is extended to Alex Wolf and Sally Jaskold at Merrill/Prentice Hall and to Jean Delaney, who, as our liaison with the publisher, guided and coordinated the mechanics of this book from prospectus to production.

In addition, the following acknowledgments are made:

Judith Simpson: My most sincere thanks to the six exceptional women who saw the validity in writing this book and agreed to take the unique, collaborative voyage with me. Appreciation for their contribution to the book goes to all my former students, as well as to Jill Hessinger, Mia Marsh, Steven Appler, and others in both the graduate and undergraduate programs at the SUNY College at Buffalo. They taught me much and allowed me to use their words and works freely in my chapters. To friends, colleagues, and family, especially my husband, Joseph, special thanks for support and patience. Thank you to Meryl Meisler and Mario Asaro for the unrestricted use of their photography and to Nancy Weekly, the Charles Rumsey curator at the Burchfield-Penney Center for the Arts, Buffalo, New York, for her cooperation in selecting images from the permanent collection that are used throughout the book.

Jean Delaney: Thanks to my husband, Don, my daughter, Laura, and my colleagues and good friends in Maryland, Missouri, and Milwaukee for their encouragement and support; to my art students in Canton, Ohio, St. Mary's and Baltimore County (Maryland), and Southwest Missouri State University, whom I have taught and learned from since I began my journey in art education in 1954; and to my preservice art educators for the unit plans, lesson plans, and artwork they contributed to Chapter 4.

Karen Carroll would like to acknowledge the inspirational teachers, students, and colleagues she has worked with in Houston, TX; Providence, RI; New York City; and the state of Maryland, whose artful choices have informed her teaching and enriched the content of her chapter. Special recognition is given to mentors David Baker, Irving Kaufman, and Al Hurwitz. She thanks the following people, who read various versions in process and provided invaluable feedback: Ellen Dissanayake, Charles Dorn, Renee Sandell, Barry Schauck, and Shirley Glick. The following teachers contributed wonderful teaching ideas and artwork for Chapter 3: Amy

Ruopp, Russell Harris, Donna Basik, Tara Breslin, Michael DeAgro, Mary Hennessey, Andrew Katz, Ann Marie Lyddane, Susan Lowe, Mary Mark Munday, Pam McLoughlin, LaVerne Miers-Bond, Aileen Pugliese, Monica Rastigar, Michele Salamony, and Christina Sundvall. The artwork of the following students appears in Chapter 3: Ameenah, Casey, Naomi Basik, Todd Brooks, Dylan Blank, Terry Bowman, Ann Beasley, Robert Chila, Joseph Chong, Carlos Cid, Nick Santa Croce, Ashley Cunningham, Edwin Davisson, Sunni Diggs, Rachel Dorenfeld, Brandon Ellifritz, Kristan Farley, Jessica Foudes, Stephen Gangi, Alena Groopman, Danny Haught, Rebecca Hamilton, Steve Hoffer, Erika Huber, Darryl Kelly, Evan Kirkland, Amanda Korman, Julia Liu, John Lucke, Sherri Matthews, Calib Meyers, Deven Redd, Jennifer Ray, Cory Reith, Matt Rouse, Peter Sanderson-Kilchenstein, Jeremy Stanton, Logan Turner, Dakota Turnell, Mark Wendell, Kim Williams, and Joseph Yi.

Jan Olson: I would like to thank all who have willingly shared their stories with me throughout my long and rewarding teaching career. My students, my colleagues, my family, and my friends have all taught me to value the concept of story in each of our lives. I especially want to thank my husband, Alan, for his unwavering support. Without his encouragement, my message would never have been committed to the printed word!

Cheryl Hamilton: "Couldn't we just make a book instead of writing one?" I want to acknowledge the support of my six co-authors and friends who may have felt likewise and thought our message was important to share with preservice teachers of art. I have learned much about writing, computers, and myself through this experience. My family, friends, and colleagues also provided invaluable support. Dr. David Baker influenced my interest in the topic of artistic strategies by encouraging the exploration of drawing as a tool for learning, which I've done in the schools of Milwaukee, Wisconsin, and Wichita, Kansas. Teachers of art in both urban areas as well as in Normal, Illinois, Madison, Wisconsin, Lawrence, Kansas, and Buffalo, New York, have offered insights to classroom use of these strategies and lots of examples. The students in these K-12 schools, as well as my own preservice students at Wichita State University, Marquette University, and the University of Wisconsin-Milwaukee, have been willing to share their experiences and results of employing artistic behaviors. I appreciate their generosity of spirit. Specifically, I include Dr. Lorraine Pflaumer, who shared her own journal-keeping research; Diane Koeppel-Horn, who reviewed my early drafts; and the teachers at Buckner Visual and Performing Arts Magnet school, who welcome me in their hallways and classrooms with my camera.

Sandra Kay: As students fuel my passion for the profession, the sustenance for intellectual inquiry is provided by dialogues with valued colleagues. My line of thought is strengthened by treasured discussions with the following mentors and friends: A. Harry Passow, Abraham J. Tannenbaum, Ed Feldman, Francoys Gagne, Maxine Greene, Howard Gruber, Peter London, Moe Stein, and the Creativity Group at TC. Special thanks to Francoys Gagne and Moe Stein for their comments on earlier drafts, Kathy Arroyave for assistance with the visuals, the participants in the research study on creative thought, my family and friends, especially Jean Maxson, for her long-term support and enthusiasm, Carson Rutter, the editors I worked with at Prentice Hall, and the co-authors of this book, who took the meaning of collaboration to new heights.

Marianne Kerlavage: A 7-year-old child once said to me that she "was really thankful that she had so many people to be thankful for." I share that sentiment in that many people made my contributions to this book possible and I am thankful that they were there. Many thanks to my co-authors for making me believe that I had something to say and gave me the opportunity to say it; to my family, especially my husband and parents, who unfailingly supported my efforts even when they thought I was wrong; to Kate Green for her encouragement and support and her ability to help me create order out of chaos; and to the students who have enriched my life and made the knowledge I share about development real.

Brief Contents

Contents

PART 2   *Choices for Creating Meaning   73*

CHAPTER 3   *Cultivating Artistic Behaviors   75*

Contents

CHAPTER 4   Engaging Learners with Art Images   115

CHAPTER 5   Encouraging Visual Storytelling   163

CHAPTER 6   *Using Artistic Strategies   207*

CHAPTER 7   *Shaping Elegant Problems for Visual Thinking   259*

CHAPTER 8   *Designing Units for Conceptual Thinking*   *289*

PART 1

Teacher as Choice Maker

CHAPTER 1

Choosing to Become a Teacher of Art

Judith W. Simpson
Boston University

with contributions from all authors

Guiding Questions

- Why should you choose to become a teacher of art?
- Why should you explore a range of instructional curriculum choices?
- What must be considered in choice making?
- What do you need to know to become a teacher of art?

The intent of this book is to provide the opportunity for examination and reflection about the role of the art educator into the 21st century. We also present options for making appropriate choices for meaningful teaching in this and the next millennium. None of the chapters is meant to be discrete—no one chapter is a teaching model unto itself. Rather, you will find that several ideas from various chapters may be integrated to help you develop a philosophy leading to your own style of teaching.

Each chapter examines specific ways of thinking about teaching art. Each deals with art content, considers the importance of knowing the learner in order to teach for meaning, and refers to affective and cognitive learning processes. Affective learning generally involves the emotions, whereas cognitive learning is associated with the process of knowing. Both modes operate in all learning and must be considered when planning teaching strategies.

Eleanor Duckworth (1996) reminds us that there is no "best way" to teach. She supports her statement with a strong argument that there is a "vast array" of ways people learn. Information provided by Duckworth and other researchers on learning suggests that even though art making is characteristically idiosyncratic, art teachers still need to provide multiple ways for students to understand content and to respond to ideas visually. With this in mind, it is recommended that this book be used as a topic-by-topic text. You should visit and revisit certain chapters throughout a normal semester course, as well as, perhaps, within the construct of several art education courses.

In an effort to present information that leads to meaningful teaching, we address these issues: the need for understanding the learner; the need to think about ways of cultivating artistic behavior in students; ways of looking at and talking about art with learners of all ages; the use of narrative in teaching art; the importance of using visual strategies in teaching; the shaping of problems to encourage visual thinking; and the design of units based on concepts. Each chapter includes ideas on theory and practice, providing examples of lessons and units applicable to the design of plans and instructional strategies. In many instances, text is "borrowed" from the ideas of art education majors.

✺ Why Should You Choose to Become a Teacher of Art?

You have already made an extremely important choice by deciding to think about becoming a teacher of art. Career choices are based on a very complex mix of values, beliefs, and attitudes, and seldom does any one factor get examined in depth. Choices may be deliberate or spontaneous. They may be informed, intuitive, or guided by others. Informed career choices are made through the deliberate study of a profession. Intuitive choices are based on our thoughts and feelings and can be more spontaneous than deliberate. Sometimes, other people help us to make choices; parents, guidance counselors, and art teachers may comment that teaching is a great career for the visually talented. A course about using art concepts in elementary classrooms may have convinced you that visual strategies enhance the meaning of most any subject taught to young children. In any event, career choices and teaching choices are governed by a set of circumstances, peculiar to and different for each individual.

Why should you become a teacher of art? This was the first in a series of weekly reflective questions assigned to a group of art education seniors. One student began her response this way: "I believe this is a very good question; however, I have often found myself wondering why I wasn't asked this several semesters ago!" She went on to say that she believed her dual interests in art and children were her major reasons for choosing to enter an art education program.

Other students talked about influences that former art teachers had on their career choice. One student said, "I had really great art teachers. . . . A strong reason for my becoming a teacher of art is simply that I want to make a difference in the lives of other children as was done for me."

Another student said, "Becoming a teacher of art is a path which will allow me to continue to explore [art] while encouraging and facilitating exploration and under-

Teacher Rick Peterson encourages children to explore paper-making techniques.

Collection of Jean Delaney.

standing by others." She also said that she had been influenced by former teachers whom she felt had *not* emphasized the importance of art in "everyone's life."

Some students admitted that they sought the financial security that a teaching career could promise. "It was in my third year of fine arts that I actually began to give education some serious consideration; I began to see a degree in fine arts as not being of any worth once I entered the work force," one student said. The same student concluded his answer with this statement: "One year later, I can say I am more involved. . . . I realize my studies in the arts and my own art [have] something to offer to my future students."

In many districts, the teaching of art in the early elementary grades becomes the responsibility of the classroom teacher. Knowing the importance of art in the development of the child and the use of art as a learning tool helps elementary teachers formulate their own reasons for including art in their daily planning.

When asked the question "Why should you become a teacher of art?" several elementary education majors each had a different answer. One responded, "I will teach art to promote self-esteem, creativity, and visual learning. I believe it [art] helps kids learn to think and make decisions." Another student said, "I will use art to enhance my students' understanding of themselves, others, and other subjects. It will be an added tool I can use." A third student stated, "Everyone should know they have the ability to create in some form. Also to 'connect' visual and verbal learning and enhance education as a whole—besides, it's fun." Another simply answered, "I will teach art because it helps students to learn."

We share these comments because the choice to teach art within your elementary curriculum influences your formulation of a teaching philosophy. Your reasons for becoming a teacher of art may be similar to those stated by other students or elementary teachers, or perhaps you have other reasons. The question "Why should I choose to be a teacher of art?" is to be asked continually. As your teaching experience and content knowledge change, so will your answer.

Why Should You Explore a Range of Instructional Curriculum Choices?

The more we explore choices for teaching, the more we practice our skills, and the more we know about students, the more it becomes apparent that our philosophy evolves throughout the process of teaching.

Beginning with early childhood, art can play a critical role in the cognitive and affective development of learners. Choosing to include visual strategies and opportunities for learning about and through art must start in preschool and continue throughout the 12 years of elementary and secondary education. The reasons for making art an important part of the curriculum are explained in each of the chapters. Teachers must make choices on many issues during their careers: the amount of time art will occupy in the curriculum; the developmental appropriateness of lessons; the kinds of explorations with ideas and media available to learners; the images and objects used to support lessons; ways to use personal stories in art; visual strategies to enhance understanding; the use of challenging visual problems and the design of curriculum that encourages learners to think.

Since the choices we make are not without curricular constraints, we refer to the National Visual Arts Standards (National Art Education Association, 1994) in the exemplary units and lessons throughout this book (see also the appendix). These references are intended to reinforce the idea that there are many ways to meet standards and assessment expectations.

Standards

Standards in art education do not dictate a course of study. Rather, they are written to achieve consistent quality of education throughout art programs across the country.

Decision making is aided by teacher Nicole Kremenski.

Smedley Manion.

There are two types of standards: content and achievement. Content standards state what learners should know and be able to do. Achievement standards state what levels of understanding and competency should be expected from students upon the completion of grades 4, 8, and 12.

Results are the objective of standards. Determining how to fulfill the National Visual Arts Standards is a shared responsibility. State frameworks for art education organize the scope and sequence of art content so it is relevant to the standards; districts outline explicit content and appropriate methods, materials, and resources for local schools; and art teachers design specific unit and lesson plans that relate to district goals, state frameworks, and national standards (National Art Education Association, 1995).

Art teachers are expected to fulfill six broad content standards in which students should demonstrate proficiency:

1. Understanding and applying media, techniques, and processes
2. Using knowledge of structures and functions
3. Choosing and evaluating a range of subject matter, symbols, and ideas
4. Understanding the visual arts in relation to history and culture
5. Reflecting upon and assessing the characteristics and merits of their work and the work of others
6. Making connections between visual arts and other disciplines

The achievement standards outline expectancies for each content standard. For example, the fourth content standard implies that K–4 teachers should introduce the idea that artworks belong to certain cultures and that the students should be expected to recognize and be able to talk about them. By grade 8, learners should understand the context surrounding specific works; by grade 12, they should know the meaning of artwork within the society in terms of history, aesthetics, and its interrelatedness of purpose or function within a culture. How students reach these levels of achievement is determined by the choices teachers make.

Exploring Choices

A productive way for you to begin to think about various choices is to make use of your own frame of reference. What do you recall about your own learning experiences in art?

Early experiences influence our learning habits and attitudes. If children are encouraged to make marks and use visual tools for play and exploration, generally they will like to draw. Some spend more time at it than others. Many are encouraged by parents; others are left to find their own level of interest in developing graphic skills and abilities. In the primary school years, classroom teachers may choose to use the art corner as a reward for finishing academic seatwork. Or, making art may involve following directions to complete patterned images, coloring, or making objects to take home to Mom. Drawing is seldom taught in the early school years, although children can be encouraged to see and to draw what they think they see. Meaningful lessons that encourage drawing within the context of another subject are prevalent in curricula where art is considered a basic. Seldom does this occur in traditional settings where each discipline is taught singly. Drawing in the early grades

Teacher Monica Rastegar listens to her student talk about drawing.

Karen Carroll.

generally involves making pictures using early schema that children develop as their visual symbolic vocabulary.

The authors have chosen to share some of the experiences that influenced why and how they became interested in exploring their chapter topics in depth. They list certain questions that they would like you to consider before reading the book.

What are your earliest memories of making art? Do you remember developing a set of symbols? Can you recall your earliest school experiences?

Marianne Kerlavage, author of Chapter 2, "Understanding the Learner," recalled an early experience that is still the subject of inquiry she finds most challenging:

I taught art at all levels of public school for 23 years. Art, teaching, and making art are all very important to me. I have drawn for as long as I can remember. It seems as though some of my earliest memories have something to do with drawing. When I was 4, I tried out a new orange crayon on my mother's expensive imported wallpaper. This event was one of the few artistic endeavors I undertook which was *not* appreciated. As important as drawing was to me, teaching art was not something that I thought about until I was influenced by an energetic, enthusiastic art teacher my senior year in high school.

Since becoming a professor in higher education and being more involved in research, I have continued to be fascinated with why humans draw, paint, sculpt, and create images throughout their lives. The focus of my chapter is [on] examining why I needed to make marks on my mother's wallpaper and how all of us begin with mark making and possibly evolve into creative, artistic thinkers later in life. Each of us has a unique developmental journey that is a result of the culture we live in, the family we share, the schools we attend, the experiences we have, and the events we encounter. The way we think about, develop an interest in, and make art is influenced by all our predetermined, educational, and environmental input. I feel that it is important that teachers of art understand all of these factors.

Although art in elementary and middle schools is yet to play a role equal to that of other subjects in terms of scheduling, the importance of people making art is becoming better understood. Dissanayake (1988) introduced us to the idea of art as a behavior, a "making special" inherent in the human species. Making art is a personal process of a very complex nature. When exposed to a variety of media and techniques, people seek to develop those areas of expertise in which they are the most comfortable. Teachers of art have to choose from a variety of courses that allow them to explore various media. Teachers also have to choose materials and techniques appropriate for learners.

A discussion about a found object sculpture takes place between teacher Maren Olson and an intent learner.

Karen Carroll.

What abilities for making art have you been able to develop thus far? What materials do you use? How have you found art helpful or pleasurable?

Karen Carroll, author of Chapter 3, "Cultivating Artistic Behaviors," has these thoughts to share:

I came to write the chapter on cultivating artistic behaviors as a result of my experiences with both teaching and program development. I have found thinking about art as a behavior expands our sense of the significance of the arts in education and in life. It also helps resolve many of the pedagogical and philosophical issues. When we think of art as behavior, we can integrate the needs of learners with the processes or behaviors of art and broad body of knowledge art represents.

I also see that, in addition to art specialists, many classroom teachers carry the responsibility for teaching art. Classroom teachers not only have an affinity for "making things" but hunger for a broad repertoire of ways they can facilitate learning. Classroom teachers know the value of multiple learning strategies which allow different strengths of learners to emerge and want to use artistic behaviors as part of their teaching repertoire. I would like to inspire you to learn as much as you can about drawing, visual form, materials, and visual ways of thinking as you'll need to feel comfortable integrating them into your regular teaching routines and perhaps into your own life.

A vast range of images across cultures describes the history of art. Technology in the form of CD-ROM and the World Wide Web, as well as new considerations and broadened definitions of what art is, have increased the plethora of imagery available to

High school students work with teacher Jamie Steiger to illustrate a myth of their choice.

Collection of Jean Delaney.

teachers of art. We have unlimited choices from which to select content for lessons. Images and objects we choose often are related to our own preferences and experiences.

What experiences have you had with art images and objects? What kind of objects and images do you enjoy?

Chapter 4, "Engaging Learners with Art Images," is authored by Jean Delaney. These are her thoughts:

My interest in making and responding to art has a long history. My earliest memory of making art is of a Christmas Day when I was about 4 years old and received a box filled with art supplies from my aunt and uncle. I can still remember sitting on the floor in the sun porch drawing, cutting, and pasting all day. Although I never had any art classes in elementary or high school, I continued to fill sketchbooks with drawings. We lived only 20 miles from New York City, and my friends and I went to the Greenwich Village art show every spring and made many visits to the Museum of Modern Art. I'll never forget the impact of seeing for the first time Picasso's "Guernica." Although I started college as a journalism major because I loved to write and felt somewhat insecure about my background in art making, I soon decided to become an art teacher. I have taught in public schools and college for more than 25 years and I still love it!

In my chapter I discuss factors that affect engagement. I also describe some models for helping K–12 learners understand art images and construct personal meaning that helps them to understand themselves, others, and the world around them. Experiences with these learners have made it clear to me that you cannot overstate the value of knowing your students, having a depth of knowledge about the artist and the artwork, and finding ways to connect your students with art images.

Each of us has a story. Art has played a different role in each of our lives. For some, as one student said, "it was the only place in school where I felt I could succeed." For others it may have been an escape, a primary mode of expression, an intimate friend, a compulsion.

What is your personal story?

Chapter 5, "Encouraging Visual Storytelling," is authored by Janet Olson. She talks about her interest in story and narrative art:

My scholarly and professional interest in story and narrative art began about 16 years ago. Brent and Marjorie Wilson from Penn State University conducted one of their research projects at my K–8 elementary school. After teaching art for many years, I found their research particularly inspiring. The

Teacher Carolyn Grimsley checks the work of a "story-teller."

Karen Carroll.

Wilsons were interested in the kinds of visual stories students would choose to express and whether a drawing program that focused on narrative drawing skills would enable them to "tell" even more complex visual stories. Recently, I wondered whether my fascination for story goes back much further than I'd originally realized. I believe that as a young child my most creative work was accomplished during my own private time or in collaboration with my neighborhood friends, rather than at school. We created endless puppet productions with found objects, such as wooden orange crates, clothespins, pieces of cloth remnants, yarn, paint, and so on. During each change of season, our backyards were redesigned to provide elaborate settings for ever-changing narratives. The spring rain helped us to create our very own muddy "Pearl Harbor Mess," including ships, waterways, roads, trucks, tanks, soldiers, and lots of action! We were the children of World War II and, consequently, through story we tried to make sense of what we heard adults speaking about. Summer flowers and the luscious green grass provided the stage and backdrop for numerous plays, which included elaborate costumes and props. The clothesline was perfect for supporting a sheet or blanket curtain. During the fall and winter, leaves and snow offered new narrative possibilities. We built elaborate rooms, houses, and characters for our never-ending stories. Art experiences in school, on the other hand, were much more directed, more of a "cookie cutter" approach with all finished projects expected to look much the same. Such expectations simply didn't take full advantage of the rich imagination of childhood. Although I always enjoyed my art classes at school, I now realize that it was the creative collaboration with childhood friends and the backdrop of my neighborhood that provided the foundation for my interest in art as narrative.

Learning is as individual as art making. Children who are visual learners often find lack of success in traditional settings where linear, sequential teaching methodology is the norm. "I see" is seldom literally the equivalent for "I understand." Art teachers often make assumptions that because they teach a visual subject, they are teaching visually. They can also be guilty of thinking that everyone learns most effectively the same way they do.

What do you know about how you learn "best"?

Cheryl Hamilton describes artistic learning strategies in Chapter 6. Here she shares her reasons for directing her research in this area:

I hear and I forget

I see and I remember

I do and I understand

This proverb has been attributed to more than one culture and I believe applies to more than one group of people. In fact, it offers a rationale for

The use of multiple sources to find one's own images is displayed by teacher Linda Kies.

Marianne Kerlavage.

teaching art and adding the options of seeing and doing to traditional lecture strategies in order to increase memory, experience, and comprehension for all learners. These strategies are techniques to make our shared communication concrete and to make our thinking visible to ourselves and others. Although our views are shared verbally and visually throughout societies that are locally, regionally, nationally, and internationally based, our global "information age" is connected more often through image than language. Therefore, it is imperative that our students develop the tools to understand and communicate through visual information.

Communication has always been more than a passing interest of mine. My choice was to talk anywhere, to anybody, and at all times. But spoken words do not last. They are not concrete, as marks are. I learned that marks are the results of actions that are seen. This influenced my decision, when I was 6, to become an artist and a teacher. My childhood problem was to combine the seeing and doing of the artistic process with the verbal communication of the teacher. I was lucky and had many classroom teachers of art who allowed, encouraged, and included artistic strategies in their teaching. They understood that not all children learn in the same way and that offering a variety of approaches to conceptual knowledge would build experiences, assist in translating them across disciplines, and aid in comprehension. In doing further research on this subject in several schools, I found that some teachers recognize the contribution that artistic strategies can make to learning and that some do not. I share these insights in Chapter 6 and invite you to apply this information to your own learning and future teaching.

The level of challenge in an assignment can either frustrate or excite learners. Student frustration can be the result of a problem that is either too complex or too simple. Excitement occurs when projects are interesting and related in some way to the learner and when there is an opportunity for a variety of ways to succeed.

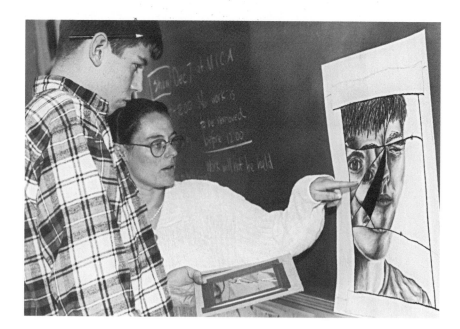

Teacher Amy Ruopp discusses ways of making a student's fractured self-portrait better.

Karen Carroll.

What kind of problems, projects, or assignments do you find interesting, and why?

Sandra Kay explains the origin of her interest in the subject of "Shaping Elegant Problems for Visual Thinking," Chapter 7:

My father spent his life imagining built environments for people. Holding a piece of cloth, my grandmother would see my next dress. My mother fabricated incredible bedtime stories. One neighbor illustrated Walt Disney cartoons. Another made jewelry out of sheets of silver in her home studio. Imagination was an everyday tool of thought for everyone as far back as I can remember. Designing was a way of life. But it was my elementary art teacher who showed me the magic of sharing the joy of meaning-making with others. At 7, I told my father that I wanted to be an art teacher.

The concept of shaping problems designed for visual thinking probably began during my first year of teaching high school studio art, crafts, and ceramics courses. Some of my students were academically as well as artistically talented. Friends would accompany them in the studio during the free periods they used to work on an assignment. Some of these friends were seriously interested in art but afraid to take a class because they did not perceive themselves as talented enough to maintain their grade point average. Creative ideas were miraculous to them. When I designed the courses so that students could contract for a grade by achieving technical mastery while pursuing a certain number of problems at various difficulty levels, the other honor students appeared on my class rosters. The mainstreamed students from special education classes also responded well to the format. The art majors challenged the problems with unique contributions.

When we stare at a blank sheet of paper or a lump of clay, we see mind pictures; often, a series of half-shaped images are projected on our internal screens. The process of selection from several "pictures" begins—winnowing, narrowing, amplifying, associating, identifying, and clarifying. Eventually the first mark on paper is made or the first piece is pulled away from a ball of clay. Not all learners are familiar with this process, and not all are confident about beginning. Some will seize upon the first idea they have, and others will not be satisfied with any of their thoughts. Teachers need to design lessons that help students to connect ideas and images in their minds.

Where do your best ideas come from?

In Chapter 8, "Designing Units for Conceptual Thinking," Judith Simpson addresses the notion of helping students to connect ideas through teaching strategies and learning processes expressed throughout the book. Teaching conceptually creates an environment where students can construct meaning. They can see ideas expressed in various forms and cultures and relate them to their personal set of thoughts and visual statements. Here is what Judith has to say:

Since I became an art teacher in the early 1970s, I have thought of curricula as "pearls of wisdom" rolling throughout 12 years without the string! Students in my high school classes could not connect art or art making to themselves, to their other academic subjects, or to the world in general. My efforts to work with colleagues in other subject areas led me to believe that when we correlated ideas, students benefited greatly from experiences that required a visual/verbal synthesis pattern of thinking. The process of examining a concept through multiple lenses clearly enhanced their understanding of art and the subjects with which it was paired.

The importance of context also became clear to me. Knowing something about the conditions surrounding the maker of art was critical to the level of understanding of the finished product, whether it was student work or that of a celebrated artist. In "Designing Units for Conceptual Thinking," I discuss how to connect art to real students from real worlds.

What Must Be Considered in Choice Making?

The role of a teacher is to afford all students the opportunity to find meaning in that which he or she is asked to study. As Dewey (1910/1991) stated:

> Everything the teacher does, as well as the manner in which he does it, incites the child to respond in some way or other, and each response tends to set the child's attitude in some way or other. (p. 47)

Art teachers are charged with the responsibility of providing opportunities for students to think concretely, abstractly, metaphorically, and inquisitively about content and art making. We have the opportunity to incite children to respond to art conceptually, contextually, critically, aesthetically, and productively.

How Do I Start?

What are the characteristics of a good art teacher? Frequently we pattern ourselves after a teacher we respected. Chances are the memory of a particular person is based on our own successful interactions with that person. It is a good idea to think critically and analytically about a mentor's success with all students, not just with ourselves. Analysis of the whole learning environment allows objectivity to reveal which characteristics really made the teacher outstanding. Those characteristics can be incorporated into our own teaching style and contribute to the formation of our own philosophy.

Once the characteristics of a good art teacher have been personally defined, it is time to think about learners. The more opportunities there are for interacting with school-age children, the easier it is to parallel what is learned about them in texts with what they actually do. Knowing about the nature of learners is critical to planning for teaching. Observation is often not enough—actually working with children provides one with a more realistic basis for understanding how they think, act, and respond in learning situations. After teaching an inner-city class of seventh graders, a preservice art education major wrote:

Teacher Ray Parris shares examples of student books with his sixth graders.

Karen Carroll.

> One really needs to understand kids and the situations that revolve around their problems. Two girls fought in class today and were yanked out by the principal. The fight was about something very insignificant. These kids have a lot of tension and anger in them.

Not all seventh-grade students are tense and angry, but the students in that specific class were. Knowing this could help the teacher to design lessons that use those emotions productively rather than ignoring them. Having experience with several seventh graders in different situations also allows a teacher to realize that those are not the predominant characteristics of all adolescents. What have been your experiences with children? How could experiences working with children be valuable to you? How can you find ways to do more active work with learners?

 ## What Do You Need to Know to Become a Teacher of Art?

What About Art Content?

Art is a complex subject that has been defined and redefined time and again over the course of history. The body of knowledge embedded in the visual arts is so vast that learning about all of it is not possible. Despite the enormity of the task, art teachers are still required to define what they think art is. Before we can teach others, we have to know as much as we can about art ourselves.

Here is an example of why our knowledge about art must be solid: A preservice teacher, talking to a group of special-needs learners about a Dali painting, was caught off guard by the comment, "He got ears and floating dogs in it, maybe dreams do make sense." The image had neither ears nor floating dogs. Fortunately, the teacher was comfortable with his own knowledge of the work and said, "You know, I hadn't thought about that, but this is how dreams play tricks with your memory." He went on to talk of surrealism in a manner that took advantage of the child's statement and that helped the rest of the class to think, again, about memory as a tool for their own production of a dream statement.

Often we do not have the luxury of exploring each period of art in depth. Many times formal courses in art history stop short of here and now, leaving an important part of the definition of art uninformed. Sources for learning more about art may need to be personally expanded to include reading critics' columns, attending gallery openings, going to museums more frequently, getting together with others and sharing subscriptions to current art magazines, viewing videos about artists, reading artists' biographies, and generally becoming more immersed in the subject you intend to teach. What do you need to do to expand your knowledge of art content? Have you thought about studying anthropology? What do you know about art from small-scale societies and about hiddenstream art?

What About Art Making?

Teaching about art through making art is an exciting challenge. There are many ways of working with school-age children, many avenues to take to teach them the processes and content of art. Often teachers are required to investigate techniques, media, and methods they have not formally gravitated toward studying. Many school art curricula include photography, video filmmaking, desktop publishing, and computer graphics, for example. Prospective teachers need to go beyond their favorite media. They need to investigate a broad range of two- and three-dimensional materials and be ready to adapt what is learned in studio courses to school art materials. What choices do you need to make to expand your art-making knowledge? One student responded in the following way:

> As far as [studio] experience goes, you can never have enough. The more you experiment the better you become in your art making. . . . You need to discover what materials will best convey the message you are trying to get across. . . . If there are no options, thinking is limited and in turn the creative process is halted.

Another says:

> My experience and expertise lie strongly in ceramics. I have been working with clay for only a year and a half, but in that short time I have been completely consumed by it. . . . Drawing and painting were always very special to me. They still are, I feel very competent in two-dimensional work and would feel very comfortable teaching it. . . . Areas I still have to explore are printmaking, paper making, welding, video, and fabric design. There just isn't enough time. . . . To me the creative process is [expressed through] a vehicle . . . different materials are faster than others. To me, clay is the vehicle. To others it might be paint, printmaking, dancing, or music. Love your vehicle!

Photography students ask teacher Jennifer Stabnick's advice about printing.

Eli Vonnegut.

These statements indicate that it may be worthwhile to think about your own areas of expertise and how your creativity, in relationship to teaching, is affected by your experiences with various media. Many studio areas need to be understood in preparation for teaching.

Things you discover about yourself can inform your future work in the classroom and help you to make meaningful choices about what and how to teach. In sorting out your own beliefs, areas of knowledge, and technical skills, what you learn allows you to begin to expand your reason for choosing to become a teacher of art and to grow in the areas that will best serve your goals.

SUMMARY

As you travel throughout the book, you will begin to explore several ways teachers of art may become more integrated into the mainstream of curriculum planning; more responsible for the art-making, critical thinking, and creative problem-solving development of learners; and more responsive to learners' needs.

Guiding questions introduce each chapter. Please think about your answers to the questions before and after you read the chapter. Think about why each topic is important. Think about how the ideas presented can help you to become a teacher of art who is aware of the necessity of art education for all children. Students want to know—they need to know—the purpose and meaning behind what teachers ask them to do. Your choices can help create meaning for learners.

SUGGESTED ACTIVITIES

∼   Begin a journal in which you keep your responses to the book's questions and those you formulate as you move through the book. Additional entry ideas include the following: personal time lines, a map of your journey through the book, a visual of your thoughts, a diagram of the steps toward your finding new meaning, drawings.

∼   Begin a collection of slides and videos and make a **quick time movie** of children doing lessons that reflect choices explained in this book.

∼   Begin a collection of children's artwork that reflects the concepts covered in this book.

Reflection is one of the most valuable tools a teacher has. Keeping a documentary of your thoughts allows you to see where you have been, where you are, and where you are going.

ANNOTATED RESOURCES

Dewey, J. (1910/1991). *How we think.* Buffalo, NY: Prometheus Books.
The noted educational philosopher John Dewey addresses the importance of critical thinking and the educator's role in training people to think well. The correlation between the curiosity, imagination, and experimentation required by the scientist and the natural learning characteristics of children provides a rationale and venue for teaching how to think.

Dissanayake, E. (1988). *What is art for?* Seattle, WA: University of Washington Press.
The author presents a case for art as a distinctly human form of expression. She has said that she takes an "anthro, bio, physio, psycho, sociological point of view" of art as "making special."

Duckworth, E. (1996). *"The having of wonderful ideas" and other essays on teaching and learning* (2nd ed.). New York: Teachers College Press.
Eleanor Duckworth's extensive research on the work of developmental psychologist Jean Piaget has provoked her own studies based on Piaget's theories. Through her research, she confirms that children learn in many different ways and reach plateaus of knowing through a variety of teaching strategies.

National Art Education Association. (1994). *The national visual arts standards.* Reston, VA: Author.
This document presents the reasons for art education; the structure of content and achievement standards; and a description of learners' expectations for the standards at levels K–4, 5–8, and 9–12. (See also the appendix to this book.)

National Art Education Association. (1995). *Visual arts education reform handbook: Suggested policy perspectives on art content and student learning in art education.* Reston, VA: Author.
This resource describes various kinds of art content and discusses relationships among content, functions, techniques, and facts to the visual arts standards. Assessment and curriculum alignment are also addressed.

KEY TERM

Quick time movie   Imported images (slides, video, digital camera), sound, and text combined through software programs. Such a movie can be stored on a disk and shown on your computer screen or projected through an LCD panel onto a large screen. Digital editing software, such as *Adobe Premier,* may be used for making quick time movies. Movies made by others may be downloaded from the World Wide Web and viewed using *Movie Player* and certain shareware.

CHAPTER 2

Understanding the Learner

Marianne S. Kerlavage
Millersville University of Pennsylvania

Guiding Questions

~ What ways do we have for thinking developmentally about learners?

~ How does graphic, symbolic, artistic language develop?

~ How do contextual influences affect development?

~ Why is it important to have a holistic conception of development?

Figures 2.1–2.8 illustrate the unfolding of a remarkable system of visual communication. The process begins with initial mark making and progresses toward the type of artistic expressions represented by a work by van Gogh, one of the world's most well known artists. While our interests may center on artistic development and the quality of visual communication, this is only part of the total development of the learner.

In this chapter I describe the path that the learner takes in graphic and artistic development and the influences that affect that journey.

Jessica, 3 years old, explains to her mother that the black marks and meandering lines she made on her paper (see Figure 2.1) are a picture of "animals we saw at the zoo." Jessica's drawing contains no images that are recognizable to adults, but for her these marks have meaning and represent her initial attempts to represent her world visually.

23

Figure 2.1
"Animals We Saw at the Zoo," 3-year-old Jessica's controlled line drawing

Collection of the author.

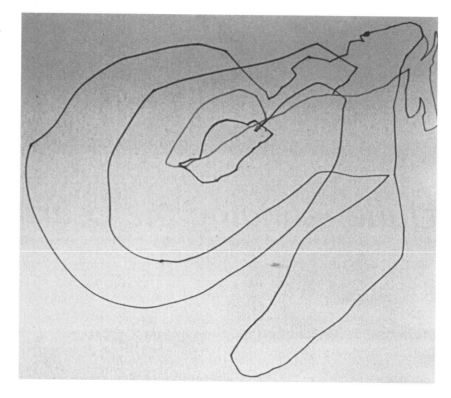

Figure 2.1
"Animals We Saw at the Zoo," 3-year-old Jessica's controlled line drawing

Collection of the author.

Alex, 4 years old, has drawn a picture of himself, which his older brother refers to as "Mr. Potato Head" (see Figure 2.2). For Alex, this drawing is a move toward making images that are recognizable symbols to others.

A gorilla "grows" across three pieces of paper as 9-year-old Patrick attempts to "show what a gorilla looks like" (see Figure 2.3). While his drawing is detailed and

Figure 2.2
"Mr. Potato Head," 4-year-old Alex's self-portrait

Collection of the author.

Figure 2.3
"The Gorilla," 9-year-old Patrick's drawing

Collection of the author.

recognizable, it is not an attempt to draw realistically. Instead, it is a symbolic representation of a gorilla.

Danna, 11 years old, worked on her drawing of a costumed classmate for a long time (see Figure 2.4). She kept revising and changing it, then handed it to me and said: "Here it is, but it's not very good." Danna is not satisfied with her drawing; she is not yet able to accomplish the realistic portrayal she is after.

As seen in this three-dimensional work (Figure 2.5), 13-year-old Jimmy is beginning to develop the ability to think abstractly and portray imagery in an abstract way. He is able to go beyond a realistic portrayal.

While Jimmy seems able to move to a new level of thought in a three-dimensional form, he is still not satisfied with his ability to draw realistically. This drawing (see Figure 2.6) was one of six that he did in his visual journal, but he considers it unacceptable. He says, "I like to draw but I just can't do it. When I work with clay, though, it just feels right."

In drawing her self-portrait, 17-year-old Iris attempted to portray her feelings of loneliness. She wanted to "go beyond just a drawing of my face to show how alone I often feel." Although in the finished drawing her eyes are open, in the first draft of

Figure 2.4
"The Clown," a drawing of a classmate done by 11-year-old Danna

Collection of the author.

Figure 2.5
"Myself," ceramic sculpture by Jimmy, age 13

Collection of the author.

Figure 2.6
"My Sister," 13-year-old Jimmy's
line drawing of his sister
Collection of the author.

Figure 2.7
17-year-old Iris's self-portrait
Collection of the author.

27

Figure 2.8
Peasant of the Camargue, by Vincent van Gogh, 1888. Brown ink over graphite on woven paper.

Courtesy of the Fogg Art Museum. Harvard University Art Museums. Bequest of Grenville L. Winthrop.

the portrait her *eyes* are closed and her face is sad, to show how much she missed her family in Costa Rica (see Figure 2.7).

Vincent van Gogh's drawing *Peasant of the Camargue* (see Figure 2.8) is the artist's attempt to draw not a mathematically correct head but the general expression—in short, life (Uitert, 1978, p. 21).

What Ways Do We Have for Thinking Developmentally About Learners? A Holistic Portrait of Learners

To form a clear picture of our learners, we need to understand all areas of growth that make up a holistic portrait of our students. This will enable us to more clearly understand the influences on artistic development. Developmental research in many fields has provided us with theories that offer insight into what behavior we might see at various stages and how we would define each area of cognitive, emotional/moral, social, language, physical/perceptual, and aesthetic development.

Cognitive Development

The area of development that has received the most research attention is that of cognition. Cognition is the act of knowing or perceiving. Processes and products that lead to knowing include such mental activities as symbolizing, remembering, creating, problem solving, fantasizing, and categorizing. The development of these mental abilities is vital to the growth of graphic and artistic understanding. There are many theories of cognitive development, and it is important to understand some concepts gleaned from the research that directly affect our knowledge of artistic growth.

Stage theory, greatly influenced by the work of Viktor Lowenfeld (1952) in art and Jean Piaget (1926, 1951; with B. Inhelder, 1967, 1969) in psychology, suggests that development proceeds through clearly defined stages as children, through direct action, discover the shortcomings of their current thinking and revise it to better fit the external world. They move from initial simple cognition to metacognition, which enables them to understand aspects of thought itself. More recent stage theory, such as the information processing of Case (1985) and Fischer (1987), reinterprets these ideas by suggesting that while children's development occurs in defined sequential stages, children encode, transform, and organize diverse information in different ways and progress at varying rates.

Sociocultural theory (Vygotsky, 1986) maintains that cognitive development does not occur as independent learning but is a socially mediated process through which children move in various sequences. According to sociocultural theory, learning is affected by two factors: the culture, which defines the learning deemed necessary, and the surroundings, which provide social interaction.

The theory of multiple intelligence (Gardner, 1985, 1990) suggests that not only is development uneven and individual but that specific domains of cognition exist. Each domain is defined by unique processing operations that allow individuals to solve problems, create products, and discover new ideas.

In summary, then, cognitive growth travels through stages, is influenced by culture and surroundings, and is defined differently for every individual.

Emotional/Moral Development

A growing body of research indicates that the emotions play a central role in all areas of development. Influenced by the early work of Freud (1974) and Erikson (1950, 1968), three major viewpoints have guided research and definition of emotional development: behaviorism, social learning theory, and a functionalist view. These views and more recent work by Goleman (1994) help us to realize that emotional development occurs sequentially; is a result of conditioning, modeling, and the cognitive processing of new information; and is a central adaptive force in all aspects of human growth.

The theories provided by Kohlberg (1984) and Piaget and Inhelder (1969) define moral development. They also suggest that decisions concerning right and wrong are reached by actively thinking about them first concretely and intuitively and then in a more complex, abstract way.

Social Development

Social development, or social cognition, refers to the development of an understanding of the self, other people, and social relationships. This development is highly complex and evolves very early. Social understanding (Selman, 1980) develops from an understanding of concrete social reality (understanding one's own behavior) to abstract metacognitive social understanding (participating in complex social situations and understanding others' thoughts and behaviors). The ability to get along with and understand others is strongly influenced by gender and ethnicity.

Language Development

Language, which is the basis for human communication, is one of the most phenomenal achievements of human beings. An infant quickly learns to communicate with caregivers and rapidly develops a spoken vocabulary. Three theories provide differing accounts of how this phenomenal achievement occurs. The behaviorist perspective (Skinner, 1957) suggests that language is learned through conditioning and imitation. The nativist perspective (Chomsky, 1969, 1976) suggests that children are biologically equipped to develop language. An interactionist perspective suggests that both innate abilities and social context need to be combined to facilitate language development (Berk, 1994).

Physical/Perceptual Development

Humans go through a relatively long period of physical development to reach their adult height, weight, and sensory faculties. Gains in height and weight are rapid during infancy, slow and steady during middle childhood, and rapid during puberty, leading up to full adult size (Gesell, 1933). Changes in skeletal growth do not follow the same chronological pattern as that of other body systems. Body systems such as that of the brain, sex organs, and lymph nodes have their own developmental timetables (Berk, 1994). Development of perceptual and sensory modes also follows defined sequences, moving gradually from simple to complex understanding.

Aesthetic Development

In addition to making art and artlike objects, learners also view, interact with, and gain understanding of their art, the art of others, and the world around them, which we will define as aesthetic understanding. Many theorists (Parsons, 1987; Hobbs & Salome, 1991; Housen, 1983) have suggested that children and adults go through several stages in developing an understanding and appreciation of art objects. While the names of the stages may differ, there is some agreement concerning the pattern of aesthetic development. Aesthetic development is defined more by the changes that occur in understanding and by experiences with works of art than by age.

The holistic view of the learner—which includes cognitive, emotional/moral, social, language, physical/perceptual, and aesthetic development—provides a base of information for looking at and understanding the influences on sequential development of artistic imagery.

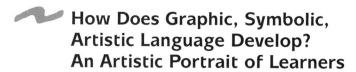

How Does Graphic, Symbolic, Artistic Language Develop? An Artistic Portrait of Learners

The early images created by children are symbols rather than artistic representations. An understanding of the way these visual symbols develop is vital when making choices for structuring art experiences. Symbols are profound expressions of human nature. They occur in all cultures, in all time periods, and in varying degrees of complexity. Human communication depends largely on signs in the form of spoken and written words, images, and gestures. Each culture develops its own forms of communication within these symbol systems. Thus the sounds we make, the words and numbers we write, the gestures we make, and the images we draw are all symbols designed to convey information.

Children begin early in their lives to attempt communication through image, sound, and gesture. All three are symbolic forms of communication that are used interchangeably at a young age. As children develop, each symbol system becomes a distinct form of communication and increases in complexity. Visual symbols evolve gradually, and only after visual communication is well established do children begin to think of their drawn imagery as art.

We will investigate six stages of development, which I have named mark making, early symbol making, symbol making, emerging expertise, artistic challenges, and artistic thinking. As there is little agreement on exactly how children develop artistically, the designation of stages and the interpretation that follows is based on a synthesis of research provided by Lowenfeld (1952), Kellogg (1967, 1969, 1970), Goodnow (1977), Arnheim (1969, 1989), Burton (1980a–d), Golomb (1974), and Gardner (1980, 1985, 1990).

Mark Making (Ages 2–4)

The initial stage of artistic development begins with the making of accidental marks and progresses toward the production of recognizable visual symbols. It is the foundation for all that happens later in the visual arts and in the production of all visual symbols. Research shows that these early marks form the basis for what children will understand about numbers, letters, and images (Kellogg, 1969; Schickedanz, 1986). When children are given ample opportunity to develop their mark-making skills they often perform better academically (Baker, 1995).

Within the stage of mark making, four distinct behaviors can be observed: manipulation, uncontrolled marking, controlled marking, and planned (or named) marking. Children frequently travel back and forth between these behaviors in an attempt to create meaning for their marks and constructions.

Manipulation.   Children begin manipulating tools to make marks long before they are aware of what they are doing. The kinesthetic movement of banging marking tools on surfaces begins as a pleasurable activity. When children attend to the marks, they are making a visual language.

The "picture" that 22-month-old Melody created on a piece of paper (see Figure 2.9) has no recognizable symbols. It is merely dots on a page, and Melody did not see the marks, nor was she really aware of what she was doing. She merely enjoyed the kinesthetic experience of grasping an implement in her fist and manipulating it to bang on a surface.

These initial marks, which generally occur during the process of hitting some tool against a surface, are often referred to as **bang dots**. The surface, the tool, and the material used are not important, so sculpting with spaghetti, smashing peas with a spoon, and making dots and meandering lines with a marker provide the same kind of satisfaction for children. Children at this stage have an avid interest in all kinds of tools, which they grip with the whole hand and control with whole-arm movements. Children eventually realize that something is left behind when the tool hits the surface, and they become fascinated with their marks.

Figure 2.9
Melody's line manipulation

Collection of the author.

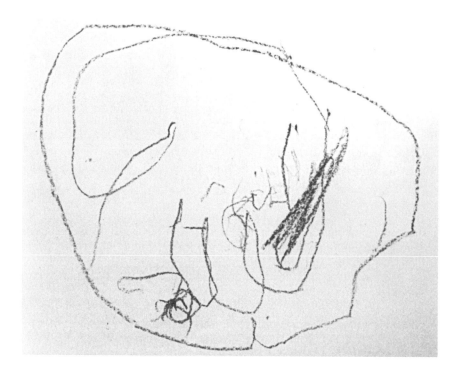

Uncontrolled marking. After making a series of kinesthetic "banging pictures," Melody began to realize that there was a connection between her marks and the action of banging on the surface. She then began to fill pages with manipulated line formations (Figure 2.10).

At this point, Melody's marks, like those of most children at this stage, were still primarily kinesthetically uncontrolled and, for the most part, unintentional. However, she now watches the process of mark making and begins to experiment with a variety of marks that result from different arm movements.

Each mark holds an immediate, if temporary, fascination. New variations will appear quickly and will often overlay the lines and marks made moments before. Recognizable shapes and images are usually accidental. Marks are seldom contained within a border, since children have not yet developed an understanding of the figure–ground relationship or a spatial sensibility. The tool used is still of little importance, although the best interaction occurs through the use of drawing implements or brushes, which leave easily seen marks.

Children recognize different colors at this point but seldom choose to use colors with forethought. They may overlay many different colors (see Color Plate 2.1) and enjoy experimenting with line. Children also enjoy the kinesthetic activity of modeling materials and may begin to form shapes with soft plasticine, line up blocks, and "build" three-dimensional structures.

Controlled marking.   Melody continued to draw and observe her results, and gradually the lines and forms became more consistent. She began to make a conscious effort to control her marks and assign meaning to them. She titled this drawing (Figure 2.11) "Flowers" after she finished.

In the process of acting on materials, and through observation and experimentation, Melody realizes that the surface and the mark are different. This establishment

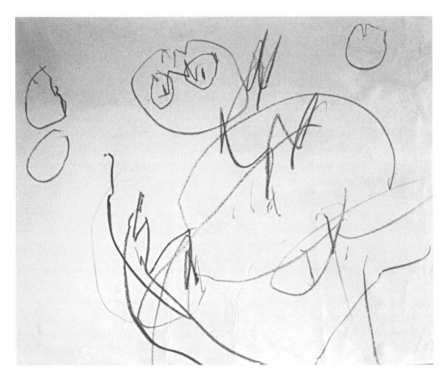

Figure 2.10
Melody's kinesthetic manipulation

Collection of the author.

of a figure–ground relationship is the next big step in the development of visual communication and is vital to continued symbol development. Without the development of a figure–ground concept, children may be unable to develop or recognize visual, verbal, and arithmetic symbols.

A growing ability to direct the course of the hand and the eye and an increased ability to use wrist motion provide greater control of the marks. As a result, various

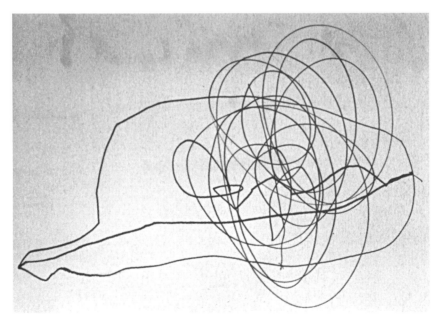

Figure 2.11
"Flowers"—Melody names her marks.

Collection of the author.

lines appear, along with simple geometric shapes formed from massed lines. Marks are now drawn as separate images and repeated again and again. This experimentation leads toward the creation of a beginning vocabulary of visual symbols.

Children now recognize the edges of the page, and while marks are placed randomly with little spatial organization they seldom go off the edge. This stage also marks the beginning of preferential choices of tool, surface, and color. Choices are usually based on the tools and surfaces that will provide the best visible results. Children will also begin to use different colors for each experimentation (see Color Plate 2.2) so that they may more easily recognize individual marks.

Usually at this stage children begin to identify their marks. Often after completing a drawing, painting, or construction they name their manipulations and will invent stories or "romance" (Gardner, 1980) about them. Although naming will not be consistent, this is a first step in the development of visual vocabulary, for the child now realizes that marks have meaning.

Planned (or named) marking.   Although Melody's drawings do not contain recognizable symbols, her work is now carefully thought out and drawn with intention. Melody told her father she was going to draw "mommy and me at the store" before she began to draw the image in Figure 2.12.

Melody has developed fine motor skill, which allows her to hold her marking tool with her fingers, giving her better control of her marks. Having established greater control, she begins to pay more attention to the actual shape of the forms resulting from her graphic manipulations. At some point she drew a single line around the massed lines, forming a simple geometric shape. This outlining behavior

Figure 2.12
"Mommy and Me at the Store"— Melody plans her drawing.

Collection of the author.

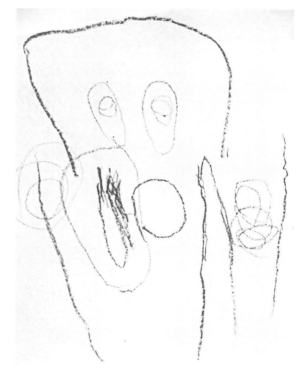

is the first incidence of mark making that is actually intentional and represents a big step in the progress toward making recognizable visual symbols (Kellogg, 1970).

When closed shapes are achieved, children begin to experiment with various ways of combining them, stacking them (Figure 2.13), and changing their sizes. They now work with intention. They preplan drawings, choose preferred tools and media, consider the placement of items on the page, and use color according to defined preference. The use of space is still haphazard and based on the amount of space remaining rather than on an understanding of composition. Color is identified with specific shapes as part of their naming process (Kerlavage, 1995b), but color decisions are generally made according to preference (see Color Plate 2.3). Showing preferences for tools, media, and marking surfaces continues; choice is usually influenced by controllability and visibility.

Visual development in the mark-making stage begins with initial unintentional marks and ends with the appearance of geometric shapes and consistent naming. By the end of this stage, children master the ability to make a dot, a straight line, and a closed form and are able to combine these forms into complex formations, which are the basis for all visual communication (Kellogg, 1970).

Figure 2.13
"Owl"—Melody stacks her shapes, and "owl" appears.

Collection of the author.

Relationship of Mark-Making Behavior to Holistic Development

The period from 2 to 4 years of age is a time when children move from babyhood to childhood, and it is a time of dramatic change in all areas of development.

Cognitive development.   By age 2, children have 70% of adult brain capacity, with primary motor and sensory areas developing rapidly. In the beginning of the mark-making stage they cannot direct and control their own thinking, so they are unaware of the marks they make by the banging of a tool on a surface. External stimuli, such as the noise from banging, initiates cognitive processing, aiding development of an awareness of the marks they make.

When they begin to recognize marks, children make associations between their actions and the creation of the mark. Brain responses and associations grow rapidly, and marks become shapes and named symbols. The ability to make judgments and associations gradually increases through experiential opportunities and social interaction. Complex thinking begins, but while there may be connections made between ideas, there is no overall integration coordinated around a single concept. Children are still unable to organize thinking systematically, and they cannot consistently direct or coordinate their own thinking. Therefore they are able to form consistent shapes and line formations and give them meaning but are not yet able to create recognizable symbols.

Attention span is limited, and there is little ability to handle complex tasks, so children work quickly and in spurts. As children begin to reflect upon their actions and are able to understand some events after they occur, the ability to consciously act on new information and develop representational thought increases. This gain marks the passage from primarily sensory learning to the onset of reasoning, facilitating a move from unformed marks to the beginnings of symbolic representation.

Emotional/moral development.   Children begin to understand the concept of right and wrong at this stage but have little skill at self-regulating their behavior. Many of their actions are based on instant gratification, which is observable in the kinesthetic involvement with marks. As the ability to self-regulate behavior increases, children are also able to move from strict kinesthetic involvement with materials to planned action upon them.

Social development.   In the mark-making stage, children base much of their social understanding on how the people who make up their world behave. By the age of 2 they have developed the ability to interact with others, are able to define characteristics that identify individuals, and begin to form friendships. This ability to interact with others and verbalize thoughts is necessary for children to develop the concept that marks have meaning.

Language development.   When they begin to communicate visually during the mark-making stage, children also begin to develop their ability to communicate verbally. By experimenting with sound and words they discover which ones receive the response they want. Once a few words are established, their vocabulary quickly increases to include several hundred words. Single-action words lead to combinations of words and then to full sentences, although children do not always have a clear understanding of meaning. The ability to define grammatical rules is also emerging. Increasing ability to communicate verbally also helps children to sort out their visual communication. As they identify meaning in spoken words, they begin to develop a concept of meaning in the images they make.

Physical/perceptual development.   Children quadruple in height between birth and age 2, after which time their growth slows to about two or three inches a year. Dramatic increases in motor skill and coordination occur during the period from age 2 to 4. At the beginning of the mark-making stage, children have little motor control, tools are grabbed in the fist, and marks are limited to the up-and-down motion of the arm. As gross motor skills increase, children begin to include the large arm motions used in making uncontrolled marks. Controlled marks occur when large-muscle control and increased hand–eye coordination develops, and the emergence of fine motor skill produces a change of grip on the tool from grabbing with the whole hand to holding it with the fingers. With more flexibility, children can form simple shapes.

Aesthetic development.   In the mark-making stage, children's aesthetic understanding is based on their sensory response to the visual world. They are curious, egocentric, open to new experiences, react to the moment, have not developed a complete definition of symbol, and respond to all kinds of visual stimuli—including visual images—kinesthetically and viscerally (Kerlavage, 1995a). They also react positively to abstract, nonobjective works and objects that contain bright, highly saturated, contrasting colors and simple patterns and composition.

Children are usually unable to verbalize their reasons for preference of an art image at this stage. When they do make preference statements they center on naming the color and pattern formations, much as they do their own work, by relating them to objects and feelings in their known world. They are unable to distinguish artists' styles, define different media used in artwork, or explain why an artist might have created a work.

Early Symbol Making (Ages 4–7)

As children enter preschool, kindergarten, and early elementary school, they begin to develop and expand their initial visual vocabulary. In the early years of school, graphic development is marked by the child's search for representative schema. Lowenfeld (1952) defines **schema** as a representation with no intentional experience expressed; rather, it is a symbol for the thing itself. Arnheim (1969) states that children are not attempting to represent reality but instead to create an economic equivalent for what they know of the world. Some of the first recognizable symbols produced, both two- and three-dimensionally, include a radial or sun form, a simple human figure equivalent, and letter and number shapes.

Jason's drawing (see Figure 2.14), like those of most children at this stage, is an early representation of the human form often referred to as a tadpole. This image usually consists of a circular head/body with arms and legs protruding from it and facial features contained within it. Children often invent simple, multiple-use symbols for other common objects found in their world (such as houses, trees, and flowers), and with minor embellishments the tadpole figure may also serve as a symbol for animals or birds. Radials and people appear remarkably similar in Lakisha's drawing (see Figure 2.15).

Figure 2.14
This drawing, "Jason's Family, with His Dog and Uncle Jimmy's Cat," shows 4-year-old Jason's first symbols. They all look very similar but are "named" differently.

Collection of the author.

Throughout this stage, symbols undergo constant change as children continually search for clearer representations. Embellishments and color changes that seem necessary to identify the symbol are added. A figure may have no arms yet may have large ears with earrings attached to represent Mom. The same figure may also be drawn without the earrings to show the difference between Mom and Dad (Figure 2.16).

Figure 2.15
"Sunny Day," 4-and-a-half-year-old Lakisha's drawing with multiple radials

Collection of the author.

Figure 2.16
"Dad and Mom"—A child's drawing of Dad and Mom are differentiated by the addition of earrings where the arms used to be.

Collection of the author.

Between the ages of 4 and 7, children also begin to use different types of visual symbols. Letter and number forms will appear to float on the page along with graphic symbols. These forms are not actually used as letters and numbers; they are experiments with line formations and will ultimately become words and numbers (Figure 2.17).

During this stage the development of a vocabulary of visual symbols is of primary importance, and children give little attention to the development of spatial understanding or to the realistic use of color. Objects are placed on a surface in terms of continuity, each with its own space and with placement and proportion determined by available space. Objects float in space and are attached neither to each other nor to a baseline (Figure 2.18).

Figure 2.17
"My House"—Name letters and objects float on the page.

Collection of the author.

Figure 2.18
"Vacation"—Cliff's figures float on the page and seem unconnected.

Collection of the author.

Children also begin to develop an understanding of three-dimensional space (see Photo 2.1) and now model and construct upright, freestanding forms (Golomb, 1974).

Various preferences develop during this stage. Choice of color is determined primarily by preference, not realism. Children may begin to assign specific colors to symbols as a way of denoting differences (see Color Plate 2.3). They also develop definite preferences for marking tools and surfaces, usually based on ease of use and on the clarity of image that results.

Chelsey's drawing of a trip to the zoo (see Color Plate 2.4) shows her with her mother riding Sarah the camel. This is a good example of how far children travel in

Photo 2.1
A young child models her "person."

Collection of the author.

developing a system of symbolic representation during the early symbol-making stage. By the end of this stage they have developed a beginning vocabulary of basic visual symbols and have created broad symbols for categories of objects, as well as subcategories of embellished symbols within them.

Although choice of color depends primarily on preference, children begin to select more realistic color during this stage. Their drawings clearly begin to communicate meaning and represent visual images of objects in the world. For example, Chelsey remembered a pattern on the camel's red blanket and chose to make the outline of the blanket red with some blue flowers. Indications of background and spatial organization appear, and clear differences among pictures, letters, and numbers appear.

Relationship of Early Symbol-Making Behavior to Holistic Development

The period from 4 to 7 years old is marked by many changes in all areas of development that directly affect the way teachers of art should make choices for curricular activities.

Cognitive development.   For most children, these years are marked by the beginnings of symbolic and representational thought. At this stage, children's minds are in constant motion. They experiment and try new ideas, conceptualize and construct more complex thoughts, and continually modify concepts. They are able to call up information from their expanding memory, exercise mental strategies, create mental imagery, and form centralized conceptual structures. They still have a problem differentiating between internal and external realities (thus, fantasy, make-believe, and dreams, in the children's minds, are real), they ascribe thoughts and feelings to inanimate objects, and they have no clear notion of the causes and purposes of things.

Children in the early elementary grades usually center on only one aspect of a problem at a time and are typically egocentric, based on themselves and their own immediate world. They also have difficulty taking other viewpoints into account, and they express knowledge of time and place as "here and now."

As children devise various symbol systems—including spoken words, drawn images, numbers, and letters—to represent objects, they apply them in various contexts. However, these representations are, in essence, prototypes and invented languages, frequently understood only by the children themselves. Through constant experimentation and comparison with others, children begin to establish accepted forms and manners of thought processes and mental products. As children develop logical thought, they begin to clearly establish images, symbols, concepts, and rules through conscious application of perception, memory, generation of ideas, evaluation of concepts, reasoning, and free association.

Emotional/moral development.   As the ability to communicate improves and understanding of causes and consequences becomes more clear, children are better able to self-regulate their behavior. Self-control leads to a better understanding of other points of view and an increased ability to make more complex decisions about behavior, which leads to the development of coping mechanisms. Children will develop a sense of fair play and the ability to share, but much of their compliance to rules is self-serving.

Social development.   During the early symbol-making stage, children begin to assume a variety of social roles. Whereas before their social world was contained primarily within a small family group, they must now define their role in schools and peer groups as well. Friendships based on shared feelings and interests become important. Gender differences and cultural origins also begin to be a part of social interaction, and children's personality traits begin to emerge. They begin to compare themselves with others and recognize differences and similarities. The development of an understanding of similarities and differences among individuals facilitates the sharing of a developing visual schema with others, thus increasing their visual vocabulary.

Language development.   By the time children are 4 years old they have gained the ability to engage in conversational speech. They can participate in give-and-take discussions, which requires them to understand the other speaker's topic and think of ways to participate effectively. Children are also able to understand and use vocabulary that has multiple meanings. As children discuss their drawings and constructions with others, they begin to identify ways to increase the complexity of the meaning contained in their imagery.

Physical/perceptual development.   The physical change that most affects children's artistic growth is the development of fine motor skills, with increased small-muscle control and the integration and coordination of large- and small-muscle activity. This broadens the scope of art-making materials that can be used and helps to make it possible for children to refine their initial symbols.

Perceptual abilities and the ability to distinguish between two- and three-dimensional objects increase also. As seen in Figure 2.19, children still have limited ability in organizing visual space. Each image has a specified space on the page, but the various items do not work together in creating a complete picture.

Aesthetic development.   As children develop a sense of what a symbol is, their aesthetic involvement with art images becomes less sensorial and more dependent on subject matter. Children move from an intuitive response to color and pattern toward decisions about art objects and images based on the reality of the image. They are attracted to, and more easily interact with, works that have simple realism

Figure 2.19
"The Art Teacher," an embellished "tadpole" and a story about art class

Collection of the author.

and contain few objects. There is little attention to style and recognition of individual artists, and when asked to place artworks in groups children at this age will order them by subject matter or theme.

Young children begin to develop skills allowing them to make judgments about their own art, the art created by their peers, and the artworks of adult artists but are frequently not able to give exact reasons for choices, nor do they consistently respond to work for the same reasons. They are able to acknowledge other viewpoints, but they base interaction on their own responses. This stage is marked by a reliance on concrete information such as theme, simple realism, and the perceived beauty of the work. Moreover, the story in the painting holds greater importance than expressive or design qualities of the work.

Symbol Making (Ages 7–9)

This stage of development covers the first few years of formal schooling in most Western societies. Artistically it is when children most enjoy their art and produce work that is most appealing to adults. It is important to note, however, that children are not really creating art but are working on developing a complex system of visual communication and are frequently more interested in the process of making than the resulting product.

The move into the symbol-making stage is visually identifiable in several ways. First, human figures have a distinct head and torso. Learners may accomplish this either by stacking several shapes (see Figure 2.20) or by creating a contour outline

Figure 2.20
"Bobby"—Bobby's portrait shows a series of shapes stacked to form a figure.

Collection of the author.

(see Figure 2.21). Another characteristic of this stage is the improvement in visual organization. Objects may be anchored to a visual or assumed baseline, and children may compose objects into pictures (see Figure 2.22).

A third area that identifies this stage is color. Objects are no longer assigned arbitrary colors but are instead given a specific symbolic color that is based on realistic color of the object. The sun is always yellow and the grass is always green (see Color Plate 2.5), but children are not using natural color.

The way symbols are drawn remains remarkably unchanged throughout this stage (see Figures 2.23 and 2.24). Each symbol is revised and refined, and many new symbols are added to the visual vocabulary. However, once children personalize a symbol to suit themselves, they move on to other problems.

The symbol-making stage is also marked by a great deal of attention to solving spatial issues. When children enter this stage, they generally are using a single baseline in their drawings to anchor all objects. This one line will not allow them to place as many objects in their pictures as they would like, so multiple baselines with multiple anchors appear (see Figure 2.25).

Children at this stage will devise many rules or graphic principles (Wilson & Wilson, 1982) to solve spatial or drawing problems. They will use whatever means are acceptable to themselves to translate a three-dimensional world into symbolic form and to see that images do not touch, overlap, or go off the page. As a result we see foldout drawings (see Figure 2.26); X-ray drawings, which show the inside and the outside of objects at the same time (see Figure 2.27); multiple-viewpoint draw-

Figure 2.21
Jessica's figure drawing shows a "cookie cutter" outline drawing of a figure.

Collection of the author.

Figure 2.22
"Spring"—Mary composes her picture of spring using many images. The ideas connect, but they are not all placed along a baseline.

Collection of the author.

Figure 2.23
"Christine"—Christine draws a self-portrait in first grade.

Collection of the author.

Figure 2.24
"Christine"—Christine draws a
self-portrait in third grade.

Collection of the author.

Figure 2.25
"Trees"—This painting reflects
the child's reliance on a baseline
for the trees, but we now see
the grass going beyond the tree
line.

Collection of the author.

Figure 2.28
"Indian Village"—The student
shows us the entire Indian village
from the air.

ings; and bird's-eye views, which show scenes from the air (see Figure 2.28). We
often see combinations of these conventions as the children solve spatial problems in
their own unique ways.

The themes of children's artwork are usually narrative (see Figure 2.29).
Whether they work with two- or three-dimensional materials, children create art
about themselves and their world. Themes will often be repeated over and over as
they attempt to develop and refine their symbols and solve spatial problems.

Figure 2.29
"Moon Landing"—A fourth-grade
child tells a story through his
drawing, which represents a visual
narrative of a moon landing.

Relationship of Symbol-Making Behavior to Holistic Development

Cognitive development. In the symbol-making stage, thought processes begin to resemble those of an adult, and reasoning becomes more logical, flexible, and organized. However, these changes occur only in relation to concrete, tangible information, and children still have limited ability to think abstractly. Learners can now categorize information better, which enables them to think through the steps of a problem and coordinate several features of a task at the same time. They also develop the ability to reverse their thought processes by going through a series of decisions and returning to the starting point.

It is also during this stage that children begin to develop spatial concepts of time, distance, and speed. Spatial understanding helps to formalize children's symbolization. Symbols are separated into distinct categories, each with its own identity and function, and meanings and representations become consistent, as well as closely aligned with cultural expectations. Invented language disappears, and fantasy and make-believe are easily distinguished from reality.

Emotional/moral development. Between ages 7 and 9, children develop the ability to self-regulate their behavior and are able to construct behavioral strategies without adult direction. These learners can consider multiple sources for the emotional behavior of others, and they can internalize societal norms for behavior that have been developed through a system of reward and punishment and adult authority.

Social development. As school broadens children's social contact, they develop new strategies for dealing with various groups of people. They will often develop separate forms of social behavior based on very different rules set by various groups. They will also realize that there are different social rules for academic settings, for games, and for social groups. In the art room, for example, children will attempt to understand what the teacher wants, instead of just freely interacting with materials.

In the symbol-making stage, children will also develop a well-defined sense of self. They understand themselves better and are able to make comparisons between themselves and others.

Language development. By the time they enter school, children have a vocabulary of approximately 14,000 words. They can understand words by definition and have developed the ability to differentiate the subtle differences in pronunciation and meaning. Learners are able to become involved in complex conversations with several speakers, which opens up the possibility of in-depth discussions about their artwork and can inform children's continued artistic development. This development makes it possible to introduce children to the vocabulary of art and enables them to learn, remember, and apply the vocabulary necessary for technical development and for critically discussing the aesthetics and history of art.

Physical/perceptual development. Children continue to increase their fine, small, and gross motor skills and are able to combine them into complex physical activity. Their hand–eye coordination has become well developed, which enables children to begin to see depth, understand proportion and perspective, and clearly differentiate between two- and three-dimensional space.

Aesthetic development.   Learners from ages 7 to 9 are still primarily dependent on concrete information when they view or discuss works of art. They believe that the purpose of making a work of art is to record something or represent a person or object. They state their preferences very clearly and are able to give reasons for their choices. If asked to repeat a preference task, they will usually order choices in the same way and respond with similar reasons for them (Baker & Kerlavage, 1989).

Children in this stage cannot truly understand exact historical time, but they can place works along a continuum and in historical sequence. To some extent they are beginning to discern differences in the style of artworks, are able to sort works of art according to the artist or the medium used, and can discern between two- and three-dimensional works.

Emerging Expertise (Ages 9–11)

Artwork at this stage shows an emerging sense of a need for expertise, and it is marked by a move from art as symbolic communication toward art as a creative endeavor. This stage, which Lowenfeld (1957) referred to as "Dawning Realism," is frequently marked by a dissatisfaction with art as representative schema and the realization that artworks are instead realistic or abstract representations of the world. Young people cease to use their artlike productions as visual communication and begin the move toward artistic involvement with art and art-making material. For many, the move occurs before they have the skill to accomplish it. Thus the stage is defined by the constant, frustrating struggle to develop the expertise to "make art."

The drawings that students now produce seem to regress. Figures are stiff but frequently more proportionately accurate and attempt to show movement and action. Figures and objects are drawn from various viewpoints rather than just a frontal view. Dissatisfaction and lack of expertise lead to the use of cartoon-like drawings and the creation of "shorthand" images such as stick people or V birds. The young artist will often work on one particular artistic problem—say, a figure or a spatial problem—while leaving the rest of the page empty or filling it in quickly with little attention to accuracy or detail.

Figure 2.30
"Christmas Eve"—Space is treated in a more realistic way, with a developing understanding of three-dimensional space.

Collection of the author.

One visual cue indicating a new way of thinking artistically is the appearance of a horizon line, which takes the place of the many multiple baselines (see Figure 2.30). We now see the appearance of a foreground, middle ground, and background.

Awareness of proportion and perspective also becomes apparent as young artists become aware that the picture plane can be flexible and that an object is complete even though not all of it is represented. As seen in Valerie's drawing of her dual ambition for a future career (see Color Plate 2.6), there is also a beginning use of abstract thought in the way the split figure is represented.

The themes and content of artwork undergo change during this stage. In previous stages, themes centered on the students themselves and their immediate world; now the emphasis is on social issues, fantasy, observational drawing, and design exercises. Gender differences in the images and themes drawn also become apparent. The drawings of girls will often include hearts, rainbows, animals (particularly horses), domestic scenes, or fashion models (Figure 2.31). Drawings that boys create are more action oriented and focus on superheroes (Figure 2.32), wars, and supercharged vehicles as themes.

Young artists move away from the objective, symbolic use of color toward a subjective, realistic use of color. This is also a time when students may eliminate color from their work as they struggle to develop realistic imagery or solve spatial problems.

Preferences for specific tools and media become very strong. Students do not willingly use any two-dimensional material that they cannot totally control or that will not allow for maximum rendering of detail. Young artists' use of three-dimensional

Figure 2.31
"Ann the Rock Star"—Ann draws herself as a rock star on a Hollywood talk show.

Collection of the author.

Figure 2.32
"Captain Adam"—Adam draws himself as a superhero who saves the world.

Collection of the author.

media is more free because they have not set the same standards for reality as they have in their two-dimensional work.

The stage of emerging expertise is also marked by the beginnings of considered use of design principles. However, the move away from an innate use of design toward an artistic application often makes the work less visually appealing.

This stage is a critical one in artistic development. It is vital that as teachers we understand the huge challenges facing these students and realize our role in aiding their development. The learners' changing definitions of what art making is about and their frustration with a lack of artistic expertise move many of them away from an interest in the visual arts.

Relationship of Emerging Expertise Behavior to Holistic Development

Cognitive development.   Cognitively, this stage is a transitional one as learners move toward an adult form of reasoning. Learners develop an understanding of abstract concepts based on concrete examples, and they expand their attempts to define how individual reasoning fits into the agenda of peer groups and the school and community culture. There is a continuation of growth in the capacity to think logically, to be flexible in accepting various solutions to a problem, and to organize and apply thought to problem solving.

This stage marks the beginning of active metacognition—that is, the awareness of various aspects of thought that affect performance (Berk, 1994, p. 291). It is during the emerging expertise stage that youngsters become aware of their own cognitive ability to process information and develop strategies that facilitate or impede performance. These changes in thought processes facilitate a move away from the concrete representation of symbols toward attempts to interpret or reproduce real objects.

Emotional/moral development.   When young people move into the adult world of complex emotional and moral decision making, they begin to have autonomy. Learners are now more self-governed and must take responsibility for their actions. They must negotiate right and wrong behavior and emotional response in a large variety of situations and realize that expectations from peers may be different from those of adults in authority. Between 9 and 11 years of age, students also become aware that rules set by adults are not always adhered to by them, and they begin to develop a personal set of rules. Ideals concerning right and wrong emerge, and they may experience difficulty coordinating their ideals with what is real. These ideals also influence students' ability to accept the artwork they create as good when they compare it with the ideal they wanted to produce.

Social development.   Development in the stage of emerging expertise is further complicated by peer influence and greater awareness of self with regard to gender. Learners at this age are highly influenced by their peers, and group membership and acceptance by a widening circle of friends are very important. Rules that govern group behavior become important, and children often subordinate themselves to the group in an attempt to fit in.

The desire to fit into the group also means that students make social comparisons and define their talents based on the accomplishments of others. This may lead to a drop in self-esteem. Children identify some students as "good artists" and then have difficulty participating in art activities in which they feel inadequate. Some children who believe their talent will make them less acceptable to the group may also lose interest in art.

Language development.   By the age of 10, most children have developed the adult capacity to use language. They are able to use metaphor, understand multiple meanings, detect humor and sarcasm, and have developed a fairly complete vocabulary. They have also developed metalinguistic awareness, which means they are able to think about language as a system (Berk, 1994). This enables the students to understand how messages are communicated, apply grammatical rules, and understand puns, riddles, and nonsense words. Their increased ability and confidence in communicating verbally is another reason their artwork changes from being symbolic communication to being the result of a desire to create art in new ways.

Physical/perceptual development.   Although cognitive change is rapid, there is a lull in physical growth at this time, which contributes to the frustration learners have with their artwork. Cognitive advances aid in developing an adult perspective about the appearance of their art, but their physical and perceptual immaturity leaves them without the skill to accomplish their goals. Without sound drawing instruction and practice at this stage, students cannot develop the skill needed to move on developmentally.

Aesthetic development.   In the stage of emerging expertise, learners begin to develop the ability to think abstractly and are thus able to perceive and appreciate the expressive and stylistic aspects of artworks. Preference for realistic imagery still dominates, but interest in works with subtle and dark color, complicated compositions, and expressive messages appears (Baker & Kerlavage, 1989). There is recognition that different media produce different expressive and stylistic imagery and that the same subject can be interpreted in a variety of ways.

Students also begin to analyze and define their preferences for art images based on expressive and artistic factors. They begin to perceive that making a work of art is a way of expressing feelings and emotions, not just a method for recording stories. Learners can differentiate among a photo, a reproduced painting, and a sculpture, and they develop a preference for styles or media in artworks. Their ability to interpret and explain differences in an individual artist's style and artistic interpretation is also developing. An expanded concept of time enables them to place events and situations in proper historical sequence and to distinguish and classify artworks by time periods.

Artistic Challenges (Ages 11–13)

This stage often marks the end of most students' involvement in formal art education. For others it marks the beginning of understanding the challenges involved in making art as an artist. It is defined by the need to develop the skill to produce art. Students at this stage will move from unconscious imaginative activity to critical awareness, develop visual attention to reality, express dissatisfaction with their visual representations, and place increasing emphasis on the final product rather than the working process.

Greater attention to proportion and action, an understanding of three-dimensional space, realistic use of color, and development of an aesthetic concept of design are characteristic of the stage of artistic challenges. In an attempt to become more proficient in these areas, students set standards for what they consider good art. As a result, many individuals face an artistic crisis at this time involving a lack of self-confidence in their ability to produce work that meets those standards. Many students learn best when they track their own artistic growth, rather than by comparing what they are doing with more talented classmates or with their own preconceived notion of good art.

The sense of three-dimensional space in their two-dimensional work becomes fairly well developed. Students will attempt to show the relation of objects to space through change of placement, diminishing size, figure/object proportion, and simple perspective, and they consciously attempt to apply the elements and principles of design to their work.

Learners at this age move away from strict narrative drawing. They prefer to draw from observation rather than from imagination, and they like to have examples and models from which to work. There is also increasing emphasis on the expressive quality of their work, on presenting various viewpoints, and on experimenting with altering reality. Social issues, worldviews, and emotions replace personal themes as the content of their work (see Figure 2.33).

Experimentation is a key concept for students at this stage. It aids them in their constant attempts to develop a greater understanding of the way art is produced. When they render, model, use color, choose materials, or design space they are going beyond realistically portraying images. They begin to work expressively, create mood in a work, or use design creatively. In 12-year-old Nathaniel's drawing of a

Figure 2.33
"The Wind Will Blow It Clean"—
The student addresses an environmental issue in this artwork.

Collection of the author.

house (see Color Plate 2.7), the student is not attempting a strict interpretation of reality but is using rendering, color, and composition in an expressive way.

In the artistic challenges stage, students have a strong interest in drawing, painting, and modeling the human figure, and yet it is also when they have the least confidence in their ability to do it well. They will spend a great deal of time experimenting with their images in various media to increase skill (see Figures 2.34 and 2.35).

Tools and materials also present artistic challenges to these students. Learners want to gain skill with as many materials as possible, and they want to develop an understanding of how each medium and tool can be used to produce the best artistic effects.

Figure 2.34
"Face in a Crowd"—Emily draws many faces in an attempt to refine her skill.

Collection of the author.

Figure 2.35
"Mandy"—Emily created this portrait of her best friend after many "practice drawings" in her journal.

Collection of the author.

Relationship of Artistic Challenges Behavior to Holistic Development

Cognitive development.   Although the ability to think abstractly is not yet fully developed, learners no longer require concrete information to engage in thought. They can solve problems by considering all possible factors that may affect the outcome and then test their solutions to see which ones will work best. These learners are at the beginning of a cognitive shift from concrete to abstract thought, and they will be inconsistent in their approach to solving problems. This affects their artwork in that they will move back to previous stages in an attempt to solve an artistic problem. They need to sort through a great deal of information, which can cause frustration. They will often deal effectively with a design, drawing, or color problem but have difficulty solving all these in a single work.

Emotional/moral development.   Emotions tend to be on a roller coaster of highs and lows during the early stages of adolescence. Attempting to reconcile the differences in their roles as children and their roles as adults causes great confusion and is often reflected in a lack of emotional control.

In previous stages, adults established rules of behavior. Later, the influence of peers and the desire to be accepted brought changes in the rules. Now, learners are attempting to establish their own definitions of right and wrong. For example, students know that the amount of special paper is limited, and they have been told that only one piece is available to them. However, they feel a need to redo their artwork. They are thus faced with the dilemma of choosing between following the rule they know to be right and taking a new piece of paper so they can complete the assignment to their satisfaction.

Social development.   All the rules for social behavior that developed in earlier stages are suddenly called into question as students, in transition between childhood and adulthood, attempt to establish their role in an adult world.

They also become aware of changing sexual roles as they move into the teenage years, and they will often dissolve opposite-sex friendships and become actively involved with same-sex groups to help define these changing roles. Competition becomes a big part of group interaction as young people test their abilities against each other. Students at this stage may develop low self-esteem if they are not included in the "right" group, and there is also less tolerance for individual differences. Individual friendships often fluctuate, but many young people of this age have at least one best friend with whom to share problems.

The search for autonomy also affects students' roles within the family and their response to authority. Young people want to be independent of parents and establish their own identity. This frequently runs counter to adult expectations and causes conflict.

All these complicated social changes will affect student behavior in the art room. They will also affect student participation in art activities, their choice of themes for artwork, and their overall interest in art.

Language development.   The number of vocabulary words has now reached about 30,000, and learners have added many abstract words that allow them to communicate on a fairly adult level. Slang words, colloquialisms, and invented words with meaning to a particular group also become a common part of young adolescent language.

Physical/perceptual development.   By the end of this stage, most children will have entered puberty, a time of rapid body growth and the beginnings of sexual characteristics. Preadolescents go through tremendous developmental changes with the onset of puberty. It is also a time marked by extremes as some youngsters will mature earlier and much more quickly than others.

Girls usually go through growth spurts early, with many of them reaching their adult height by age 13. Boys physically develop much later, generally beginning their growth spurts toward the end of this stage. For girls who mature very early and boys who mature very late this can be a very difficult time. Rapid growth also affects coordination. For many young people, coordination lags behind physical growth, which makes it difficult for them to control their bodies and makes simple tasks complex. This frustrates them in their attempts to create artwork that meets their own expectations. Modeling and construction activities, which are not as dependent on exact physical control, are often more successful than two-dimensional activities.

Aesthetic development.   The primary focus of aesthetic investigation for students of this age is to begin to understand how and why artists produce the works they do. With this focus, they can also begin to develop their own sense of artistic expression. Learners are still attracted primarily to realistic works, but they are able to appreciate many styles of artwork. Early adolescents can analyze work through the elements and principles of design; identify individual artists by style; recognize the media and technique used; place artworks in stylistic or historical periods; and apply information gained through inquiry to their own work.

Artistic Thinking (Ages 14–17)

The stage of artistic thinking marks entry into the adult world. As adolescents reach an adult understanding of the artistic process, they begin to make art from the perspective of the mature artist. Whereas previous stages were defined by art as symbol and as interpretation of reality, in this stage art becomes a creative process.

Subject matter is open ended and covers everything from detailed realistic renderings (see Figure 2.36) to abstract works (see Figure 2.37). Social issues, emotional outlets, and skill development serve as motivation for producing a wide variety of images. Work becomes more individual as young artists begin to develop a personal style and are less influenced by peers.

The adolescent artist has developed a degree of skill with many media in previous stages and is now intent on refining those skills and applying them in the most effective manner to achieve artistic effect. Artists in this stage will use tools and media to express emotion or portray a specific idea rather than just as a way of portraying reality. They will also be interested in experimenting with media to discover how they can be used most effectively. Young artists will try out the same idea with a variety of two- and three-dimensional media (see Figures 2.38 and 2.39).

Figure 2.36
"Pottsville View"—Kate, age 16, does a realistic rendering of her neighborhood.

Collection of the author.

Figure 2.37
"Pottsville as Van Gogh Sees It"—J.P., age 15, does a monoprint of an imaginative view of his hometown.

Collection of the author.

Students will portray objects and people from a variety of viewpoints and unusual perspectives or intentionally distort them (see Figure 2.40). They also may leave some objects incomplete or show only parts of things for artistic or emotional effect.

An understanding of space, color, and design emerges, which enables the student to use these artistic conventions creatively. Color, for example, is used for its emotional or expressive qualities (see Color Plate 2.8), as well as to interpret reality as close to nature as possible (see Color Plate 2.9).

Figure 2.38
"The Thinker"—Megan, age 17, models a form of "The Thinker" in clay.

Collection of the author.

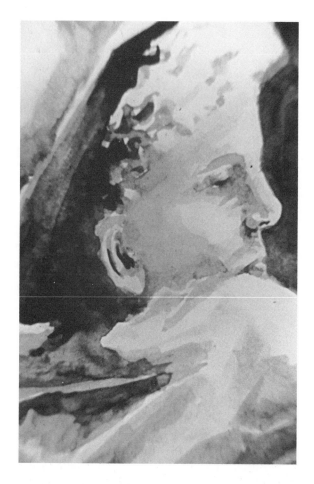

Figure 2.39
"The Thinker"—Megan repeats her Thinker theme in watercolor and ink.

Collection of the author.

Figure 2.40
"Mrs. Indara"—A high school student chooses an unusual angle to draw the posed model.

Collection of the author.

Relationship of Artistic Thinking Behavior to Holistic Development

Cognitive development. The ability to think abstractly is fully developed by this stage, and students have a strong capacity for metacognitive activity. They are fairly competent at monitoring their own cognitive activity for consistency, for gaps in information that need to be filled, and for the accuracy of application. Adolescents are able to draw a great deal of information from memory, sort it easily, and ascertain how new information fits into their preexisting knowledge base. They can think logically about both concrete and abstract information.

These advances make it possible for students to work and think in an artistic, creative manner. They can now analyze their ability and knowledge about art and art making and form strategies for moving to a higher level of artistic involvement.

Emotional/moral development. The onset of puberty causes tremendous emotional upheavals. Hormonal changes, the lack of a clear understanding of their new role, and the stress of fitting in creates difficulty in controlling their emotions. By age 17 or 18, adolescents' emotions have stabilized and their control has improved. Adolescents believe that they are special and unique and that no one else, especially adults, can understand them. They also believe that they are invulnerable to danger, and have difficulty foreseeing the consequences of their actions.

Social development. Social development can also be very complicated at this age. Adolescents need to develop a sense of self and a sense of social self as part of a community. They are concerned about how they appear to others but need to integrate their own identities, desires, and skills with what is perceived to be acceptable. This can lead to confusion and makes young people susceptible to gangs and cults, which give definition to identity roles. Adolescents may also experiment with, and sometimes adopt, such risky behavior as smoking, using alcohol or other drugs, and engaging in early sexual activity. There is a high rate of suicide as they live in the present and cannot always see long-range solutions to problems nor fully comprehend the results of their actions. Conflict with adult authority arises as adolescents attempt to define their role in an adult world.

The most difficult social change involves defining new roles of social interaction with the opposite sex. It seems that suddenly all the rules change. Increasing sexual awareness and desire make it difficult to establish acceptable social behavior, and this is compounded by the messages society delivers. Dating is accepted, even encouraged, and yet sexual involvement is discouraged. The mass media continually send sexual images and messages, yet society's rules suggest sexual restraint.

The need for continuing friendships and for looking to a variety of role models also becomes important during early adolescence. Friendships, usually with same-sex peers, become stronger and more important as they provide a sounding board for solving social problems. Teens seek role models to help define what they will become. This becomes complicated, as society provides few exemplary models.

Language development. Language development for most teens has reached adult levels. Other than continued additions to their vocabulary, little change occurs.

Physical/perceptual development. Adolescents will reach adult physical and sexual maturity during this stage, but there is a great deal of individual difference as to when that occurs. After rapid growth ceases, coordination and motor control are refined. Teens gain greater control of their physical actions, and their strength and flexibility increases. They become more involved and increase their skill and technique in artwork as manual dexterity improves and they gain confidence in their physical abilities.

As puberty ends and teens become sexually mature, they establish their sexual identity, and 1–4% of teens realize that they may be gay. Physical appearance becomes increasingly important to both young men and young women, and many become sexually active. To meet the idealized standards of strength and beauty, some teens will develop eating disorders to lose weight or use steroids to build muscles.

Aesthetic development.   During the stage of artistic thinking, adolescents begin to analyze works of art from the point of view of the artist. They are able to understand the complexity of artistic activity and appreciate works on the basis of their emotional value, portrayal of an idea, or use of media rather than on their rendering of reality. Young artists are also able to analyze works for their value in contributing to the development of their own artistic understanding and personal style.

How Do Contextual Influences Affect Development? Seeing the Child in Context

One of the first things you will discover when you begin to observe children and young adults is that there is a great deal of variability in how they fit into the developmental portrait. The developmental stages involve large generalities, and many learners will not fit certain patterns of development. They may be faster or slower in reaching identified "milestones" because other factors affect them and influence ways they develop.

Each individual learner develops within a context that will affect that development. If we are to make appropriate choices for teaching and creating meaningful experiences in art education for all students, we need to understand all the influences on their development.

Family Context

The biggest influence on development, especially for young children, is the family. Learners obtain academic habits and value structures toward education from their families. Children whose families encourage and help them with learner activities seem to perform better and achieve more in school. For example, young children who have access to art materials and are encouraged to draw at home do well not only in art but also in academic subjects (Baker, 1995).

Children's families may also have values and customs that are different from those of the school community. They can range from something as obvious as a different language spoken at home to more subtle issues, such as a less structured form of discipline. One of the first things children generally do when they enter school is negotiate the differences between home and school.

Family structure can also influence children's development. The number of children in the family and a child's position in the sibling order can affect the way children learn. Older children may receive more attention from adults or may have early responsibility for younger siblings and thus mature more quickly. Younger children may either have the disadvantage of being ignored by adults and older siblings or benefit from lots of attention from family members. The traditional nuclear family is no longer the norm, and nontraditional family structures (such as single-parent families and extended families) are becoming more common. Whether children come from a nuclear family or not, the structure of that family will affect their development.

Serious problems within families also may affect student learning. Many children face difficulties in school as a result of physical, mental, or sexual abuse; alcohol- or drug-addicted family members; parents out of work; or family members with serious psychological problems.

School Context

The context with which you will be most familiar is that of the school, which is a community with rules and regulations all its own. It is a society within a society and may have values very different from those of the community within which it exists. Learners are often evaluated by criteria set largely by white, middle-class educators, and educational excellence is defined by test scores of academic ability. Although these standards are adequate for many students, a large segment of the population is not well served by them.

Learning styles. Researchers have begun to pay attention to the fact that all students do not learn in the same way. According to Grant and Sleeter (1988), teaching, learning, and assessment have traditionally been designed for learning styles that focus on tasks rather than personal orientation; parts rather than the whole; formal and nonpersonal attributes; decontextualized information; linear thinking patterns; nonemotional, sedentary behavior; long attention spans; use of Standard English; ability to communicate without contextual reference or nonverbal cues; and formal rules, schedules, preplanning, and structure. Students whose learning styles do not fit within this framework will have difficulty demonstrating what they know.

Many theories on learning styles (including analytical, relational, passive, active, global, individual, field-dependent, and field-independent) question this traditional bias and suggest that there are multiple ways of learning. Gardner (1985) identifies seven types of intelligence: linguistic, logical-mathematical, musical, spatial, bodily kinesthetic, and two forms of personal intelligence—interpersonal and intrapersonal. He suggests that students function in all the intelligences but that each has a higher degree of development in one or more areas. Schools tend to be structured to benefit those who are highly oriented toward learning in the linguistic and logical-mathematical modes. Samples (1987) and McCarthy (1981) suggest that emphasis on rationality and logical scientific thought ignores the way most people learn and impedes the development of creative thought and creative problem-solving skills.

Language arts researchers suggest that, although many children learn verbally by processing information through verbal cues, others are visual learners and thus process information best through nonverbal cues. Many gifted artists have been visual learners and have had difficulty in traditional school programs. In contrast, highly verbal learners may have trouble developing their art ability. Olson (1992) suggests strategies that aid both types of learners in developing visual and verbal skills.

Many theories explain the variety of ways students learn. It is important that you clearly understand that there is no one way of learning and therefore no "best" way to deliver information to learners.

Learners with special needs.   Students whose skills deviate from the established norm are frequently labeled special-needs children and are often placed in special classes. These children may have any of a variety of special needs, including learning disabilities; attention deficit syndrome; mental handicaps; and physical, visual, or hearing impairments. Today's laws, however, mandate that all children have a right to an education in the least restrictive environment; therefore, most children, regardless of special need, will be part of an art class. Their challenges may be either minimal or profound, but in all cases these learners will need special consideration. Special-needs children do well in art. In fact, some, like 18-year-old Mandy (see Color Plate 2.10), who is hearing impaired, and Jeffrey (see Figure 2.41), a high school student who is learning disabled and reading at a third-grade level, may be exceptional young artists.

Remember that, as a teacher, you must evaluate what each student is able to do. Once current strengths and challenges are understood, lessons that are flexible and adaptable to individual student needs will accommodate the different challenges students face (Henley, 1992).

Gifted learners.   Students talented in the visual arts are often excluded from special programs. Most programs for gifted students are based on academic test scores that define high abilities in verbal and mathematics-based subjects, which are often not the strengths of visually gifted students.

Kimberlee was placed in a special kindergarten because she was considered developmentally delayed. Small for her age, she entered first grade delayed in beginning to read and write. However, her artistic ability is far superior to that of children many years older than she is. Art teachers can provide special opportunities for such children through the regular classroom or through special classes at the elementary and middle school levels. Because art is usually an elective at the high school level, advanced classes can benefit visually gifted students. It is vital that the talents of

Figure 2.41
"Self-portrait"—Jeffrey is a high school student who reads at or below a third-grade level but shows exceptional ability in the art room.

Collection of the author.

gifted students are recognized, nurtured, and challenged. Doing so will help these students achieve their potential in areas of strength and subsequently may foster growth in other areas as well.

It is also necessary to take note that students may be gifted in one particular area of art. Some may be exceptionally talented with two-dimensional media but have limited ability with sculptural materials. Conversely, a student with a well-developed spatial sense may do exceptional work in three-dimensional areas but have little talent when drawing or painting.

Learning styles and exceptionalities can be identified and often determine how a student is perceived in a school context. Judgments about learning styles, development, and valued skills are often based on a teacher's knowledge and educational history.

Community Context

The United States is made up of a large and diverse population. However, schools tend to be structured on white, middle-class, Protestant, Eurocentric, male norms (Cremin, 1988). These norms often do not fit with certain learners' backgrounds and can create a major area of incompatibility and conflict.

Cultural and ethnic influence.   Students come from a variety of cultural and ethnic backgrounds and may exhibit behaviors and attitudes that the mainstream culture devalues (Hale-Benson, 1986). Such differences include ethnic or racial cultural norms, as well as religious and community attitudes. Students in urban schools live in community cultures that can be very different than suburban and rural cultures.

Anthropologists have stated that discontinuities between one set of cultural practices and another can be confusing to anyone who must make a transition between the two. When learners come from homes whose culture is different from the culture of the school, they may be confused, frightened, or unsure of themselves. They may become angry if they are reprimanded for doing or saying something acceptable to their culture but not to the school's.

Students cannot be expected to function well in a school culture without understanding its value structure; nor can teachers do their jobs well without knowledge of the culture children live in at home. For example, Mexican American children live in a cultural community that is people oriented. They often have large extended families, and sharing and cooperating among members is common. However, in the school community, learners are expected to be task oriented and to work quietly and independently, behaviors not common to their culture. The result may lead to a high dropout rate for these learners (Grant & Sleeter, 1988).

Teachers raised and educated in cultures different from those of their students may devalue behaviors different from their own. For example, African Americans grow up in a culture that is highly charged emotionally and very people oriented. The ability to communicate extensively nonverbally as well as verbally often develops from this kind of environment. Much is communicated with body language, hand movements, and dress. As a result, children may have advanced motor skills and thus be more physically active than their classmates from other cultures. Teachers who are not raised in this culture and do not have a knowledge of it are likely to reprimand the child for not sitting still and paying attention rather than valuing their energy, expressiveness, and interest in communication (Hale-Benson, 1986). By understanding and recognizing the differences and similarities among cultures and capitalizing on them as educational resources, we can create cultural compatibility.

It is also important to realize that culture may influence the definition of art. We have the opportunity to give our students a true understanding of the beauty in all cultures and a chance to develop a better understanding of their own. As teachers of art we can share with students the richness of many cultures through the study of art.

Socioeconomic influence.   One in four children in America lives in poverty. These children are frequently hungry and possibly malnourished, may live in substandard housing and have inadequate medical care, and may face violence in the home and surroundings or deal with the consequences of drug and alcohol abuse. They may also have little access to learning materials such as books, crayons, and educational toys when they are young. These factors will frequently cause developmental delays and physical or mental handicaps, and they certainly do not prepare students to learn in traditional schools.

The largest percentage of poor children lives in urban centers. In addition to living in home environments that often do not adequately provide for basic needs, they attend schools that do not provide education relevant to them. The schools are often designed to emphasize their perceived inadequacies—that is, to correct what society feels they cannot do. Poor children—in particular, poor, urban, minority children—are disproportionately represented in special-needs classes and have lower test scores and higher dropout rates than children from higher socioeconomic classes. Researchers are beginning to suggest that this may have more to do with inadequate, inappropriate school curricula than with the deficiency of the learners.

As teachers of art, you need to be aware that poor urban children may come to you underprepared by traditional educational standards, but they bring a wealth of knowledge often untapped. By gaining a knowledge of what your students are capable of and helping them to understand their potential, you will aid them in increasing their learning abilities.

We have looked at many ways the contextual influences on learners affect their development. As a teacher of art, you will need to develop as complete an understanding as possible of the outside influences that will affect the learners in your classroom. You will need to develop a knowledge of the community within which you teach, its ethnic and racial makeup, its economic status, and the family structures from which your students come. You cannot know everything about all your students, but you can develop skills to aid you in developing art programs and in using teaching methods that will reach your students. Also, by gaining knowledge of development and the factors that influence it, you can help students to understand their own learning potential and encourage them to be self-directed learners.

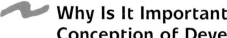

Why Is It Important to Have a Holistic Conception of Development?

Creating meaning through art for your students will require you, as a teacher, to make many choices directly related to how well you know and understand your students. Throughout this chapter we have looked at all aspects of child and adolescent growth and development in an attempt to develop a full portrait of the learners you will teach. Developing this portrait was like gradually adding pieces to a giant puzzle. Each piece gives you greater understanding. The better you understand the total developmental portrait of the students you teach, the more effective their learning will become. As a teacher, it should be your goal to define what each of your students knows and is able to do and then help them progress toward the next step of development. By knowing all the influences that will advance or retard their growth, you can organize artistic learning to meet the artistic needs and developmental place of all your students.

THEORY INTO PRACTICE

In this chapter we have looked at the various types of development and developmental change through which students traverse. We have seen how learners change from their earliest mark-making endeavors until they reach the stage of artistic thinking. Once we understand the learner from a theoretical standpoint, we need to develop strategies for application in classrooms. You have been given many suggestions on how to begin to investigate and understand developmental issues. In subsequent chapters, you will be exposed to a variety of curriculum planning formats. The intent of this chapter is not to provide you with a specific planning format but rather to suggest issues that will need to be considered when designing developmentally appropriate practice. While planning formats may be varied, most would include at least these four components: goals, activities, materials, and assessment. Therefore, we need to ask what developmental issues will affect how we decide what students will learn (goals), what they will do (activities), what they will need to accomplish tasks (materials), and how we will know what they have learned (assessment). The students in one class may fall into various developmental categories. Thus, a plan must be capable of crossing developmental levels. This can be accomplished if in developing the plan we take into consideration all aspects of holistic development. The changes in cognitive understanding, emotional maturity, social development, language skills, and physical and perceptual growth will need to be considered as strongly as artistic and aesthetic development.

Learning goals can facilitate a wide variety of developmental characteristics if they are clear, well stated, and flexible enough to allow for various developmental differences. In stating a goal, indicate exactly what learning will take place, but allow for students to meet the criteria in several ways. The following statement might be used for a lesson on self-portraits: "Students will be able to complete accurate portraits of themselves." This goal allows for different abilities and developmental places. For example, students whose physical development or artistic growth limited their understanding of all the needed components of the human form could still reach the goal. Their portrait would be as "accurate" as they could make it. On the other hand, a statement such as "Students will be able to discuss the abstract qualities of their own and others' work" is much more prescriptive. This statement could cross a number of developmental levels but would require the cognitive ability to think abstractly.

In designing what students will do to accomplish the goals, you will also need to be aware of the holistic developmental picture. You can design lessons or activities that cover one developmental stage, but you may want to always include a section that allows you to list adaptations for students who are either advanced or delayed in their development. So if the activity was to have students create a monoprint self-portrait, you could easily set up an open-ended activity that allowed for students of various developmental abilities to successfully complete the task. The basic components of the lesson, the use of monoprinting techniques, the understanding of the human form, the discussion of various artists' styles of self-portraits, and the use of color and composition would be appropriate for children in almost any grade. The differences that would be seen would be based on the complexity of the task and each student's creative problem-solving abilities. You could teach this lesson successfully to 25 learners with as many developmental portraits.

No art lesson can be accomplished without consideration of the materials students will use. In the monoprint self-portrait lesson, decisions on material use would be dictated the most by physical development. With a younger child whose fine motor skill is not fully developed, a monoprint portrait could be achieved using fingerpaint. As the students develop, they can be introduced to more complicated material requiring more highly developed technical skills. It is hoped that at the upper stages students are able to choose materials based on their knowledge of technique and on their intent to create a specific artistic statement.

Assessing students' learning is as important as deciding what they will do. All assessment is based on clearly stated goals and an understanding of developmental capabilities. Returning to our earlier goal statement ("Students will be able to complete accurate portraits of themselves"), you would need to consider several things. First, the definition of "accurate portrait" will be very different across stages. The early symbol-making child will have created an accurate portrait if it shows a developed human symbol. The student in the artistic thinking stage will have created an accurate portrait if it shows not just a realistic image but also an emotional or interpretive quality. Each is "accurate" within the developmental schema of the learner.

Theory that becomes appropriate practice is dependent on each teacher developing a complete understanding of his or her students and being able to match learning activities with learning potentials.

SUMMARY

The intent of this chapter was to develop a complete, holistic portrait of learners of all ages. To accomplish this, we addressed four questions, the first of which asks: What ways do we have for thinking developmentally about learners? We have looked at many areas of development: cognitive, emotional/moral, social, language, physical/perceptual, and aesthetic. Each of these has been discussed to define a picture of all phases of development and to develop an understanding of the relationships that exist among them. We have attempted to help you realize that overall development affects artistic development and that lags in any one area of development will influence growth in every other area.

The second question—How does graphic, symbolic, artistic language develop?—was addressed through the presentation of six stages of development. In discussing theses stages we saw the move from initial mark making at around age 2 to the development of artistic skill in high school. We also looked at how each area of development influenced artistic growth.

How do contextual influences affect development? The third question looked at ways learners are influenced by the world around them. The contexts of family, school, and community all affect growth as strongly but not as obviously as do the developmental stages. For total development to occur we need a clear understanding of all influences on students.

Why is it important to have a holistic conception of development? This was the final question addressed. Throughout the chapter the point has been made that without a clear understanding of developmental place, teachers cannot provide instruction that meets the needs of students. Also, when students understand and recognize their own levels of artistic development they are better able to move forward. Having gained an overall portrait of your learners, you can now begin to see how and why they make art and what influences their growth and development. Subsequent chapters will extend your knowledge and understanding of learners, art, and teaching.

ADVANTAGES AND CHALLENGES OF MAKING THIS CHOICE

The advantages and challenges to understanding the learners you will teach in art classes are many and varied. It is important to note that many of the advantages of this form of choice making will create many of the challenges.

Advantages to Understanding the Learner

The advantages to understanding the learner have been discussed frequently throughout the chapter. Perhaps the primary advantage is that your understanding of all aspects of development will aid you in planning learning activities that further the growth of your students. It is important to realize that in working with students in an art class we recognize the many factors affecting their ability to create and appreciate art. The movement from one stage of development to another is dependent on the concomitant growth and change in each individual area. Therefore, if we understand the portrait of a student holistically, we will understand how lags or developments in one area affect, positively or negatively, advancement in another.

The advantage to understanding all the components that make up the portrait of the learner for each stage helps to define a "typical" student. This definition helps the teacher of art to understand how students will move through the stages and that they will move in different ways and at different rates. Knowledge of each stage thus allows for changes in instruction and interaction that meet individual student needs and facilitates the move from one stage to the next.

Challenges to Understanding the Learner

How to apply what you have learned about holistic development to your teaching of art will be your biggest challenge. After developing a portrait of the "typical" learner within each stage, it will be necessary to discover how each individual student fits into the overall portrait. It will frequently be impossible to quickly get to know all your students in this way. You will probably develop strategies for gaining a picture of whole groups of students first and then gradually decipher how individual students' portraits will be different from their same-age peers.

It will be necessary for you to realize that all the information provided about each stage is not intended as assessment criteria for each student to meet. The definition of developmental place should be used to help students move forward and not as a hypothetical norm that when not reached means a student is failing in some way. The challenge thus becomes one of using the developmental information to help students move forward while not setting standards that all students must reach in the same exact way and time frame.

As you create a developmental portrait of your students, you will be challenged to set goals that are educationally meaningful and yet allow for the diversity of student capabilities. You will continually be torn between what you believe learners should know about art and art making at a certain age and how that learning becomes developmentally appropriate for each learner.

ACTION PLAN FOR INSTRUCTIONAL DECISION MAKING

- ～ *Develop* a complete understanding of the learners with whom you will work.
- ～ *Read* about development and developmental issues.
- ～ *Observe* behaviors.
- ～ *Watch* children make art.
- ～ *Record* your learning.
- ～ *Become* a teacher/researcher who uses data to increase your teaching skills.

DISCUSSION QUESTIONS

1. Imagine that you are the art teacher for a third-grade class. Your class is made up of a very diverse population of students from many cultural backgrounds and developmental places. How would you ascertain their abilities in art, and how would you plan lessons to meet their goals?

2. In your high school Art I class, you have many students going through adolescent crises. How might their artwork reflect what they are going through, and how might art activities help them through this difficult transition to adulthood?

3. Very young children (kindergarten and preschool) go through many changes as they move from mark making to early symbol making. Describe in your own words each area of holistic development that leads to the emergence of representative symbols. How are they interrelated? How might the lag or advancement in one area of development influence other areas?

4. If you have a clear understanding of the developmental place of the students in the emerging expertise stage, how would this knowledge help you assist the students in moving to the next stage of artistic growth?

5. How will you create a holistic portrait of the learners in your classes? What will you need to know about them, and how will you apply your knowledge?

6. As a teacher of art, why do you think the knowledge of holistic development is important in providing appropriate instruction for your students?

SUGGESTED ACTIVITIES

For Understanding the Learner Holistically

To extend and refine your understanding, you might consider beginning a journal in which you can note the main points of holistic development discussed here. You could then note your experiences, including the following:

~ Describe the experiences you have had with children thus far and analyze how your understanding of them changes.

~ Develop an individual portrait of a learner by describing holistically an individual you know well.

~ Make contact with schools and children so that you can observe learners in the classroom. Observe their behavior in an organized manner; then see how well the holistic portrait is reflected in the real world.

~ Collect several representative artworks from each of the five developmental stages and compare them with the developmental information provided. Explain what influences may have caused change and growth.

~ Look at the artwork of same-age children and see if you can ascertain what developmental delays or advances may have caused the differences in their artworks.

For Understanding the Learner Contextually

~ As a journal activity, collect drawings from the members of several families done at about the same age and see if there are differences in development.

~ Look at the artistic levels of your own family and suggest reasons for variability and similarity.

~ Investigate two styles of learning and write a comparison in your journal.

~ Compare artwork done with different styles of learners.

~ Collect drawings from special-needs children, define their learning challenges, and compare the work with that of same-age children. How would you help these challenged students reach their potential?

~ Compare the artwork of children defined as gifted and talented with that of their same-age peers. Decide how you might change lessons to meet their needs.

~ Discuss your educational profile. How do you learn? What are your successes and failures? What are your strengths and weaknesses as an artist and a student?

~ Reflect on how teachers and peers responded to you in your education, or describe someone who was different and subsequently was treated differently. For example, think about a child who looked different from everyone else because he or she was very tall or heavy or had bright red hair. How was that child treated? How did you sometimes feel different from others?

~ Ask students from various cultures to discuss objects they define as art.

~ Compare artwork to see if there is a cultural influence on what and how it is created.

ANNOTATED RESOURCES

Arnheim, R. (1989). *Thoughts on art education*. Los Angeles: Getty Center for Education in the Arts.
This book will introduce you to Rudolph Arnheim's philosophy and ideas about art and development.

Berk, L. (1994). *Child development* (3rd ed.). Boston, MA: Allyn and Bacon.
This textbook presents a good overview of all aspects of the growth and development of children.

Fein, S. (1991). *Heidi's horse*. Worcester, MA: Heinemann Press.
Fein presents a visual portrait of the development of one symbol drawn during the years of one young artist.

Gardner, H. (1980). *Artful scribbles: The significance of children's drawings*. New York: Basic Books.
This book gives an overview of artistic development as observed in two children.

Gardner, H. (1990). *Art education and human development*. Los Angeles: Getty Center for Education in the Arts.
Gardner presents developmental theory from psychology, with special emphasis on ideas that affect artistic development and education.

Golomb, C. (1974). *Young children's sculpture and drawing: A study in representational development*. Cambridge, MA: Harvard University Press.
This is one of the few books that looks at the development of children's ability to work with three-dimensional art forms.

Kellogg, R. (1970). *Analyzing children's art*. Palo Alto, CA: Mayfield Publishing.
Kellogg presents her ideas on the early development of children's art. The book is illustrated with many examples of children's art.

Lowenfeld, V. (1952). *Creative and mental growth* (2nd ed.). New York: Macmillan.
This book represents one of the strongest influences on our understanding of the artistic and creative development of children. Lowenfeld presents stages of development that form the basis for much of today's knowledge about children's art. For the best understanding of his work, read one of the first three editions.

Piaget, J., & Inhelder, B. (1969). *The psychology of the child*. New York: Basic Books.
Jean Piaget wrote many books on various aspects of child development that greatly influenced current research on stage theory. This book presents a definitive summary of these aspects.

KEY TERMS

Bang dots   Initial marks, which generally occur during the process of hitting some tool against a surface, that children produce during the mark-making stage of artistic development.

Schema   A representation with no intentional experience expressed; a symbol for the thing itself.

PART **2** *Choices for Creating Meaning*

CHAPTER 3

Cultivating Artistic Behaviors

Karen Lee Carroll
Maryland Institute, College of Art

Guiding Questions

~ Why think of art as a behavior?

~ How can artistic behaviors contribute to the creation of meaning?

~ How can investigations of form and material be connected to feeling and meaning?

~ How can the motivation to represent lead to the development of visual symbolic language?

~ How can visual and artistic modes of thought and expression be cultivated?

Given the instinctive and natural way that mark-making, drawing, and making behaviors emerge in early childhood, why do most learners eventually stop drawing and making? The young child brings to school many natural propensities: a love of mark making; an interest in tools; a desire to make, construct, and build; an affinity for storytelling; a love of imaginative play; and the understanding that marks can carry meaning. What happens to these inherent human propensities depends a great deal on the choices teachers make.

In Chapter 2, you had the opportunity to think about the nature and needs of learners. The intent of Chapter 3 is to introduce **artistic behaviors** as different ways of integrating making and thinking that artists, designers, and visual thinkers have used to construct meaning. To do so, I propose that we begin by thinking about art as behavior and about teaching art as the cultivation of artistic behaviors. The more comprehensive and masterful the command of artistic behaviors, the more likely it is that visual modes of thought and expression will be chosen as a way of constructing meaning in school, outside of school, and later in society as adults. The reverse is also true. If we fail to cultivate artistic behaviors, the innate, human propensities to make things, use visual language, think visually, and give visual expression to our thoughts and feelings will atrophy.

Why Think of Art as a Behavior?

Although *everyone* has a notion of what the word *art* means, it is a slippery concept—one hard to pin down. Usually, art makes us think of objects, things we can see—like paintings (on canvases, walls, vases, bodies), sculptures (carved or modeled), ceramic vessels, and woven textiles. Some find art in only certain kinds of paintings, sculptures, and ceramic vessels—for these observers, art is a quality (like skill, beauty, craftsmanship, elaboration, and spiritual or other significance) that defines art.

In this chapter we will think of art as behavior. More specifically, we will consider art as artistic behavior—what we do when we make art or make something artfully. If there were a word such as *artify,* we might use that. In other words, the interest is shifted from objects and their qualities to the behaviors or processes and to the purposes fulfilled by that engagement. Rather than asking "How do we teach art?" I ask "How do we cultivate artistic behavior in our learners?"

Art has evolved as a primary mode of thought and expression. Artistic behaviors such as making special objects and forms of visual display for community celebrations have long been integral to the visual sharing of communal beliefs and values in traditional societies. Artistic behaviors have also come to serve the needs of individuals in search of their own identities and have made it possible for individuals and groups to record, respond to, shape, personalize, and critique the world of experience. When artful processes of thinking and image making are applied to life's endeavors, life itself becomes more satisfying and fulfilling.

How Can Artistic Behaviors Contribute to the Creation of Meaning?

The habits of mind and the ways of working artfully that artists employ as part of a process of creating meaning emanate from modes of visual thought and expression. The roots of these artistic behaviors are seen in infancy and early childhood, and they are found in the activities of traditional societies. The manner in which artistic behaviors develop can be seen by looking at the work of children and young people, who, by nature, are **visual learners** and whose affinity for this mode of thought and expression is so strong that they educate themselves. But it can be seen among all learners where a strong art program cultivates artistic behaviors within the context of

COLOR PLATE 2.1

Melody painted one kinesthetic manipulation over another.

Collection of the author.

COLOR PLATE 2.2

Melody showed an ability to plan and place her painted lines.

Collection of the author.

COLOR PLATE 2.3

Melody chose her favorite colors for each object she painted.

Collection of the author.

COLOR PLATE 2.4

"Sarah the Camel"— Chelsey French, age 5, drew a picture of a trip to the zoo.

Collection of Judith Simpson.

COLOR PLATE 2.5

"27 Pine Street"—Second grader Thad drew his house.

Collection of the author.

COLOR PLATE 2.7

"The House in My Dreams"— Nathaniel, 12 years old, created an imaginative rendering of a house.

Collection of the author.

COLOR PLATE 2.8

"Who Am I?"—Twelfth grader Eduardo created a self-portrait using color and line to show his confusion about life.

Collection of the author.

COLOR PLATE 2.10

"Mandy, Self Portrait"—Mandy, age 18, showed that she has a well-developed visual sense despite her hearing loss.

Collection of the author.

COLOR PLATE 2.9

In this watercolor 16-year-old Kim used color to realistically define the items in her still life.

Collection of the author.

COLOR PLATE 3.1

"Today We Will Make a Still Life," by a fifth-grade student, involved drawing objects from observation.

Collection of the author.

COLOR PLATE 3.2

"The Queen of Chocolate," by a third-grade girl.

Collection of the author.

COLOR PLATE 3.3

A detail from the narrative by a high school student honoring the role her parents have played in her life and recognizing her own accomplishments in school.

Collection of the author.

COLOR PLATE 3.4

A seventh grader combined the soft qualities of fiber, warm inviting colors, and a symbol for a house to make a weaving that suggests ideas about comfort and home.

Collection of the author.

COLOR PLATE 3.6

This narrative drawing by a sixth grader honors significant others in this child's life ("My uncle, mom, and dad are my heroes") and tells a story: "In a dollar store, I found a $50 bill. I was real young but I managed to find it under the counter while my mom paid for one item. My mom made me give it to the poor."

Collection of the author.

COLOR PLATE 3.5

Visual concepts such as "touching" helped this kindergarten student use his schema for people to create the feeling of a crowd.

Collection of the author.

COLOR PLATE 3.7

A seventh grader's watercolor drawing from observation.

Collection of the author.

COLOR PLATE 3.9

This metaphorical image was made by a high school student in response to the invitation to create a visual metaphor for a childhood memory that held special significance. This image stands as a metaphor for a painful childhood accident.

Collection of the author.

COLOR PLATE 3.8

This second grader's watercolor-and-crayon drawing can be considered a visual metaphor for "the city" because of the way it provides a structure for thinking about certain highlights and aspects of the city.

Collection of the author.

COLOR PLATE 4.1

Tag, 1961, by Walter A. Prochownik (born 1932). Oil on canvas, 60.25 x 40.125 in.

What ideas or feelings are communicated in this art image? How?

The Charles Rand Penney Collection of Western New York Art at the Burchfield-Penney Art Center, Buffalo State College, Buffalo, New York.

COLOR PLATE 4.2

Five Capital Executions in China: Flaying, 1992, by Zhi Lin. Charcoal, ink wash, acrylic, screenprint on canvas, and ribbons, 144 x 84 in.

What is your response to this artwork? Why? What postmodern strategies did the artist use? What feelings are generated as you respond to the artwork?

Courtesy of the artist.

COLOR PLATE 4.4

Five Capital Executions in China: Firing Squad, 1995, by Zhi Lin. Charcoal, ink wash, acrylic, screenprint on canvas, and ribbons, 144 x 84 in.

How does the use of color and space contribute to the meaning of this artwork? What do you see in the crowd that seems out of place in the scene?

Courtesy of the artist.

COLOR PLATE 4.3

Five Capital Executions in China: Decapitation, 1994, by Zhi Lin. Charcoal, ink wash, acrylic, screenprint on canvas, and ribbons, 144 x 84 in.

What symbols has the artist used in this art image? How do they affect the meaning?

Courtesy of the artist.

COLOR PLATE 4.5

The Destructive Periods in Russia During Stalin's (Communist) and Deniken's (Monarchist) Leadership, 1988, by Tanya Ganson (1910-1993). Oil on canvas, 16.25 x 20.25 in.

How does the childlike style of this painting affect your response to it? What feelings are generated by the colors and shapes?

Collection of the Burchfield-Penney Art Center, Buffalo State College, Buffalo, New York. Gift of Kevin and Rise Kulik.

COLOR PLATE 4.6

The Sneak, 1989, by Joyce J. Scott. Sculptural neckpiece of glass beads and thread, two-drop peyote stitch, 5.5 x 13.5 x 11 in.

A murder victim, her attacker, and observers of the crime are portrayed in the medium of glass beads. Why do you think Scott chose this medium? What devices did she use to communicate the horror of urban violence?

Collection of the artist.

COLOR PLATE 4.8

Hometown Hunger, 1986, by Christy Rupp (born 1949). Steel, plaster, and paint, 33 x 64 x 24 in.

How does this artist use metaphor to communicate her message about the effect of industry on farmers?

Collection of the Burchfield-Penney Art Center, Buffalo State College, Buffalo, New York. Gift of the artist.

COLOR PLATE 4.7

Greenscape, 1982, by Bob Booth (born 1952). Birch and mixed media, 40.5 x 21 x 21 in.

What environmental concerns does this artwork address? How?

The Charles Rand Penney Collection of Western New York Art at the Burchfield-Penney Art Center, Buffalo State College, Buffalo, New York.

COLOR PLATE 4.9

Three-dimensional interpretation of Matisse's *Still Life in the Studio, Nice,* by Kelli Nunn. Tempera paint on cardboard and mixed media, 15 x 15 in.

Collection of the artist.

COLOR PLATE 4.10

Three-dimensional interpretation of Cassatt's *Little Girl in a Blue Armchair,* by Faye Martin Clifton. Tempera paint on cardboard, 13 x 15 x 10 in.

Postcard reproduction of *Little Girl in a Blue Armchair,* by Mary Cassatt, 1878, oil on canvas, 35.5. x 51.125 in.; framed 45 x 60.75 x 2.25 in.

Collection of Mr. and Mrs. Paul Mellon, ©1996 Board of Trustees, National Gallery of Art, Washington, D.C.

COLOR PLATE 4.11

Three-dimensional interpretation of Morisot's *In the Dining Room,* by Bradney Willingham. Tempera on cardboard, 13 x 12 x 12 in.

Postcard reproduction of Berthe Morisot, *In the Dining Room,* 1886, oil on canvas, 24.125 x 19.75 in.; framed 31 x 26.5 in.

Chester Dale Collection, ©1996 Board of Trustees, National Gallery of Art, Washington, D.C.

COLOR PLATE 4.12

The Garden, by Jessica Lillard. Tempera paint on paper, 18 x 24 in.

Artwork from the 1994-1996 Crayola® Dream-Makers™ Collection. Crayola® is a registered trademark of Binney & Smith, Inc., used with permission.

COLOR PLATE 4.13

Josephine, by Miriam Shapiro, 1986. Cutout paper, 86 x 66 in.

How does Shapiro communicate a sense of energy in this artwork?

Private collection. Courtesy Steinbaum Krauss Gallery, New York.

both the art curriculum and the larger curriculum of the schools. When this happens, the making of art contributes meaning to the entire educational process, as well as to the individual lives of our learners. To understand the full range of choices a teacher has, we need a way of thinking about art.

The following conception of art is useful for thinking about both making art and teaching. If we think of art as visual language, embedded in significant form and material, making thought and feeling visible (Carroll, 1987), we have a three-part conception that is sufficiently open ended to accommodate a wide range of possibilities. In particular, this conception of art is useful because it integrates the search for visual form in which to embody thought, feeling, and idea with a command of symbolic language in which visual symbols are used to create meaning. Each part of this conception has something specific to lend to the whole.

Finding Meaning Through Visual Form and Material

The notion of art as **significant form** (Cassirer, 1972; Langer, 1953b) refers to the way thoughts, feelings, and ideas are embedded in **sensuous materials** and given visual shape and form. Together, form and material are transformed into a language that carries its own meanings. What makes visual form significant is its power to attract attention and to communicate or express a whole set of feelings and ideas in a nonverbal manner.

Compare two still lifes, one drawn with chalks and the other drawn with pen (see Color Plate 3.1 and Figure 3.1). The objects in the chalk drawing are rendered

Figure 3.1
"Still Life in Pen," by a sixth-grade student

softly; the still life in pen uses lines to describe forms and materials that are dry, even brittle. The chalk drawing speaks gently of smooth solid forms, while the pen drawing speaks energetically about different textures and natural materials.

Young children have a natural curiosity about materials, and they willingly play with them to see what they can do (Szekely, 1988). In many ways, artists try to keep this sense of curiosity and play alive in their own investigations and admit that the best ideas are often found through accidents, which present possibilities not thought of otherwise. Thus, orchestrating investigations of materials is an important part of making art. Developing an understanding of how visual form, combined with materials, creates meaning is also critical to the art-making process. The profound pleasure that can come from working with art materials, processes, and forms is a central motivational force for both artists and learners.

Finding Meaning Through Visual Symbolic Language

The notion of art as a **symbolic language** (Goodman, 1968; Gombrich, 1969; Gardner, 1980; Golomb, 1992) suggests that art is like other languages and involves the mastery of vocabulary, grammar, and form. In the case of the visual arts, learning to draw realistically can be thought of as one example of learning the **conventions** of art's symbolic language. The language of Western drawing involves practice with techniques for drawing different kinds of subject matter, rendering form, showing perspective, and dealing with specific kinds of representational problems, such as foreshortening (see Figure 3.2). A command of Western drawing conventions makes it

Figure 3.2
Foreshortened figure drawing by a middle school student

possible to create the illusion of depth and form, or what is called the third dimension, on a two-dimensional, or flat, surface.

There are other symbol systems besides the conventions of Western drawing to consider. Take, for example, the vocabulary of forms used by the Northwest Coast Indians, which has been handed down through the years from one carver to another. In this case, the carver learns the forms that are expected by the culture, their mythological meanings, and the techniques needed for carving (Boas, 1955). Artists may also invent (as did Kandinsky in his paintings and Frank Lloyd Wright in his buildings) a personal vocabulary of forms that they use symbolically to represent ideas and worldviews. Thus, developing visual symbolic language is a central task in making art. In part, it involves learning the conventions of existing visual systems. For many artists it is also a matter of developing a personal and even unique vocabulary of symbols and forms that carry meaning.

Finding Meaning Through Visual and Artistic Modes of Thought and Feeling

The notion of art as a way of knowing, thinking, and feeling focuses attention on the ways art makes thought visible. Value is assigned to art precisely for its alternative way of thinking (Cassirer, 1972; Langer, 1953b), which is different from more linear forms of thought. Because of the way art integrates intuitive and rational thought and unites the emotions with cognition, it becomes a powerful process for coming to know what one thinks (Arnheim, 1962) and feels (London, 1989).

Art-making processes can accommodate many different ways of thinking (Dorn, 1994; John-Steiner, 1985). For example, the act of drawing activates the search for knowledge, bringing into focus visual information about structure, form, and detail. In a different way, an intuitive search with symbolic language, form, and materials can lead to discoveries and new insights (Arieti, 1976; Szekely, 1988; London, 1989, 1994). Art is also a way of thinking visually and spatially (Dixon, 1983; Kay 1991). Solving visual problems, solving problems visually, making problems visible, and generating visual problems are all variations of creative thinking (Eisner, 1972; Goodnow, 1977; Roukes, 1988; Gablik, 1991). While the process of making results in thinking and feeling, the product of art can be regarded as thought and feeling made visible.

Finding Meaning Through Multiple Modes of Thought and Expression

In many ways, art is similar to other modes of thought and expression. Verbal and written forms of expression involve forms such as poems and plays constructed with the materials of words with sounds, colors, shapes, voices, and action. To develop writing skills, students are encouraged to develop a rich vocabulary of words and to experiment with poetic, dramatic, and other artful forms of writing. As a result, thoughts and feelings can be given form and shape. Mathematics and science are other modes of thought and expression, each with their own languages of symbols and forms.

Yet visual, mathematical, scientific, and verbal modes of thought and expression are distinctly valuable because each one accommodates different ideas and perceptions and can lead to different insights or understandings. Consider how a visual

Figure 3.3
A child's map of her neighborhood

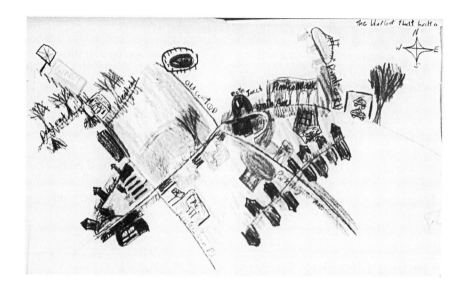

map brings to light different information than a set of verbal directions because it provides a sense of spatial relationships and orientation (see Figure 3.3). A poem told in words as well as images has twice the power of words or images alone because of the way the sounds, action, and feeling are heightened and reinforced (see Figure 3.4).

Teachers are beginning to understand that these modes of thought and expression are not only different from each other but complementary. The practices of combining image and text (Olson, 1992) and using visual strategies for instruction give teachers more ways of reaching students with different learning styles. The recognition of different learning styles and multiple intelligences (Guilford, 1967; Gardner, 1985) is consistent with the idea of employing different modes of thought and expression for their own distinct value as well as their value in relationship with each other. The ways emotion and cognition work together to help the brain learn, remember, organize, and make sense out of experience suggest that artistic modes of thought and expression, and artistic behaviors, should take a more central position in the curriculum (Sylwester, 1995; Goleman, 1994). How might this look in practice?

Figure 3.4
A first grader's poem–shape book: "My shapes are going to the fair where they can ride the ferris [wheel] round and round and round."

THEORY INTO PRACTICE

Time Portal Portraits

Russell Harris was student teaching in a city elementary school. His third-grade students had been introduced to information about the kings and queens of Africa. A painter himself, Russell decided to design a painting unit that would build on this information. He invited his students to step back through a portal in time by creating painted portraits of themselves embellished with special touches as would befit kings and queens. Russell demonstrated painting techniques, and the work began.

As the students were working, Russell urged them to think about the royal persons they were creating portraits of and the stories they might have to tell. When they completed their images, they were invited to put their stories into writing. Observing this lesson, I noted that one young artist had portrayed her royal figure as having blowing hair (see Color Plate 3.2). When it came time to share the stories they had written, Ashley Cunningham offered the following:

> I am the queen of Chocolateland. I even make chocolate. We sleep on chocolate. We also eat from chocolate spoons and forks. I [am] from the past. We also made chocolate history.

As Ashley was telling her story about Chocolateland, someone asked her about the blowing hair. Thinking on her feet, she spontaneously offered that the hair was blowing from the cool breezes that kept the chocolate from melting.

Personal Narratives

Amy Ruopp, in working with narrative formats with her middle schoolers (Ruopp, 1996), had been using a variety of tasks to prepare students for making their own narrative images. These tasks included reflective questions dealing with significant others and formative moments in their lives. The piece in Figure 3.5 (see

Figure 3.5
Sunni Diggs's "Personal Narrative"

also Color Plate 3.3 for a detail of this figure) was done by a 15-year-old high school student taking a special class in narrative drawing with Amy.

The format that Amy introduced draws on Faith Ringgold's story quilts for a number of conventions: the possibility of representing the self more than once in a narrative image; the use of mixed points of view; the merging of different moments in time; the inclusion of quiltlike borders, which add additional symbolic information to the completed work; and the inclusion of text as part of the image. The following text appears in Sunni Diggs's border:

> My mother guides me into school and leads me to a world in which I know nothing about. While eight years old and entering the third grade, I moved from a school that was about 90% black to a school that had 95% white students. I seemed to manage for seven years. Here I am, standing in front of the goals that I want to achieve in my lifetime. Looking beyond into the future, I can see these goals as someday becoming my greatest accomplishments and crowning glories. Yes, this is my father. I feel he is determined to achieve the American dream for himself and his family. He's working hard at getting that flag to the top. As you can see, it doesn't have far to go.

Three-Part Conception of Making Art

The meanings found in these two examples are indeed personal. In the first, a young girl has imagined herself as a royal character and set herself into an imaginary land where, of course, chocolate abounds. Perhaps that alone is sufficient to suggest she has created her own meaning. But the experience pushed a little further, offering her the opportunity to write and then share a story. In watching her construct on the spot a justification for the blowing hair, one could almost see her wheels turning. Both she and the class were delighted to know that she could think such thoughts.

In the case of the personal narrative, we have an image that is loaded with reflective information. It tells of a personal journey. We see the mother escorting the child to the new school, and we also see her as she has matured into a young woman. Not only did this image have great personal meaning for the young artist, but it also deeply moved her mother when she saw it at the class exhibition. The mother related that she had not realized the way her daughter had seen what both her parents were doing to help her. Thus, we have an image that is not only meaningful to the maker but is of special value to her parents as well.

If we probe a little deeper, we see that both art encounters involved experiences with sensuous materials and interesting visual forms. Russell's students not only made painterly paintings but could embellish them by adding sequins. Amy's students combined drawing and painting materials with fabric and collage materials using Ringgold's quilt format. Sunni added cloth from Africa as well as hearts and other designs to personalize the border. Both teachers challenged students with problems of visual representation appropriate to their level of artistic development. Russell's learners concentrated on depicting the face, whereas the more complex narrative image made use of more advanced skills in drawing. Figures in the narrative are shown from different points of view, and three different images have been merged together into a whole. Finally, both teachers presented opportunities to think reflectively and creatively. Envisioning the self as royalty provided the young artist with a sense of self-esteem. Thinking new thoughts, as a result of having made an image, proved to be a special form of discovery and delight. For Sunni, telling her story, looking at her journey, and seeing the roles others have played in her life became a way of recognizing and synthesizing formative experiences, personal strengths, and goals.

The manner in which these two students have discovered their own meanings illustrates the three dimensions of the making act, which I believe are intimately related to the creation of meaning: the use of sensuous materials and significant form, the use of symbolic visual language, and the use of visual modes of thought and feeling. This three-part conception of making art can help us think about what is involved in the process of making art and the ways teachers can nurture and guide the development of artistic behaviors. In the following three sections, we will explore some of the choices teachers have if they aim to develop artistic behaviors with their learners.

How Can Investigations of Form and Material Be Connected to Feeling and Meaning?

Nurturing Natural Artistic Behaviors

Teachers have long recognized that young children and learners of all ages are drawn to making things and working with materials. I have also found that classroom teachers and art teachers share an avid interest in making things. The pleasures of making and the personal satisfaction and social rewards of doing so are strong motivational factors for learners of all ages, including adults. Human beings, by their nature, like to make things special (Dissanayake, 1988), and both children and artists have especially wonderful ideas about how that might be accomplished. As art materials and visual form are intimately linked in the process of creating meaning, it is impossible, for example, to practice making visual form without working with materials. And working with materials results in the creation of forms. Nevertheless, it may serve our purposes to take a look first at each of these separately before considering how to orchestrate investigations that make the connection to feeling and meaning.

Finding Meaning in Materials

Children are great collectors and organizers of materials (Szekely, 1988). They find them in the most unlikely places and generate creative ideas with minimal means. For example, two sixth graders demonstrated an inventiveness with found and everyday materials to make fantasy vehicles (see Figure 3.6). Artists, too, are drawn to materials. Studios are full of found objects and all kinds of raw materials for creative endeavors. Artists spend time organizing their tools and materials almost as a premeditative exercise for the process of making. Pass art materials out to students before instructions are given and you will have lost their attention, as minds and hands quickly succumb to the gravitational pull of materials. All this suggests that materials have their own seductive powers and are part of the reason art can be so compelling.

It is not often recognized that materials have the capacity to carry their own meanings. For example, materials such as yarn and clay have unique qualities. When a weaving is constructed out of wool, it has different meanings than one made of painted

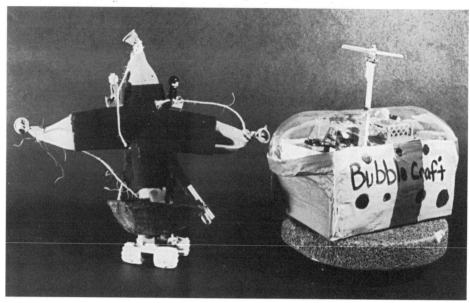

Figure 3.6
Fantasy vehicles made by sixth graders

sticks, even though both prospects have interesting possibilities. The weaving in Color Plate 3.4 takes a solid, large-scale object (the house) and changes it by representing it as a woven image, soft to the touch and small in scale. It connects the idea of a house with the ideas of warmth and comfort. A pot made of clay (see Photo 3.1) carries very

Photo 3.1
12-year-old boy making a ceramic pot

different meanings. While the material begins organically and is technically alive in its wet state, fire and heat turn it into something hard, solid, and stable. Ideas about containers are connected to ideas about durability and permanency.

Both clay and wool, like many materials, have long histories associated with their use by different cultures in history and around the world. Some tools and materials have short histories, yet they still hold important meanings. For example, computer-generated images have meanings attached to a technologically advanced society. To use a given material is to call upon its associated use in time and culture. Materials may be used in ways consistent with traditional ways of making, or they can be used in very different ways in a effort to create dramatically new meanings.

It is also possible to think about feelings communicated by materials and processes. Two faces, made by children of the same class, demonstrate how the same subject matter and even similar feelings can be achieved differently by changing the materials. One first grader has used feathers and three-dimensional shapes of cut paper to speak with a feeling of exuberance (see Figure 3.7a). Shapes vary in color and texture and explode off the page with a sense of playful innovation. In contrast, a drawn portrait (see Figure 3.7b) achieves a similar yet different feeling of intensity with its actively and vigorously drawn lines and shapes.

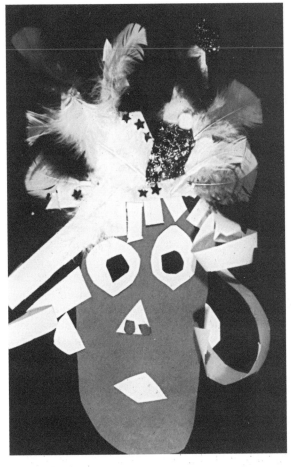

Figure 3.7a
Collage portrait by a first-grade student

Figure 3.7b
Drawn portrait by a first-grade student

Developing a repertoire of ideas about materials.   On one hand, we want learners to know what ideas can be accommodated by a wide variety of materials, tools, processes, and techniques. This has sometimes led to a smorgasbord kind of thinking in which new materials are presented each time a class meets. On the other hand, evidence shows that extended practice with a more limited range of materials leads to a higher level of mastery and more sophisticated ideas. Most artists know that they regress in their representational skills every time they switch to a new medium. It takes time to get to know how to use the tools, to find out what a medium can do, and to begin to make some connection between the medium and the ideas it might carry.

A good example of extended work with a drawing medium can be seen in Figure 3.8. Third graders were invited to make tunnel books using colored pencils. The medium was chosen because it was the best solution for preserving the level of detail in drawing the children wanted while at the same time affording them the opportunity to work in color. As labor intensive as the project was, there was pleasure in mark making and discovering what new colors could be made by blending and mixing. The additional use of cutaway foregrounds and middle grounds to reveal a background made these three-dimensional book constructions a great success. Monkeys swing from the trees. Animals stalk in the forests. Whole environments are created with both depth and detail. Investigations of materials should be balanced between extended opportunities with selected materials (as illustrated in these tunnel books) and more short-term exploratory experiences.

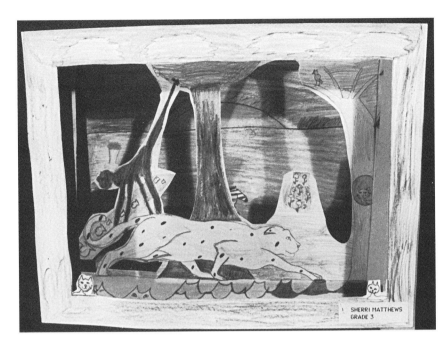

Figure 3.8
"Jungle Tunnel Book," by a third grader

Finding Meaning in Visual Form

Art teachers use a formal language to describe, analyze, and interpret **visual form**. Since the beginning of the 20th century, the **elements of art and the principles of design**, first set forth by Dow (1899), have been a pillar of practice in art education. Art problems have been designed for experimentation with the elements of line, shape, color, texture, and value, as well as the different ways of organizing a composition through unity, balance, and opposition. The elements and principles have evolved just enough so that almost *every* design book has a slightly different version. (For contemporary examples, see Roukes [1988] and Stoops and Samuelson [1983].) While some teachers and artists think of these elements and principles as the "rules of art," they are more accurately one set of terms useful in the description and analysis of visual material and form.

Other formal languages exist. Itten (1963) taught at the Bauhaus in Germany and developed a theory of visual form based on the study of contrasting **visual concepts**. In studying how one concept was opposite of another, both concepts and the meaning they carry could be better understood. For example, high was studied in contrast to low, soft to hard, curved to straight. This vocabulary of opposites—including sophisticated concepts such as spiral and concentric, parallel and branching, open and closed, rough and smooth—can be mastered by children as young as 3 and 4 years old if they are explored with clear examples and through a variety of activities. Figure 3.9 shows an example of clay tiles made by first graders exploring the concepts of rough and smooth. Part of the instructional process includes playing with words, acting out various concepts physically, finding examples in the environment, connecting visual forms with feeling and meaning, and using the form in both two- and three-dimensional materials (see Townley, 1978).

Research reinforces the notion that young children understand form before other visual qualities such as color (Golomb, 1992). Visual concepts can be taught to

Figure 3.9
Clay tiles by first graders showing both rough and smooth qualities

children who are still in the mark-making or early symbolic stages prior to the beginnings of a basic symbol system for drawing people, animals, or houses. In the
process of sorting and classifying visual form according to perceived characteristics,
children are developing **cognitive concepts,** which underpin more **abstract
thinking** (Arnheim, 1989). These concepts are essential for understanding more
about the complexities of experience. Recognizing, for example, that open or closed
forms (such as doors and windows) carry meanings, possibly of danger or welcome,
helps young learners navigate the world more intelligently. When children not only
begin to see how visual forms are alike and different but associate feeling and meaning with them, they have a more sophisticated language for thinking and talking
about the world of experience (see Color Plate 3.5). They are also better prepared
for the more abstract ideas that are to come in the larger curriculum. As well, they
might become emotionally intelligent—aware of their feelings and the way visual
form contributes to them.

     Investigations using a formal language of visual concepts and explorations that
integrate looking with touching, moving, and making can make a major contribution to
the cognitive and emotional development of learners, as well as to their artistic growth
(Baker, 1991a, 1994). Such investigations have even more value if they are connected
with feeling and meaning. New language presents itself as new concepts come to light
through science and technology. Roukes (1988), for example, presents language for
describing the substructure of design and unseen forces at work in nature.

Orchestrating Investigations with Form and Material: Making the Connection to Feeling and Meaning

Just as this book is concerned with teachers' choices, it is important to help learners
consider the choices they have with materials and for creating visual form. Their
choices will have meaning. Dialogue with learners is especially important (Burton,
1980a, 1980b): calling attention to possibilities, asking for ideas, engaging thoughtful

Figure 3.10
Paper collage with letters and yarn by a kindergarten student

preparation for even simple tasks such as kindergarten collages made with shapes and letters. Before a kindergarten student made the collage shown in Figure 3.10, the class talked about where they could put shapes and letters and invested time rearranging parts prior to gluing.

Attending to choices with materials and visual form contributes significantly to the understanding that, through choices, materials can be transformed to carry new meanings (Burton, 1980a). One also comes to understand that it is through choices that different meanings can be found and created. Very often, it is only a matter of taking an additional step. The charcoal drawing shown in Figure 3.11, made by a middle schooler, employs **nonrepresentational form**. It offers an opportunity to ask: What possible meanings might we see here? How might this drawing be a metaphor for some meaning or feeling?

 How Can the Motivation to Represent Lead to the Development of Visual Symbolic Language?

Nurturing Natural Artistic Behaviors

While drawing seems to be a natural behavior for young children—a spontaneous, even an instinctive, activity—the same is not true for older learners and adults. Many associate drawing ability with notions of natural talent or ability rather than training

Figure 3.11
Nonrepresentational charcoal drawing by a middle school student

and education. Most adults see themselves in one camp or the other: the drawers or the nondrawers, the artistically talented or the nonartistically talented. Many teachers have a fear of drawing; drawing anxiety has even been noticed among art teachers. Most children, as well, soon lose confidence in their drawing. Why is this the case? Is there another way of thinking about drawing so that the natural human propensity to make marks, use tools, and create meaning graphically and symbolically might be cultivated in the schools?

Artistic behaviors rooted in pleasure.   The drawing behaviors that begin in early childhood are rooted in the kinesthetic pleasures of mark making and natural affinities for tools, which continue to fund the drawing act throughout its development. Early drawers may not even be looking at their drawing so much as enjoying the pleasure of moving their arms over a surface with a tool. Very soon, however, they become fascinated with the marks they are making and will put down a marker that has run dry or find the end of the pen that leaves a mark. At first, children are interested in making marks on any surface: their clothes and shoes, walls and furniture. They have to be taught to use paper and gradually become aware of the edges that define the drawing space. The resulting marks delight children, and they are eager to share their marks with others. The human fascination with tools causes children to further explore these possibilities.

Discovering that marks can carry meaning.   The discovery that marks can carry meaning signals the beginning of visual symbolic language (Burton, 1980a; Winner, 1982; Golomb, 1992). This insight usually occurs before any recognizable equivalent has yet been drawn. Young drawers name their markings and practice making more marks (Lowenfeld, 1957). Watching young children handle marking tools reminds us of how much effort it takes to develop the coordination to hold and control them and how much practice it takes to first make basic shapes such as the circle. Yet, children pursue mark making with a strong sense of purpose (Gardner, 1980), as though something from the inside were directing it and pulling it forward.

The motivation to represent.　As children learn how to make shapes by enclosing a form with a line, the possibilities of representation dramatically increase. The symbols that begin to take shape are economical equivalents that have sufficient correspondence to the structure of their referent to signify them. Thus, a person is a tall form with a circle on top. Soon, children have a vocabulary of basic forms with which they can make equivalents, such as people, houses, and animals. Research suggests that this entire process is propelled forward by the possibilities of representation (Golomb, 1992). Adults can encourage children to draw different kinds of forms and to try different kinds of drawing tasks (Goodnow, 1977; Golomb, 1992) (see Figure 3.12). It becomes clear that the young learners are indeed thinking and solving problems as they draw.

Principles guiding representation.　Children's drawings look the way they do because certain principles serve as guides to the drawing process (Wilson & Wilson, 1982). For example, children have an affinity for drawing equivalents that are economical yet show important visual information. Thus, they are likely to draw frontal views of people and houses because from that view, maximum information can be depicted. They begin to observe perpendicular and symmetrical principles in organizing the picture plane. They make their **schema** or symbols more flexible by observing a kind of plastic principle, in which limbs can be extended to reach balls or objects. Where do these principles come from? In part, they appear to be related to the conceptual and cognitive development of the child. They are also related to the process of learning the conventions of drawing. In short, children are learning how to draw. How they solve drawing problems is influenced by what they have discovered

Figure 3.12

Two drawings by the same first grader. *Left:* Spontaneous drawings of people using the schema the artist has developed. *Right:* A drawing from dictation in which parts of the body were named, one by one, so the student could draw them.

on their own and what models of representation they have been exposed to. They can learn from their own practice, their peers, teachers, the popular culture, and art.

Learning to solve drawing problems.   Rather than thinking about drawing as simply the unfolding of a natural ability (as it appears to be for developmentally advanced drawers who progress quickly), teachers can think about drawing as solving different kinds of representational problems. How can children get more visual information into their schema? How can drawings become more expressive and interesting? How can the possibilities of representation—in particular, the narrative impulse—motivate children to further the development of their graphic, symbolic vocabulary and grammar?

The narrative impulse.   The need to tell stories acts as a powerful motivation for both the visual arts and the language arts, and it is certainly not limited to childhood. Because an idea wants so badly to be expressed, learners are inclined to solve representational problems. Cultivating and directing this impulse, teachers can orchestrate opportunities for **narrative drawing,** or visual storytelling, as a way of developing symbolic language, while serving the fundamental needs that all learners have to map their journeys, tell their stories, and dream their dreams. But teachers can do more than just provide the opportunity to draw stories. They can provide practice with different narrative drawing techniques so that children can make a variety of characters; show action; use different points of view; develop interesting settings with time of day, season, or year and weather; and create special effects (see Color Plate 3.6) (Olson, 1992; Wilson & Olson, 1979). They can learn from art created by others, including their peers, illustrators of children's books, and established artists. (Chapter 5 takes a more in-depth look at the human need to tell stories.)

Multiple Strategies for Teaching Drawing

Studies of childhood works by artists tell us that learning to draw involves simultaneous practice with multiple strategies for making images (Duncum, 1984; Pariser, 1985; Carroll, 1994). The young Edvard Munch, artist of the well-known image *The Scream*, drew narratively as a child, working alongside his brother making storybooks. His interest in narrative art continued throughout adolescence (illustrating images for novels) and into adulthood. At the same time he was drawing narratively, he was also teaching himself to draw from observation, first with simple objects and interiors of his home, later with landscapes, and finally with figures and faces. He also practiced image making by copying master works of art (Carroll, 1994). We know from other research that young image makers have sought out models for new ways of drawing, copying from peers, artists, and popular culture (Duncum, 1984).

Practice with multiple strategies for drawing and image making can begin in the early grades, where examining objects closely and guiding children through the drawing process can give young drawers more visual information to factor into their existing schemas. Working from memory and experience, using previsualization or association dialogues to activate passive knowledge (Lowenfeld, 1957; Burton, 1980c), can help learners make more interesting and unusual images about everyday activities and special events (see Figures 3.13 and 3.14).

Themes that spark the interest of learners have a particular way of unearthing unusual drawing solutions and fuller images (Hurwitz & El-Bassiouny, 1993) (see Figures 3.15 and 3.16). Using works of art as a springboard for image making helps

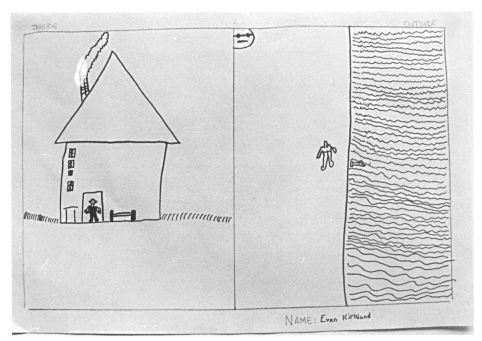

Figure 3.13
A previsualized drawing by a second grader. *Left:* "Inside." *Right:* An aerial view, "Outside," at the beach.

Figure 3.14
A previsualized drawing by a second grader. *Left:* "Inside" a house. *Right:* "Inside an airplane which is Outside."

Figure 3.15
A crayon-and-watercolor narrative drawing by a third grader entitled "He Shattered It to Pieces"

Figure 3.16
Narrative drawing by a middle school student reflecting on his family's reaction to the birth of another child

students by providing a start for an image as well as models and techniques for more interesting stylistic possibilities (Wilson, Hurwitz, & Wilson, 1987; Aukerman, 1991, 1992, 1993, 1994) (see Figures 3.17a and 3.17b). (See Chapter 4 for a more in-depth look at engaging learners with works of art.)

Critical passages in drawing development.   Often adults are so enamored with the vividness of children's early art that they are reticent to interfere with the natural unfolding of the drawing act. Many assume that because children are drawing with schemas or symbols they cannot draw from observation. Quite the opposite is often true (see Figures 3.18a, 3.18b, 3.19a, and 3.19b). Confidence in drawing wanes during the early years of school because basic schematic forms of representation begin to fail the ideas children want to portray. A natural bridge between the schematic drawing of first grade and the more realistic drawing styles of middle school can be constructed with narrative drawing techniques that show children ways of making their schema more flexible and their narrative devices more dramatic and full (Olson, 1992; Ruopp, 1996).

Beginning in about the fourth grade, **contour line drawing** can connect the child's increasing capacity for observation with a process for slowing down the eye and coordinating the movement of the eye with the movement of the hand (Edwards, 1989). Practice with drawing small objects sharpens the capacity to observe structures and details (Gainer & Child, 1986). A window of opportunity for

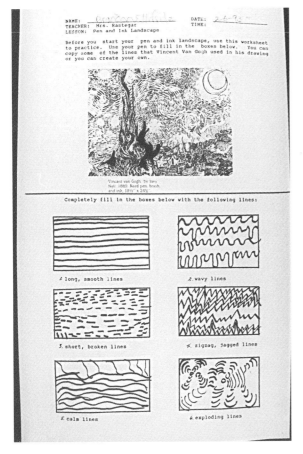

Figure 3.17a

A worksheet for practicing some of the lines used by van Gogh in his *Starry Night*, a warm-up exercise for students in preparation for making drawings with pen and ink

Figure 3.17b
Three sample drawings by fifth graders using the same conventions borrowed from van Gogh but put to individual use portraying a memory of being out in nature

Figure 3.18a
A second grader's drawing from memory

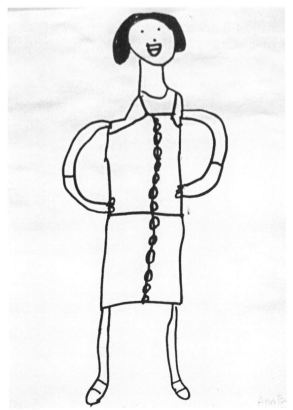

Figure 3.18b
The same student who drew Figure 3.18a drew this figure, the same day, drawing from observation.

Figure 3.19a
A fifth grader's drawing from memory

Figure 3.19b
The same student who drew Figure 3.19a drew this figure, the same day, drawing from observation.

98

drawing faces and figures from observation can be found in the middle years, between the sixth and the ninth grades. Various drawing techniques, including **blind and modified contour line drawing** and the use of **formulas** and **sighting techniques**, help sort out proportions in faces and figures, making them look more "real" and "right" (Burton, 1980d) (see Figures 3.20 and 3.21 and Color Plate 3.7).

The **representational accuracy** crisis that occurs in early adolescence is yet another critical passage in drawing development. The crisis is about representation, and the desired end is a convincing likeness or a believable rendering of the three-dimensional world on a two-dimensional surface (see Figures 3.22 and 3.23). Many adults, including most teachers and even some art students, are still caught in the representational crisis, unable to meet this expectation. Being stuck here can bring one's artistic development to a standstill. Safe passage through this crisis gives permission to continue artistically, to take expressive risks, and to confidently think like an artist. What makes for safe passage? Most learners, including those with more natural affinity for representation, respond very positively to instruction on the techniques of drawing from observation. Given that we now have well-developed methods that have been proved successful with even the most reluctant drawers (Edwards, 1986; Dodson, 1985), there is no reason for teachers not to aim to make observational drawing a goal for both themselves and their students. (For sources of instructional methods, see the Annotated Resources at the end of this chapter.)

Beyond convincing likenesses.　　What lies beyond drawing realistic and convincing likenesses of the observed world? Because adolescents have a great affinity for the power and technique associated with representational accuracy, they can finesse their

Figure 3.20
A sixth grader's drawing using water-soluble fine-point markers working with contour line to achieve a drawing that looks "real" and "right"

Figure 3.21
Two figure drawings by seventh graders working from observation with contour line and paying attention to how the placement of the figure in space gives context and meaning to the image

Figure 3.22
Profile drawing by an eighth-grade student as one of a series of lessons based on Edwards's *Drawing on the Right Side of the Brain*

Figure 3.23
Final project, a self-portrait by the same student who drew Figure 3.22

observational skills in drawing and other two-dimensional media, such as painting and printmaking, as well as three-dimensional forms such as sculpture in clay, wire, and wood. Yet the exciting prospects of greater expressive powers, which can serve the feeling life and conceptual powers awakening in adolescence, lie beyond representational accuracy. Expressive and innovative styles, as well as the possibilities of symbolic and **metaphorical representation,** await. The capacity of art making to accommodate a range of visual modes of thought and expression is the focus of our next section.

For the moment, pause and reconsider assumptions you may be living with. Is drawing a matter of talent or education or some combination of the two? Certainly some learners will be developmentally advanced drawers, and many who show an affinity for drawing may be first and foremost visual learners (Olson, 1992). Some learners will demonstrate their intelligence best through drawing. Although some will experience difficulty drawing, the odds are that the majority can learn to draw and use visual symbolic imagery, by itself or in concert with other symbolic languages, as viable and productive modes of thought and expression.

～ How Can Visual and Artistic Modes of Thought and Expression Be Cultivated?

Nurturing Artistic Behaviors

So far, we have looked at a number of human propensities and artistic behaviors that can be cultivated in the schools so that art-making processes can lead students to the construction of their own meanings. Human beings have an affinity for materials that can be given shape and form. It is natural to want to make things special, especially objects and events that have personal or collective meaning (Dissanayake, 1988, 1992). Artists, craftspersons, designers, folk artists, and learners of all ages have worked with materials to make the ordinary extraordinary. Artful making reveals care, intent, purpose, and the desire to make something visually compelling to the self and others, calling into play both reason and intuition, as well as thought and feeling.

From Pleasure to Mastery

Part of the meaning in making resides in the pleasures afforded by the process of making (Dissanayake, 1995). Often likened to a journey that makes the trip worthwhile, the act of making leads to thoughts and feelings not otherwise possible (Simpson, 1995). Pleasure comes from making contact with tactile and sensuous materials; working with different kinds of techniques, processes, and tools; solving different kinds of problems; and discovering unexpected possibilities. A complex process or extended project develops discipline and the ability to delay gratification because making something artful takes time, thought, intuition, and effort.

Sometimes, the act of making takes place within the context of a group or community, where work is done side by side or in collaboration. The social benefits of making art with others can give it special meaning (see Figures 3.24 and 3.25 and Photo 3.2). On the other hand, the process may accommodate a solo journey and reward the maker with solitude. The experience of meeting challenges, solving problems, thinking new thoughts, and recognizing deeper feelings keeps makers coming back for more. Such heady experiences make us feel good.

From Perception to Cognitive and Emotional Growth

While human beings have the capacity to develop fine powers of visual discrimination, sight is both the fastest and the least accurate of our senses (Ackerman, 1991).

Figure 3.24
This painting by an elementary student captures not only the still life but the other children sitting around it, a reminder of the very social nature of art making that children enjoy.

Photo 3.2
A banner made through a collaborative process and hung in the middle school for all to enjoy

Figure 3.25
This was a collaborative project made by 14 high school students. The project involved starting with raw wool, carding and stamping it to make felt, forming shapes, and assembling the quilt. The surface was embellished with stitchery as the students (half young women and half young men) enjoyed the social benefits of their own "felt-quilting bee."

It needs to be supplemented by other sensory information and can be sharpened through the processes of making images. Infants are attracted to the visual world and begin learning to attend to form; they learn to edit visual stimuli so they can focus on important aspects and navigate the world spatially and visually. Artistic behaviors give us ways of being in the world and attending to it. We can draw the visual world in order to know it. In touching and shaping materials to make images and objects, we can think about the meaning in form (see Color Plate 3.8).

From Equivalents to Metaphors

We have also made note of the human propensity to use symbol systems to create meaning. Visual symbolic language makes it possible to create equivalents, to communicate visually with each other, and to open a dialogue between the work and the maker and between the maker and the viewer. Young children start out making equivalents. As their conceptual powers develop, metaphorical thinking becomes possible. All art might be thought of metaphorically, presenting and re-presenting reality. Metaphors help us make sense out of our experience. They are characterized by coherent structures in which certain features are highlighted and others recede or are hidden (Lakoff & Johnson, 1980). Image making is a way of creating visual metaphors that can deal with such essential questions as Who am I? Where am I going? What journey have I traveled? What have I experienced? (London, 1989).

Figure 3.26
These two metaphorical sculptures were made in response to a unit on archeology and art. After going on a "dig" and unearthing a "relic," reassembling and speculating on the relic's meaning, the relic became a model for constructing one's own "Metaphorical Sculpture." The sculpture in the foreground represents a deer, an animal with personal significance for its 12-year-old maker.

Through creating, sharing, and exploring the meanings in visual metaphors, learners can discover deeper and more satisfying reasons for making art (see Figure 3.26 and Color Plate 3.9). (Chapter 8 will take a more in-depth look at the conceptual and metaphorical possibilities of making art.)

From Solving Problems to Forming Problems

Human beings like to solve problems. Our minds are capable of imagining the past and the present. We have the capacity to think about how the world might be otherwise. We are designers and problem solvers by our nature, perfecting our tools, always looking for better ways to do and make things. The capacity to understand systems, manage resources, and think visually and creatively are among the skills most sought in the workplace (U.S. Dept. of Labor, 1991). In cultivating artistic behaviors, we can develop all these skills (see Figures 3.27 and 3.28). (Chapter 6 will take a more in-depth look at visual and artistic strategies for thinking.)

Creative problems range from the highly structured to the open ended. Creative thinking can take many different forms. Problems such as moving people around can be solved visually through signage, color coding, and the design of space. Some problems are already visual in nature and offer visual challenges (such as how two unlike ideas, concepts, objects, or images can be merged into a new one). Some problems are social and can be made visible through art. Having students form their own problems should happen as often as possible on a small scale and progressively increase as the result of a developmental curriculum. Deciding how to use resources, focus energies, do research, generate ideas, test possible solutions, and give visual form to their ideas prepares learners to both search for and find their own meanings. (Chapter 7 will focus on the formation of elegant problems.)

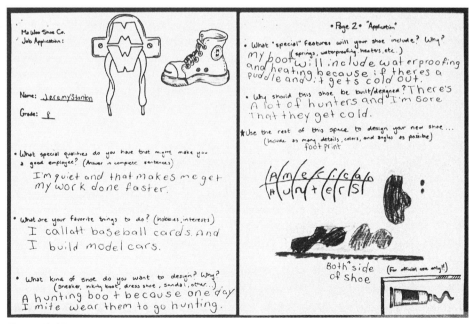

Figure 3.27
Application for employment as a creative shoe designer

From Surface Knowledge to Meaningfulness

Brain research suggests that the construction of meaning is related to the depth of
information processing (Caine & Caine, 1991). Art-making processes offer opportunities to test and even push beyond the limits of one's knowledge, awareness, and
expertise (Eisner, 1991). The world of experience—schooling in particular—is loaded
with partially processed information. Learners gather bits of information in science,
social studies, history, and other subjects. What if artistic behaviors were cultivated so
that learners could process newly found information visually and artfully? Could
making art provide a way of expanding and assessing learning? Through the
processes of making images, objects, books, constructions, design solutions, and
exhibitions, learners not only revisit and explore ideas and concepts. They also create
artful holding forms as a way of preserving and documenting the development of
their ideas, feelings, insights, and discoveries. In making such connections, the curriculum becomes an integrated whole (Jacobs, 1989). (See Figure 3.29.)

Different kinds of meaning.   Making art can give meaning to the learning
process and community. Art making has served individual artists as they have sought
to find and claim an identity, map their journeys, tell their stories, get power over
their thoughts and feelings, mix with others, and dream their dreams (Lippard,
1990). Why should it not be put to work to serve the developmental and contextual
needs of learners? Art-making processes can also give meaning to community
through collaboration (Hurwitz, 1993). Evidence suggests that the needs of the educational community are well served by creating an artful culture and climate in which
learners can discover how they are alike while at the same time honoring differences
(OMG, 1991; Oddleifson, 1994). And if the art-making process demands an integration of reason with intuition, thought with feeling, it can be put to work to resolve
longstanding disagreements in education that have led to unproductive polarizations.

Figure 3.29
In a simple but straightforward art lesson, third graders were invited to take new information from their study of bugs and make monoprints. The students eagerly offered the names for all the bug parts, but the art lesson took them a step further in considering how those parts might look from different points of view and where bugs might live in an environment. The drawings were turned into monoprints—artful records of the learning that had occurred in both science and art.

With artistic behaviors, it becomes possible to integrate the needs and interests of the learner with the larger content of the curriculum.

SUMMARY

Thinking about art as behavior shifts attention from objects and their qualities to human propensities and behaviors as well as to the purposes fulfilled by making art. The process of creating meaning through art has three interrelated dimensions: the use of sensuous materials and significant form, the use of symbolic visual language, and the use of visual modes of thought and feeling.

A comprehensive program that cultivates artistic behaviors can prepare learners to find their own meanings. It will have made them familiar with a variety of materials and processes and connected visual form to feeling and meaning. It will have kept symbolic language alive and growing. It will have introduced learners to artists, designers, and visual thinkers who model visual ways of working and thinking. As such, it will have prepared students to make informed choices. It will not leave them outside the process of making as merely an appreciator of what others can do or make; neither will it leave them without visual ways of knowing what they think and feel. Rather, through the cultivation of artistic behaviors, they will come to know that they can create meaning and enrich their lives through the processes of artful making.

Artistic behaviors can serve the developmental and contextual needs of individuals, groups of learners, and the whole learning community, contributing to a climate in which learners can discover how all are alike yet individually special. In particular, visual learners stand to benefit from opportunities to use their strengths and preferred learning styles in school. Equally important is how all learners can benefit by developing and using visual modes of thought and expression. Giving artistic behaviors a more central role in education may also help resolve longstanding polarities in educational theory and practice, uniting reason with intuition, cognition with emotion, and the curriculum with the learner.

ADVANTAGES AND CHALLENGES OF MAKING THIS CHOICE

Meeting Developmental and Contextual Needs of Learners

If learners are invited to create their own meanings through the making of art, they will learn how to use visual thought and forms of expression as a way of forming visual metaphors for their identities, stories, journeys, ideas, feelings, and dreams. These visual metaphors offer learners significant ways of discovering, organizing, and expressing what they think, know, and feel. Substantial practice and experience with visual forms of thought and expression will help learners know when and how making images and objects might serve their needs and give them the confidence and artistic behaviors to do so.

Some immediate ends are served by cultivating the artistic behaviors of learners for the purpose of creating their own meanings through making art. For some learners it will provide a significant or alternative way of coming to know what they think and feel. It can also provide a way of attending to the world of experience, even a way of being in the world. For some, it will provide an important means for imagining a better world. For many, it can build the confidence to continue learning. For all, it can suggest ways to make work and leisure more satisfying. It may help some envision themselves in careers where visual thought and expression are paramount, and it suggests that we consider the ways artistic behaviors might make all vocations, avocations, and life endeavors more productive and satisfying.

Advocating for Visual Learners and Visual Learning

If visual thought and expression are cultivated through the processes of making images and objects, visual learners will have a way of using and demonstrating their intelligence—for themselves and for others. As this visual intelligence gains recognition and support, confidence will build and bridges can then be constructed to other forms of thought and expression. The fate of many learners who struggle so hard with written forms of thought and expression might be turned around. As well, the processes of visual thought and expression will serve to expand, enrich, reinforce, and stimulate the learning of all students. The goal should be to facilitate movement among different symbol systems and forms of thought and expression as it best serves each student's learning style and needs.

A Window of Opportunity

If learners are encouraged to give visual form to their thoughts and ideas, adults will have another window into the lives their children and students live. Art, as well, might be served by giving greater recognition to the manner in which young people give form to their ideas and feelings. Making art provides an unusual window into the mind, the way it perceives the world, and the manner in which it constructs, reconstructs, and imagines possibilities. That educators and parents might miss this opportunity to know young people better seems tragic, compounded by the fact that without nurture, the natural propensities to make and give visual form to ideas and feelings will lie dormant or may even atrophy. Thus, making art with learners is a window of opportunity, and, fortunately, the window of opportunity for making art extends throughout a learner's journey from early childhood to young adulthood. Knowing that there are critical passages and successful teaching methods can help teachers support and guide artistic growth and development.

Meeting the Needs of the Learning Community

As an added advantage, the cultivation of artistic behaviors and meaningful encounters with making art can provide education with processes to resolve longstanding questions and debates. As far back as the time of Aristotle and Plato, philosophers and educators have sought to understand the relationship between reason and intuition, objective and subjective thought, exploration and play with mastery and technique, and universal and communal needs with the unique needs of individuals. In the processes of making art, all these facets of human behavior and need are united. One cannot engage meaningfully in the art-making process without balancing and integrating reason with intuition, play with technique, objective thought with subjective feeling.

Further, the process of making art can affirm both the ways humans are alike and the ways individuals are unique and special. It can accommodate subject matter and content as well as the learner's own interests. Perhaps it might suffice to say that when learners find their own meanings through the making of images and objects, they give new meaning to the whole process of education.

Cultivating visual and artistic modes of thought and expression requires an understanding of both the *nature* of artistic behaviors and how they might be *nurtured*. It requires both knowledge of learners and expertise in making art. Only then can the teacher become an artful mediator between the world of the learner and the world of art, knowing how the many and diverse possibilities for making art might serve developmental and contextual needs.

ACTION PLAN FOR INSTRUCTIONAL DECISION MAKING

Our three-part conception of art gives us a way of thinking about the responsibilities of the teacher of art, questions to ask in making instructional choices, and key questions useful in evaluating the results of art-making encounters. First, how can we look at the responsibilities of the teacher of art?

Responsibilities of the Teacher of Art

The teacher of art is one who develops a repertoire of ideas about materials as well as an understanding of the ways that form communicates meaning. Such a teacher shapes investigations with different materials and helps learners connect visual form with feeling and meaning.

The teacher of art is one who cultivates the inherent propensity to use visual, graphic, and three-dimensional symbol systems. Such a teacher works to keep visual, graphic language alive and growing and understands that visual, symbolic behaviors include many forms, styles, and media.

The teacher of art is one who helps learners think visually and creatively, making visible their thoughts, feelings, and ideas by using symbolic language, form, and materials. Such a teacher employs a wide variety of strategies for engaging students in different kinds of visual thinking and problem solving. This teacher understands that the capacity to think visually is deeply connected to the mastery of symbolic language and a knowledge of form and material.

Making Instructional Choices

Whether plans call for a single lesson, a more complex series of lessons, a unit, a more extended project, or a course across grade levels or interdisciplinary connections, we can ask the following questions:

~ How will visual form and materials be investigated and connected to feeling and meaning?

~ How will symbolic language be developed?

~ What processes will be used to generate and investigate thoughts and ideas and to discover feelings? What options will be made available so that thoughts, feelings, and ideas can be given visual form?

Evaluating Instructional Choices
for the Meanings They Create

By attending to the results of instruction, including both the learning process and its product, and by exploring **qualitative questions** with students, teachers can assess the real value that making art has for students. We can ask the following questions:

~ What ideas and discoveries as well as skills and processes resulted from the investigation and creation of meaning through visual form and materials?

~ In what ways has visual symbolic language developed in concert with the effort to express certain ideas, thoughts, and feelings?

~ What meanings have been discovered or created through the processes of making art?

DISCUSSION QUESTIONS

1. How might an early childhood program that emphasizes the exploration of visual concepts and art materials give learners a head start in school?

2. How can the ability to draw be developed through instruction? What methods might be used to help learners solve different kinds of drawing problems?

3. What might you think about as you plan a lesson or unit that will lead learners to find their own meanings?

4. How might you evaluate an art lesson or unit for the meaning it created?

SUGGESTED ACTIVITIES

Journal Writing

Describe your personal history with making art, starting with your earliest memories of drawing and playing with materials. Trace that history through your activities at home and at school. Consider what has influenced your art making along the way. In what ways are you satisfied with the encouragement and education you received for making art? Is there anything you wish had been different?

Analyze your present strengths and interests in making art. What expertise do you currently have, and what expertise would you like to develop? Make a plan for strengthening your studio expertise.

Visualize yourself as a teacher. What will be in the teaching repertoire you take into the classroom with you? What modes of thought and expression are you likely to emphasize most and least, and why?

Observing and Analyzing Practice

Find an opportunity to observe someone teaching art. During the observation, pay particular attention to the art-making process and the problem students are given. In your journal, reflect on the observation. Use the three-part conception of art and the evaluative questions to analyze what you observed. In what ways were materials and visual forms investigated? Was meaning connected to visual form and material? Was symbolic language developed through the lesson or unit? What kind of thinking, through making, did you witness? What kinds of meaning resulted from the teaching you observed?

As an alternative to observing teaching, look at a copy of *School Arts* magazine. Take one or more articles and do the same kind of analysis, looking for ways the encounter with making art was orchestrated and for the meaning learners were able to create.

Searching for Pedagogical Models

Teachers are always shopping for ideas. Now is the time to begin shopping for teaching methods and strategies. Select an area of interest to you and search out resource books and articles that describe teaching methods. Begin a section in your journal that deals with teaching strategies for making art.

Experiment with one of the methods you have found. See if it can strengthen your own work in some way. Add sketches and reflective notes to the information you are compiling in your journal.

ANNOTATED RESOURCES

Developing an Understanding of Form and Materials

Edwards, B. (1986). *Drawing on the artist within*. Los Angeles: Tarcher.
  Edwards's guide includes strategies for analog drawing in which feeling is associated with visual form.

Herman, G. N., & Hollingsworth, P. (1992). *Kinetic kaleidoscope: Exploring movement and energy in the visual arts*. Tucson, AZ: Zephyr Press.
   This book makes the connection between the formal languages of dance movement and visual art. It presents ideas for exploring visual concepts in art through movement.

London, P. (1994). *Step outside: Community-based art education*. Portsmouth, NH: Heinemann.
   This book proposes ways to use the community as a primary educational resource for teaching. It describes a broad range of activities that involve the search for materials and ideas in the world inhabited by learners.

Roukes, N. (1988). *Design synectics*. Worcester, MA: Davis.
   This book acknowledges a substructure of design that includes the visual representation of unseen forces and ways of grouping as well as the visual language associated with the elements and principles of design and "visual analogistics," or the way art systems mimic nature.

Townley, M. (1978). *Another look* (Teachers' ed.). Reading, MA: Addison-Wesley.
   This guide is divided into Levels A, B, and C and is useful with children four years old and older. Visual concepts are approached through the study of contrasts, using examples from nature, the world of children, and art. These are explored by comparing and contrasting, identifying and sorting, and acting out and making movement, as well as by word play, practice with two- and three-dimensional materials, and thematic units. It emphasizes the association of feeling and meaning with visual form.

Developing Symbolic Language

Dodson, B. (1985). *Keys to drawing*. Cincinnati: North Light.
   This is a beautifully illustrated book setting forward a program for drawing from observation. It includes excellent pointers for students and models for self-evaluation.

Edwards, B. (1989). *Drawing on the right side of the brain*. Los Angeles: Tarcher.
   This book describes hemispheric brain theory as it applies to drawing and sets forth an illustrated, sequential program for developing skills for drawing from observation.

Olson, J. (1992). *Envisioning writing: Toward an integration of drawing and writing*. Portsmouth, NH: Heinemann.
   Part I deals with a method for teaching narrative drawing and its relationship to the language arts program and the needs of special education students. Part II discusses historical grounds and current practices related to the integration of drawing and writing.

Wilson, B., Hurwitz, A., & Wilson, M. (1987). *Teaching drawing from art*. Worcester, MA: Davis.
   This is an illustrated guide for teaching a comprehensive drawing program. It includes strategies and ideas for working from art, observation, built and natural forms, memory, and verbal forms to visual forms.

Developing Ways of Thinking and Knowing

London, P. (1989). *No more secondhand art.* Boston: Shambhala.
> *This guide proposes ways to make art a natural means of expression. It includes examples of creative encounters as a stimulus for working intuitively and metaphorically.*

Roukes, N. (1988). *Design synectics.* Worcester, MA: Davis.
> *This book sets forth synectics as a theory of creativity based on disruptive thought, identifies "trigger mechanisms" for transforming a stimulus into perceptions that emerge as concepts for art and design, and illustrates a wide variety of ideas for studio action.*

KEY TERMS

Abstract thinking   A form of thinking that is more conceptual than concrete, focusing on important points or aspects

Artistic behaviors   Artful ways of working and habits of mind that integrate making and thinking and result in visual form

Cognitive concepts   Generalizations derived from classifying, sorting, comparing, and contrasting qualities and attributes; as such, cognitive concepts provide a way of thinking about similarities and differences as well as associated feelings and meanings

Contour line drawing   A form of linear drawing that concentrates on the perception of edges and forms; **blind contour drawing** involves looking only at the subject, not the paper; **modified contour line drawing** combines looking at the object while drawing with checking the progress on paper; the intent of contour line drawing is to slow down the process of looking and to coordinate the movement of the *eye* with the movement of the hand

Conventions of drawing   Ways of drawing and rendering form that have developed over time (e.g., conventions for showing depth include overlapping, diminution of sizes, and one- and two-point perspective)

Elements of art and principles of design   Formal language for describing visual form; traditional elements included line, value, and color—contemporary versions usually include line, shape, color, texture, and value; the principles of design include ways that visual form can be organized to achieve unity, balance, and/or opposition

Formulas for drawing   Visual diagrams that show the relationships of the parts to the whole (e.g., a formula for the face helps locate the eyes, ears, mouth, nose, eyebrows, and hair)

Metaphorical representation   The use of metaphors to create visual images that can represent ideas, concepts, and feelings; metaphors are constructs that have coherent structure, highlighting some things and hiding others, and are thus useful in making sense of experience

Narrative drawing   A way of telling stories visually; a narrative drawing can consist of a single image or a sequence of images

Nonrepresentational form   A visual image without realistic references, usually constructed with shapes, lines, values, textures, and color

Qualitative questions   Inquiries about qualities or values, as opposed to quantitative questions, which ask "How much?"

Representational accuracy   A style of art in which the goal is to render an image or object realistically and with as much accuracy and detail as possible

Schema   A symbol or visual equivalent for a form; a child's schema is likely to be simple, whereas an adult's schema might be either economical or more complex

Sensuous materials   A notion in philosophy and aesthetics that refers to the compelling nature of tactile and visual materials in art that have their own meanings

Sighting techniques   Ways of measuring and comparing the size and angular relationships of parts of a whole; with one eye closed and a pencil in an extended hand, comparative measurements can be taken against the pencil, noting proportional relationships and relative angles (e.g., with sighting techniques, one can check to see if the space between the eyes of a portrait subject is the same width as the eye itself)

Significant form   A notion in philosophy and aesthetics suggesting that form has meaning

Symbolic language   A language that uses signs and symbols to refer to or denote meaning

Visual concepts   Descriptive qualities of form and structure (such as straight and curved, open and closed, spiral and concentric)

Visual form   Visual and spatial attributes (including shape, line, texture, color, value, volume, and/or space) that have relationships within a given whole

Visual learners   Those whose preferred style of learning, thinking, and expressing is visual; these learners respond well to (and use) diagrams, models, maps, drawings, and visual examples as a way of knowing and thinking

CHAPTER 4

Engaging Learners with Art Images

Jean M. Delaney
Southwest Missouri State University

Guiding Questions

- What is art?
- Why should experiences with art images be provided for students?
- How can you engage learners with art images?
- What factors affect engagement?
- How can you structure experiences so learners can create meaning through art?

Engaging learners is about getting them involved to the point where they push the boundaries and go beyond what is required. Motivation grabs students' interest and gets them excited about what they are going to do, but engagement takes this excitement to another level. According to *Webster's New Collegiate Dictionary* (8th ed.), *motivation* means "to provide with motive; impel; . . . excite"; *engagement* is defined as "to interlock with: to begin and carry on an enterprise. . . . ; actively involved in or committed to . . . being in gear." If students are engaged, they take personal ownership of their learning, so engaging learners is a key ingredient of good teaching.

Engaging learners with art images is the major focus of this chapter. But first you need a wealth of information about art itself and the purposes it has served for human beings in various cultures throughout time. Cultures throughout the world have created images and objects that are the products of artistic behaviors. We can't teach art without them. Before you can engage learners with this artwork, you need to know about the culture and about the art. Even within a single society, art may be defined in more than one way, and ideas about art also change over time. While some kinds of art are important in one era, others may be valued in a later era. When you encounter a work of art, you view it through your own personal and cultural values, which may be different from those expressed in the images or objects. To really understand the art of a culture, you need to know why the work was valued in that culture.

Various fields of study, called **disciplines,** can help you understand the art of different cultures. Ideas from anthropology provide information about art in small-scale societies. Other disciplines, such as art history, aesthetics, and art criticism, can help you understand how art in Western society has changed over time and why it has been valued. Because information from these disciplines is critical for understanding what art is and has been in various cultures and times, I'll discuss them in relation to both small-scale societies and more complex ones.

First I present an anthropologist's view of art, then a biobehavioral view, and finally views about art in Western cultures. Each view will be presented in terms of the disciplines that inform them. Rationales for providing experiences with art images, factors that affect engagement, and ways you can engage learners and structure experiences with art images will follow the discussion of art in small-scale and complex societies. (While at least one course in the history of Western art is generally required for preservice art educators, a course in the art of small-scale societies is less likely to be mandated. Since the art of these societies is an important part of art education, the view of art from an anthropological perspective will be more extensive than that of art in the Western world.)

~ What Is Art?

Art is a difficult concept to define, and all art is value laden. Values are learned, often unconsciously, through the experiences and relationships in which you have been immersed throughout your life. These experiences also fund your response to art images and the meaning that you derive from them.

As referred to earlier, people in different disciplines often view art differently. In *Art as Experience* (1934), the American philosopher and educator John Dewey suggested that the power of an art image to communicate feelings, ideas, and meanings is grounded in the lived experiences we bring to the encounter with an art image or object. He stated that viewing art is an active experience, not a passive one: "Language exists only when it is listened to as well as spoken. . . . The work of art is complete only as it works in the experience of others than the one who created it" (p. 106). The Russian novelist and philosopher Leo Tolstoy (1898) defined art as communication, stating that it is a way "one man consciously . . . hands on to others feelings he has lived through, so that others are infected by these feelings and experience them" (p. 108).

Considering art from an anthropological view provides further ideas.

An Anthropological View of Art

Small-scale societies. Cultural anthropologists, in studying human beings and their cultures, look for patterns in the similarities and differences between cultures. They attempt to see a society on its own terms and through its own values, rather than from their own viewpoints. Some anthropologists use the term *small-scale* rather than *primitive* to describe cultures that have fewer members and simpler technology than more complex cultures. The word *primitive* implies that these societies are less advanced and that our own culture is superior to them. Richard Anderson (1989), a cultural anthropologist, suggests that this is not necessarily so. He states that the only real difference between these small-scale societies and a complex one— the difference between "them" and "us"—is *scale*. In his view, large may be different from small, but it is not necessarily better.

The term **ethnocentrism** is used to describe the attitude that one's own race or culture is superior to that of others. Those with an ethnocentric attitude consider the art of small-scale societies primitive and crude and view their own society's art as more highly developed. In contrast to this ethnocentric attitude is one called **cultural relativism,** which suggests that we should not judge all art by the same standards. While small- and large-scale societies are different, they are also alike in many ways. If we attempt to see the commonalities between cultures, rather than just focusing on the differences, we can begin to identify some artistic behaviors that cut across cultural boundaries and are common to all human beings, regardless of when or where they live.

Art, the artist, and society. In many small-scale societies, there is no term for what we call "art" because in such societies all art has a utilitarian purpose. It satisfies spiritual, ethical, or practical needs. A magical or spiritual function is attributed to some images and objects, and there may be no distinction made between the object itself and its use in ritual. Objects used in rituals are considered important more for their spiritual value than for their materialistic worth. The object or image itself may be made of impermanent materials (such as Navajo sand paintings), and the artwork may be destroyed during a ceremony or ritual. The value is in the power of the symbolic meaning embedded in the object through the behavior of ritual or ceremonial making. That is, the process itself and the symbols used may be more important than the art object itself.

According to Anderson, art in small-scale societies is "not created 'for art's sake' but as an integral part of religious, social, and political life" (1989, p. 21). Contemporary art from these societies continues to tell stories and portray spiritual relationships between people and their environment. In *Keeping Our Stories Alive,* Hood (1995) explains that the art of Inuit peoples of northwestern Canada (see Figures 4.1 and 4.2) "often depicts the people themselves, in a communication with the spirit world designed to bring success in the crucial activities of life. . . . [T]heir arts are not only traditional but also contemporary expressions of their way of life" (p. 9).

Images and objects in these societies are often created collaboratively, and the names of individual artists may not be as important as they are in more complex societies, where some people may specialize in art making. Each person in a small-scale society has more than one role, and someone skilled in artistic behaviors also "hunts and gathers along with the other adult members of his or her sex" (Anderson, 1989, p. 7).

Complex and small-scale societies differ in the number of people they contain, the purposes for art images and objects, and the extent to which members of the

Figure 4.1
Hunter with Helping Spirit, by Kiawa Ashoona, 1994, Cape Dorset, NT, Canada. Serpentine stone, 25.5 x 14.25 x 8.5 in. How does this sculpture, created by a contemporary Inuit artist, relate to the traditional value and purpose of art in small-scale societies?

Northwest Company Inuit Art Marketing Service, Rexdale, Ontario.

Figure 4.2
Community Life, by Luke Anowtalik, 1994, Arviat, NT, Canada. Caribou antler, 14 x 15.5 x 17 in. What does this sculpture communicate about life in small-scale societies? How does the artist's use of the medium relay this message to the viewer?

Northwest Company Inuit Art Marketing Service, Rexdale, Ontario.

group specialize in art making. However, commonalities also exist in the social structure and in the artworks made in these societies. Both groups have developed their own institutions, rituals, and answers to perennial human questions; family structures for socializing their children; and ethical standards and value systems for acceptable behaviors (Anderson, 1989). Both groups also use some form of visual and performing arts for rituals and celebrations to commemorate special events. Cultures throughout the world have immortalized their leaders and heroes through the arts, and both small-scale and complex societies have created masks to transform themselves.

While the art of each culture has unique characteristics we can appreciate, looking at commonalities across cultures can help avoid ethnocentrism and may increase understanding. It takes preparation to lead students in searching for knowledge about a culture. Researching the context of the artwork and translating that information into specific goals and strategies are two important steps in the process.

Researching contextual knowledge.   The context in which an art image or object is created provides a window into purposes it served and reasons it is valued. In-depth research will help you develop a strong knowledge base about a culture and enable you to guide your students with confidence. With more than a shallow understanding of a culture, students may see how the art of a small-scale society relates to their own lives and cultures. It may also help avoid trivializing the images and objects of that culture.

In a unit entitled "Life Tellers: An Excursion into Contemporary Aboriginal Art," one of my students gathered information from several sources. He synthesized his research in a resource paper as a basis for introducing students to the art of this culture. In this excerpt from his paper, Keith talks about "Dreamtime," the basis for Australian Aboriginal history, spirit belief, ancestral knowledge, and culture:

> Contemporary Aboriginal art includes visual narratives of Dreamtime stories or symbolic maps of tribal lands. Traditionally, artists may only depict "Dreamtime" stories which they "own." Ownership is determined through one's place of conception or birth or through kinship. Dreamtime is largely an oral tradition of stories describing the journeys of the Aborigines' supernatural ancestors whose actions formed the Australian landscape. Contemporary Aboriginal artists hide their symbolic references in the mist of dots and overdots which characterize their art. (Ballard, 1995)

Translating information into understanding.   Armed with information on Dreamtime and other information, as well as slides he would use to introduce students to these art forms, Keith developed a unit plan. His goals were for students to define symbolism and narration in art, recognize a part of themselves in historical or contemporary cultures, and explain relationships among artist, artwork, and environment. The goals address the fourth National Visual Arts Standard: understanding the visual arts in relation to history and cultures. They also fulfill some achievement standards for grades 5–8 and 9–12 by helping learners see commonalities and differences among art and the purposes it serves in various cultures and in their own world.

One of the lesson options Keith developed is for students to create an art object that maps out a part of their life (see Chapter 6, "Using Artistic Strategies") and write a statement explaining the symbolism and story. Key concepts for students to know include ideas such as the following: "symbolism is subjective and varies between people and between cultures; law, religion and art are inseparable for many cultures; art has the ability to empower its creators, its viewers, and the society in which it was generated" (Ballard, 1995).

Symbol systems, storytelling, and the regional nature of stories are universal phenomena. Storytelling through the arts has always been a way for humans to share their experiences (see Chapter 5, "Encouraging Visual Storytelling"). Every culture in the world has practiced some form of art. Research can help you make connections between the art of other cultures and the lives of your students, which can broaden their understanding.

The small-scale, or tribal, stage of Western art lasted for more than 40,000 years. The heritage of Western civilization is only about 3,000 years old, and contemporary notions of art in this culture are only about 200 years old. The majority of so-called art in the Western world was created during the tribal period, so investigating the art of small-scale societies is a very important part of art education.

Looking at art from an anthropological perspective has provided some insight into the values that underlie art in these cultures. Our next perspective considers what may be a common basis for art in both small-scale and complex societies.

A Biobehavioral View of Art

What is art for?   Chapters 1 and 3 introduced you to Ellen Dissanayake's ideas. She researched concepts about art through the disciplines of cultural and physical anthropology, ethology, cognitive and developmental psychology, evolutionary biology, Western cultural history, and aesthetics. In *What Is Art For?* (1988), Dissanayake presented a biobehavioral view of art and proposed that a common behavior may underlie the creation of art in all human cultures. Her thesis is that in traditional, small-scale cultures the use of the arts in rituals helped preserve information that was important for group survival. Ideas and feelings embedded in traditional symbols were made memorable through rituals and helped to develop the group cohesiveness that is essential for survival in these small groups.

In our culture we also have rituals that help us remember important ideas and cohere our society. Events such as the Fourth of July to commemorate our nation's independence and Memorial Day to honor those who died in our wars are rituals, not art. But the arts for these rituals provide the symbols that play an important part in generating feelings and ideas. Music, parades, floats, costumes, and fireworks all help to make the celebrations memorable and special.

Making special.   Dissanayake states that rituals and art making are both related to a genetic tendency she calls "making special." She thinks that this universal behavior evolved in humans because of its survival value. Dissanayake considers making special just as identifiably human as our ability to speak. She feels that communal rituals—enhanced by the visual arts, music, dance, and theater—have made important events memorable and special for people throughout time. Making special involves creating something with reflection, special care, and concern. It goes beyond just the utilitarian functions by involving the embellishment of objects in ways that promote feelings about them. A major characteristic of this behavior is the intent of the maker to do something beyond the ordinary:

> One intends by making special *to place the activity or artifact in a "realm" different from the everyday* . . . [and] both artist and perceiver often feel that in art they have an intimate connection with a world that is different from if not superior to ordinary experience. (Dissanayake, 1988, p. 92)

Both ritual and art can transform our experience, but Dissanayake maintains that "it is not art . . . but making special that has been evolutionarily or socially or culturally important" (1992, p. 56).

The behaviors of art.   Like any adaptive behavior of human beings, artistic behavior has more than one form. While aggressive behaviors include activities like defending territories and making threats, artistic behaviors include making special, as well as activities like drawing, painting, singing, dancing, acting, writing poetry, and engaging in other art forms. When we celebrate special occasions such as birthdays and holidays, we embellish the events by preparing special foods, making traditional decorations, and creating symbolic objects that have meaning to our family group.

Your classes will include students with many different cultural backgrounds. Letting them verbally and visually share family traditions for celebrating a holiday or other special occasion can open the door for cross-cultural understanding as well as appreciation of cultural differences. Behaviors that focus on meaningful activities related to the real experiences of your students can promote more thoughtful reflection about themselves and their world than activities based on holiday clichés. Art as the behavior of making special focuses on the process of art making and the way it serves human beings, rather than just on the art object itself. It can provide a link between the art of small-scale societies and art created in more complex ones.

Dissanayake's research defines art in a broad sense and allows us to consider diverse forms of art from various cultures as artistic behaviors of making special. It also helps explain why art and life are intertwined in small-scale societies. Making special is a major focus in these societies, and art is a natural part of life. While traditional forms are still appreciated, art also changes over time. Artists in these societies use art to reflect their current lives as well their past. Like the Inuit artists of Canada, "they dwell in the contemporary world but honor traditions that trace back thousands of years" (Hood, 1995, p. 8).

A Western View of Art

Information from the discipline of cultural anthropology helps to understand art in small-scale societies, and Dissanayake used several bodies of knowledge in her research. Ideas from three other disciplines—art history, aesthetics, and art criticism—can help you understand how art has changed in the Western world from the classical era to postmodern times.

Art history.   This body of knowledge focuses on the study of artists, styles, movements, and art forms. Art historians research, write about, and interpret art and artists. They each have a point of view, and histories of art may be biased in their coverage of artists and art forms. The issue of bias has been a concern in art education. The major focus in histories of Western art has been on **fine art**. Some art educators feel that **popular art, folk art,** and the **hiddenstream art** of women and other minorities have been neglected because they are outside of **mainstream art** (Collins, 1987; Collins & Sandell, 1988). While they recognize the importance of fine art and that it fosters **cultural literacy,** some art educators feel that the scope of many art histories is not broad enough and is also culturally biased (Lanier, 1987).

As an art educator, you need to be aware that, like all accounts of historical events, art history is limited by the viewpoint of the author. Just as versions of contemporary events can vary, different versions of art history vary in the extent to which they include work of different cultures and the work of women and other minorities.

Aesthetics.   Philosophers who argue about and develop theories about art and the artistic experience are called aestheticians. This discipline, which emerged in the 18th century, is defined by Lankford (1992) as "concepts for understanding the nature of art" (p. 4). Aesthetics deals with two major areas: theories of the aesthetic and theories of art (Dickie, Sclafani, & Roblin, 1989).

Theories of the aesthetic.   Concepts in this area of aesthetics are focused on our response to art. If we think of *anesthetic* as something that eliminates feeling, we can see that the opposite term, *aesthetic,* has to do with generating feeling. Ideas about art and beauty have been a topic of discussion in Western art history since the time of classical Greece. Plato considered beauty as an objective ideal, not something influenced by personal feelings (Dickie et al., 1989). Later theorists defined beauty as something more subjective, based on personal taste and sense perceptions.

Aesthetic values and notions of beauty vary across peoples and cultures. For example, the Yoruban culture of Nigeria values "coolness, composure, even . . . a certain detachment . . . [and] dislikes emotions or violence in the facial expressions and gestures of their sculpture" (Buser, 1995, p. 8). The aesthetic of any individual or culture is influenced by life experiences.

In the 19th century the concept of aesthetic attitude was introduced. This involves "blocking out," or becoming detached from, the real-life qualities of something and focusing on its aesthetic qualities as much as possible. Stolnitz (1960) defines aesthetic attitude as contemplating and focusing attention on an art image for its own sake, not for any purpose it might serve.

An artistically talented high school student in an art mentoring program described an experience that exemplifies this attitude. Nathan told his mentor that he was beginning to look at things differently. He related how he became entranced with the colors a ray of light produced on a water spigot and kept watching as it changed. This aesthetic view bypassed the function of the water spigot to focus on its aesthetic qualities. An aesthetic attitude is considered by some as a prerequisite for an aesthetic experience, which involves feelings of awe and delight, and is an integral part of some forms of art criticism.

Theories of art.   Both Plato and Aristotle felt that artworks were imitations of things in the world (Battin, Fisher, Moore, & Silvers, 1989). The idea that art should imitate nature is the basis for **imitationalism,** or the **mimetic theory of art,** which suggests that to be called "art" a work must represent things realistically. **Instrumentalism,** or the **pragmatic theory of art,** values practical functions of art for society more than it values realism.

In the late 19th and early 20th centuries, new forms of art emerged that were very different from earlier ones, and new aesthetic theories were developed to deal with them. **Expressive theory** suggests that to be called "art," an image or object must express emotion and that communication of strong feelings is valued more than realism. **Formalism** focuses primarily on the way the art elements and design principles are used to achieve a unified expression. In this view, a painting is an arrangement of colors, shapes, and lines on a two-dimensional surface, not a window to the real world. The portrayal of content is not as important as the form of the art image or the arrangement of art elements and design principles.

Later in the 20th century, art continued to be redefined, and other theories emerged. The **open concept theory** states that art cannot even be defined, because there are no specific conditions that can clearly identify an image or object as art. In contrast, the **institutional theory** accepts as art anything that experts in the **art world** say is art (Dickie et al., 1989). **Contextualism** is concerned primarily with the context in which the art was created, **semiotic theory** focuses on interpreting signs and symbols in an attempt to identify the meaning of an artwork, and **critical theory** is concerned with the hidden agenda, or underlying meaning, of an artwork in relation to social issues.

Hart (1991) contrasts the basic tenets of Western aesthetics with those used to judge non-Western artwork. The former values individuality, uniqueness, permanence, and form, but non-Western cultures may not value individuality as much because work is often a collective effort. Tradition is more important in these cultures than uniqueness, and the work is often destroyed during a ritual, so permanence is not a critical consideration. Finally, the content and the meaning of the artwork is valued over the form.

Aesthetic theories play an important role in the judgment phase of art criticism, but every aesthetic theory may not be appropriate for judging all kinds of art. There has been disagreement in the art education literature concerning the notion that formalism can be used as a universal aesthetic standard to judge the art of any culture (Delaney, 1992). Some suggest that the dominance of formalism is a kind of "cultural imperialism" (Johnson, 1988), an ethnocentric view that assumes this Western aesthetic theory is more profound than those used by non-Western cultures (Anderson, 1989). Others see formalism as "an aesthetic of the masterpiece" (Krukowski, 1990, p. 130) that focuses on the aesthetic pleasures of art appreciation, while contextualism is more concerned with art appreciation as cognition.

Formalism has also been criticized for too much focus on the analysis of design principles and not enough on the meaning of the artwork and the cultural message that it conveys (Nadaner, 1985; Efland, 1987). In contrast to formalism, which focuses on intrinsic qualities, contextualist and semiotic theories of art consider both intrinsic and extrinsic aspects of an artwork. These theories are considered more appropriate for understanding non-Western art because they delve into the function that art served in the society and focus on understanding the content and meaning of symbols used in the context of that culture.

Art criticism.   Professional art critics write and talk about how an artwork is organized or executed and what it expresses or symbolizes; then they judge its worth in relation to others in that style or era. Critics each have their own style and may not follow a specific model. Reading what an art critic has to say about a work of art can provide students with new insights. Art educators have developed several models that simplify the critical process for students by defining specific steps. Most models include some kind of description, analysis, interpretation, and judgment. Five models were visible in art education literature from 1980 to 1992: the Feldman model; variations on the Feldman model; the aesthetic scanning model; phenomenological models; and deconstructive models. Feldman's model and variations on it were cited more than any other model (Delaney, 1992).

The Feldman model.   Edmund Feldman's model stresses what has been called a formalist approach, a view that focuses on analyzing how the elements and principles are used to communicate ideas and feelings. Feldman feels that the most important thing for students to learn is why the artwork affects them. He thinks that knowing what it is in the artwork that generates a response is more important than information about the context of the artwork (1992). There are four sequential steps in Feldman's model: description—saying what you see; formal analysis—identifying relationships among what you saw; interpretation—looking for the meaning; and judgment—ranking the artwork by comparing it with others like it. Feldman suggests formalist, expressivist, and instrumentalist theories of art as helpful in the final step of judgment.

Variations on the Feldman model.   Some art educators have tailored Feldman's model to suit their own needs and deleted some steps or added new ones. Feinstein (1989) proposes the elements of description, analysis of form, metaphorical interpretation, and judgment. Zeller (1984) uses a developmental approach with different steps added at each level: identification and description for primary grades; analysis and interpretation for fifth through eighth grades; and judgment or evaluation for junior and senior high. Many of these variations leave out the judgment step for younger learners (Delaney, 1992).

Aesthetic scanning model.   Broudy (1987) states that his aesthetic scanning model enhances the skill of "aesthetic perception," which, "unlike the ordinary variety[,] has to be especially attentive to the sensory content of the image" (p. 49). His model involves describing and discussing four different characteristics of an artwork: sensory properties—colors, shapes, textures, and lines; formal properties—the organization of sensory properties; technical properties—materials and processes used to create the artwork; and expressive properties—those that contribute to the mood or feeling of the artwork.

Phenomenological models.   The number and name of steps vary in phenomenological models, but **bracketing,** which is similar to the aesthetic attitude, appears in most. Lankford (1984) proposes five steps: receptiveness—avoiding preconceptions; orienting—determining how physical conditions might affect response and trying to set up a relationship with the artwork; bracketing—consciously focusing on its qualities to interpret its meaning; interpretive analysis—describing the interaction among visual, representational, and symbolic elements and feelings they generate to interpret its meaning; and synthesis—a final interpretation of the artwork's significance in light of experiences with it. In addition to the step of bracketing, experiencing and understanding both the surface qualities and aspects of the content of the artwork are often part of phenomenological models.

Deconstructive models.   The major focus of deconstructive models is on questioning what an art image communicates. Contextual, semiotic, and critical theory may be applied to understand the message an image communicates. Raising consciousness by deconstructing the hidden agenda in artwork is the goal of this model of art criticism. Questions are often used to get to the underlying ideas, but they will differ depending on the artwork.

Fred Wilson, an artist of African American and Carib descent, used work from the Maryland Historical Society in his installation "Mining the Museum" (see Figures 4.3 and 4.4). He intended "to extract the buried presence of racial minorities by planting emotionally explosive historical material to raise consciousness" (Stein, 1993, pp. 112–113).

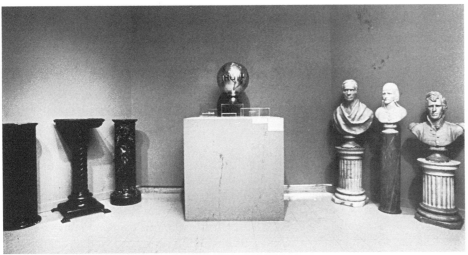

Figure 4.3
Pedestals, by Fred Wilson, 1992. Mixed media exhibited in "Mining the Museum," an installation by Wilson at the Maryland Historical Society in conjunction with the Museum for Contemporary Arts. What postmodern strategies does Wilson use in this entrance to the exhibition? What ideas does it communicate? How?

Photo by Jeff D. Goldman.

Figure 4.4
Metalwork: 1793–1870, by Fred Wilson, 1992. Mixed media exhibited in "Mining the Museum," an installation by Wilson at the Maryland Historical Society in conjunction with the Museum for Contemporary Arts. Questions for viewing this exhibit were: What is it? Where is it? Why? How is it used? For whom is it created? For whom does it exist? Who is represented? How are they represented? Who is doing the telling? the hearing? (Corrin, 1992). What message does Wilson communicate? How does the title add to the meaning?

Photo by Jeff D. Goldman.

Each art criticism model focuses on different issues, and the meaning students derive from the experience might differ according to the model of art criticism employed. You might want to use more than one model of art criticism to reveal different facets of the same art image.

This review of ideas about art history, aesthetics, and art criticism can help you understand issues discussed in this brief survey of art in the Western world. I'll introduce you to how the definition and purpose of art have changed since classical times.

Definition and Purpose of Art

Classical art.   The legacy of Greek and Roman art continues to influence the Western world more than 2,000 years after the fall of the Roman Empire (Preble & Preble, 1994). Art in this era was valued for how it glorified man and imitated nature, but it served instrumental purposes as well in both Greece and Rome. The Western world benefited from these ideas, and the fall of Rome did not destroy this legacy.

Medieval art.   In addition to the legacy from Rome and Greece, medieval art felt the influence of ideas from invaders who swarmed Europe and the eastern portion of the Roman empire. Early Christians used symbols about their beliefs to tell stories through images and objects to educate an illiterate populace. Imitation was less important than the instrumental purposes art served, and the names of artists who created magnificent stained glass windows and other art images and objects were seldom known.

Renaissance art.   After the Middle Ages, interest in classical ideas was revived, and a focus on the individual emerged. A burst of patronage for the arts by rich merchants fostered artistic activity. Symbols continued to communicate ideas and Christian beliefs. Realism and the ideals of classicism were combined with humanistic emotions by Michelangelo, Leonardo da Vinci, Raphael, and others whose works are still considered masterpieces.

Revolution and change.   Dramatic changes occurred in society and art in the 18th century. Preble and Preble (1994) call it "the most significant shift . . . since the Neolithic agricultural revolution ten thousand years earlier" (p. 372). New nations were formed and the Industrial Revolution changed life in many ways. Photography opened new ways of seeing, and mechanical reproduction made artwork less expensive and more accessible. David's neoclassicism, Géricault's romanticism, and Goya's images of man's inhumanity to man recorded the era. A view of art very different from prior views, and difficult for many to understand, emerged with the advent of modernism.

Modernism.   New technologies and advances in transportation, communication, and science changed the way the world was viewed. They also changed the purpose and form of art and the way art was viewed. Museums were built in this era, and fine art gained a more elitist status than other kinds of art.

Art for art's sake.   In form and purpose, art in the modern era is very different from art in small-scale societies. Art for art's sake suggests that art does not need to serve any purpose other than providing aesthetic enjoyment to the viewer. This view differs from earlier instrumental and imitationalist views. New knowledge in science and psychology expanded views of reality, and the invention of the camera provided other ways to record life. Artists looked for new ways to represent experiences, and a series of -isms that emerged required new ways of defining art.

Imitationalist and instrumental theories of art continued to be important, but innovation in art became valued more than tradition. New styles such as impressionism, postimpressionism, expressionism, cubism, surrealism, futurism, and constructivism emerged. Formalist, expressive, open concept, and institutional theories helped to define why the new forms were art and gave art critics new ways of interpreting art. Work created by Monet, Cézanne, van Gogh, Picasso, Matisse, and others provided viewers with different ways of seeing the world in the first half of the 20th century.

In the second half of the century, styles such as abstract expressionism, pop art, minimalism, conceptual art, photorealism, and installation art emerged. The work of Pollock, Frankenthaler, Rauschenberg, Warhol, Stella, Neel, Close, Hanson, Estes, Beuys, and others provided us with more ways for perceiving the world. Kissick (1993) reports that **avant garde** work in this era was abstract and large and focused on formal qualities. A new breed of realistic painters worked from photographs, and "color field painters" were interested in "unifying the picture plane in a more resonant, less overtly physical manner, producing eloquent expressions of harmony, balance, and equilibrium" (pp. 406–407).

In *Tag* (see Color Plate 4.1), Walter Prochownik combines a color field technique with a tiny group of figures at the very top of this large, vertical painting. While representational content is included, the primary focus is on the field of color, which provides a sense of almost infinite space.

Postmodernism. Changes in technology and society helped to precipitate the emergence of another new approach to art, called postmodernism. Computers have changed the very notion of painting, and video cameras and other electronic media have changed the way we communicate. Artists such as Nam June Paik, Jenny Holzer, and others have used these new media as well as the mass media in their work. Work by some postmodern artists, such as Baselitz, Kiefer, and Schnabel, is subjective and expressive. Other artists, such as Salle and Levine, may appropriate work by earlier artists. They often present their art in ways that speak more to societal issues than to formal issues, and they may change our response to a familiar artwork.

Postmodern art started in reaction to what some saw as a view of art that was too narrow. Risatti (1990) states that "the strictly formal interests of Modernism seemed . . . insufficient and insensitive in the face of social and cultural concern" (p. xiii). Postmodernism is a complex concept that is not easily defined. It focuses on art for society's sake more than art for art's sake, and it exhibits a pluralistic approach to art. Embedded in these issues is a sense of responsibility to raise consciousness about society's problems and the environment, a reaction to the emphasis on formal elements in modernism, and an echoing of traditional art forms.

Art for society's sake. In *Has Modernism Failed?*, Suzi Gablik (1984) suggested that a focus on individuality and artistic freedom has changed the concept of art. She maintains that many artists "doubt that it was ever meant to be organically integrated with society" (p. 119). However, in *The Reenchantment of Art* (1991), Gablik cites a transition from "aesthetic attitudes . . . that art has no 'useful' role to play", to a new direction that "reflects a will to *participate* socially . . . a significant shift from *objects to relationships*" (p. 7). While a focus on aesthetic attitude and formal qualities continues to be valued, artists with a postmodern focus are more concerned with raising consciousness about social, political, environmental, and gender issues. They use metaphor, juxtaposition, narrative, parody, and other devices designed to make the viewer aware of specific concerns.

A pluralistic perspective.   Acceptance of a broader range of art and the postmodern practice of appropriating or "quoting" earlier art work in a contemporary work reflect a sense of pluralism. In *Mixed Blessings: New Art in a Multicultural America,* Lucy Lippard notes a need to move away from the idea of our society as a melting pot to the metaphor of a "soup in which the ingredients retain their own forms and flavors" (1990, p. 5). Postmodernists question the notion of cultural literacy in a multicultural society. They want recognition for a wider range of art that includes fine art, popular art, folk art, and the work of women and other minorities.

This pluralistic perspective is also apparent in contemporary approaches to architecture. When postmodern architects design a new building for a community, they often borrow architectural features from existing buildings in the community in an attempt to create a link between the character of the old buildings and the new structure. This attitude is similar to that expressed by Inuit artists of Canada who look forward and backward in their art by honoring past traditions but also reflecting contemporary life (Hood, 1995).

Raising consciousness.   The work of many contemporary artists attempts to raise awareness about issues that affect our society. Fred Wilson revealed how museums can perpetuate prejudice (refer back to Figures 4.3 and 4.4). Zhi Lin (1996), a Chinese artist, feels that art should be more than just beautiful. He says, "I want to . . . wake up my countrymen who were and are the audience of the killing grounds. I want to raise the social awareness of the situation in China and the world" (p. 1). He does this in a series of paintings called *Five Capital Executions in China.*

In the first three works of this series (see Color Plates 4.2–4.4), Zhi appropriates methods and symbols from both Western painting and traditional Chinese painting. Contradictory images give the execution scene a festival aura and "remind us of our own participation in the crowd that either cheers or ignores the ignorance of our society and ourselves" (p. 2). He prints a 4,000-year-old Chinese symbol over a 16th-century-style painting, frames his academic work in Chinese folk art style, and uses a raised Tibetan Buddhist red curtain "as a symbolic challenge to the tradition that domestic shame should not be made public" (p. 2).

Artworks created by Tanya Ganson also depict the inhumanity of humans to one another and raise our consciousness about social issues. Ganson portrays memories of herself as a Jewish child during the Russian civil war and depicts the violence, chaos, and horror she witnessed before her flight from Russia (Color Plate 4.5). Ganson says, "I try to express with a brush the fear; the pain of leaving my girlfriends [behind in Russia]" (1996, p. 1). African American artist Joyce Scott uses beaded jewelry to tell a contemporary story of violent urban crime in *The Sneek* (Color Plate 4.6). Robert Booth is concerned about environmental issues in *Greenscape* (Color Plate 4.7), and Christy Rupp uses metaphor to protest industry's consumption of the American agricultural tradition in *Hometown Hunger* (Color Plate 4.8).

Postmodern art packs powerful social messages, and some of these images may not be appropriate for younger students. Older students can interpret and understand a wider range of art images.

In the next section, one of the rationales for providing experiences with art images addresses the importance of considering developmental issues when you use art images (*see* Chapter 2, "Understanding the Learner," for a discussion of developmental stages in art education).

Why Should Experiences with Art Images Be Provided for Students?

Three basic positions—object centered, society centered, and child centered—suggest different rationales for providing experiences with art images. An object-centered position, also called an essentialist philosophy, focuses on the masterpieces of Western European art so students can become familiar with these exemplars of fine art and achieve cultural literacy. A society-centered position focuses on a wide range of art images that reflect the diverse nature of our society. Experiences with them are provided so students can recognize themselves in art images and identify what they communicate about our society. The developmental appropriateness of images and how they are used is the focus for the child-centered position.

All three rationales are important, and all three can provide something of value in a well-balanced art program. Students should be familiar with Western European masterpieces. They represent the heritage of many people whose parents emigrated to America. However, a broader definition of art that goes beyond the melting pot theory of assimilation into American culture is important for recognizing cultural diversity. Fine, popular, and folk art from any culture and time can help students understand and think critically about contemporary issues that affect their world. Your students' learning will depend on how you structure the experience. Content that secondary students like may be inappropriate for the primary level. Developmental issues are important when you choose art images and structure experiences with them. A well-balanced art program considers this view with an object-centered or society-centered one, depending upon the goals and objectives of a unit.

How Can You Engage Learners with Art Images?

I said earlier that engaging learners gets them involved so they become self-motivated. You want to generate this kind of engagement in your art classes, and you know it has happened when students don't want to stop at the end of the class. Several factors affect engagement with art images, and the way you structure the encounter affects what the students derive from the experience. Students in one of my eighth-grade classes became so involved with art images that many went beyond the assignment of mixing colors in the image and wanted to render the whole artwork. They started calling it "their" image and wanted to buy it for their bedroom. What generated this kind of engagement?

What Factors Affect Engagement?

Factors that got my students involved included my understanding of them, the classroom environment I created, and the teaching strategies that I used.

Understanding Learners

Viktor Lowenfeld wrote that "motivation is meaningful if it is adequate to the developmental level and is keyed to specific interests of the child" (1957, p. 47). To engage students, you need to know where they are in the developmental sequence (see Chapter 2). You also need to be aware of what their interests are and what kinds of experiences—both individual and cultural—they bring to the classroom.

Information about cultural heritage can be very helpful. Knapp (1995) suggests that using cultural background "as a resource for learning and actively or proactively addressing the cultural dimension" (p. 200) increases the possibility of engagement. A survey can provide you with information about your students and help guide your planning.

My students were in eighth grade, a transition period for adolescents. It can be a tough time for some, and they like to make their own decisions. Guided by knowledge gained from my survey and personal experiences with these students, I encouraged them to choose an image from some that I thought might interest them. You'll have many different students, and you can't understand all of them. If you try to see each one as an individual, and look for ways to connect with them, you will reach some of your students.

Creating a Learning Environment

Before formal schooling was initiated in the 19th century with the advent of the Common School Movement, children learned in their own communities. Most learning today is separated from this context (Kornhabe & Gardner, 1991). Extending your classroom into the community (London, 1994) is one possibility. In a walking tour of their neighborhood, students in Boyd-Berry Elementary School in Missouri learned about architectural styles from an architect (see Chapter 8). While this real-life experience engaged the students, it's not always possible for teachers to go outside the classroom. They must rely on art images instead.

Displaying all kinds of visual images is a key factor in engaging learners. I've found that students learn as much from the visuals in my classroom as they do from what I say. In the color unit I used a large color-value wheel as a concept visual to generate dialogue about hue, value, and intensity. Depicting ideas about art visually and verbally allows more students access to information for talking about art. Process, product, concept, and art history visuals; objectives for a unit; and other information displayed on the blackboard, bulletin board, or "mini gallery" (see Photos 4.1–4.6) all enrich the learning environment.

Selecting Pedagogical Strategies

The strategies you use to introduce ideas about art images are also important. **Pedagogy** is the art or science of teaching. It deals with how you translate information to help students learn. Research indicates that some strategies work better than others, and it is "important for learners to construct their own knowledge . . . rather than giving it to them ready-made" (Barth, 1991, p. 115). Providing choices for students, planning hands-on activities, using dialogue, and encouraging reflection are all strategies that help to engage learners.

Allowing choices enhances the possibility of connecting with students. Making their own choice of an art image gave my eighth graders a chance to use ones that

Photo 4.1
Display of concept visuals. The color-value wheel and the visual-verbal depictions of design principles make the meaning of these concepts more understandable. Examples of letter styles, and a process visual for teaching text lettering, are accessible for students who need help, and the "Artcabulary" display on the bulletin board familiarizes students with words they need to know. Visuals like these can help make your classroom an environment for learning.

Author's collection.

interested them. Sharing ideas through dialogue and experimenting with hue, value, and intensity helped them to construct their own understanding of color. Dialogue is also useful in assessing learning, because it allows students to reflect upon what they have done and critique their success (Burton, 1992). Other pedagogical strategies can generate both individual and group reflection.

"T,P,S" and "K,W,L" are two strategies that help to encourage reflection. In T,P,S, a question is posed; students *Think*, then they *Pair* with someone to compare answers, and pairs *Share* ideas with the class. In K,W,L, students tell what they *Know* about a topic, what they *Want* to know, and what they *Learned*. The final step can be an assessment. These strategies empower students, let you know what they bring to the lesson, provide new information, and encourage engagement.

Ernest Goldstein (1986a) modeled good pedagogy in guiding one of my sixth-grade classes in a search for clues in Edward Hicks's *Peaceable Kingdom* (see Figure 4.5). Hands wagged furiously as students found information they wanted to share, and questions he posed kept them going back to the image for answers. Goldstein's open-ended dialogue encouraged participation and engaged students. A thank-you note one student wrote shows the power of engagement.

Goldstein's intent was to help students enter and derive meaning from this art image. One student, Keisha, had a response to the experience that apparently reflected something in her life. She wrote, "That lamb better be careful about laying down next to the lion. She might get hurt." I was concerned about this response and

Photo 4.2

Bulletin boards are a useful tool for introducing unit themes and displaying student work. If they are not available, consider hanging work mounted on cardboard from the ceiling with fishing line. Putting drawings, paintings, masks, or reproductions on both sides doubles the display possibility, and air currents make both sides visible. The concept visuals above the bulletin boards imaginatively depict the art elements and can be referred to by all during dialogue about the artwork. Having supply boxes, water containers, and brush racks near each work table will simplify management of tools and materials.

Author's collection.

Photo 4.3

Bulletin board display for eighth-grade drawing unit

Author's collection.

Photo 4.4
Visuals of design principles, a statement about the value of art, and the theme for each middle school class are displayed above objectives and visuals for current projects. This provides students with an overview of what they will do, and it is helpful on PTA night as a way to communicate your program to parents both visually and verbally.

Author's collection.

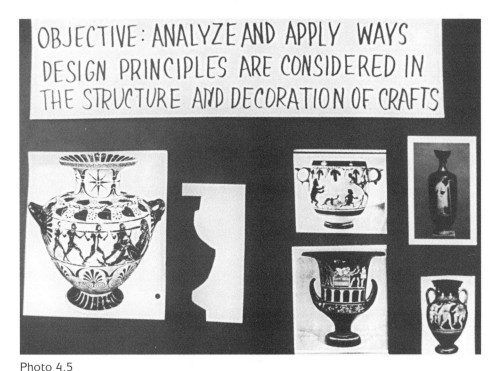

Photo 4.5
Visuals for Greek pottery unit. Art history visuals are an important ingredient for teaching art. This display introduces students to the unit objective, and the art history visuals provide a focus for discussion of characteristics of Greek pottery. The sample template, a product/process visual, helps students see how to control form in hand-built pottery.

Author's collection.

Photo 4.6
Notes for students, concept visuals, and a visual-verbal art history display about the kinds of art make this classroom a learning environment.

Author's collection.

Figure 4.5
Peaceable Kingdom, by Edward Hicks, ca. 1834. Canvas, 29.375 x 35.5 in.

Gift of Edgar William and Bernice Chrysler Garbisch, ©1996 Board of Trustees, National Gallery of Art, Washington, D.C.

shared the information with the school counselor, who said it validated his prior suspicion of abuse. We can never be aware of all that students bring to the classroom. Dialogue about art images can cause students to reflect upon many different issues. Listen to them. Knowing your students, making your classroom a learning tool, and using good teaching strategies all engage learners. The next step is to structure the experiences so they are meaningful.

 How Can You Structure Experiences So Learners Can Create Meaning Through Art?

Structuring an experience with art images involves four basic choices: the objectives it will serve; the content you will use; the processes you select for teaching; and the models you choose for the experience. The choices you make will affect student engagement and will also affect the possibility for them to create meaning through art. These choices are not necessarily sequential, but they often must begin with curricular demands.

Objectives

Goals are a general description of what students need to know and be able to do over time. Specific goals, mandated in local curriculum guides, may be derived from national standards and state goals. Concepts and skills are cumulative, and requirements increase at each level. You generally have freedom to choose the sequence in which you fulfill these goals at each level, but you must work toward helping students achieve all the goals in your curriculum. Objectives translate goals into the specific functions that a particular lesson will serve.

Seven different functions proposed by art educators for experiences with art images were synthesized in a content analysis of art education literature from 1980 to 1991 (Delaney, 1992). They included "raising consciousness; aesthetic appreciation; meaning and value; recognizing cultural literacy; recognizing cultural diversity; knowledge about art history; and thinking and behaving like an artist" (p. 143). They incorporate a range of behaviors. You will create your own objectives, appropriate for units and lessons you design. Developmental issues are important to consider in planning objectives and in selecting the content.

Content

The specific art images or objects you select are the content for an experience. Your rationale for providing the experience with art images, developmental issues, the function you want them to serve, and availability of images will affect your choice of content. Some subject matter may be too difficult for young children. You wouldn't consider asking second graders to read *War and Peace* because their limited experience and level of cognitive development would make it too difficult for them to understand. These constraints also apply to art images.

Look for art images that seem to be appropriate for the developmental level, the kinds of experiences students are likely to have had, and their personal interests. Younger children may not even know the difference between a reproduction and a painting, so you will need to help them understand even this basic information. Showing them original oil and watercolor paintings can help them understand the differences. Developmental issues also affect how students understand art images (see Chapter 2). They will interpret art images from a personal view based on their world. Images dealing with topics related to this world help engage students at this level. Older students can work with a wider variety of art images and take a broader perspective, but to engage them you still need to make a connection between the art image and the students' lived experiences.

Art images are available in many different forms, such as slides, reproductions, and overhead transparencies. Computers also provide access to a broad range of images from around the world on the Internet and the World Wide Web. If budget constraints limit your resources, used books, calendars, and postcards can provide an affordable source for reproductions. With any form of art image you introduce, you need to help students understand the distortions of size and color that change it from the original.

Processes

Howard Gardner's theory of multiple intelligence (Gardner, 1983, 1990) can provide you with insight into different ways of knowing. Verbal, visual, kinesthetic, musical, dramatic, and many other types of processes can be used in working with art images, and more than one process can be combined in an experience. There are numerous ways to engage learners with art images. They include (but are not limited to) looking at art; talking about art; making art about art; and interpreting art metaphorically, visually, spatially, contextually, and through music, movement, and drama. All the senses can be involved in learning. Choosing processes that focus on the strengths of learners can help them understand what you want them to know and be able to do. By planning experiences that utilize more than one process, you increase the possibility for more students to be successful. This is especially true when you are working with students who have special needs. Armstrong (1994) suggests that focusing on the strengths rather than the disabilities of special-needs students gives us a different perspective and may help us to "see that disabilities occur in only a part of a student's life" (p. 138). In *Multiple Intelligences for the Classroom,* he translates Gardner's theory into practical strategies for all students.

Multisensory processes.   An interrelated arts learning experience can help students interpret art images through more than one process. Invoking kinesthetic, musical, visual, and verbal intelligences to understand artwork is fun to do. It also engages students in an active, physical way; increases their perceptual skills; and helps them understand relationships among movement, gesture, music, words, and visual properties. This multisensory data provides ways to derive meaning from artwork.

Making a linear tracing to define the focus and rhythm of movements; creating a tableau of the image by replicating the positions of people; or representing objects musically, visually, and verbally engages students in discovering for themselves what the artwork is about. Taking a Polaroid picture of each tableau provides feedback that helps students assess how well they captured the mood and movement in the image. Selecting music and having students create a dance related to the art image, write words that the people might say, or create a story about what they see and dramatize the incident could provide new insights into the art image and encourage student involvement with realistic, abstract, or nonobjective art images.

Using art images as a resource for art making is another possibility. By translating the ideas and feelings embedded in an art image into their own artwork, students can learn *through* as well as *about* art. Students can imagine and depict events that might have preceded or followed what is in an art image. Several artworks can be the source of imagery for a pastiche, an artistic composition made up of pieces from different artworks. This borrowing process is a postmodern technique that can communicate new ideas and feelings by giving a new twist to familiar imagery. Interpreting art can be done kinesthetically, spatially, through movement, or by translating a two-dimensional image into a three-dimensional object. Making a three-dimensional interpretation of an art image helps learners with the concept of foreground, middle ground, and background (Baker, 1989). To help my preservice art educators recognize the value of this approach for students they would teach, I had them try the process. The assignment was purposefully ambiguous. I wanted each student to set his or her own problem and make personal decisions concerning the choice of the content and form. Each one took a slightly different approach.

Kelli Nunn's interpretation of a Matisse painting, *Still Life in the Studio, Nice* (see Color Plate 4.9), is like a stage set. Each of the dimensions is enclosed in a box connected with slots and tabs. The completed construction is "framed" with black cardboard, which creates ambiguity between the two-dimensional "picture frame" and the three-dimensional space of the stage set. Kelli explained that she put the frontal plane on a slant "to emphasize that it was going back in space" (Nunn, 1995). The fabric for the curtain is real, and a real mirror represents what Matisse had painted. She experimented with light to create shadows within the structure, an effective idea that I had not even considered.

Faye Martin's spatial interpretation of Mary Cassatt's *Little Girl in a Blue Armchair* (see Color Plate 4.10) is presented in a more open form. Each piece of furniture is separately slotted into the base, and the background has only two sides. Through this spatial interpretation, Faye allows us to see and experience the actual space from more than one angle, which could help students who have difficulty conceptualizing spatial dimensions.

Bradney Willingham's representation of Berthe Morisot's *In the Dining Room* (see Color Plate 4.11) combines a stage set box like Kelli's with the individual slotting that Faye used. His interpretation allows viewers to move visually through the construction and see the spatial qualities of three dimensions. Another student, Steve, represented Hokusai's *The Wave* by creating a U-shaped wooden form with deep slots gouged in the sides to hold separate flat depictions of the foreground, middle ground, and background.

Through this experience, students learned the problems and possibilities of a visual-spatial representation and also came to know the artist's style and the art image in another way. Choosing processes that implement various ways of knowing can increase the possibility that students will become engaged, be successful, and derive meaning from the experience.

The theory of experientialist cognition supports the idea that human bodily experiences influence our response to art images. Lakoff (1988) proposes that "meaningful conceptual structures arise from . . . the structured nature of the body and social experience" (p. 121). The idea that our experiences influence how we perceive and relate to art images is similar to ideas that Dewey expressed in *Art as Experience* (1934).

Stake and Kerr (1995) suggest that different media can reveal different aspects of our experience as human beings, and our "perception is colored by tacit knowledge, both personally and culturally constructed. . . . [T]he viewer hangs these images in his or her mind, confronting other images already there, reshaping the edges of experience" (p. 57). Art images can activate memories and provide insight into personal experiences, as Keisha's response to Hicks's painting illustrated. Interrelated arts approaches increase the possibility that learners will connect with an artwork.

Models.   The model, or form of an experience, is the way you actually shape and structure the content and processes to achieve the objective you want. Research into art history, inquiry about aesthetic issues, and the models of art criticism introduced earlier can be used in many of the models introduced in this section. However, developmental issues should be considered. An "art in the dark" slide lecture, which many of you have endured to learn about art history, is generally not appropriate in K–12 classrooms. You also may need to simplify the form and topic of aesthetic inquiry and art criticism for younger students. Formal art criticism models introduced earlier may not be appropriate for some levels. Feldman (1992) states that a fundamental tool for art criticism is "wide acquaintance with art, especially the kind we expect to judge" (p. 471). High school students may be familiar with a large enough body of work to pass judgments. Those in elementary and middle school generally are not, so informal models work better at these levels.

In this section you'll encounter informal models for working with art images, as well as cooperative learning models, computer-based models, and integrated models. After identifying basic characteristics of each category, I'll describe examples of specific models for each one. Ideas about art history, aesthetics, art criticism, and art making can be introduced in all models, and any content or process can be used. As you read, consider other models you might develop!

Informal models.   Informal models are tools for acquainting learners with a wide range of art images and helping them develop perceptual skills. These models can also provide experiences with art history and aesthetics or aspects of art criticism, such as describing artworks or analyzing them. The major characteristic of this category is a lack of specific, formal steps in the process. Four informal models will be introduced: familiarizing, living with art, games, and critical studies.

Familiarizing is an informal model that focuses primarily on introducing students to artwork and increasing perceptual abilities. Even very young children can look at an artwork, describe what they see, and relate the content and feelings it communicates to their personal experiences. Talking about art is important. At any level, combining talking about art with creating objects or images based on ideas and feelings about an art image can provide deeper understanding.

Anything that engages learners in concentrated interaction with art images can familiarize them with art and set the stage for later learning through art. For example, a Missouri art teacher familiarized her sixth graders with van Gogh's *Starry Night.* Students talked about the artist, the era, the image, its content, reasons the artist might have painted it the way he did, the colors used, and the feelings conveyed. Then they created an image that reflected van Gogh's style. Eleven-year-old Jessica Lillard's painting (see Color Plate 4.12) reflects his style, as well as Jessica herself and her memory of another van Gogh painting, *Sunflowers.* Her painting was selected to appear on the cover of *School Arts* magazine and was also one of 80 selected from 1,400 entrants in the central region to be exhibited at Epcot Center in Disney World.

Living with art is an informal model with one consistent feature: experiences with an art image extend over a period of time. It can be a few weeks or a full semester. The "Bag It" approach (Baker, 1989) works well with upper elementary and middle school students, because they like to collect things. Students are given a postcard reproduction in a Baggie and told to gather things related to it, such as color swatches, words, textures, or other images. They write a statement about how and why these things relate to the artwork, and then they create an image that reflects the meaning derived from the art image. This model is flexible and generates many different responses. It encourages learners to interpret an art image metaphorically when they represent it and talk about the symbolism they use.

My college students lived with a randomly selected art image for several weeks. They described their initial response; gathered things related to it; considered aesthetic qualities; researched the artist, artwork, and era; and created an image reflecting a similar mood or idea. Finally, they interpreted the art image, anchoring their ideas in the image itself and in their own personal experiences that might have affected their responses.

One student, Jamie, wrote about van Gogh's *Three Pair of Shoes*, beginning with her initial response: "Wow, what a boring postcard I have to live with for three weeks!" (Steiger, 1995). Later she discussed how the brush strokes projected "a tired, used feeling" to her: "Although the shoes are sitting in a group, they still look lonely and separate. . . . The only shoe upside down . . . makes for a sense of . . . wanting to belong." Her close relationship with her family influenced her interpretation, and she said: "One of my initial reactions was that the shoes were painted of family." She decided that it was not three pairs of shoes, "rather it is of six single shoes. The shoes signify Vincent and his siblings." Research into van Gogh's life and work gave her this insight. Jamie wrote:

> After knowing a lot more about his life and sort of analyzing this image through his eyes, this is my final interpretation. . . . The shoes represent three brothers and three sisters. . . . One of the last shoes, Vincent's, is upside-down. I feel this is a cry for help. (Steiger, 1995)

When she presented her paper to the class, Jamie described her excitement when she arrived at the insight that led to a personal and metaphorical interpretation of the artwork. The longer time frame and multiple processes help to engage learners in this model.

Using games about art is an informal model that is fun for all ages. Commercial games are available, or you can invent art games yourself, based on ones familiar to students. They can help young students develop perceptual skills and understand art images, and older ones are challenged by them.

A game called "Concept Formation" works at any level and can be structured to introduce or reinforce any concept. Using three artworks that incorporate a concept (such as primary colors) and one that does not, a leader points to the images, saying Yes to those that have it and No to those that do not. Whoever guesses first gets to be the next leader. This focus on concepts helps students develop the vocabulary needed to articulate responses to art.

In the game of "Mystery," the leader gives clues about an art image, and players try to figure out which specific image it is. Clues are based only on art elements and principles, expressive qualities, or techniques, not on subject matter. "Mystery" can be used to review for a test or reinforce understanding of concepts.

Using puzzles to teach aesthetic concepts makes a game of a sometimes difficult discipline. Battin (1994) introduces case studies focused on aesthetic issues and provides questions that help the students think critically about the cases. Dialogue is moderated by the teacher. Students must justify their positions, and they learn that more than one answer is possible. Some of the cases may need to be adapted for younger students.

A unit that incorporates an informal approach to art history through construction of a miniature golf course was created by one of my preservice students. Called "Putt Art," this secondary level unit was inspired by "Putt-Modernism," an exhibition at the Kemper Museum of Contemporary Art and Design in Kansas City. John's goals are to help high school students become familiar with specific historical periods of art and their relationship to current issues and capable of applying two-dimensional design to three-dimensional mixed media. He introduces ideas about these goals through dialogue and visuals. Students would choose and research a period of art history, then design and create usable miniature golf holes that related to art history and current issues (Hooker, 1996).

The product visual that John created helped him understand problems his students might encounter. It is a usable miniature golf hole with the definition of pop art on the ramp leading to the hole. His issue was environmental concerns. Everything he used to build the golf hole was created from recycled material. He painted an image of Jim Morrison of The Doors on an old car door and used discarded plywood to construct a strip with four holes. One directed the ball into the actual hole and earned points for the player. The others channeled it in the opposite direction and the player lost points.

This informal games model involves students in art history research, lets them make something that is fun and usable, and addresses ideas about art and social issues. It would be a challenging and engaging unit for high school students and covers information related to the National Visual Arts Standards 1, 3, and 4. John's assessment strategies included in-process and oral critiques, peer and self-evaluations, and an essay test on the art history period selected for study. He developed a five-point rubric for evaluation of student work.

A miniature golf game was also the strategy for seventh- and eighth-grade classes in the Milwaukee Public Schools (see Photos 4.7–4.9). The golf holes these middle school students designed in the "Art Golf" project were smaller than those high school students would make in the "Putt Art" unit, and they were made of

Photo 4.7
Milwaukee Public Schools seventh- and eighth-grade students' "Art Golf"

Courtesy of Cheryl Hamilton collection.

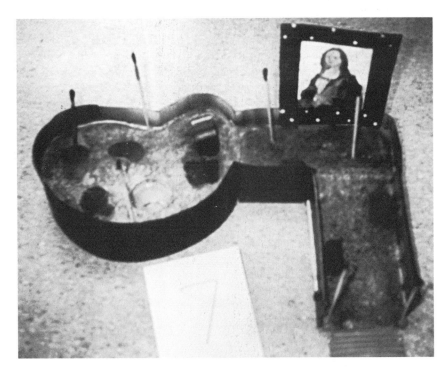

Photo 4.8
Milwaukee Public Schools seventh- and eighth-grade students' "Mona Lisa Golf Hole"

Courtesy of Cheryl Hamilton collection.

papier-mâché rather than wood. However, they did incorporate images and ideas about art in a game format.

The critical studies model is an informal one originating in Great Britain. Thistlewood (1991) states that "*Critical Studies* is now an accepted abbreviated term for those parts of the art and design curriculum . . . that embrace art history, aesthetic theories, and the social, economic, political, religious and numerous other contexts" (p. x). Contextual, technical, critical, aesthetic, and various other issues are combined with art making in this model.

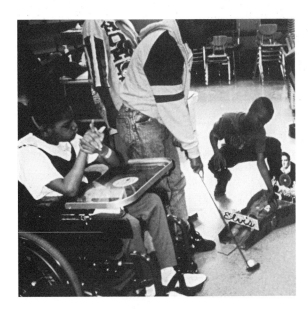

Photo 4.9
Milwaukee Public Schools seventh-and eighth-grade students trying out the "Art Golf" game

Courtesy of Cheryl Hamilton collection.

The model that I designed for eighth-grade students incorporated aesthetic, contextual, cultural, social, economic, and technical issues concerning folding screens. I was inspired by an exhibition at the National Gallery of Art that included work by artists from various eras and countries in a wide variety of materials. The possibilities for design seemed endless, and I started to consider how I might use screens to help students understand factors that influence the design of craft objects and the way the function of an object might differ across cultures.

It was a while before I finished researching the information and translating it into a unit that included processes for looking at, talking about, analyzing, webbing ideas about (see Chapter 6), making art about, and reading about art. Translating the research into understanding also involved creating a directed reading activity, which used questions as an advance organizer.

THEORY INTO PRACTICE

The Folding Image: From the 17th to the 20th Century

National Content Standards
1, 2, 4, 5, 6

Achievement Standards
5–8

Goal:	Analyze and interpret factors that influence artists in designing craft objects.
Learning Strategy:	Research the design of folding screens by artists from various cultures to analyze factors that influenced their design. Consider these factors in the design of a miniature folding screen for a specific function in your life.
Objective 1:	Identify factors that influence the design of craft objects.
Introduction:	What factors influence the design of craft objects? Dialogue about the question and model webbing by analyzing factors that influence the design of doors. Use posters of the *Doors of Boston* and the *Doors of New Orleans*.
Directed Reading Activity:	Read about the history of folding screens to discover: Who invented them? How and why do Chinese and Japanese screens differ? What purposes have folding screens served? How have culture and environment influenced their design? Discuss answers to questions. View slides of folding screens from various cultures and use a webbing activity sheet to analyze aesthetic, formal, and technical qualities of the folding screens. Consider the number of panels, their shapes, the way they were unified, and the materials used.
Closure:	Share and compare results of the analysis of folding screens.

Objective 2:	Identify ideas for design of a folding screen.
Introduction:	Review and Dialogue: Which principles are most important in designing a folding screen? Why? What choices do artists have in creating a folding screen? What materials might be used?
Activity:	Sketch at least two to three ideas for a screen and list possible materials.
Closure:	Share ideas and critique idea sketches of folding screens.
Objectives 3–5:	Identify and use various materials in the design and construction of a miniature folding screen.
Introduction:	Dialogue about the question: What might be the limitations and possibilities of the materials you plan to use? Demonstrate safe procedures for using tools and equipment. Identify criteria for a well-made craft object.
Activity:	Experiment with a variety of materials to discover their potential and limitations for designing your miniature folding screen.
Closure:	Share discoveries about materials and processes. Dialogue about problems and possible solutions. Critique work in process.
Objective 6:	Assess strengths and weaknesses of miniature folding screens.
Introduction:	Review assessment criteria for folding screens.
Activity:	Write the following: a self-critique of completed screen; a personal statement about the process and product; a description of how your experiences, interests, environment, and culture influenced your design; and a description of the function your screen will serve in your life (50 points).
Closure:	Critique selected screens as a group. Consider what works well and why it does, what doesn't work and why, and how you would suggest addressing the problems.
Assessment Criteria:	Is the screen well constructed? Are the materials appropriate for the design? Are sections related to create a unified whole? Does the screen reflect the artist's interests, experiences, culture, or environment? Can it serve its intended purpose? (10 points each).
Evaluation:	Based on self-critique and assessment criteria (100 points possible).

Many materials were available for experimentation in this unit: leather scraps, colored straws, cardboard, tissue paper, cellophane, and others. Students worked through the materials and set their own problems. The ambiguity of the unit and the many possibilities for designing a screen made it engaging and exciting for my most able students. It was also a challenge to develop an aesthetically pleasing and functional way to join the panels. Some students enjoyed experimenting with the materials and came up with creative solutions (see Figures 4.6–4.9), and others worked from sketches and translated them into materials. It was a very successful unit for many of my eighth graders, and I was pleased with the extent of energy they invested in problem solving and achieving results.

Figure 4.6
Moonlight, by Baltimore County Public Schools eighth-grade student. Cardboard, construction paper, and leather, 12 x 16 x 3 in.

Author's collection.

Figure 4.7
Seagulls, by Baltimore County Public Schools eighth-grade student. Wood, paper, and drinking straw, 14 x 18 x 4 in.

Author's collection.

Figure 4.8
Wind Surfing, by Baltimore County Public Schools eighth-grade student. Colored tissue paper and flexible drinking straws, 14 x 21 x 5 in.

Author's collection.

Figure 4.9
Flaming Colors, by Baltimore County Public Schools eighth-grade student. Colored construction paper and cardboard, 18 x 12 x 4 in.

Author's collection.

My less able students also became engaged with the webbing and the slides. However, it was clear that many of them were overwhelmed with the number of choices and the ambiguity of the problem. I needed to make some adaptions for them to achieve success, so I limited materials and provided precut mat board. Students could change the contour, design the sections, connect the pieces any way they wanted, or simply fold cardboard and create a design on it (see Figures 4.10 and 4.11). With a tighter structure, they became more engaged and solved problems they set for themselves.

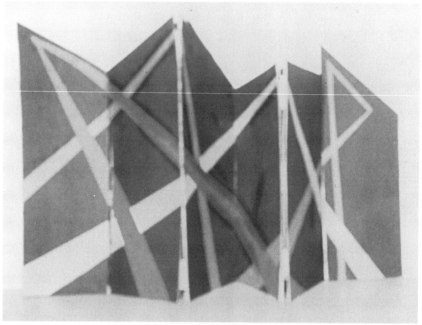

Figure 4.10
Dynamic Directions, by Baltimore County Public Schools eighth-grade student. Construction paper and cardboard, 14 x 21 x 3 in.

Author's collection.

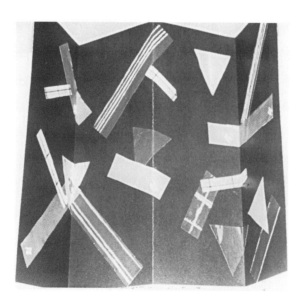

Figure 4.11
Lines and Shapes, by Baltimore County Public Schools eighth-grade student. Wallpaper, construction paper, and cardboard, 16 x 14 x 3 in.

Author's collection.

Cooperative learning models. Models in this category all include some kind of collaborative work between students. The extent to which tasks are defined, the number of groups, and the size of each group may vary. Members may be assigned by the teacher, selected randomly, or chosen by the students. If you select members, you can pull "outsider" students into a group and assign tasks based on each member's strengths. Random selection changes groupings each time. Students usually choose to work with their friends. However, varying the makeup of groups provides the opportunity for them to learn more about, as well as from, one another.

Cooperative learning is an effective model for structuring an experience at any level. Students like to socialize with their peers, and they favor working in groups. Responsibilities are shared. Students have a chance to construct their own understanding through research and hands-on experiences, then share their insights with other groups. The class can cover a broader range of material or can look at the same topic from different viewpoints, in a shorter time period.

One of my former students taught a high school ceramics class about ancient cultures through a cooperative learning model that grew from her personal experiences on an archaeological dig in Israel. Elizabeth introduced her class to archaeology and art history by bringing in actual artifacts she had dug up. Her unit plan addresses five National Visual Arts Content Standards: 1, 3, 4, 5, and 6. Objectives for the unit were that students become acquainted with the history of ceramics, be able to identify how archaeologists use artifacts to draw conclusions about a culture, and cooperate in a group to learn about ceramic arts of a specific ancient culture (Barker, 1995).

Elizabeth introduced students to various cultures through slides and artifacts; then she broke the class into groups. Each group chose a specific culture from the past to research and wrote a one-page report; each member replicated an actual artifact from that culture. The supply managers made sure everyone had the supplies and tools they needed each day. The researchers gathered data on the subject and gave each member source information about an artifact and a copy of it to use as a model. The writer used the researcher's information to write a report about where and when the people lived, how they supported themselves, what kinds of objects they made, what function they served, what their religious beliefs were, and why their culture disappeared. The speaker taught the rest of the class what the group learned.

Self, peer, and teacher assessment was based on how well each member did his or her assigned job and what the quality was of their ceramic artifact replica and glaze application. Points were assigned to each of these criteria for evaluation of the project. After this experience, each student's idea of a ceramic figure or vessel was enlarged through the hands-on activity as well as the research. Through their cooperation, they learned about many ancient cultures (see Photo 4.10 and Figures 4.12 and 4.13).

This was not dry, boring art history. These students in a rural Missouri high school had little or no knowledge about archaeology before this unit. They were teaching their parents about it before the unit was over! Although students replicated an object, rather than creating their own, the process helped them "walk in the shoes" of people from that culture. A follow-up lesson could build on this experience by having students create an object of their own for a function in their lives that somehow connected to the function and form of their artifacts.

Photo 4.10
High school student Julie Stoll glazing pottery based on research about the Inca culture

Courtesy of Elizabeth G. Barker, art teacher, Lebanon High School, Missouri.

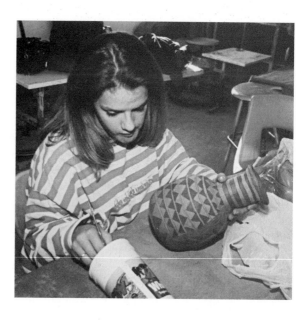

Figure 4.12
Animal figure created by Lebanon High School student based on research about pottery in ancient Persia

Courtesy of Elizabeth G. Barker, art teacher, Lebanon High School, Missouri.

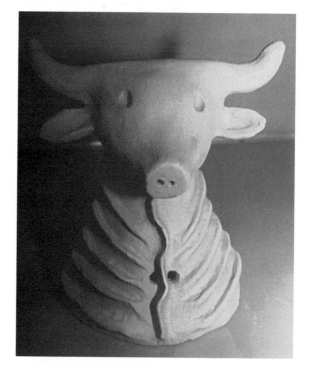

Figure 4.13
Imaginary creature created by Lebanon High School student based on research about pottery in Thailand

Courtesy of Elizabeth G. Barker, art teacher, Lebanon High School, Missouri.

Computer-based models. The Internet and the World Wide Web provide access to museums and galleries and collections of art that are impossible to see except through this electronic medium. Directories that can help you identify and locate them are available (Taylor & Ryan, 1995). These resources increase your storehouse of information and images, and the potential for electronic media is vast. One California teacher described a project that intended to "explore the relationship between art and emerging technologies, such as Virtual Reality" (Sakatani, 1996).

A unit plan developed by one of my students includes two possible computer-based models: one for middle school and one for high school students. Alissa's goals were for students to "know and use art media, methods, tools and problem solving processes, recognize and employ elements and principles of design, and demonstrate understanding of personal, group, and cultural relationships and interactions with art" (Donaldson, 1996, p. 1). The unit plan addresses National Visual Arts Content Standards 1, 2, 3, and 4; the achievement standards for grades 5–8; and the achievement standards at the proficient level for grades 9–12.

In the middle school plan, "Exploring Current Issues with 19th and 20th Century Media," Alissa wants students to brainstorm current issues and research information about them on the Internet, then view slides of work by artists who "documented current issues of their periods using the technology of the time" (p. 3). Each student is required to generate five pages of research from the Internet on their topic and then use the computer and camera as tools to create a poster about it. In the high school lesson, "Hot Topics Explored with the Latest Tech!" students do a "net-search" to look at current photography and print three photographs that intrigue them. Then they choose a school or community issue and create a photographic composition that explains their position through the use of multiple images. Finally, they summarize their issues and write an artist's statement about their work. Teacher and peer reviews provide in-process assessment, and a rubric is used for summative assessment and evaluation of the high school lesson plan:

4 Completed on time. Excellent craftsmanship: no spots on photos from development; appropriate level of contrast; no obvious flaws from scanning and slicing photos. Two or more elements or principles of design used in designing the format of a poster that promotes awareness of the current issue; a clear and original artist's statement.

3 Completed on time. Good craftsmanship with only one or two spots on photos from development; level of contrast is almost exact; few noticeable flaws from scanning and slicing photos. Two or more elements or principles of design used in designing the format of the poster. Artist's statement is evident and original.

2 Completed within a week of project due date. Photographs have several spots from development; contrast level is too gray; noticeable flaws from scanning and slicing photos. One element or principle of design used in designing the format of the poster. Artist's statement was attempted but unclear; some originality evident.

1 Completed after a week of the project due date. Photographs are spotted and streaked; contrast filters not used; glaring flaws from scanning and slicing photos.

These approaches to the computer provide some direction on how this model might be used to work with art images. Ideas and possibilities for computer models will continue to be expanded.

Integrated models.   These models are probably the most familiar ones of all. They all address National Visual Art Standard 6, because this model connects learning in art with learning in other areas. I'll describe three examples of integrated curricula. Two involved my collaboration with middle school English and social studies teachers; the third, proposed by one of my students for the middle school level, involves social studies, art, and science.

In a unit designed to integrate art and English, I wanted students to develop skill in a watercolor technique, identify proportions of the human figure, and explore lettering styles. Seventh graders are energetic, and Miriam Shapiro's dynamic cutout figures interested them (see Color Plate 4.13). After looking at and talking about the way Shapiro achieved movement and her use of color, each student chose an activity they wanted to depict.

When students knew what they wanted to do, I introduced them to wet-in-wet watercolor technique. They selected appropriate colors for a background, then began their figure by considering the proportions and drawing each part separately on cardboard.

After cutting out the parts, the students played with them to get the action they wanted. Using a collage technique helped them become more confident and successful in getting it to look "right," which is a concern at this level. Students posed for one another and brought in equipment, such as scuba gear and skateboards, as models. They created clothing, hair, and other accessories from various materials, then glued the separate parts of the figure to the background in an action pose. Next, they explored lettering styles and created a poem about their figure using Cinquain, a form of poetry they learned in English class (see Figures 4.14–4.19). The poem was lettered on strips of paper to avoid ruining the painting with a misspelled word or an ink spill. Concepts about poetry were reinforced, and students became familiar with the style and qualities of Shapiro's work.

An integrated unit for sixth grade focused on Japanese art and culture. The social studies teacher and I introduced concepts about Japan in the same time period. Working on the same topic in two classes gave students an opportunity to

Figure 4.14

Dance, by Baltimore County Public Schools seventh-grade student. Watercolor, cut paper, and ink, 18 x 24 in.

Author's collection.

Figure 4.15
Skydiver, by Baltimore County
Public Schools seventh-grade
student. Watercolor, cut paper,
and ink, 18 x 24 in.

Author's collection.

Figure 4.16
Skate, by Baltimore County Public Schools seventh-grade student. Watercolor, cut paper, and
ink, 18 x 24 in.

Author's collection.

Figure 4.17
Michael Jordan, by Baltimore County Public Schools seventh-grade student. Watercolor, cut paper, and ink, 18 x 24 in.

Author's collection.

Figure 4.18
Scuba Diver, by Baltimore County Public Schools seventh-grade student. Watercolor, cut paper, and ink, 24 x 18 in.

Author's collection.

teach each teacher what the other one had taught. They learned about the environment, architecture, and culture of Japan from different perspectives in each class. Content issues, the use of space in Japanese art, and the place art has in Japanese homes were introduced in art class. The geography, climate, and history of Japan were introduced in social studies. Haiku poetry and Japanese words were discussed in both classes. Each student created a watercolor painting of animals in an environment (see Figures 4.20–4.23) using a horizontal or vertical format, and they lettered a haiku poem and Japanese characters related to their painting.

Kelli Nunn's goals for her secondary unit, called "Art in Your Environment," address National Visual Arts Standards 1, 2, 3, and 6. Her purpose was to "help students develop skills in making judgements about the design of everyday objects and ordinary environments [and] . . . become more observant of their environment" (Nunn, 1995, p. 1). She drew support for her rationale from this statement by Paston (1973):

> Through the visual arts, the individual is involved in understanding the world he lives in, thus encouraging him to react to things he sees and feels. When he interprets these feelings, emotions, and insights through visual materials, he can often influence not only himself, but the community and culture as well; for when we express our ideas in art we involve ourselves in both the examinations and appraisal of works of art and the development of aesthetic problem-solving behaviors. (p. 23)

Kelli's strategy was for students to "look at examples of how different artists have represented their environments in different styles and mediums . . . [and] research a chosen subject and express an understanding of its environment by constructing a 3-D representation of it" (Nunn, 1995, p. 9). She would show and discuss work by Bearden, Ringgold, Grooms, Christo, and Smithson. Students would have a directed reading activity about Faith Ringgold's *Tar Beach* and a period to research their subjects (an animal or a person in their environments) in the library. Materials

Figure 4.20
Grizzly Bear, by Baltimore County Public Schools sixth-grade student. Watercolor, cut paper, and ink, 18 x 24 in.

Author's collection.

could include shoe boxes, paper, paint, found objects, markers, and clay to create a diorama of the environment and a model of an animal or person. Peer and self critiques provide in-process assessment, and summative assessment and evaluations are based on the artist's statement, completion of the assignment, and extent of adherence to criteria. This unit integrates art, science, social studies, and language arts and reinforces concepts in each area. Integrated units may take extra time to plan, but the results are worth it.

SUMMARY

Art can be defined in many ways, and definitions of art are influenced by culture, values, and personal experiences. Because ideas about what art is differ across cultures, it is critical for art teachers to research the context of a work before introducing

Figure 4.21
Birds Sing Happily, by Baltimore County Public Schools sixth-grade student. Watercolor, cut paper, and ink, 18 x 24 in.

Author's collection.

Figure 4.22
Vicious Tiger Eyes, by Baltimore County Public Schools sixth-grade student. Watercolor, cut paper, and ink, 18 x 24 in.

Author's collection.

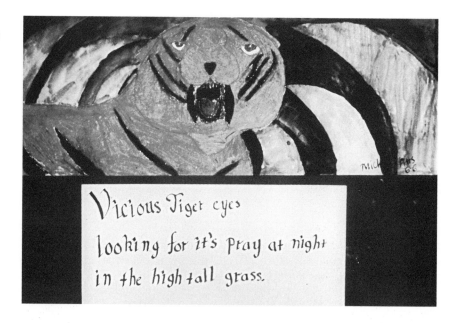

156

Bats are wonderful
The brown bat fly in
dark sky.

Figure 4.23
Bats Are Wonderful, by Baltimore County Public Schools sixth-grade student. Watercolor, cut paper, and ink, 18 x 24 in.

Author's collection.

it to students. The art of small-scale societies is an important part of art education, and it requires preparation to understand how it is valued and what purposes it serves in these societies. Looking at art as a behavior, which includes "making special," provides a way to consider commonalities across diverse cultures.

Anthropology helps us to understand the art of small-scale societies, and the disciplines of art history, aesthetics, and art criticism can give us insight into how art has been defined in larger cultures of the Western world. Each discipline enlarges our understanding in a different way. Art history provides contextual information. In aesthetics, theories that explain why something is called "art" are discussed, and formal models of art criticism provide approaches for deriving meaning from art images. Art in the Western world has changed dramatically since the classical era, and the recent emergence of postmodernism has moved away from the "art for art's sake" view of modernism to a view that is concerned with how artists can raise consciousness about social, environmental, and gender issues.

Experiences with art images from both Western and non-Western cultures and small-scale and complex societies are important. They may be centered on societal issues, on learning about specific art images and objects, or on the child. Each of these rationales is important in a well-balanced art program. However, you need to know your students and make connections between the curriculum you teach, the world of the student, and the world of art. Your understanding of the learner, the extent to which you create an environment for learning, and your selection of pedagogical strategies all affect student engagement.

Structuring experiences with art images so learners can create meaning is a creative process that involves many choices. Your selection of the objectives, content, processes, and models and your creation of unit and lesson plans that translate researched information and consider the developmental level, experiences, and interests of the learner will all affect the extent to which learners can derive meaning from experiences with art images. Translating information into understanding requires hard work. There are advantages in engaging learners with art images, but there are also challenges in the process.

ADVANTAGES AND CHALLENGES OF MAKING THIS CHOICE

The advantages implicit in this choice are numerous. There is a big difference between engaging students and just teaching them, and you will be very aware of it when it occurs. Think back to your very best teachers. What were they like? Did they give you a chance to figure things out, or did they tell you what to do? How did you feel in either case? The discovery of ideas through a challenging and hands-on activity, supported by knowledge and skill development, can be exhilarating for the student and rewarding for the teacher.

Giving information to students and structuring experiences in a closed way that permits little latitude for personal decision making does not achieve the engagement that occurs with an open-ended approach. Guiding your learners—being sure that there is time and space for their ideas to emerge and for them to search and find solutions to problems they set for themselves—establishes an atmosphere charged with doing, sharing, looking, analyzing, and learning. If students are responsible for their own learning, the class is not quiet, but it is an exciting place to be!

Engaging learners involves the challenge of in-depth research, but you need to know about more than just the culture and the artwork. Finding out about your students' interests, experiences, and cultural background helps you to design strategies that make a connection with their world. This involves time and effort, and so does creating a classroom environment that helps students learn, but these factors can make a difference in how they learn. Allowing choices, using dialogue, and shaping experiences so students construct their own understanding through active involvement and reflection all affect engagement.

Structuring the experiences involves many different choices. What goals and objectives do you want to achieve? What content and processes will help your students achieve them? What model will you use? Once you make these decisions, you have the challenge of researching and planning lessons to implement them. This involves more choices. What do students need to know and be able to do to achieve the goals? Will you incorporate reading and writing? How will you design objectives to teach both knowledge and skills? What learning strategy will you use? Why is it appropriate? How is your rationale for teaching this lesson to this level supported in the literature? How can you adapt lessons for special-needs students? How will you assess and evaluate learning? Is it worth it to do all this, just to engage students?

ACTION PLAN FOR INSTRUCTIONAL DECISION MAKING

～ *Identify* the characteristics of the learner.

～ *Define* the objective for the experience.

～ *Choose* the content, topic, or theme for the experience.

～ *Do research* necessary to provide in-depth knowledge.

～ *Select* the processes and models you will use.

～ *Structure* the experience to allow individual choices.

～ *Develop* active learning strategies to engage the learner.

～ *Select* appropriate images and processes.

～ *Create* a context for learning to occur.

～ *Plan* assessment strategies and evaluation criteria.

DISCUSSION QUESTIONS

1. How would you define art? Does this definition fit all art?

2. Why is research about the context of art important? How much is needed? Why? Where can you find resources?

3. How could defining art as a behavior provide connections between large- and small-scale societies?

4. How can you enrich your knowledge of aesthetics? art criticism? Which formal model of art criticism appeals to you? Why?

5. What do you think is the most difficult part of engaging learners with art images? Why? How can you make it work?

SUGGESTED ACTIVITIES

1. Select an art image or object that appeals to you and interpret it using each of the formal art criticism models. Compare results.

2. Research a small-scale society collaboratively, make slides, synopsize your research, create unit and lesson plans, arrange to teach them at a local school, and videotape your presentation.

3. List your favorite artworks and analyze commonalities of those you like best. Define your personal aesthetic preferences and consider how you might use this process with students.

4. Select an art image that doesn't appeal to you. Interpret its meaning over time. Compare your initial and final responses.

5. Consider how you might translate the content, form, and meaning of work in a museum exhibit into a unit for a specific level.

6. Work collaboratively to select a universal theme expressed in the art of many cultures. Collect art images on the theme, create a unit plan, and plan a sequence of lessons based on it.

ANNOTATED RESOURCES

Books

Anderson, R. (1989). *Art in small scale societies.* Englewood Cliffs, NJ: Prentice Hall.
This book provides theoretical information about art in six different societies and explanations of symbolism.

Armstrong, T. (1994). *Multiple intelligences in the classroom.* Alexandria, VA: Association for Supervision and Curriculum Development.
This guide describes strategies for using multisensory processes for teaching, learning, and assessment.

Battin, M. P., Fisher, J., Moore, R., & Silvers, A.(1989). *Puzzles about art: An aesthetics casebook.* New York: St. Martin's Press.
Specific case studies related to aesthetic issues are included here.

Gablik, S. (1991). *The reenchantment of art.* New York: Thames and Hudson.
The author provides images and ideas about current approaches to art that reflect a change toward art for society's sake.

Herman, G. N., & Hollingsworth, P. (1992). *Kinetic kaleidoscope.* Tucson, AZ: Zephyr Press.
The authors describe various ways to interpret art through movement.

Lippard, L. (1990). *Mixed blessings: New art in a multicultural America.* New York: Pantheon Books.
The author introduces a wide range of artwork that is replete with social commentary and representative of the various cultures that make up America.

Stephens, K. (1994). *Learning through art and artifacts.* London: Hodder & Stoughton Educational.
Stephens lists strategies and approaches for introducing young children to art images.

Taylor, R. (1987). *Educating for art: Critical response and development.* Essex, England: Longman Group.
This book examines the critical studies approach and provides examples.

Thistlewood, D. (Ed.) (1991). *Critical studies in art and design education.* Portsmouth, NH: Heinemann.
This anthology of information provides many different approaches to teaching art history, art criticism, and art making in ways that integrate academic and hands-on learning.

Other Resources

Art Education, published by NAEA, is a valuable resource for reproductions of artworks and strategies for using them.

Binney & Smith. 1100 Church Lane, P.O. Box 431, Easton, PA 18044-0431. This company provides thematic-based guides for its biennial Crayola® Dream-Makers™ event at a reasonable price; the guides include ideas for implementing the theme and reproductions based on it.

Local museum libraries often have resources available to borrow. They may have slide sets, exhibition catalogues from other museums, and packets of hands-on resources about art and artifacts for the classroom.

The National Gallery of Art loans and sells reproductions, slides, videos, and filmstrips about art.

The Shorewood Collection of reproductions provides a catalog of more than 800 art images. It also has available a guide to the reproductions, as well as one that provides information about the artists. Write to: Shorewood Fine Art Reproductions, 27 Glen Road, Sandy Hook, CT 06482. Tel. (800) 494-3824.

Other sources for art images include but are not limited to the following: outdated calendars and notecards from gift shops; old art appreciation books from used book stores; issues of Art News *and other illustrated magazines; catalogs of exhibitions; downloaded images from the Internet and World Wide Web; and, for popular art, images and advertisements from any magazine or newspaper.*

KEY TERMS

Art world   The group of people who are involved in the business of art or the arts. In the visual arts they include those who sell, make, write about, or talk about art, such as artists, art critics, aestheticians, art historians, art gallery owners, and museum directors.

Avant garde   Artwork that takes a new direction in art and moves away from what is currently accepted. This type of work may be harder to understand because it is on the cutting edge of the art world; it is often predictive of styles that follow.

Bracketing   Looking at an artwork with an attitude that focuses only on the work itself and its aesthetic qualities and blocks out all else. This is a step in most phenomenological models of art criticism.

Contextualism   This theory of art focuses on the need to understand the context in which an artwork was created in order to fully understand its meaning. Information about the culture of the artwork, experiences in the artist's life, issues prevalent in the society and in the art world during the era, and any other information that might help clarify the meaning of the image or object are sought out and used to interpret the art.

Critical theory   A theory of art that focuses on the underlying meaning or hidden agenda that may not be apparent. By deconstructing the artwork, the real meaning is discovered; social issues are an important focus in this theory.

Cultural literacy   This involves being knowledgeable about the art masterpieces of Western European cultures.

Cultural relativism   This approach to art examines work in light of the values of the people by whom and the culture in which it was created. Taking a culturally relative position implies that you will try to avoid looking at and judging an artwork in terms of the aesthetic values of your own culture and will judge it instead by values that relate to the artist's culture.

Disciplines   Bodies of knowledge that relate to a specific field of study, each of which may include several disciplines. Art education draws on knowledge from a number of disciplines, including aesthetics, art history, art criticism, and art production, as well as archaeology, cultural anthropology, psychology, and others.

Ethnocentrism   A point of view that considers one's own culture, and thus artwork, superior to that of other peoples. This view is the opposite of cultural relativism.

Expressive theory   Stresses the expression of emotions as a criteria for judging an artwork

Fine art   The acknowledged masterpieces of Western European art. This kind of art is displayed in museums and art galleries, is often available in reproductions, and is created by people who have been trained as artists.

Folk art   The work of untrained artists who create images and objects more for their own pleasure than for profit. This kind of art has a long tradition in many cultures, and traditional patterns or symbols are often preferred.

Formalism   The theory of art that focuses primarily on the way the elements and principles of design are organized and unified. Formalists attend to what is in the artwork itself rather than any factors in the context that might affect the meaning.

Hiddenstream art   Artwork created by women and other minorities. This term was coined during the 1980s in an effort to include these groups in art education curricula.

Imitationalism   This theory, also called the mimetic theory of art, judges art according to how real it looks. If it doesn't look real, it's not art.

Institutional theory   The major criteria used to judge art according to this theory is whether the experts call it art. The institution called the art world is the decision maker, and if those in the art world say it is art, then this theory accepts it as art.

Instrumentalism   According this theory, art should serve a purpose. The purposes may vary, but the practical nature of art and the way it serves a society are the focus (also called the *pragmatic theory of art*).

Mainstream art   Artworks that are created by influential artists, accepted and valued by the art world, and present in many museums; the opposite of hiddenstream art

Mimetic theory   See *imitationalism.*

Open concept theory   Some aestheticians assert that art has changed so much in the modern era that defining what it is has become impossible. This theory contends that there is no set of criteria that can be used to judge all the various forms of art, and therefore art is an open concept that cannot be defined.

Pedagogy   The art or science of teaching

Popular art   Art created primarily for commercial reasons (therefore also called *commercial art*). CD covers, posters, advertisements, T-shirt designs, music videos, and many other art forms are included in this category.

Pragmatic theory   See *instrumentalism.*

Semiotic theory   An art theory that focuses on the interpretation of signs and symbols. Semiotics examines signs and symbols in words and images as a way to interpret the meaning of an artwork.

Symbol system   Refers to the way ideas are communicated in each of the "ways of knowing" in Gardner's theory of multiple intelligences (e.g., words are the symbol system for verbal intelligence, and movements are the symbol system for kinesthetic intelligence)

CHAPTER 5

Encouraging Visual Storytelling

Janet L. Olson
Boston University

Guiding Questions

~ What is a story?

~ Who tells stories?

~ Why is storytelling important?

~ How does storytelling develop?

~ Why should art teachers be concerned about verbalization?

~ What Is a Story?

Everyone has a story to tell! In fact, everyone has many stories to tell. **Storytelling** is an important part of being human. I suspect that on many occasions, you have shared your experiences with friends and family in the form of a story. I'm sure you will continue to do so, simply because it is a natural and effective way to communicate thoughts, insights, and experiences to others.

The *American College Dictionary* (1956) defines a **story** as "narrative, either true or fictitious, in prose or verse, designed to interest or amuse the hearer or reader" and as "a narration of the events in the life of a person or the existence of a thing, or such events as a subject for narration." This definition assumes that the concept of story involves only words—I argue that stories are expressed most naturally with both visual and verbal languages. Historically, this was particularly the case during the Middle Ages, when Bible stories and historical events were transmitted to illiterate parishioners through the use of altar paintings, stained glass windows, tapestries, and monumental sculptures.

The famous Bayeux Tapestry, for example, illustrates in great detail the story of the Battle of Hastings, which occurred on October 14, 1066. Seventy-nine panels transmit the story of how William the Conqueror became the King of England by defeating King Harold. The story is vividly told with images that include elaborate costume, action, and human expression. The 15th-century Spanish altarpiece titled *Retable of St. Michael and Gargano* is also an excellent example of how art was used in churches to educate the unschooled population (see Figure 5.1). The two images at the highest point of the altarpiece depict the Annunciation. According to Goldstein (1986b), the remaining four images read from left to right and tell this story:

> Christ ordered St. Michael and his angels to battle, an arrow shot at the bull owned by Gargano because it refused to descend from a cave on Mt. Gargano, St. Michael and his angels overpowering Satan, and the arrow miraculously returning to pierce the archer's eye and the arrival of the Bishop to explain that the bull was sent by St. Michael himself to mark the site of a church to be dedicated to him. (p. 22)

 ## Who Tells Stories?

Using both the image and the word to tell stories has continued to be a powerful and effective practice throughout history to communicate a range of personal experiences and insights to others. In the past, **storytellers** drew their experiences on the walls of caves and composed parables to transmit moral lessons. Today, when we share

Figure 5.1
Retable of St. Michael and Gargano, by anonymous Spanish artist, 1453

Milwaukee Museum of Art, gift of Friends of Art. Used by permission.

experiences with family members or friends around the dinner table, a campfire, or the office water cooler; when we recall family events for grandchildren to appreciate, read bedtime stories, or look through family photo albums; when we share events or insights with strangers via the Internet; when we volunteer to participate on radio or television talk shows; even when we are called as witnesses in a court of law—we are telling stories. Stories will always be an integral part of our lives. They are part of our natural language ability and an important, effective means of communication. Stories are critical to our humanity. To emphasize the extent of this phenomenon, Susan Engel (1995) explained her experience as a graduate student:

> I asked students how many stories they told in a typical day. Many of them said none or perhaps one. Then I asked them to keep a record for twenty-four hours of the stories they told. They all arrived at the next class session surprised with their own results. They said they had told anywhere from five to thirty-eight stories in the day, and felt that, if anything, they had missed some. (p. 5)

The arts have played an important role in the preservation of our stories. Literature, poetry, theater, music, dance, and the visual arts have been the primary means of preserving our history and our stories for all to share and from which to gain insight and understanding. Throughout time and across all cultures, stories preserve human experiences in the most unique and personal way. Life is composed of a complex design of characters, settings, and plots, as William Shakespeare so eloquently expressed when he wrote, in *As You Like It*: "All the world's a stage. And all the men and women merely players."

Why Is Storytelling Important?

If human beings are natural storytellers (Coles, 1989; Bruner, 1986; Engel, 1995; Wilson & Wilson, 1982), there must be a reason, a basic human need, for this to be so. Dyson and Genishi (1990) explain that "children, like adults, use narratives to shape and reshape their lives, imagining what could have or should have happened, as well as what did happen" (p. 2) (see Figures 5.2–5.4 and Color Plate 5.1).

Brent and Marjorie Wilson (1982) extend the discussion on the importance of story by stating that narrative "becomes a means for the child to understand himself and the world with which he must cope. . . . [T]he child, in his own stories, is creating situations that are suited entirely to his own needs and desires, that deal directly, though symbolically, with his own immediate concerns" (p. 102) (see Figure 5.5).

Telling stories is, therefore, an important and effective way for people of all ages and all cultures to order, reflect upon, and make sense of their life experiences. Stories help people to understand themselves, to shed some light on the events of their lives and their unique and special places in the world. Stories also help people to reflect upon their relationships with others and their responsibilities as citizens of the world community. Simply stated, stories help people to understand themselves and others. Retelling their own life experiences helps people to understand the universal human condition and to be part of the universal human family.

Although all people naturally engage in the act of storytelling, they often don't recognize their own experiences as sufficiently compelling or insightful to document and to share with others. Several years ago, an elderly woman participated in a poetry workshop offered at a nearby community center in New York City. For a number of sessions, she didn't think she had anything important to write about. Then one day she brought

Figure 5.2
"My Dog Is Shaking Water Off,"
by a kindergarten student

Collection of the author.

Figure 5.3
"I Dreamt a Scary Lion Woke Me Up," by a first-grade student

Collection of the author.

Figure 5.4
"My Shopping Trip to the Mall,"
by a fifth-grade student

Collection of the author.

Figure 5.5
"An Imagined Battle," by a sixth-grade student

Collection of the author.

in a sensitive and poignant drawing of a cockroach and an accompanying poem. When she was asked why she chose a cockroach as her subject, she simply explained that it was the only living creature that ever came to visit her. I never forgot her story.

Wondering about the relationship between life and story, the author John Barth (1995) begins one of his short stories with the following inquiry:

> It has occurred to Ms. Mimi Adler, whom I like a lot, to wonder whether people reflectively think of their lives as stories because from birth to death they are exposed to so many narratives of every sort, or whether, contrariwise, our notion of what a "story" is, in every age and culture, reflects an innately dramatistic sense of life: a feature of the biological evolution of the human brain and of human consciousness, which appears to be essentially of a scenario-making character.

Is it true that we generally believe our own personal experiences don't qualify as "real" stories? Do we think that our stories are not dramatic or important enough to qualify as experiences or insights worth committing to paper? Do we think that they're not worthy of sharing with others? As teachers, if we do not value our own stories, most likely we will not value the stories of our students either.

If teachers do not show interest in the lives and stories of their students, if they do not encourage students to tell their stories, are they then suggesting that the students and their lives are not particularly important? This certainly can be the result if storytelling is not encouraged and nurtured regularly in the school setting.

A few years ago, the fourth-grade language arts curriculum in my school district was changed quite dramatically. Whereas students used to be asked to write stories of fantasy and fiction, they were now asked to write stories based on real-life experiences. Teachers were instructed to have their students write about the daily events of their lives. The teachers became very discouraged when students said they couldn't think of anything to write about; and when students did write, they simply skimmed the surface of their daily routines. For example, they would write something like, "I got up in the morning, had breakfast, went to school, came home, played with my brother, ate dinner, watched TV and went to bed."

To focus on the numerous details and the depth and meaning of a particular experience, I suggested that students keep a small sketchbook with them at all times and be encouraged to draw a series of pictures each week of specific events—even the seemingly uneventful experiences like "helping my Dad clean up the yard," "playing Monopoly with my sister," and "going grocery shopping." These drawings became an important resource for story ideas, especially when a student couldn't think of anything to write about. During conferences with students, teachers would ask to see their sketchbooks, which became a rich resource for conversation and ultimately for writing interesting stories. The real stories of their lives were valued and elevated to a high level of appreciation and importance.

Art and Story

I believe that the most important purpose of art is to tell a story—to share one's interests and concerns, one's personal view of the world, one's joys and sorrows, to touch the life of another. I argue that the vast majority of art either relates to story in and of itself or relates in some way to the individual artist's life and is therefore a part of the artist's personal narrative. All art encompasses a story, in one way or another. Even works that do not initially appear to be narrative in content can often be related to narrative if one is familiar with the life of the artist.

Figure 5.6
Composition in White, Black and Red, by Piet Mondrian, 1936

The Museum of Modern Art, New York. Gift of the Advisory Committee. Used by permission.

For example, Piet Mondrian's *Composition in White, Black, and Red* and *Broadway Boogie Woogie* (Figures 5.6 and 5.7) relate directly to the narrative of the artist's life. Bennett Schiff (1995), former art editor for *Smithsonian* magazine, wrote recently that in both Mondrian's life and his art he searched for peace, harmony, and balance. Mondrian held a deep philosophical belief that by employing mathematics he could live in balance and harmony with the universe. Consequently, through his art he tried to demonstrate visually that this harmony between the whole and its parts was possible. Mondrian was also a very good dancer and was particularly interested in American music, rhythm, and the popular dances of his time, such as the two-step, the shimmy, the Charleston, and, of course, the boogie-woogie. He lived in New York City from 1940 until his death in 1944. Both of these paintings are examples of how works that appear to be nonobjective are in fact narrative, and they are obviously an important part of Mondrian's personal story.

Another poignant example of art expressing life's narrative can be found in the work of Willem de Kooning. His early and midlife work is filled with thick, powerful color and dramatic brushwork that expresses an energetic and active view of life (see Figure 5.8). As de Kooning progressively became the victim of Alzheimer's disease, his painting gradually expressed the state of his mind. The empty, white negative spaces became dramatically more prominent in his work, even to the point of becoming the dominant element. This emphasis on the negative—the spaces being outlined with lines of thin color—reflects his own mental deterioration.

During an interview recorded on videotape and presented at the National Gallery of Art at a recent exhibition of the artist's work, de Kooning described his most recent painting process. He explained that he retraces the lines of his compositions repeatedly, over and over. This behavior is indicative of the Alzheimer patient. In an attempt to not get lost or to not lose their grips on daily routine and reality, the victims of Alzheimer's disease repeat endlessly the simplest of daily processes. De Kooning's final works are a powerful expression of his daily life, the personal story of being swallowed up by the empty negatives.[1]

---

[1] Permission to publish an image from de Kooning's late paintings was denied by the conservators of his estate. They are particularly sensitive about connecting these works to his Alzheimer's disease and feel it is a premature conclusion. No doubt they are also concerned with preserving the economic value of the work.

Figure 5.7
Broadway Boogie Woogie, by Piet Mondrian, 1942–1943

The Museum of Modern Art, New York, given anonymously. Used by permission.

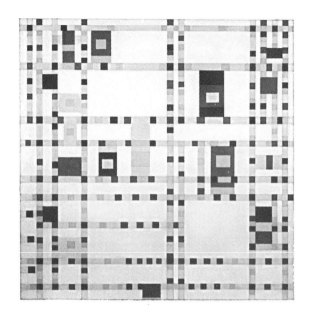

Figure 5.8
Woman I, by Willem de Kooning, 1950–1952

The Museum of Modern Art, New York. Used by permission.

It becomes increasingly clear that the selected images—the favored elements and forms of expression—of individual artists are closely related to their personal narratives. Even though most art historians would not generally categorize certain artists' works—such as works by Joseph Albers, Elaine de Kooning, Helen Frankenthaler, Hans Hoffman, and Jackson Pollock—as narrative, I suspect that direct connections to their life experiences could, in fact, be made rather easily in the case of each and every artist.

It is human nature to investigate issues that are of personal concern or of particular relevance to one's own life. For instance, it is not unusual for educators to focus on academic issues that relate directly to their own personal histories. Teachers teach from their own backgrounds and are often passionate about issues that are particularly important parts of their stories. It is not unusual for special education teachers to have had a personal struggle with a disability or the disability of a close friend or family member. Teachers who focus on the needs of gifted and talented students are often gifted or talented themselves. Educators often search for educational answers to the problems they experienced as learners. Similarly, the issues that are carved out or focused upon by artists influence their body of work and are an important and relevant component of the individual artist's life story.

If one is able to accept nonobjective art as part of one's life story and therefore a piece of life's narrative, then it is rather easy to place all other forms of artistic expression into a narrative context. Portraiture and figure studies can be viewed as a cast of characters; landscapes, seascapes, cityscapes, interiors, and architectural images can be viewed as a vast variety of settings; and still lifes and various individual objects can be viewed as various props in one's daily life. An image composed of all these elements—including characters, a setting, and some props—such as *Hark! The Lark,* by Winslow Homer, could be considered a moment in time or a moment in a story (see Figure 5.9). A sequence of such moments, several images, or a body of related work could be considered a plot or a fully developed narrative. Thus, all art relates to story in one way or another.

Figure 5.9
Hark! The Lark, by Winslow Homer, 1882

Milwaukee Museum of Art, gift of Frederick Layton. Used by permission.

The Need to Hear and See the Stories of Others

I've referred to the concept of culture several times in the chapter so far. **Culture** can be considered a common and/or shared set of experiences and values. Both visual and verbal stories from other cultures—as well as stories shared by friends, classmates, and family members—can provide your students with a natural pathway toward understanding their unique place in the world and their relationship to others. The histories of art and literature can provide a wealth of source material for you to draw upon as models for your students.

Artists and writers.   The stories expressed by artists such as Rembrandt, Cassatt, Rivera, and Lawrence and writers such as Shakespeare, Melville, Alcott, and Baldwin are obviously excellent educational models for students. But what about the numerous artists and writers who actually use more than one form of expression to tell their stories—artists who do creative writing and writers who make art? These artists and writers offer a unique view of the partnership between the word and the image, as well as a more complete view of their lives. Using such artists as educational models and drawing attention to their creative processes can enable students to understand the value of both forms of expression in their own development. Such models help students to understand that visual art and literature are not such strange bedfellows—nor are such works created magically, out of the blue. Both are the result of the artist or the writer choosing the most appropriate form of expression at a given time. Without this total picture, students are left with the inaccurate assumption that visual artists express their stories with only visual imagery and that writers express their experiences only with words. Students need to understand that both visual and verbal languages are available as tools for self-expression and that it is not unusual for visual artists and writers to use both forms of expression to tell their stories.

Michelangelo, William Blake, Edvard Munch, George Bellows, Kathe Kollwitz, Paul Klee, Ben Shahn, Wassily Kandinsky, Jennifer Bartlett, and Faith Ringgold are but a few examples of the many visual artists who have used verbal expression to tell their stories. It is truly eye opening to discover and identify the vast numbers of visual artists who choose to express themselves verbally (see Figures 5.10–5.12). At various times, these visual artists chose to write poems that stand alone on their own literary merits. We know very little of this phenomenon, primarily because of educational specialization. Educators have become so specialized that they rarely understand how their own subject areas relate to other areas of study. Art educators, for example, have believed so thoroughly in the **"art for art's sake"** philosophy that many

Figure 5.10
"The Scream," a poem by Edvard Munch

© Oslo Kommunes Kunstsamlinger. Reprinted from *Words and Images of Edvard Munch,* © 1986 by Bente Torjusen. With permission from Chelsea Green Publishing Company, White River Junction, Vermont.

I walked along the road with two friends—
and the sun went down
The sky suddenly became blood—and I felt
as if a breath of sadness
I stopped—leaned against the railing
tired to death
Over the blue-black fjord and city lay clouds of dripping
steaming blood
My friends walked on and I was left in
fear with an open wound in my breast.
     a great scream went through nature

A Thing or Two

A fish went deeper and deeper into the water. It was silver. The water blue. I followed it with my eyes. The fish went deeper and deeper. But I could still see it. I couldn't see it anymore. I could still see it, when I couldn't see it. Yes, yes I saw the fish. Yes, yes I saw it. I saw it. I saw it. I saw it. I saw it. I saw it. I saw it.
A white horse on long legs stood quietly. The sky was blue. The legs were long. The horse was motionless. Its mane hung down and didn't move. The horse stood motionless on its long legs. But it was alive. Not a twitch of a muscle, no quivering skin. It was alive.
Yes, yes. It was alive.
In the wide meadow grew a flower. The flower was blue. There was only one flower in the wide meadow.
Yes, yes, yes. It was there.

Figure 5.11
"A Thing or Two," a poem by Wassily Kandinsky, 1912

Reprinted from *Sounds* (1981), by Wassily Kandinsky, © translation by Elizabeth R. Napier, Yale University Press. Used by permission.

bristle at the mere mention or possibility that art can be instrumental in the learning process of another subject. Without an understanding of how art relates to all areas of the curriculum and, consequently, how art relates to all areas of their lives, students will never develop to the point where they value art for its own sake. Art for art's sake might be a noble goal of art education, but it must be the result of a good education, not the beginning.

If teachers do not know how to begin the journey, students will never reach the destination. Teachers must recognize and understand the need for specific learning skills that will make it possible for students to reach their full potential as learners. Otherwise, students will never develop the appreciation for art that we as art teachers hope for. Understanding the relationship between visual and verbal expression is one

Figure 5.12
"Evening Land," a poem by Egon Schiele, 1914

Reprinted from *I, Eternal Child* (1985), by Egon Schiele, translation by Anselm Hollo, Grove Press/Wheatland Corporation. Used by permission.

I have seen swaying fields
cut by tiny jagged edges
of thousands of vanishing points on yellow,
mirror ponds and soft clouds.
Curving, the mountains bent down
and enveloped airs made of veils.
I smelled the sun.
Now the blue evening had come,
sang and first showed me the fields.
Red glow still flowed around a blue mountain.
I was surrounded in dream by all the manifold fragrances.

Evening Land

of these important skills. It is very unusual for art teachers and art historians to explore and present to their students the important role that writing plays in the artistic process of visual artists. Are they uninterested, or is it simply a matter of not understanding?

Conversely, language arts teachers frequently have little interest in the drawings, paintings, and sculptures executed by writers. And even though they understand the importance of mental imagery in the writing process, they rarely ask students to commit this visual thinking to paper or other materials, such as paint or clay. Yet many writers—those who work with both visual and verbal forms of expression—could serve as models. A brief sampling of notable writers who have made visual art an integral part of their personal expression includes John Updike, Edgar Allen Poe (see Figure 5.13), Federico Garcia Lorca, Dylan Thomas, Anne Sexton (see Figure 5.14), T. S. Eliot, Gunter Grass, e. e. cummings (see Figure 5.15), Henry Miller, Johann Wolfgang Goethe, and Harriet Beecher Stowe (see Figure 5.16). Does this oversight demonstrate a lack of interest or understanding? Or have language arts teachers simply overlooked an important element of the creative process? Goethe once said:

> We ought to talk less and draw more. I personally should like to remove speech altogether and communicate everything I have to say in sketches. My poor little bit of sketching is priceless to me; it helped my conception of material things; one's mind rises more quickly to general ideas, if one looks at objects more precisely and keenly. (Hjerter, 1986, p. 16)

Becoming more fully aware of artists who write and writers who make art can provide profound insights for educators. To introduce students to artist-writers and

Figure 5.13
Portrait of Elmira Royster Shelton, purportedly drawn by Edgar Allen Poe, 1845

Lilly Library, Indiana University, Bloomington, Indiana. Used by permission.

Figure 5.14
Self-Portrait, a painting by Anne
Sexton

Ransom Humanities Research Center,
University of Texas at Austin. Used by
permission.

Figure 5.15
Self-Portrait, a painting by e. e.
cummings, 1945

Ransom Humanities Research Center,
University of Texas at Austin. Used by
permission.

Figure 5.16
White Magnolias, a watercolor
by Harriet Beecher Stowe, after
1867

The Harriet Beecher Stowe Center,
Hartford, Connecticut. Used by permission.

their stories helps to humanize the artistic process. Students will soon realize that they
are attracted to particular works that they can relate to personally, forming a close
bond with the artist or the writer. Only when both forms of expression are sought out
and valued will a complete picture of the creative process and the artist-writer be
understood by students. Their "stories" simply will not be complete without this
understanding! As educators, we need to keep all options open, for the sake of our
students and their learning.

Stories and other world cultures.   Stories about or originating from another
culture can also promote a great deal of insight and understanding for your students. The oral and visual traditions of all world cultures have relied primarily on
the stories, rituals, and history of these cultures. Storytellers have always been
respected and valued members of society. Unfortunately, when other cultures are
included in the school curriculum, they are most often studied from the perspective
of how foreign they are to us. The focus is often on differences rather than similarities. I don't believe this approach helps to promote understanding, tolerance, or
even appreciation.

　　To focus first on our universal similarities establishes a strong foundation upon
which to build the desired level of appreciation, respect, and understanding for our
unique differences. The stories of any given culture can provide the vehicle for this
understanding. Since there are so many common experiences that people of all cul-

tures share, why would we attempt to educate students by focusing on our differences? A short list of common human experiences and themes could include the following:

celebrations (birthdays, weddings, etc.)

sports/games

family concerns (births, deaths, homes, etc.)

architecture

illness/health care

food preparation

agriculture

dress/adornment

emotions (happiness, sadness, fear, etc.)

pets

worship

travel

language

dreams

love

reproduction/sex

conflict/aggression

wealth/poverty

music

dance/visual arts/literature

I'm sure you can think of many more common experiences to add to this list.

It's absolutely essential that art teachers become familiar with artists and writers who represent a broad range of cultures. Language arts teachers and school and public librarians can be very helpful in identifying appropriate material and resources for use in your classroom. For starters, artists from non-European cultures include the following:

Fernando Botero (Colombia)

Ana Mercedes Hoyos (Colombia)

Hector Hyppolite (Haiti)

K. Hokusai (Japan)

Frida Kahlo (Mexico)

Roberto Matta (Chile)

Diego Rivera (Mexico)

Pajaro (Venezuela)

I. M. Pei (China)

Toeko Tatsuno (Japan)

Carlos Zerpa (Venezuela)

Zhu Qizhan (China)

Rufino Tamayo (Mexico)

Writers from non-European cultures include these:

Isabel Allende (Chile)

Mario Vargas Llosa (Peru)

Salman Rushdie (Pakistan)

Derek Walcott (West Indies)

Stories of friends and classmates.   With the United States being the most culturally diverse nation in the world, sharing one's stories with friends and peers seems to be the most natural and effective way to build respect and appreciation within the classroom. American schools reflect a growing diversity of races, cultures, languages, religious affiliations, social classes, abilities, disabilities, and values. Each category can be defined as an independent "culture" within the overall American culture. Banks (1994) indicates that "the increasing recognition of diversity within American society poses a significant challenge: how to create a cohesive and democratic society while at the same time allowing citizens to maintain their ethnic, cultural, socioeconomic, and primordial identities" (p. 4). This is a crucial issue for educators today. I believe cultural diversity can exist positively and productively not only when students are nurtured and encouraged to understand and respect differences but also when they understand the common bonds that unite us as human beings. Sharing one's stories is a natural way to accomplish this task. American artists who represent minority cultures include the following:

Romare Bearden (African American)

John Biggers (African American)

Mel Chin (Asian American)

Robert Colescott (African American)

Jacob Lawrence (African American)

Maya Ling Lin (Asian American)

Maria Martinez (Native American)

Horace Pippin (African American)

Faith Ringgold (African American)

Fritz Scholder (Native American)

Joyce Scott (African American)

Juane Quick-to-See Smith (Native American)

Carrie Weems (African American)

American writers who represent minority cultures include these:

Maya Angelo (African American)

James Baldwin (African American)

Carlos Castenada (Mexican American)

Louise Erdrich (Native American)

Langston Hughes (African American)

Toni Morrison (African American)

Amy Tan (Asian American)

Alice Walker (African American)

Richard Wright (African American)

A Partnership Between Visual and Verbal Expression

Visual and verbal forms of expression are simply two sides of the same coin, each contributing to the value and purpose of story. The concept of story is the inherent and natural link between the image and the word and enables a full range of expression and communication.

Whether one chooses to express personal insights, observations, and experiences with words, images, or a combination of both, choice of expression is important and should always be offered and encouraged as an option. If one fully understands that one form of expression can effectively inform the other, it becomes increasingly clear and essential that teachers should nurture and encourage learning through the use of both visual and verbal languages in all classrooms, including the art room. Research tells us that a close partnership between visual and verbal languages enables many students to perform at a much higher level of visual and verbal literacy (Olson, 1992; Fountas & Olson, 1996). Without the benefit of both languages for expression, students do not have the opportunity to realize their full potential as artists, writers, and learners. Students at all age levels ought to be encouraged to move back and forth between visual and verbal languages, to think and problem solve in both languages, and, finally, to weave both forms of expression together to tell their stories fully, completely, and most effectively. Only then will they be able to benefit from the special and unique insights that each language can provide.

When art teachers and language arts teachers understand the close relationship they have with each other, especially around the concept of story, they can share insights and strategies that will help them to facilitate a broad range of learning in their classrooms. And just as art teachers and classroom teachers should have knowledge of the artistic growth and development of children (see Chapter 2, "Understanding the Learner"), they should also have an understanding of the development of storytelling skills so they can design challenging and appropriate strategies for their students.

How Does Storytelling Develop?

How children develop oral ability and how they develop the ability to tell stories are not the same issue. According to Glazer (1989), babies from birth to 1 year of age experiment with sounds. They coo and babble, and at about 6 months their sounds—such as "Da Da" and "Bow Wow"—begin to take on meaning. From 1 to 2 years of age, children begin to put two words together, such as "Me up" and "Me go." By the end of 3 years of age, children can use about 1,000 words and are able to string many more words together in a more traditional form (e.g., many words can be used to describe one object, such as the family dog: "She big," "She brown," "She jump," "She soft"). Between 4 and 5 years of age, children are able to use complex sentence structure, including pronouns, adjectives, adverbs, possessives, and plurals. Children at this age have acquired most of the elements of adult language and have a vocabulary of about 3,000 words. Between the ages of 5 and 6, according to Glazer (1989), children have acquired language skills similar to adults, with most rules of grammar already in place.

This entire sequence of oral development is very similar to the sequence of artistic development, but the steps are not necessarily accomplished at the same ages. The babbling stage is similar to the mark-making stage, when children experiment with making marks. The stage of putting two words together is similar to when children begin to combine their marks to make radials, suns, or their first tadpoles. The stage of stringing more words together is similar to the early symbol-making stage of development, when children are expanding their visual vocabularies but do not yet place images into a realistic frame of reference. The phase of fully developed grammatical construction is similar to the symbol-making stage of visual development, when children are able to compose the entire picture plane. Children will continue to develop by adding to both their visual and verbal vocabularies and to the complexity of each expressive language.

The ability to tell a verbal story requires another level of language analysis. According to Applebee (1978), the ability to tell a story begins with what he calls the "spectator role" of language. Using language for looking on rather than for participating in begins as early as infancy (experimentation with babbling) but is more fully developed at about the age of 2 and a half years. Sighting a study by Weir (1962), Applebee describes how the spectator role of language first begins when children are alone in their cribs and produce pre-sleep monologues (e.g., a boy 2 and a half years old designates a toy, such as a Teddy bear, as his audience and uses language to talk to the toy, without the benefit of any social interchange). During these monologues, the child functions happily in an imaginary world. Applebee describes a second characteristic of the spectator role as the ability to order experience. At 2 and a half years, children are sensitive to the rhythm of language and can repeat in rondo-like patterns a sequence of experiences, such as "See the doggie here. See the doggie. I see the doggie. Kitty likes doggie" (p. 35).

Applebee discusses further that as early as 2 and a half years old, many children are able to respond appropriately when asked to "Tell me a story." They begin with a formal opening or a title, they end with a formal closing, and they consistently use the past tense during the telling of the story. At 2 and a half, children already recognize that to tell a story is different from other uses of language.

Great differences in story structure occur between 2 and a half and 5 years of age. When the child is 2 and a half, stories are generally expressive reports on events closely bound to the child's world of experience. For example, "The daddy works in the bank. And Mommy cooks breakfast. Then we get up and get dressed" (Applebee, 1978, p. 37). By the age of 5, a clearly distinguished story with attention to the sound of language develops—for example, "Once upon a time there were four cowboys. One was named Wilson, one was named Ashton, one was called Cheney. They all shot holdups and killed rattlesnakes and they ate them" (p. 37).

Many more changes take place in storytelling between 2 and a half and 5 years of age. One of the most significant is the change from understanding story as history alone (experiences that have happened in the past) to understanding that story can be fictional, or imagined. Children begin to distinguish between what is "real" and what is "just a story." Applebee describes how a child at 4 years and 2 months explains that a book about England is not really England because it is just paper. By the age of 5, the issue of what is real and not real is an important issue. Previously, all stories were accepted as fact and cannot be changed (a child at the age of 2 years and 8 months corrected her mother each time she skipped a part or changed the wording of a familiar story).

To be willing to change a story requires an understanding of what is real and what is fictitious. Applebee describes a child at 6 years and 9 months who was unable or unwilling to change the ending of *Sleeping Beauty* because "you can't rub out the words" (p. 39). The distinction between truth and untruth is a very important concept in the development of storytelling. Applebee explains:

As long as stories are seen as true, or at least (as in nonsense) simply an inversion of the true, they can only present the child with the world as it is, a world to be assimilated and reconciled as best the child is able. It is only after the story has emerged as a fiction that it can begin a new journey toward a role in the exploration of the world not as it is but as it might be, a world which poses alternatives rather than declared certainties. (1978, p. 41)

Applebee reminds us that even though children at the age of 6 begin to address the issue of true stories and made-up stories, it will be a few more years before most children expect stories to be fictional. Not until the age of 9 do most children fully understand this concept. Before this age, children often argue or defend the truth or untruth of a particular story character, such as Snow White or Little Red Riding Hood. Gradually and by the age of 9, children develop rather specific expectations about characters. For example, the introduction of a wolf creates the expectation of a character that is fierce, mean, hungry, and cunning. These expectations are the result of meeting these characters in both fictitious and real situations.

The issue of fact or fiction makes the spectator role of language a useful way to extend a child's limited experience. Applebee explains:

The stories they hear help them to acquire expectations about what the world is like—its vocabulary and syntax as well as its people and places—without the distracting pressure of separating the real from the make-believe. And though they will eventually learn that some of this world is only fiction, it is specific characters and specific events which will be rejected; the recurrent patterns of values, the stable expectations about the roles and relationships which are part of their culture, will remain. It is these underlying patterns, not the witches and giants which give them their concrete form, which make stories an important agent of socialization, one of many modes through which the young are taught the values and standards of their elders. (1978, pp. 52–53)

Applebee is in close agreement with Bettelheim (1977) and Bennett (1993) in this regard, each believing strongly that the stories seen and heard during childhood help children to gain insight and understanding for living successfully, productively, and morally in the world community.

Applebee explains further that a child's storytelling ability develops from a basic poetic form and the reexperiencing of the story in the retelling of it. This is characteristic of the very young child, who is able to build more complex and advanced narrative structures and reorganize and classify experiences. Gradually, children are able to remove themselves from their immediate experiences, which significantly broadens the range of story options.

Preadolescents (9–12 years) develop the ability to distance themselves from story content that poses any sort of threat to their sense of reality. They are concerned with summarizing the action, and they acquire the ability to categorize a story as an adventure, a love story, a mystery, or other type. Adolescence (13 years and older) represents a radical shift in story orientation. Applebee explains:

Instead of being preoccupied with stabilizing their impressions, individuals become concerned with analyzing "how the world works," and in turn considering how it might work differently. This leads to inquiry in virtually all fields of human endeavor—from science on the one hand to politics on the other. In effect, the adolescent replaces the younger child's sense of "what is" with a new sense of "what might be." (p. 108)

In conclusion, it is essential that teachers understand the close relationship between visual and verbal language development, as well as the way we naturally acquire the ability to tell stories. Without this developmental foundation, curriculum goals may be inappropriate, unrealistic, and unreachable. A child-centered curriculum always considers developmental issues first and subject-centered goals second. When developmental considerations are not placed first, the subject goals can never be achieved. To be effective, teachers must have a well-informed sense of the learning process.

Listening, Discussing, and Caring

Using stories and themes to stimulate artistic expression of personal stories and experiences requires that you develop good dialogue skills, including listening, questioning, and, above all, projecting an attitude of genuine caring. Dialogue strategies can include an entire class, a smaller group of students, or just two people (student and student or student and teacher). The arts provide a unique opportunity for teachers to relate to students on a personal level, to learn about their interests, their concerns, their worries, and their lives. Ted Sizer (1992), founder and director of the Coalition for Essential Schools, emphasizes the necessity for personalization in the educational process. Describing committee recommendations for the ideal school, he reports:

> We believe that everyone at the school should be accorded the respect of being known well, that the particular strengths and weaknesses, worries and hopes of each young person should be understood and accommodated. Personalization is not just courtesy; it is the necessary condition for efficient and effective teaching of each student. Every teacher should know his or her students well and should have the authority to act flexibly to capitalize on the special qualities of each. (p. 143)

The primary difficulty, however, is that many teachers are not particularly good listeners; consequently, they are not effective facilitators. Teachers are generally more comfortable when they are in the position of telling students what they should know, what they should do, and what they shouldn't do. It can be a huge challenge for many teachers to be good listeners and to develop classroom strategies that build on the interests and experiences of their students.

I was recently struck by one art teacher's inability to relate to the experiences of her students (and hers is probably not an isolated case). During a workshop with a small group of inner-city elementary art teachers, I stressed the importance of designing art lessons based on the personal experiences and interests of their students. This particular art teacher declared with great emphasis, "My students have no experiences!" I found it difficult to understand what she meant, until she explained further. She said that she had instructed her students to paint a winter picture of snow-covered mountains and skiers. With a frustrated and critical tone, she explained that she ultimately discovered that her students had never been skiing. She quickly concluded that they had no experiences. I tried to help her see that her urban, low- to middle-income, mostly minority students simply didn't have the kind of winter experiences that she expected, but that didn't mean that they had no winter experiences. If the art lesson had started with a discussion of the students' winter experiences, I'm sure they would have had an abundance of experiences to share and to draw upon. Their winter experiences could have inspired a wealth of visual and verbal stories. The art teacher could have learned much about the lives of her students, and her students would have been personally involved with the artistic process. As Sizer explains, "People of all ages are likely to work harder when they feel they are valued and respected. The essence of respect is being known" (p. 122).

Translating from Visual to Verbal Expression

Critical analysis.   Providing students with a formal or structured process for criticism and analysis of an image will encourage discussion and shared insights. It will also provide a method for translating visual content to the verbal form of expression. Although there are numerous methods of art criticism (see Chapter 4, "Engaging Learners with Art Images"), I have a personal preference for Feldman's (1992) four-step process of analysis. I have found that this method is easily understood and remembered and is flexible enough to work well with students of all ages, from the very young to adult learners. The beauty of Feldman's method of critical analysis is that it generates stimulating discussion and allows room for insights based on personal experiences. It also facilitates a broad range of possibilities for translation from the visual to the verbal form of expression. This method can be used to discuss professional artwork or student work. It can be used as a classroom strategy or by individual students. This four-step method also encourages respect for each student's insights and interpretations. After identifying the artwork to be discussed by name, artist, media, and size, Feldman's four steps of critical analysis are as follows:

1. *Description.* In a classroom setting, students take turns naming what they see in the image, usually beginning with the most obvious and gradually moving to the more inconspicuous. This step often becomes a challenge for students to identify something that hasn't been seen by anyone else. I allow students to pass if they are not able to name something new.

2. *Analysis.* This step focuses on the elements and principles of design—the language of art. Obviously, the length of time devoted to this step will depend on the age and artistic background of the students.

3. *Interpretation.* This step addresses the question "What could this information mean?" It allows for some speculation, as long as it is based on a visual clue within the art object. This step can be particularly interesting because it encourages independent and creative thinking. A fourth-grade student once speculated that the door at the right in van Gogh's *Bedroom at Arles* was not used very often and was possibly a closet used for storage, based on the visual clue that the foot of the bed was in front of the door. An eighth-grade student once speculated that the man in one of Magritte's paintings was a "flasher" because he was wearing an overcoat. Using humor and exploring a wide range of possibilities keep the discussion lively and interesting for students of all ages.

4. *Evaluation and/or Judgment.* The final step sums up the discussion in a sentence or two. This step tries to answer the question "What is the meaning or the essence of this image?" A philosophical interpretation is encouraged, and numerous possible conclusions are tried out for classroom consideration.

This method of discussion and dialogue provides an excellent vehicle for translating a visual image to the verbal form of expression. Artists sometimes resist this form of translation, but as educators we cannot reject the necessity for verbal interpretation. Helping students to verbalize their insights and their understanding of an image can only elevate the value of visual expression and promote respect for differences of opinion. While this method provides a more formal, or structured, procedure, rather than simply engaging students in individual and informal dialogue, it gives students a valuable tool for analysis and often helps them achieve a level of insight that would otherwise not be possible. I encourage you as future art teachers to employ this method of translation to help your students value their own insights and experiences as related to the image being discussed. This method of discussion also helps students understand the value and power of visual imagery.

Symbolic self-portraits.   One of my favorite assignments for my preservice students, at either the college or graduate level, is to have them create a symbolic self-portrait representing their life or a portion of it. This assignment furthers their understanding of how effectively images can communicate. The self-portrait can be either two- or three-dimensional and should include a variety of collected objects or symbols that represent important parts of their personal story. The shapes, colors, textures—everything used to compose the work—should represent something important to them. This assignment is completed at home. When the projects are due, we take one or two class periods to critically analyze each work. I preface the discussion by assuring all students that they do not have to say anything about their work if they do not want to.

This is not a therapy session but rather an opportunity to hear what students' work communicates to others. The process truly emphasizes the power of the visual image and provides a vehicle for verbal translation. I generally model the discussion for the entire class with one student's work and then divide the class into smaller groups for further discussion. Each student takes a turn being the one who monitors the steps of analysis. The artist takes notes from the group discussion for later reference but does not participate in the discussion until the very end, when the group has completed its discourse. The artist is then invited to respond if he or she wishes to. I've never had a student decline comment, but I always leave that option open. Usually students are amazed by the process, by how effectively their work communicates their story.

In many cases, the works accurately communicated feelings or insights the artists weren't even aware of as they worked on their portraits. Students often gain an appreciation for the role of the unconscious in the artistic process, as well as an appreciation for using visual expression to communicate their stories. Following the group discussion, each artist writes a three- to four-page paper, following Feldman's four steps of analysis. Creative writing is encouraged, rather than simply reporting the findings. An inventive setting or narrative can be employed, as well as prose or poetic form. Emphasis is placed on the translation of meaning from the visual to the verbal form of expression. The artist is in complete control of what is included and what is dismissed as unimportant or irrelevant. I also find it interesting and informative for students to add their reflections on the entire process of translation. Figures 5.17a–5.18b and Color Plate 5.2 are examples of this assignment, including two artists' interpretations of their original sculptures, their finished pieces of creative writing, and their personal reflections on the entire process.

If you experience this process yourself, you will be exposed to the value of your own stories, the power of imagery to tell your stories, and the close relationship between the visual and verbal languages. And as I stressed earlier, if you learn to value your own stories you will in turn value the stories of your students.

The writing process.   Another strategy that I often employ with students who are preparing to be art teachers is to focus more directly on the process of writing and to compare the numerous similarities with the artistic process. I ask students to choose a piece of their own artwork—a painting, drawing, or sculpture—and to carefully go through a process of translation from the visual to the verbal form of expression, to explore and develop the narrative dimension of their chosen work. Using Murray's (1984) writing process model (see Figure 5.19), students are encouraged to create their

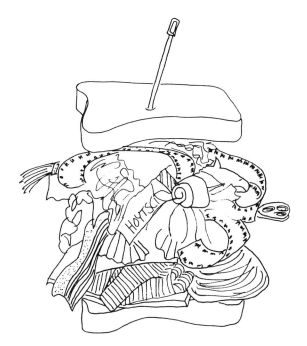

Figure 5.17a
Drawing of symbolic self-portrait sculpture, by Jennifer Stabnick, art education student

Collection of the artist.

own strategies for translation related to collecting, focusing, ordering, drafting, and clarifying the text. They are encouraged to pay close attention to each step of the process so it can be documented, shared, and understood. This is a long-term process, and students share their progress throughout their investigations. The students also give each other advice and feedback as the writing process develops. To complete the assignment, students hand in a photograph or photocopy of the original piece of artwork, the final example of creative writing, and a report that documents the entire writing process. My students are always impressed by how similar the writing process is to the artistic process. This understanding will help them as art teachers to value the image and the word as equal and necessary forms of expression. The image and the word are finally displayed together, to communicate their story more fully. Color Plate 5.3 and Figures 5.20a–5.21c are examples of the work of two students for this assignment, including a picture of the original artwork, the final piece of creative writing, and a few sample pages from the writing process documentation.

Encouraging Storytelling in the Classroom

Robert Coles (1989) recalls the saying of a busy, streetwise New Jersey doctor-writer acquaintance: "Their story, yours, mine—it's what we all carry with us on this trip we take, and we owe it to each other to respect our stories and learn from them" (p. 30). Coles points out that children too are "accumulating stories on their journey . . . and the stories [are] ones that begged to be told" (p. 30). Teachers need to give their students a full range of opportunities to tell their stories, including visual and verbal forms of expression. The classroom is an ideal environment in which to encourage the telling of students' stories. Storytelling is both an opportunity and a necessity that should be encouraged, and chances for storytelling should never be overlooked or put off until a more convenient time.

The Ebb Tide Restaurant

"No. Really Matt, I heard about this place from a friend. It's supposed to have the most interesting sandwiches. And look how pretty it is out by the ocean."

"Yeah, well if it is so great, why is it out in the middle of nowhere?" Matthew said skeptically as he grabbed Audra's hand and opened the screen door. The restaurant had a simple cottage decor. Cool blue paint layered on the old wooden floors and exposed beams hung from a tired roof line. Surrounded by sea grass and pond reeds, the structure stood, terribly weathered by nearly one hundred hurricane seasons. Matthew's feet scuffed along the sandy floor until a loose board announced their presence with a loud squeak.

"Welcome to The Ebb Tide!" shouted the waiter, "I am Ted, your waiter. Please, please have a seat at this lovely spot overlooking the ocean!" His animated face was covered with golden brown wrinkles, earned from his many days at sea checking on his lobster traps. His

①

stature was comparable to the restaurant walls that surrounded him. As he spoke, one could not help but imagine the fish stories he must have told in his heyday.

They followed Ted to the table and sat down. "Hi! My name is Audra and this is my husband, Matthew," she said, gesturing in her companion's direction.

"A pleasure to meet you both," Ted responded with a wink and a crooked smile, handing them both menus. "Please take your time looking at the menu and getting comfortable, while I get you both some water," and off he went to the kitchen.

As soon as Ted had made his way out of the room, Matthew leaned across the table. "Why the hell did you tell him our names? Are you crazy? He doesn't care about us. If he was back in the city with us, he would be just like those drivers that speed up when we try to cross the street!"

"I don't know. He seemed so friendly and I felt like being friendly. It just feels so friendly and pleasant here," Audra said with a smile, as she tried to take in the details of the room. "This town

is so beautiful. I don't know if I want to tell anyone about it or just keep the restaurant a secret."

"Well I think you are in luck. I don't think too many people would drive all this way to . . . " his eyes fixed on the house specialty. "Wow! Eat a sandwich that is ten inches tall!"

"Oh honey, I don't think you should eat anything that big!" Audra interrupted.

"I don't think I would even try to. Take a look at the description," he pointed to the top of Audra's menu. "Shells, party favors, ticket stubs, rolls of film, a frog, photographs, fabric . . . all stacked between two slices of cardboard bread," Matthew read in amazement. "Well at least there is a Chinese fortune included in there. I think you would need a little luck to digest such a sandwich!"

"It sounds like the chef has a playful imagination. There are so many textures and materials and it still manages to stay a well balanced meal," Audra said as she analyzed the ingredients.

Ted returned with two glasses of water. "I heard you talking about our chef's specialty. If this is your first time in the area, I suggest you try it!"

"It sounds like it may be fishy," Audra said

③

pointing to the description, "Shark, whale, clams, scallops . . . "

"No, it is really just a taste of life here in Quonochontaug combined with a few ingredients, characteristic of our chef's talents," Ted explains.

"It sounds wonderful, but isn't it rather large for one person? It could take a lifetime to consume so much," Audra questioned.

"The sandwich is a pretty good size, but it is actually fairly light. We here at the Ebb Tide like to think of it as a celebration of the quiet summer days and the activity and spirit of the sea!" Ted folded his leathery hands over his order slip in confidence that they were both sold on the special.

Audra and Matthew both ordered the special and enjoyed a pleasant meal filled with laughter and calming sea breezes. They spent the rest of the day enjoying the secret pleasures of Quonochontaug. They decided that the little town should be kept as a retreat from the rest of the world where they could hide from the complications of city life.

Figure 5.17b
Creative writing inspired by symbolic self-portrait sculpture, by Jennifer Stabnick, art education student

Collection of the artist.

Response

This project has been a terrific activity and lesson. The creation of the sandwich sculpture was fun to plan and research. The in-class discussion made me take close notice to the importance of deliberate placement and justifying the composition and design of the final piece. It was interesting to hear what my classmates noticed and drew from my sculpture. I can see how this activity could be beneficial at any level. This final portion, that I am now turning in, was much more enjoyable than I had thought it would be. It helped me to create conclusions for the entire project. I am finishing with a new knowledge of how art work is and can be observed.

I sit on the porch
staring up at the night sky
the wind
rips through the air
sending my long curly locks
SPINNING around my head
Behind me
through the open window
I hear a dull ripping sound
the hum I can't ignore
I turn towards the noise and notice the SPINNING
SPINNING
It's mounted to the wall
a concoction made of paper, glue, canvas
and paint

The wind dies down
and still
I stare
A pinwheel
mounted to a circle
Pictures
Images
cover the inside of the wheel
A landscape
a poem
a cartoon
a poem
A picture of a store, a bar, of rocks and a river.
Trees, leaves, a painting
a poem.
A mountain
a record album
a mountain
a pink Victorian house
A mountain
And gold—
gold paper covers the outside
reflecting
reflecting the scattered flecks of paint
randomly strewn across the circular base.
The concoction is secure
as it begins SPINNING
once again on the wall

Symmetrical and balanced

four equal parts cut out
but remain
one piece of paper
Each part contains text
and images
nothing protrudes
nothing violates the form of the pinwheel
vibrant color
separate images
they all become a blur
as it continues SPINNING
the four parts
create a solid
A solid structure
as long as it is moving
the gold refracts light
as long as it is moving
the reflections forever changing
as long as it is moving
SPINNING
yet always attached
to the sky

The sky is constant
ever present
and stable
The images—the colors
are a collection
a record of memories
all caught in the
SPINNING
Important places
familiar places
all of these places
could be called home
But home is always changing
the moving
the SPINNING
never stops
never stops long enough
to be the only home
The wind dies down
and changes direction
only pausing long enough
to collect new images
new places

new memories
And then the SPINNING continues
Dizziness is inevitable
Around and around
in a circle
always coming back
to where it began
always keeping touch
with the trail it has blazed

Literature, music, art, and nature
they're all caught up in the
SPINNING
all caught up in the circle
all part of the whole.

The whole
the inside and outside
the inside is complicated, nostalgic and emotional
the outside stays the same
reflecting its environment
adapting a new facade
as it keeps SPINNING
SPINNING
into new surroundings
All of this SPINNING
all of this motion
all of this chaos
chaos attached to the sky
the night sky
secure and peaceful
the night sky
inviting and vast
the night sky
the wonder, the stars, the heavens
all in the night sky
this
is heavenly
this
is celestial
this is celeste

Figure 5.18a

Creative writing inspired by symbolic self-portrait sculpture, by Celeste Ingraffia, art education student

Collection of the artist.

RESPONSE

Throughout the past few weeks, we have systematically participated in activities that have all created a greater appreciation for the power of imagery. By observing Munch's "Self-portrait between clock and bed" we initially learned <u>how</u> to observe imagery. The sequence of steps that we utilized were a wonderful new discovery. Knowing that you can use identification, description, analysis, interpretation, and evaluation with any piece of artwork has given me a great new way to look at things, as well as a tool I can use in the classroom. Through our own symbol collections, we were gracefully lead into our self portrait project and having completed the first step, the second step came quite easily. However, I did have a little trouble with the last part of our assignment and I think it has something to do with a comment that you made in class. Because I am a visual artist, my intent was to have my self portrait stand on its own. The elements that I included were chosen carefully and thoughtfully, and after our group discussions I felt that I had successfully accomplished what I had set out to do. Don't get me wrong, I enjoy writing, I just kind of got the feeling that I was beating a dead horse as I reiterated the class discussion throughout my poem. I almost wish we had reversed the order—written first and then created our sculptures (although logically I don't know how that would have worked out).

All in all, I feel that this entire series of activities was extremely beneficial. From the students' point of view, I enjoyed the classroom discussions and activities, and my interest in what we were doing never faded. From the future teacher's point of view, I appreciate the example you set for us—showing how all of these activities, however separate in nature, are incredibly intertwined. And from the artist's point of view, I enjoyed creating. I don't normally like working three dimensionally, but for some reason I really got into this project. Also, as an artist, something you said in class really hit me. It was one of those things, that as soon as you said it, I knew I would remember it forever. I had never really thought about this before, but you made the comment, that once you put your art out there to be viewed by the public, it is no longer <u>your</u> piece. Once an observer starts to look at it, it becomes <u>his</u> or <u>her</u> piece—and he or she will interpret it based on the visual clues. I guess I have always wanted my work to be aesthetically pleasing, and I've always carefully thought about the elements I include in a piece, but now my awareness has been lifted to another level. I am more keenly aware that what I portray visually can have entirely new meanings based on what the observer chooses to see, how he or she analyzes it, and ultimately a unique interpretation will be formed. I guess I've always known this, but somehow I'd never looked at this issue in this light before. My pinwheel may hang on the wall, or get shoved under the bed, but I can honestly say that the new, practical information I have learned these past few weeks will never (and I really mean never) collect dust.

Figure 5.18b
Personal response to symbolic self-portrait project, by Celeste Ingraffia, art education student

Before the blank page — — — — — — — — — — — — — — — — — — — → Final draft

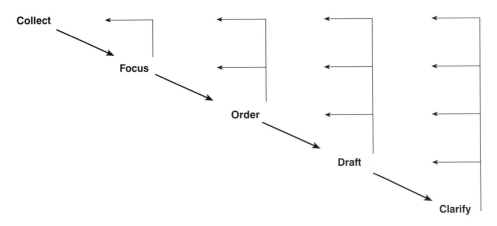

Figure 5.19
Writing process model by Donald Murray (1984, p. 9)

Used by permission.

What Will I Do?

I woke up this morning wondering what the day might be like. I could tell that the sun was out. The room was bright, the cool blue on the walls was warm, it's not an easy thing to describe. It's a free day, I thought, as I looked out the window from my bed. I could see traces of blue with gray and white, one of those milky skies. What will I do today?

It's fall and there are many things to do. It's time to prepare for the winter, but on a day like today? It's so warm and sunny. I know that last yellow rose out in the garden has a chance today, it has one last chance to blossom. The same thing happens year after year. I enjoy that last rose as much as the first. It's funny though, I don't remember the ones in the middle. What will I do today?

I know what I should do today. It's time for the rocking chairs to take that journey up to the attic, to be covered with that dusty old blanket, and wait for the warm spring air to rescue them. It is the one job that I never look forward to. What will I do today?

I know, I'll do what I like to do more than any other thing on a late October day. This is the perfect day to sit and think, or not think, but sit and rock, and enjoy what might be the last beautiful day of the fall. That's what I will do today.

Figure 5.20a
Creative writing that resulted from the writing process assignment of art education student Michael Walden

Collection of the artist.

I was very excited about starting this process. I knew what painting I would be using. I always wanted to do something more with it.

My first attempt at writing about the painting came from thinking about it. It felt very natural. It was also a day that was very similar to the day that I did the painting.

Today I am starting the writing process. The painting was in the attic in storage because we will be painting the entrance room at some point, and all the paintings are off the wall. I'm looking forward to this writing project—no determined amount of pages—always the possibility of having one page. The painting was the first thing I thought of—It's an important painting for me—you wonder why it's in the attic—no you don't—I already told you. It is interesting that I took it out today—it's the same kind of day—warm fall day, golden sun, long shadows—you have the feeling and knowledge that it won't last for much longer. It is very sunny on this porch in the fall—no leaves on the trees. There is a difference from today and when I did the painting—The rocking chairs are in the attic now.

The next piece of writing is a descriptive list. I did it without looking at the painting yet. I wanted to see what I remembered.

MEMORY LISTS

Color	Texture	Mood	Misc.
Yellow	glossy	cozy	Chime
Gold	smooth	outside cozy	Afternoon
Golden yellow	raised	natural high	4:00/3:00
Clear white	methodical	love	Turning point
Crisp white	texture	warmth	Different
Grey	paint by #s	Fall	Understand
Gray	clapboards	Autumn	To the point
Olive	scraped/	Homey	
Sage	lead paint	Sunday	
Flesh tone		There is a stew on the stove	
Blue		Some muffins too	
Khaki		The feeling of Beazer	
Museum white		Beazer just walked by	
Butter cream		A Tee shirt just out of the	
The color of shadow		dryer	
/			
ooh I like that		Pensive	

Many times in the process, I am writing about what I am writing about.

Many times in my writing, it sounds like I am having a conversation with someone, maybe the reader.

I looked at the painting again today—I think about the writing alot. I should start some creative stuff. I could start with poetry—I know I will end up feeling silly—maybe not at first. Sometimes my writing feels like a dialogue with myself—purely thoughts coming out—I like how this pen writes.

I did some work with poetry. I was not happy with what I came up with. It feels unnatural and pretentious.

The color of shadow
The color of shadow is behind me
We rock in the sunlight
The color of shadow is there,
behind me
behind us
The color of shadow is distorted
on the clapboards
behind me
behind us
We rock in the sunlight

It is interesting that this bit of writing shows up in a later piece of writing. It has a very different feeling in each one.

11-9-94

People don't understand
People don't know the life
That damn church next door—Bizy Bodys
We need a fence—can't even drink coffee without those people watching.

I am very happy with the next two pieces of writing. They started me thinking about the idea of a play.

The sun is out today. I can tell the room is bright, I think. The cool blue on the walls is warm. It's not an easy thing to describe. I'm waking up slowly—a free day. What will I do? What should I do? Is the sun out? I look from my bed out the window, it's a milky sky, I see blue and white and gray. Is the sun out? Is it warm? What will I do today?

Figure 5.20b
Selected pages from the writing process documentation of art education student Michael Walden

Collection of the artist.

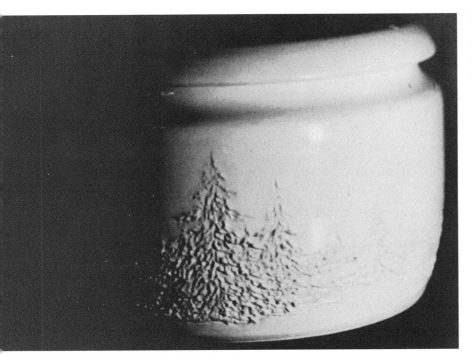

Figure 5.21a

The original piece of pottery that inspired the writing process assignment of art education student Wendy Strauch-Nelson

Collection of the artist.

Forestware

If you look carefully in the forest, you will find that little hidden rooms have been put there. They have walls and ceilings of pine boughs and a floor carpeted with smooth brown needles. Somewhere an opening seems to draw you in. Perhaps you will need to duck down under the boughs to enter. Once inside a cozy room like this, when you are lucky enough to find one, it will be quiet and still. All the surrounding sounds are muted by the insulation of the pines. You can hear the wind rustle at the periphery around you, but you won't feel it. It can't penetrate the protection of the pines. You can't even hear your own footsteps. The silence can be deafening and you open your eyes wider to compensate. You become acutely aware of everything around you. It is not a feeling of fear, however, but a pleasant alertness that makes you feel alive.

You can be all alone in your room of pines. You can even keep it a secret from everyone else and only peek out occasionally if you like. It's warm and snug inside and very, very quiet.

I have found rooms like this in the woods where I have wanted to stay for awhile; where I have even wanted to live for awhile. Here, I dream. I could live in peaceful seclusion until I was ready to leave. But I know it is impossible. Oh, I could certainly pretend to live there; perhaps even camp out there for a time. If I did, though, I'd need some food from the grocery store. I'd stir up the carpeting with my sleeping bag.

The room's other inhabitants and I would make each other very nervous. I simply don't belong there. My presence would create an unnatural tension. I can be "in" nature, encircled by it, but I can never really be a part of it. My human needs—both those I was born with and those I've since learned so well—prevent that and the room is not willing to soften its roughness in order to meet those needs.

No, it would never work. I need to be protected in a house with four sturdy walls and a door. Inside, I need my refrigerator and stove, my bed and blankets and my clothes. I need my table and chairs and I need my desk. I need my quiet studio in the basement with my kiln and wheel. I need my tools and clay there too. I need to be able to go there and be snug and warm and all alone, insulated from the world. I need my peaceful studio because when I'm there I create pots with pine trees on them. In fact the trees encircle the pots forming a never ending forest. The eye can take an imaginary journey through the maze they create. As I'm carving, I am amongst the pines. Between the trees are sunbathed meadows that invite me in further. I can imagine what might be over the next hill or behind each little group of trees.

I glaze and fire my tree pots to an icy gloss white. They depict a very cold and wintery world. Yet somewhere, hidden deep in the trees, there is a cozy little room. And in the process of creating it, I am truly a part of it.

Figure 5.21b

Creative writing that resulted from the writing process assignment of art education student Wendy Strauch-Nelson

Collection of the artist.

Writing Process

Like artwork, the process of writing is such a personal activity that I was very squeamish about trying to conform to a process other than my own. However, I have since realized that the prescribed process and my own are not that different. I use the same general steps but I don't do them all on paper. In fact before I ever sit down with a pen, much is already written. Perhaps little of it will be in my final draft but it is part of the process.

Many ideas have emerged from sleep so I never sleep without a pad of paper and pencil next to me. Often ideas come in the shower. My children have become rather accustomed to seeing mother running through the house wearing only water drops and a towel in a desperate search for paper and pencil with which to record her latest shower revelation. (They just shake their heads and continue to play.) Sometimes at 3 a.m. an idea surfaces that is too involved to jot down or save until morning and so I am forced to get up and write what must be written. That is usually how my best writing takes place—just when I least expect it and when I have other things planned.

I was also a little squeamish about someone seeing my early drafts. I have seen those of other people. They call them "sloppy copies" and yet they have words strung together in actual sentences you can read!!

However, while I had reservations about this task, I also looked forward to the job of really looking at and thinking about my pots. Over the years, I have made thousands of "Forestware" pots (tree pots for short). I had never really thought about why I make them. In fact, I had never written about any of my art work before.

First I simply studied one piece of pottery—a jar, with a lid, decorated with a carved tree design. In class I wrote a list of words:

white	covered	breakable
trees	protected	cold
encircle	carved	winter
glossy	rough	
shiny	meadows	

I ran dry rather quickly. Perhaps it was because I was working from a photo instead of the actual piece. Perhaps these pots have been a part of my life for too long for me to see something new in them. Perhaps it was because working with lists of words was foreign to me. I needed to loosen up and brainstorm, not with words but with more complete phrases and ideas. I spent some time thinking about it and then tried again. Following is my second attempt on paper: to collect and record information. Some came from little scraps of paper in my pockets, some I stored in my head, some evolved as I wrote the others down.

Some of it is in the form of vague ideas. Some are specific twists of wording that I wanted to preserve. Perhaps I spent a week thinking about it and a day or two writing things down. I haven't said what type of paper I am writing because I don't yet know.

-meadows with light (sunlight) beaming down
- invites me in, around coming
- what is over next hill?
imaginary journey—through maze
in nature but never a part of it—
can in pots—part of process/part of the work
no bugs, snakes   womb?
   Person? creature? unknown?   wraps around, never-ending—came back to where start
be warm & snug inside
venture out—in white world (snow, cold, winter)
I've been in forest that has created a
room—walls of thick pines—dark/cozy
   floor of pine needles (carpet)
where I've wanted to stay awhile
   Pretend to live awhile   hidden inside protected
insulated to create quiet; stillness
The wind can't be felt only heard at the periphery around you—
sound is
   masked
Only one there; secret
   peek out   at last found a place to go
   Wind rustles   -go through a door
   the needles   emerge amidst the stress

depth – draws in–? draws from–? what

No step is done in isolation. For example, focusing and ordering seem to be happening as I am writing down the information I've collected in my head. When I see the sentences or phrases on paper, the focus and order begin to form.

In the case of this paper, there were at least two weeks between the time I wrote down the collected little tidbits of information and when I was able to write again. However, the project was certainly not idle during that time. In the car, in the shower, even in lectures (art history, of course), I considered different approaches to focusing and ordering the paper and sent a few trial runs through my head. I dismissed the idea of poetry and fiction quickly. I simply didn't want quite that big of a challenge at this point in the semester. I also knew I wanted it to be warmer than an analysis. I liked thinking about the enclosed spaces that trees form in the woods. So on Thanksgiving evening, when I got an unexpected burst of energy, I had a fair idea of the direction I wanted to go.

The best way for me to proceed then was to get it written down. Once some words are nailed down on paper (even the wrong words), I can see it, work it, and reword it until I get what I want. Here is a copy of my first, second, third, etc., drafts—all in one worked over copy. Written in the margin are additional bits of information that had to be recorded if they were not to be immediately incorporated into the paper.

Figure 5.21c
Selected pages from the writing process documentation of art education student Wendy Strauch-Nelson

An experience that made this very clear to me occurred when I was supervising a student teacher in an urban high school art room. I was observing a drawing lesson. The young woman had put together an elaborate still life in the center of the room. She had selected an array of objects, including various bottles, jars, chairs, plants, hats, and draped fabrics. The students were seated around the still life and instructed to focus on a selected portion, a part that was of particular visual interest. Using pencil and large white drawing paper, they were to consider the placement of the objects on the page and to render a drawing as realistic as possible. A few of the students were challenged and willing to become involved, but many were simply going through the motions in a half-hearted manner, watching the clock and goofing around with their friends, tossing pencils and erasers or talking about other concerns. The student teacher was trying desperately to focus their attention on the given assignment, and she felt that they were not being particularly cooperative. As she struggled, I noticed a small group of three boys standing at the window, actively engaged in conversation. I moved closer to them and could hear that they were discussing the various cars they could see from the window parked in the school parking lot. They seemed to know who owned each car and were discussing their own experiences with a particular make of car or a similar one. They were sharing their stories! As I gradually moved closer, I indicated to them that I was interested in their discussion and their opinions about cars. I learned that they worked on their own cars after school and they were particularly interested in automotive mechanics. Their discussion was enthusiastic, informed, and personal. Later, I related my experience to the student teacher. Her view of these particular boys was that they never wanted to do the assignment and that they were troublemakers in the classroom. She had given up on them. The cooperating teacher had had similar experiences with them. I suggested that she try to engage them in conversation, as I had done, establish a rapport based on being a good listener, and try to build a curriculum based on their personal interest: cars.

If the ultimate artistic goal is to improve drawing skills, does it really matter what students draw? Automobile parts are certainly as challenging as bottles, plants, and chairs. This example also suggests that all students don't have to draw the same object at the same time. Other groups of students within the same class may prefer sports equipment or musical instruments. Maybe students ought to be encouraged to set up their own still lifes. An amazing capacity for sustained interest and concentration is possible when students are encouraged to compose a still life using objects that have personal meaning to them and relate to their lives (see Color Plate 5.4).

When teachers consistently make the decisions about what is going to be drawn, opportunities for hearing and relating to the lives of students are missed and the educational goal is severely limited. These same subjects can inspire a wide range of verbal expressions as well. Stories, poems, and descriptions can relate as easily to cars as to any other object. The connections between both forms of expression present endless possibilities.

The stories and interests of our students provide natural opportunities for educators to make meaningful connections to their lives. This knowledge and understanding ultimately informs the curriculum, making it relevant and important to each individual student. When teachers have difficulty making connections to the life experiences of their students, they often rely on their own histories and stories to inform curricula, such as the traditional choice of still life objects. This not only is unfortunate, it is a very big mistake educationally. If educators cannot make realistic connections to the lives and stories of their students, their students will never reach their full potential as learners. Their students will never learn to discuss their art in the verbal mode of expression or from their heart. The opportunity to make education relevant and meaningful will be lost.

~ Why Should Art Teachers Be Concerned About Verbalization?

Simply stated, teachers should be concerned about verbalization because there is a verbal bias in education! Intelligence in our culture and in our schools is defined primarily by verbal ability. Students who show signs of having problems with reading, writing, or even spoken language are usually tested for a suspected learning disability. The definition of *learning disabilities* has almost everything to do with language proficiency. Math is also mentioned briefly, but a deficiency in language ability is the primary indicator. The official definition of learning disabilities is as follows:

> The term "children with specific learning disabilities" means those children who have a disorder in one or more of the basic psychological processes involved in understanding or in using language, spoken or written, which disorder may manifest itself in imperfect ability to listen, think, speak, read, write, spell, or do mathematical calculations. Such disorders include such conditions as perceptual handicaps, brain injury, minimal brain dysfunction, dyslexia, and developmental aphasia. Such term does not include children who have learning problems which are primarily the result of visual, hearing, or motor handicaps, or mental retardation, or emotional disturbance, or environmental, cultural, or economic disadvantage. (Public Law 94-142, Right to Education for All Handicapped Children Act of 1975, Federal Register, USOE, 1977, p. 65083)

This definition makes it abundantly clear that language proficiency is the main goal of education. On one level, this is understandable and is the reason art teachers need to consider this broad educational goal seriously in their own curricula.

The problem with labels.   I object to the broadly accepted label *learning disabled*. To be *language disabled* would be far more accurate and less damaging to the self-esteem of the student. It would also be appropriate to coin additional terms, such as *mathematically disabled, musically disabled, drawing disabled,* and so on. I point this issue out primarily because it is often the student with highly developed visual skills who has difficulty with language expression and is consequently so labeled.

The needs of the visual learner.   It is important for art teachers to be aware of this problem so they can support the **visual learner** when diagnostic issues are being discussed. Most educators do not understand the strengths and the needs of the visual learner, and when they are frustrated with a student's lack of progress they often refer them for testing. Visual learners often need an advocate, and the art teacher is the logical person to take on that important role (Olson, 1992).

I don't mean to imply that language proficiency is not important. In fact, the opposite is true. To function effectively in our society, one must be able to read, write, and communicate well. But there are multiple pathways for reaching that goal. To assume that good language skills can be achieved by the use of words alone or even primarily with words is a false assumption for some learners. Over and over again, I have observed teachers who work with students who are struggling with language—particularly with their writing skills—and the usual solution is to require these students to do more of the same: more writing, more reading, and so on. I can't help but wonder why one would continue a strategy that doesn't seem to be working. Visual learners need the assistance of the image to reach their full verbal potential. The fact that the drawn image is not used regularly as a tool to achieve a higher level of literacy than is possible by using words alone reveals a serious lack of understanding of art as a language and a means of understanding and communicating (Olson, 1992).

Art and its relationship to other subject areas.   The verbal bias is also apparent in regard to the pecking order of subject areas. Subjects that do not rely on verbal ability are thought of as nonacademic and, consequently, less important. Generally speaking, subjects such as art, music, home economics, industrial arts, and physical education are not considered essential to a good education in the same sense as language arts, math, science, and social studies.

Historically, these nonverbal subjects are added to the curriculum when money is available and are cut back or eliminated when budgets are slim. The so-called expendable subjects are regarded as frills and generally accepted as such by many parents, teachers, and administrators. This mind-set is extremely unfortunate, primarily because it discriminates unfairly against a valuable learning and communication tool and does not recognize the power of the image and hands-on learning in the educational setting. It also discriminates against students who need these avenues to assist their learning in other subject areas. By not fully understanding art as a language and a form of communication, students are denied the benefit of the visual/verbal partnership when expressing their worldview, their view of the human condition, and their personal stories.

My views are not unique. Mitchell (1986) convincingly argues that it is a mistake "to think that we can know anything without names, images, or representations" (p. 92). And yet there is a cultural bias in the classroom that discriminates against the visual image being equal to verbal expression. Arnheim (1969) even went so far as to say that the visual image is superior to verbal expression.

The Academic Classroom

In the academic classroom, drawing is generally encouraged in the lower grades (K–2), primarily because students at this age have not acquired sufficient language skills. Gradually, as students progress through the grades, drawing is no longer encouraged, except as a reward for finishing an assignment early or in a separate art class. Rarely is a student's strength in drawing used as a tool for learning in other subject areas. Classroom teachers have admitted to me on numerous occasions that they feel a sense of guilt when a student spends a significant amount of time drawing. They feel that the student is wasting time and is not involved in a high level of thinking!

The Art Classroom

Traditionally, art curriculum has focused on the elements and principles of design (the language or structure of art) and media techniques, including drawing, painting, printmaking, sculpture, ceramics, collage, and so on. Curriculum content should also include art history (including other cultures), aesthetics, and criticism; encourage a range of subject matter; and make relevant connections to other subject areas. Each of these concerns is addressed in the recently adopted National Visual Arts Standards.

However, if children have a natural desire or need to tell their stories, I suggest that storytelling be the overall generating force of all art education curricula, representing a significant part of each unit and each lesson. Such a curriculum design would offer students the choice of expression—visual stories, verbal stories, or both. As art educators, we often search for clever or meaningful ways to relate our curriculum content to the interests of our students to capture their enthusiasm and imagination. The issue of making learning relevant would be a moot point, however, if more conventional concerns (such as the elements and principles of design, art history, aesthetics, criticism, and the teaching of media techniques) were strongly related to the concept of story and universal human themes that students of all ages could relate to. I also suggest that **verbalization** be included as a content area, to give students as much experience as possible with translating meaning from the visual to the verbal form of expression. An emphasis on verbalization can easily include dialoguing strategies and discussion related to criticism and aesthetics. As art teachers, we have traditionally focused far too much on the individual "parts" of art (including not only all those just mentioned but also subjects like trees, people, objects, and so on) rather than on the larger whole or context—the story!

I'm not suggesting that these individual issues are not important but rather that they can easily and naturally be addressed in partnership with the more inclusive concept of story. When students have a need for a particular skill or an understanding to communicate their own stories more effectively, they do not question the relevancy of the information. I have found students to be particularly eager to learn about specific artistic concerns when they understand that it will help them to express their stories more effectively.

Subject matter and classroom uncertainties.   Over the years I have noticed that more than a few art teachers are uncomfortable with uncertainties in their classrooms. Verbalization related to the concept of story can obviously cause a level of uncertainty that some art teachers will find difficult to cope with. Some art teachers attempt to eliminate the possibility of an unexpected solution to a visual problem completely by guiding their students through a step-by-step process. Teachers who control the outcome and eliminate the unexpected produce what I refer to as "cookie cutter art," with each product looking remarkably similar. Others control uncertainties by influencing their students to such an extent that the teacher is actually the artist and the students are no more than the teacher's tools. When outside judges or viewers can easily identify the student work of a given art teacher, this is the case.

When the concept of story is introduced as an overall curriculum structure, the choice of subject matter can become an area of concern, especially for teachers who have difficulty with uncertainty. Censorship of subject matter or the avoidance of troublesome issues, however, are not appropriate solutions, especially if we agree that every student deserves to be known.

American students experience a broad range of daily experiences—some happy, pleasant, and fulfilling and others difficult and troublesome. The history of art clearly demonstrates that artists throughout time have expressed personal opinions about difficult situations. If art relates to life, there will always be subject matter choices that others have difficulty relating to. A sensitive and caring art teacher can, however, arrange for help when appropriate. For example, I once had a sixth-grade student who had gradually become a discipline problem in the classroom. One day he drew an interior view of his home. The drawing included an extraordinary amount of detailed drug paraphernalia. I hesitated to discuss the drawing with him, but I brought it to the attention of the school principal. He closed his office door and explained to me that the student's father had recently been arrested for selling drugs. The family was obviously in turmoil, which explained the student's recent inappropriate behavior in the classroom. The principal assured me that the school counselor was working with the family. It's important to understand that art teachers are not art therapists, but it's also important to make sure the appropriate school personnel are alerted to any problem that may arise when students are encouraged to tell their stories.

Following this incident, I felt that I had a more comprehensive understanding of this particular student's worries and concerns. I did not impose by asking him any direct questions, but I know that my new insight was felt in the classroom in more subtle ways. I gave him much more positive attention, and, consequently, I think he knew that I understood his troublesome situation. His original drawing alerted me to his story—his visual image spoke with a loud and clear voice.

Some art teachers have told me that they will not allow certain subjects to be expressed in their art classes—for example, absolutely no violence. I generally counter the argument with, "But what if that is the life your student is experiencing?" Some of the most poignant examples of children's art have been done by young artists who have been the victims of war. Jacob Lawrence's narrative sequence titled "The Migration of the Negro," painted in 1940 and 1941, includes some powerful images of burning buildings, knife fights, clubbings, and other injustices related to the subject of race relations. Art has always been a way for people to express their own experiences. If we deny our students this understanding, then we deny them the number one purpose of art. Obviously, I would not encourage violent subject matter simply for the sake of violence, but I would not censor it either. Your students may address other uncomfortable subjects, such as abuse, teenage pregnancy, and dysfunctional families, to name a few. If this is the student's life, what better environment to express it than in the art classroom? (See Color Plate 5.5.)

As educators, we cannot pretend that these issues do not exist and that they do not relate to the educational process. If our students trust us enough to express their worries and concerns in their artwork, can we in good conscience deny them this opportunity?

I don't want to leave the impression that the use of story as a curriculum framework will open the floodgates of questionable subject matter. The vast majority of visual solutions will revolve around subject matter far less troublesome. I simply want to address the issue so that you will be prepared and alert to the range of possible experiences your students may choose to explore. My advice is to be responsive to your students, do not pry, and be a good listener. Know the limitations of your training (you are not a therapist) and rely regularly on the support services of your school system.

SUMMARY

Storytelling is a natural and vital part of being human, whether stories are expressed with images, words, or both. To use the concept of story as an art education curriculum structure may be problematic for some art teachers, but to ignore the relationship between story and art is to risk removing the human dimension from art. People of all ages tell stories, whether they're encouraged to or not. When placed appropriately in an educational environment, these narratives become powerful learning tools. The visual arts can play a critical role in the education of future generations if we do not deny students the lessons to be learned from their own stories and the stories of others. Well-educated and caring art teachers will welcome the opportunity to make a difference in the lives of their students. Only when the visual arts are understood as an essential language, capable of expressing the essence of lived experiences, will they be viewed as equal to the verbal arts. Even Plato—considered by many the first to develop a systematic, comprehensive theory of education and also a famous critic of the arts—relied on the visual metaphor of the cave in his *Republic* to teach the lesson of how the citizens of the ideal society should be educated (Cooney, Cross, & Trunk, 1993). It is our responsibility as art educators to continue to teach the power of the image. It is our shared mission!

THEORY INTO PRACTICE

What would an art curriculum structure based on the concept of story actually look like? What would the ultimate goals be for such a curriculum plan? Would such a plan meet the traditional goals of art education? Could it also meet the goals set by the National Visual Arts Standards? I believe a curriculum structure based on the concept of story actually has the potential for accomplishing much more than a more traditional plan.

The primary goal of a curriculum based on story would focus on the importance of visual imagery in the learning process and the relevancy of art in one's personal life and the lives of others. It would firmly establish an **art for learning's sake** foundation on which to build.

As students' understanding grows, the curriculum would gradually include more depth, especially in the more academic areas, such as the elements and principles of design, history, criticism, and aesthetics. Students would learn how important visual expression is in their own learning process. They would learn to value and respect the power of the image in their own lives.

Gradually, some students will elect to move beyond the personal and practical levels of appreciation and develop a depth of understanding that can embrace the "art for art's sake" point of view. This advanced level of understanding will not be achieved by all, however. As art educators, we must understand the learning process at all levels. Without this understanding, we risk turning students and colleagues off to art, rather than gradually educating them one step at a time.

The concept of story would be present in all units and all lessons with various degrees of emphasis. Story, related to a human theme, would be combined with all other content areas, including media and technique, the language or structure of art, art history (including non-European cultures), verbalization (including criticism and aesthetics), and the relationship to other subject areas. Such a structure would encourage art teachers to establish a close and caring relationship with their students; design developmentally appropriate lessons based on their students' experiences, concerns, and interests; and demonstrate flexibility and creativity when planning individual lessons.

A well-crafted unit should include each of the six content areas but not necessarily in equal proportions, such as shown in Figures 5.22 and 5.23. A lesson can take on a variety of configurations and can include more than one content area, as shown in Figure 5.24. In each unit and in individual lessons the concept of story can be present in varying degrees. It is the motivating factor. The concept of story also makes it possible for the art curriculum to involve more general educational goals, rather than be limited only to goals that are art specific. I believe such a structure would provide a much stronger model for learning than has traditionally been the case. The concept of story would provide the foundation for putting all other artistic concerns into perspective. This new curriculum structure may cause a few veteran art teachers some concern! (For more information related to the design of units and lesson plans, see Chapter 8.)

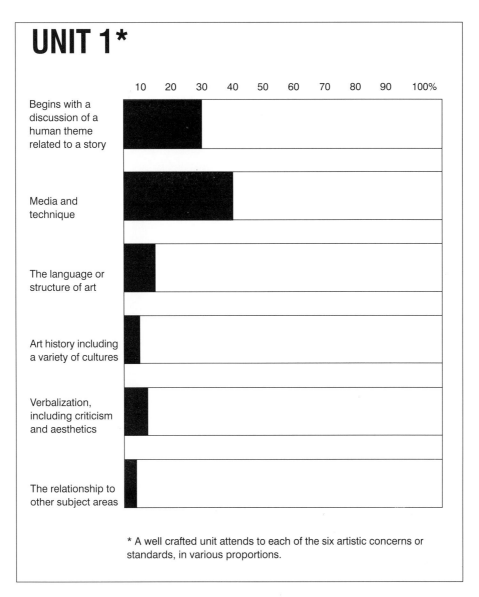

UNIT 1*

| | 10 | 20 | 30 | 40 | 50 | 60 | 70 | 80 | 90 | 100% |

Begins with a discussion of a human theme related to a story

Media and technique

The language or structure of art

Art history including a variety of cultures

Verbalization, including criticism and aesthetics

The relationship to other subject areas

* A well crafted unit attends to each of the six artistic concerns or standards, in various proportions.

Figure 5.22
A possible art education unit structure, configuration #1

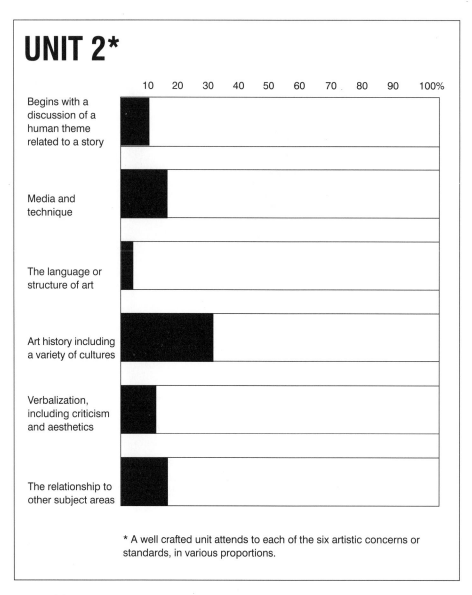

Figure 5.23
A possible art education unit structure, configuration #2

LESSON PLAN

UNIT: Travel

UNIT GOAL (educational, rather than art specific): Students should gradually become aware of the world beyond their neighborhood, in order to realize the opportunities that await them, and to help them become an active member of the world community.

PROBLEM/ACTIVITY: Students will create a painting that describes a real or imagined place they **dream** of visiting.

LESSON OBJECTIVE: Students will learn that artists have historically used their unique skills to expand their real and imagined worlds.

GRADE LEVEL: Fourth Grade

RESOURCES AND/OR MATERIALS:

tempera paint

brushes (variety of sizes)

water containers, paper towels, and paper plates (palettes)

18x24 paper

posters of selected exemplars

MOTIVATION (on a rug separated from the work site):

Opening question/statement:

Have you ever **dreamt** of visiting a special place you have never visited before?

Read a Story. Some suggestions are:

—"Where the Wild Things Are" by Maurice Sendak

—"Tar Beach" by Faith Ringgold

Introduce or Display a Variety of Artistic Exemplars, such as (but not limited to) the following:

—Paul Gauguin and his travels to Tahiti

—John Biggers and his travels to Africa

—Edward Hopper and his travels to the South Western part of the United States

—Salvador Dali's imaginary places

—Rene Magritte's imaginary worlds

Association Question/Statement:

Tell me about the place you dream of visiting (sharing).

Visualization:

Are your dreams real or imagined?

How would you travel there?

Could you paint a picture of the place you would like to travel to?

What colors will you use?

Figure 5.24
A sample lesson plan

Transition:

How will you begin your painting?

— with a small drawing?

— with the large parts? or the small parts?

— at the top? or in the middle?

PROCEDURES:

Distribution

— work tables set up with all necessary materials or students will serve as supply distributors

Time required

— two class periods (40–50 minutes each)

Clean-up

Teacher/Student Summation

— How many of you painted an imaginary place you have dreamed of visiting?

— How many of you painted a real place?

— How did your colors relate to the place that you painted?

— Share finished paintings with the class. (Individually or as a group)

EVALUATION:

What are the strengths and/or weaknesses of this lesson?

What changes or modifications will be necessary the next time I teach this lesson?

How will I determine if the students learned what I wanted them to learn? (observation, class discussion, individual discussion, etc.)

INTEGRATIVE POSSIBILITIES WITH OTHER SUBJECT AREAS:

Social Studies, painting a picture of a **real** place that was studied

Language Arts, writing a story about the painting

Science, influenced by the study of outer space or the earthly environment

NATIONAL STANDARDS ADDRESSED IN THIS LESSON:

Human Theme/Travel

Art History/Related Artists

Verbalization/During Motivation and Evaluation

Integrating the Arts/Suggestions Included

Figure 5.24, *continued*

ACTION PLAN FOR INSTRUCTIONAL DECISION MAKING

～ *Listen* thoughtfully to the stories your students share with you and the stories they share with each other.

～ *Document* the stories you hear in your classroom during the course of one hour, two hours, or a full day.

～ *Categorize* thematically the kinds of stories you hear in your classroom. (Do they relate to family, travel, friends, school experiences, a social concern, etc.?)

～ *Practice* your dialogue skills to demonstrate genuine interest and regard for the art of storytelling.

～ *Build* a learning environment that cultivates respect for both visual and verbal storytelling.

～ *Search* for specific artists whose personal stories will be of interest to your students.

～ *Create* opportunities for self-reflection.

～ *Design* units of study that will provide opportunities for your students based upon their own personal stories.

SUGGESTED ACTIVITIES

1. Keep a list of the stories you convey to another person during a 24-hour period. How many stories did you tell? Discuss your findings and your insights with your classmates.

2. Over a period of one week, keep a visual record in a small sketchbook of at least 10 experiences or events. Choose one or more of these events and write a short story that elaborates on the visual image. How important was the initial image? How did the image inform your written story?

3. Choose a favorite artist and research how his or her work relates to his or her personal story.

4. Choose a basic human experience (see suggested list on p. 177) and research how this experience has been expressed visually in at least three different cultures.

5. Write a letter to a friend that includes both visual and verbal communication and expression. Reflect on how the visual and verbal forms of expression informed each other.

6. Create a "symbolic self-portrait" (see pp. 184–188). Using Feldman's critical method, ask a group of your classmates to analyze your self-portrait. Discuss the power of the image and its relationship to both planned and subconscious communication. Also, discuss how the viewer's experience influences his or her interpretation. This process could be concluded by writing a three- to four-page analysis of your symbolic self-portrait.

7. Explore the potential of the writing process by choosing a piece of your personal artwork. Translate its meaning over a period of a week or two by using Donald Murray's writing process model (see p. 189). Conclude the process with a final piece of writing that can be presented as a partner to the artwork. Discuss your insights with your classmates.

8. Practice your listening and dialoguing skills with one young person or more who are in elementary, middle, or high school. Using Feldman's critical method (see p. 183), discuss either an art image that you have carefully selected for its narrative content or an artwork created by the student(s). Following this experience, discuss with classmates what you have learned about being a good listener, what you have learned about the student(s), and what role stories played in your discussions.

ANNOTATED RESOURCES

Bryson, N. (1981). *Word and image.* Cambridge, England: Cambridge University Press.
   This is a study of the evolution of narrative styles and the kinds of stories paintings tell. Eighteenth-century French painting is the particular focus, as it presents an entirely new approach to understanding the visual arts as a form of narrative communication.

Coles, R. (1992). *Their eyes meeting the world.* Boston: Houghton Mifflin.
   Coles is a master listener. He values the drawings and the experiences of children and is intrigued with the many ways children struggle to comprehend their world. The 50 full-color drawings reveal parts of their personal stories.

Cooper, P. (1993). *When stories come to school.* New York: Teachers and Writers Collaborative.
   This work places the concept of story at the center of an early childhood curriculum. The chapter that focuses on portraits of young storytellers is particularly interesting.

Goodman, N. (1978). *Ways of worldmaking.* Indianapolis, IN: Hackett Publishing Company.
   In this book, art is identified as a way of worldmaking. Perception, shape, color, size, and motion are addressed as a puzzle, while the definition of worldmaking is expanded to include versions and visions that are metaphorical as well as literal.

Hopkins, R. L. (1994). *Narrative schooling.* New York: Teachers College, Columbia University.
   Personal experience and experiential learning is at the center of this study. Referring to John Dewey, Hopkins builds and describes a fascinating view of a school that honors and respects each student's personal story.

Hubbard, R. (1989). *Authors of pictures, draughtsmen of words.* Portsmouth, NH: Heinemann.
   How children learn to read and to write by using both words and pictures is explored. The author explores the world of children through myth and metaphor. Many classroom examples are shared.

Jalongo, M. R., & Isenberg, J. P. (1995). *Teachers' stories: From personal narrative to professional insight.* San Francisco: Jossey-Bass Publishers.
   This book investigates how narrative can help teachers reflect on their personal beliefs and educational practices. Many examples are presented, from preschool to high school levels.

Lippard, L. R. (1990). *Mixed blessings.* New York: Pantheon Books.
   This is an excellent educational reference, providing art teachers with a breadth of visual expressions from a variety of cultures and ethnic backgrounds, including Latino, Native American, African American, and Asian American artists.

COLOR PLATE 5.4

"My Favorite Shirt and Grandpa's Lantern," by Sonja Olson, a 12th-grade student.

Collection of the artist.

COLOR PLATE 5.5

"Teen Motherhood" by J. Emmanuel Tessier, an 11th-grade student.

From "In Our Own Words," *The Boston Globe,* February 6, 1994, and under the direction of Heidi Schork, coordinating artist (Koch, 1994).

COLOR PLATE 6.1

Selected magazine pictures become resources for stories about families and friends.

Courtesy of Katie Holtzman. Collection of the author.

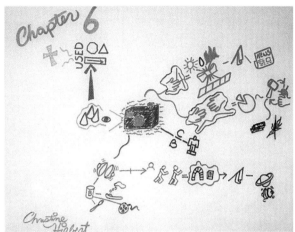

COLOR PLATE 6.2

Chapter notes are easily recalled in personal symbols for definitions of metaphor and other terms.

Courtesy of Christine Hiebert. Collection of the author.

COLOR PLATE 6.3

Looking into a spoon offers an unusual observational drawing experience.

Courtesy of Binney & Smith's Dream-Makers™ program (Florida State University 1989 exhibition). Artist: Katie Earls. Collection of the author.

COLOR PLATE 6.4

Marquetta Evans, a college student, explores thoughts and feelings through the mandala format.

Courtesy of Diane Thomas Lincoln. Collection of the author.

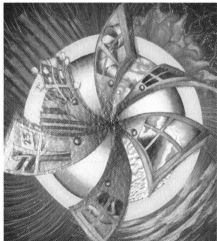

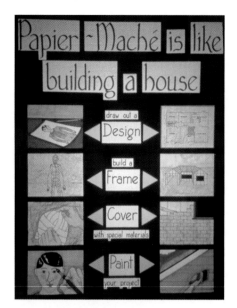

COLOR PLATE 6.5

The similarities between constructing processes are shown in this poster.

Courtesy of Helen Barnes. Collection of the author.

COLOR PLATES 6.6A-B

High school students express their memories through mixed media and collaged images. Artists: Chrystal Faucher (Color Plate 6.6A); Heather MacElwee (Color Plate 6.6B)

Courtesy of Pat Nemshock. Collection of the author.

A

B

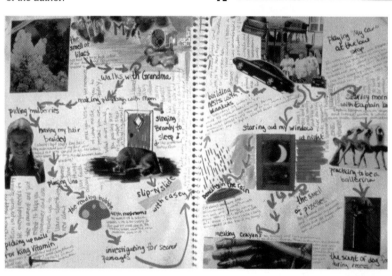

COLOR PLATE 6.7

These paintings show "before" (top) and "after" (bottom) knowledge of the ocean by second graders.

Collection of the author.

Mitchell, W. J. T. (Ed.). (1981). *On narrative.* Chicago: University of Chicago Press.
Fourteen contributors address the subject of narrative. They explore the numerous ways humans tell, understand, and use stories.

Propp, V. (1977). *Morphology of the folktale.* Austin, TX: University of Texas Press.
This is a classic study, covering the ways stories are combined and structured. History, methods, material composition, and themes are addressed.

Trousdale, A. M., Woestehoff, S. A., & Schwartz, M. (Eds.). (1994). *Give a listen: Stories of storytelling in school.* Urbana, IL: National Council of Teachers of English.
Teachers from elementary to university levels rediscover the power of oral storytelling. A broad range of experiences with story are shared.

Vygotsky, L. S. (1978). *Mind in society.* Cambridge, MA: Harvard University Press.
The Russian psychologist presents his theory of development. Known primarily for his "zone of proximal development," this work describes the value of drawing as a natural form of communication.

Wallis, B. (1987). *Blasted allegories.* Cambridge, MA: MIT Press.
This is a collection of contemporary artists' writings, both criticism and fiction. Many of the chapters relate specifically to story, such as "A Story Is Not Just a Story" and "History and Memory."

Witzling, M. (Ed.). (1991). *Voicing our visions.* New York: Universe.
This is a very interesting collection of personal writings by a variety of women artists. They are unique and powerful voices expressing both personal and aesthetic issues that shaped their lives and their personal stories.

KEY TERMS

Art for art's sake   Art produced for no other purpose than for making art; art that stands alone for its own sake—not for recording history, not for expressing a political opinion, not for the sake of understanding an issue or a concept; art that stands alone as an aesthetic object

Art for learning's sake   Art used as a vehicle for understanding; art that is not isolated from other human concerns or other subject areas; the philosophical basis for integrating the arts throughout all educational curricula

Culture   A common and/or shared set of experiences and values

Story   A visual or verbal narrative related to real experiences, imagined experiences, or a combination of both; can be presented sequentially or as an isolated moment in time

Storyteller   A person who communicates a story to others

Storytelling   The act of sharing stories, either visually or verbally

Visual learner   One who learns and understands his or her world and personal experiences primarily from images and observation

Verbalization   The process of translating meaning from the visual to the verbal mode of expression

CHAPTER 6

Using Artistic Strategies

Cheryl M. Hamilton
Wichita State University

Guiding Questions

~ What is an artistic strategy?

~ Who would use artistic strategies, and why?

~ How might artistic strategies be applied?

~ What are the challenges to using artistic strategies?

A math teacher had written the words "Pictures Help" on a geometry worksheet for his high school students. A copy of the worksheet was found in the girls' bathroom. Was the sheet lost? or discarded? Would drawing the pictures have helped the student analyze the geometry problem? Evidently, the mathematics teacher thought so or this suggestion would not have been added to the worksheet. Should we as teachers of art be concerned that this suggestion wasn't taken?

Teaching and learning create opportunities to try different procedures and techniques at all grade levels and across all subjects in the curriculum. How do artistic strategies fit within these teaching and learning structures? This depends on our explanation of these strategies and the reasons they might be chosen. The rationales for these choices vary with particular student learning needs and group teaching goals. In this chapter, types of artistic strategies and their possible functions will be described for various situations.

207

However, if we only examine rationales for choosing these options, we might assume that these strategies are in widespread use. Are they? If they are not, we need to explore why. What are the possible challenges to using these strategies, and how do perceived limitations relate to learning and teaching?

Finally, we need to assess the value of this choice in relation to art students, the total school curricular focus, community concerns, and the appropriate National Visual Arts Standards (particularly 2, 3, 5, and 6). What kinds of recommended actions are possible? Specifically, how does a teacher of art use artistic strategies and convince others of their desirability?

What Is an Artistic Strategy?

A Strategic Beginning

Why and how do we teach visual art? What is our intent? Can we be assertive and clear in engaging our students and getting our messages across? What kinds of strategies do we use in education? An **educational strategy** can be defined in various ways: as a directed way to reach a classroom or curriculum goal; a practical plan of action; a technique to solve an individual problem. The process (or behavior), not the resulting product, is the focus of an educational strategy. A **teaching strategy** can be defined as any instructional effort that obtains a specific result. A **learning strategy** involves any process that assists the student in acquiring information or understanding. A learning strategy may be initiated by the student, peers, or teachers. Both teaching and learning strategies are used in the schools. How could these strategies become artistic? How artistic are our strategies in art education?

An **artistic strategy** combines seeing and doing. It incorporates graphic images, symbols, and formats as the basis for communicating meaning instead of relying exclusively on words or numbers. Artistic strategies offer other ways of making thoughts visible to both sender and receiver. These strategies are described as visual, spatial, and tactile. Most often, the processes used in artistic strategies consist of drawing and constructing. These processes can be simple or complex; they can be accomplished quickly or developed over a longer time period. Personal or cultural symbols in several kinds of formats, from mandalas to charts and sketches, may be used. John-Steiner (1987) considers the great diversity of visual languages to include two-dimensional processes (diagrams, sketches, full illustrations) as well as three-dimensional forms that provide a range of preparational studies or forms constructed from clay or metal.

For instance, drawing as an artistic strategy is viewed as a basic behavior, not a specific result. McKim (1980) suggests that observing, visualizing, and drawing combine outer perception and inner images in concrete graphic forms. He proposes that graphic ideas provide holistic, spatial, metaphorical, and transformational opportunities. Many teachers would agree with this relationship of drawing to visual thinking.

Drawing as a training tool for thinking was mandated as part of the curriculum by the Massachusetts Drawing Act of 1870. A wide range of drawing techniques was to be demonstrated by all teachers and incorporated into other subject areas, like history, literature, and science. In 1881 Walter Smith, the first art education supervisor for Boston and Massachusetts, stated:

> What we are trying to do in our lessons is to make the children know how to draw, not how to make drawings; and I hope you see the distinction. And the great reason for

them to draw is, that the process of drawing makes ignorance visible: it is a criticism made by ourselves on our perceptions and gives physical evidence that we either think rightly, or wrongly, or even do not think at all. (Efland, 1990, p. 101)

Considering our present school curriculum, we seem to have forgotten these benefits of artistic strategies. Arnheim (1986) questions the current problem of recognizing that "drawing, painting, and sculpture, properly conceived, pose cognitive problems worthy of a good brain and every bit as exacting as a mathematical or scientific puzzle" (p. 146). Tufte (1994) describes designing information as "cognitive art" that works "at the intersection of image, word, number, art" (p. 9). What we need are broader definitions of *drawing* and the terms used to describe artistic strategies that sanction reasoning, documenting, preserving, and communicating our knowledge through them.

Terminology

What terms exist for artistic strategies? Just what are a **cluster**, a **web**, and a **map**? Is there a difference between a **chart** and a **graph**? Aren't they all drawn **diagrams**? Are we "quick-drawing" or "idea sketching" when we use these forms? Can these terms be clarified so we can use them in our teaching? Even *Webster's Encyclopedic Unabridged Dictionary of the English Language* (1989) attempts a distinction among the terms *map, chart,* and *graph* by referring to them as "representations of surfaces, areas, or facts" (p. 874): *map* refers to the surface or area; *chart* is defined as an outline map with symbols in an orderly diagram; and *graph* is described as a diagram representing information that is related in some way. As for the term *diagram,* it is defined as a chart.

Arnheim (1992) points to the basic problem of language: "True reasoning, as distinguished from mere computation, necessarily relied on imagery because language, a purely referential medium, could not serve by itself as an arena for the handling of thought objects" (p. 242). According to Buzan and Buzan (1996), the balanced use of intellectual skills would add essential elements for learning, such as visual rhythm, pattern, color, imagination, dimension, spatial awareness, wholeness, visualization, association to the linear patterning, and analysis of words and numbers. In other words, a picture is worth a thousand words.

The diagram in Figure 6.1 defines the educational functions and formats of many artistic strategies discussed in this chapter.

Teachers and learners have often coined their own terms and definitions when labeling these representational procedures. For instance, Claggett and Brown (1992) distinguish between **clustering** (**visual brainstorming**) and **mapping** (organizing ideas in words, symbols, or both). Although both processes tend to be radial in form, one allows for spontaneous, free association, whereas the other formalizes relationships in an organized manner. Buzan and Buzan (1996) describe **mind mapping** in a similar way. The initial process involves a "quick fire mind map burst," which is then reordered to show branching main ideas and subideas in a colorful, complete **Mind Map**®. Rico (1983) combines the terms **cluster** and **web** to describe a process of associating patterns around a focus word to assist writing. The terms *cluster, diagram, chart, map,* and *web* are often described as graphic or visual organizers of thought. The word **web** may be interchanged with the term **matrix** to describe a tic-tac-toe format for comparing.

Many fields also develop distinct terms for products of artistic strategies. For example, in statistics, **bar graphs**, **pictograms**, **pie charts**, and **tables** are used to list numbers and compare variables for frequency, probability, distribution, and varia-

FUNCTIONS

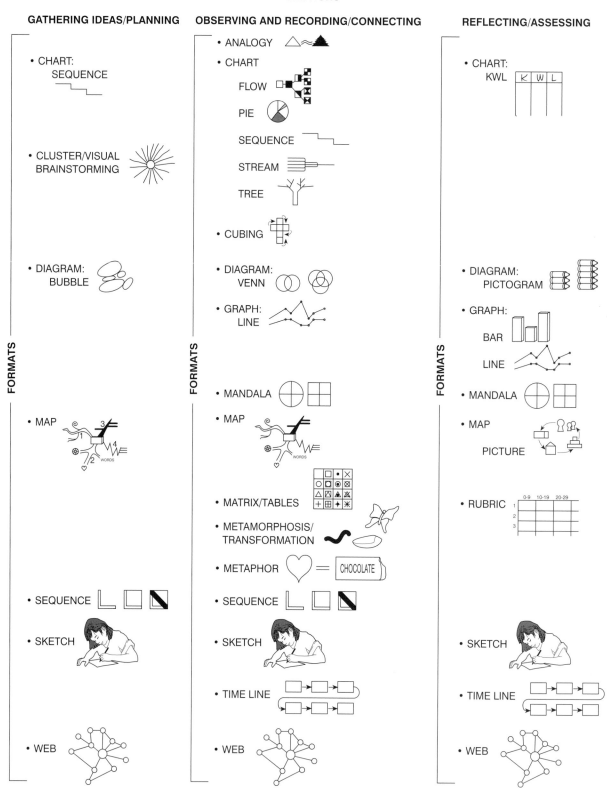

GATHERING IDEAS/PLANNING

OBSERVING AND RECORDING/CONNECTING

REFLECTING/ASSESSING

FORMATS

- CHART:
  SEQUENCE

- CLUSTER/VISUAL
  BRAINSTORMING

- DIAGRAM:
  BUBBLE

- MAP

- SEQUENCE

- SKETCH

- WEB

FORMATS

- ANALOGY
- CHART
  FLOW
  PIE
  SEQUENCE
  STREAM
  TREE
- CUBING
- DIAGRAM:
  VENN
- GRAPH:
  LINE
- MANDALA
- MAP
- MATRIX/TABLES
- METAMORPHOSIS/
  TRANSFORMATION
- METAPHOR
- SEQUENCE
- SKETCH
- TIME LINE
- WEB

FORMATS

- CHART:
  KWL

- DIAGRAM:
  PICTOGRAM

- GRAPH:
  BAR
  LINE

- MANDALA

- MAP
  PICTURE

- RUBRIC

- SKETCH

- TIME LINE

- WEB

Figure 6.1
Functions and Formats of Artistic Strategies

210

tion. In the business field, these designs are referred to as *spreadsheets*. Retail and manufacturing companies compare their economic growth and predictions of market share using pie charts and **line graphs**. **Organizational charts** visually describe many management reporting systems, while flow charts describe industrial assembly processes.

The **Venn diagram**, which is essentially two intersecting circles, is also used for showing relationships. Interconnected concepts are often shown with three or more intersecting circles. Architects sketch circles that connect to form a **bubble diagram** that translates a client's needs and movement patterns. Tracing paper is used to revise the drawn bubbles until an appropriate configuration is reached. These visual beginnings become the basis for floor plans and elevations.

Animators, filmmakers, and advertisers sketch **sequences** (called *storyboards*) to move their creatures, plots, and customers. Sports coaches draw diagrams of movement to describe their playing strategies. Sketches of crime scenes—**time lines** of events and clusters of motives—are part of many television mystery dramas.

In summary, artistic strategies are concrete visual representations of information about time, associations, objects, places, and characters. The many formats of sketching, recording, clustering, mapping, charting, and sequencing allow a wide variety of teaching and learning strategies. This definition of artistic strategies, however, does not encompass the act of **visualizing**, which involves images seen in the mind's eye (although Lazear [1991] offers some information on this process). To actually see, preserve, and share images, our artistic strategy parameters will be limited to concrete ways of communicating ideas and meaning. A strategy with such parameters probably could have assisted Tracy, a 9-year-old who described losing a visualization as the pictures in her mind began "falling off the table" (Hubbard, 1989b). A concrete form is a necessary condition for remembering and communicating.

Visual Communication

According to Hanks and Belliston (1992, p. 195), "90% of all communication goes through the eyes." Communicating to oneself and others in a personal or public way through using artistic strategies is commonplace in our lives, but often it is not recognized as significant. How often have you doodled on any convenient surface while listening on the phone or to music? What do your marks look like? Are they lines, shapes, symbols, or complicated arrangements of all these?

What do your marks mean? Some may be culturally recognizable as negative, such as a symbol with an X or a diagonal line through it. Some may express concepts and feelings that have a universal history—energy is represented by radiating lines, whereas peacefulness is represented by horizontal lines. Some marks are interpreted only as personal iconography.

Your very first mark-making efforts may have been purely physical responses to moving a crayon across a surface. But then your marks started to represent things and ideas to you and others. Your marks enabled you to communicate meaning. The connections between mark making and concept building could be termed visible thinking, thinking out loud, and problem solving in action.

Developmentally, artistic learning involves recognizing, creating, and communicating meaning through symbols, as discussed in Chapters 2 and 3. Golomb (1992) defines drawing as an act of translation requiring transference from perception to representation through a meaningful graphic language of symbols. Identifying their own graphic symbols may be the most relevant and best approach for beginning readers, as they connect personally drawn symbols with the written ones of their culture (Dyson, 1990; Kane, 1982).

Further Benefits

Besides helping us to learn to read, what are other benefits to artistic learning? Why would you need to communicate to yourself in visual, spatial, or tactile ways? Your drawing or constructing may relieve stress, help you find a focus, perhaps allow you to concentrate on a problem. Such strategies assist you in observing and remembering. They may help you reflect on your responses to ideas, people, and events. They extend your ability to plan and predict consequences. Artistic strategies aid your imagination, creativity, and understanding. In these ways, they enhance your ability to connect thoughts.

Think about situations in which you might use a visual language to talk to yourself. Artistic strategies record your ideas so you can continue them at another opportunity. This recall often leads to more graphic "playing" with the information and later innovations. You might sketch directions, choices, or relationships to see sequences or other ways ideas might flow from one to another. You might chart changes or graph data. These visual cues assist you in analyzing and synthesizing information. They also increase your knowledge of conditions and validate your feelings.

Like you, many artists, authors, and scientists have clarified their thoughts and visions through artistic strategies involving such tools as scrolls, journals, and letters (e.g., Hiroshige, Leonardo da Vinci, Goethe, e. e. cummings, Charles Darwin; see also Chapter 5). Thomas Edison began his journals of invention ideas with written notes. When those became too frustrating, he concluded his thoughts in diagrams and pictures (Young, 1992; Hanks & Belliston, 1992). Einstein acknowledged the use of images as a vehicle for developing his mathematical theories. In his morning journal, Carl Jung explored his self-concept with symbolic circular drawings called mandalas. Beatrix Potter and Charles Russell combined sketches and words to show characters and settings in their letters to friends; Russell was known to carry a lump of clay in his pocket to model his observations. Sculptors Claus Oldenburg and Coosje van Bruggen manipulate found objects like Styrofoam cups and toothpicks to explore space relationships before making formalized presentation models and drawing plans. Even in popular culture, Indiana Jones, the famous fictional archaeologist, draws information needed for his cinematic adventures in a well-worn journal held together with rubber bands.

In summary, your personal explorations with artistic strategies may assist you in discovering your capacities for thinking, planning, coping, and communicating. The process of using these strategies involves you in "making sense" and in taking responsibility for interpreting symbolic elements. This analysis and reflection leads to further understanding of yourself and validation for your views. Your ability to synthesize viewpoints may improve.

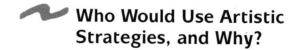 ## Who Would Use Artistic Strategies, and Why?

Would recognition of personal benefits increase the likelihood of your incorporating artistic strategies in your teaching? Who would benefit from these procedures?

Learning in Schools

According to Abbott (1997), "The understanding of learning will become a key issue of our time" (p. 9). Current educational literature indicates changes in pedagogy from a focus on lecture and text to inclusion of experiential learning opportunities for students. These "hands-on" teaching strategies may also offer more opportunities for using artistic strategies. Do you need to see and hear? Do you learn best by doing? Do you need a balance of lecture, text, and experiential formats?

To help define your own learning strategies, answer the following questions and tally your letter answers in a table (V = Visual; R = Reading/Writing; A = Aural; K = Kinesthetic). Trust your own learning preferences. Become aware of how your educational experiences affect you, both positively and negatively.

1. Recall a time in your life when you learned something like playing a new board game. Try to avoid choosing a very physical skill (e.g., riding a bike). How did you learn best? By:
    V) visual clues—pictures, diagrams, charts?
    R) written instructions?
    A) listening to somebody explain it?
    K) doing it?
2. You are not sure whether a word should be spelled "dependent" or "dependant". Do you:
    R) look it up in the dictionary?
    V) see the word in your mind and choose the best way it looks?
    A) sound it out in your mind?
    K) write both versions down?
3. You are about to give directions to a person. She is staying in a hotel in town and wants to visit your house. She has a rental car. Would you:
    V) draw a map on paper?
    A) tell her the directions?
    R) write down the directions (without a map)?
    K) collect her from the hotel in your car?
4. Apart from price, what would influence your decision to buy an optional textbook?
    K) Using a friend's copy.
    A) A friend talking about it.
    R) Skimming parts of it.
    V) It looks OK.
5. Do you prefer a lecturer/teacher who likes to use:
    R) handouts and/or a textbook?
    K) field trips, labs, practical sessions?
    V) flow diagrams, charts, slides?
    A) discussion, guest speakers? (Weimer, 1993, p. 4)

Your own experiences can guide your future planning and teaching. Consider this scenario:

Students in a university elementary education methods class in science left their visual recordings on the counter in the back of the classroom. These students were experimenting with electricity by connecting wires to a battery and light bulb and drawing their processes of trial and error on the sectioned sheets. On many sheets, several sketches were crossed out or had NO written on them until the right procedure was achieved and recorded. When I asked the professor if he always used this method, he replied that he usually handed out commercially prepared worksheets with the alternative procedures pictured and then checked by the student. He said that although these worksheets used graphic images, having the students record their own experiments through drawing was more involved and informative. This is also closer to modeling a scientific procedure.

Which way would be more useful to you: sketching a record of your experimenting, or checking a sheet of illustrated choices? Unfortunately, the professor stated that his future teachers were often more interested in finishing quickly. Therefore, they planned to use prepared worksheets, even though most of them thought the actual experimenting was more fun.

In *The Unschooled Mind: How Children Think and How Schools Should Teach*, Gardner (1991) questions the curricular stress on numbers and words, which minimizes other ways children learn. He states:

> We consign many students who fail to exhibit the proper blend [of intelligences] to the belief that they are stupid, and we do not take advantage of the ways in which multiple intelligences can be exploited to further the goals of school and the broader culture. (p. 81)

He suggests that early discovery of multiple intelligence potentials would allow for more informative intelligence profiles and for strategies to develop children's stronger areas and to supplement weaker ones. Hatch (1997) suggests that these early potentials will vary and change over time if presented in a balanced way.

Artistic strategies can be quite helpful to several of these profiles, especially those that indicate the spatial, bodily/kinesthetic, interpersonal, and intrapersonal learners (as discussed in Chapter 2). In *Seven Ways of Knowing*, Lazear (1991) offers several connections among these intelligences and visual strategies.

Various learning style theories also offer profiles to match. They are focused on the characteristic patterns people use to perceive, think, remember, and solve problems. The National Association of Secondary School Principals (NASSP) adopted a comprehensive definition of *learning style* that incorporates three theories: (1) *personality structure,* described by Jung as perception (sensing/intuition), evaluation (thinking/feeling), and orientation (introvert/extrovert) and delineated by the Myers-Briggs Type Indicator; (2) *information processing,* combining natural and environmental tendencies suggested by Gregorc and described as combinations of concrete/abstract or sequential/random mediation channels on the Style Delineator instrument for adults; and (3) *aptitude,* stressing individual traits and preference for learning process and environment identified by Dunn & Dunn's Learning Style Inventory for students in combinations of environmental, emotional, sociological, physical, and psychological areas. The NASSP definition promotes learning styles as

> the composite of characteristic cognitive, affective and physiological factors that serve as relatively stable indicators of how a learner perceives, interacts with and responds to the learning environment. It is demonstrated in that pattern of behavior and performance by which an individual approaches educational experiences. Its basis lies in the structure of neural organization and personality which both molds and is molded by human development and the learning experiences of home, school and society. (Keefe & Languis, 1983, in Keefe & Ferrell, 1990)

This definition encompasses several factors that form a multidimensional model, with eight cognitive, or information processing, elements (one of which is spatial), three perceptual responses (one of which is visual), and twelve preferences for studying and types of instruction (one of which is manipulative).

Whichever model one selects, the learning style movement "fits in with a personalized view of education appropriate to an increasingly diverse student population" (O'Neil, 1990, p. 5). Although there is controversy about how to identify and assess categories, especially regarding the reliability of tests and the claims for positive results in classroom use, Guild (1994) advises teachers to look at the big picture and use these models as a framework for decision making. She suggests that teachers could use learning style models for personal awareness, application to instruction, and diagnosis of styles and match instruction to those differences. According to Guild (in Brandt, 1990), the key issues are that "people are different, learners will respond differently to a variety of instructional methods, and we need to respect and honor the individual differences among us" (p. 12). These approaches make teaching easier, involve students more, and require less reteaching effort. "If we believe that people do learn—and have the right to learn—in a variety of ways, then we will see learning styles as a comprehensive approach guiding all educational practices" (Guild, 1994, p. 21).

The questions you answered earlier were related to physical, perceptual, and cognitive strengths. According to Weimer (1993), visual learners make up about 25–35% of the population; kinesthetic learners, about 15–25% (including 12% tactile); aural learners, 15–25%; and reading/writing learners, about 25–35%. Many students learn by using combinations of these approaches. Reaching larger percentages of learners (37–90% using these figures) is possible if artistic strategies are included in a curriculum. These strategies will surely increase the reach and recall of the particular concept taught.

Is "round" an important concept? Columbus thought so. We use it in physics, geometry, religion, song, and dance. Volk (1995) designates the sphere as the first metapattern: "We begin life as simple, floating spheres. . . . As children our minds were round. We explored in all directions" (p. 3). I once taught the concept of roundness to a workshop group of more than 60 teachers. Each teacher was given a small piece of modeling clay and was asked to make it round. They solved their problem in three different ways. Some made snakelike tubes that met to form a circle. Others rolled the clay and then flattened it out to make a pancake-like round. Several rolled the clay into a sphere.

The teachers were surprised that all three types of representations fit the criteria and illustrated the concept of round. The artistic strategy of using modeling clay allowed them to explore the material, interpret an idea in their own way, and see the results of others. Next, the teachers were asked to close their eyes and reuse the clay to form a creature who could eat and move. The first activity may have led to more flexibility in their creature formation by lessening expectations of the "right" answer or "perfect" product and by increasing confidence in their own capabilities.

In *Endangered Minds: Why Our Children Don't Think,* Healy (1990) encourages learning-by-doing strategies: "Deficits in everything from grammar to geography may be caused by teaching that bypasses the kind of instruction that could help children conceptually come to grips with the subject at hand" (p. 67). She acknowledges that children who have no drawing and scribbling experiences cannot visually locate word boundaries or consistently follow a line of print from left to right. These skills are essential for academic life. Artistic strategies can expand intellectual skills for all learners. Continuing research in brain functioning cites concrete, experiential learning through multiple symbol systems as important for literacy and transference (Cairney, 1997; Cardellichio & Field, 1997; Sternberg, 1997).

Labeled Learners

As discussed earlier, artistic strategies are particularly helpful to those who must see or do in order to learn. Often, such learners are labeled and put into categories: at risk, having learning disabilities, cognitively delayed, having attention deficit disorder, having special needs, emotionally disturbed, and needing to learn English as a Second Language (ESL). Often, these students are very frustrated and reluctant to participate in education or art making at all.

Although as a student you may not have been labeled, you most likely experienced frustration when trying to learn something new. Like Alice playing croquet with hedgehogs and flamingos, when learning something new you are in Wonderland with the Queen's confusing rules. You just don't get it. You try, but successive attempts to understand leave you feeling inept and incredibly stupid.

That's exactly how I felt in the sports medicine office discussing my lack of progress on the simple stretching exercises recommended for a knee injury. "When you feel the muscle stretch taper off, then you're doing it right," my physical therapist said. But what did that mean? For someone who was more kinesthetically aware this request might have made sense, but I didn't have a frame of reference. I overstretched and continued to damage my knee. I was so frustrated. I went back to the doctor and we explored a different strategy, a visual one called an EMG (electromyographic) procedure. I was hooked up to a computer that monitored my muscle movement. A readout of my exercising—something visual and concrete—appeared on the computer screen. The line graph displayed muscle tension in jagged peaks and relaxation in a straight line. I saw that both my legs were tense during the stretch, but when I mentally said "relax" to my right leg muscles the jagged lines immediately straightened out. Now I knew what it felt like because I *saw* the change! This visual tool clarified and affirmed my physical experience.

This is a simple example of how powerful artistic strategies are for my learning. Combined with doing and talking, it added the crucial element of seeing. I am convinced that such strategies can eliminate other learners' frustrations by making their thinking and feeling processes concrete, involving them in solutions, and supporting their learning processes.

In *Drawing Your Own Conclusions: Graphic Strategies for Reading, Writing and Thinking,* Claggett and Brown (1992), both high school English teachers, recommend several artistic strategies for reluctant writers. They focus on strategies that include making metaphors, making connections, and making sense of parts of a topic by beginning with a global view. Claggett declares that using graphics in the classroom "teaches students to think metaphorically, the primary way in which we expand our understanding of the world" (p. 5). In this program, students develop metaphorical symbols in a mandala format to understand dualities such as life and death and good and evil. They create maps to organize pivotal events and use "quick drawing" to symbolize people and places in literature assignments. The benefits for the students—be they new immigrants or labeled as learning disabled, at risk, or gifted—have included increased memory, a growing capacity to see contextual connections, self-validation, and intellectual risk taking. In addition, they have accepted the challenge to participate in and be responsible for their own learning.

I've observed teachers of cognitively delayed children generate various visuals appropriate for each student's individual development. These classroom teachers use drawing as a teaching tool. They encourage those who can draw to do so in connection with the class objectives for the day, while providing dot-to-dot or tracing materials for others. The students also cut and collage shapes for role-playing stories or comparison charts.

A school counselor describes several artistic strategies that empower her clients with emotional disturbances or attention deficit disorder to control themselves, lessen their anxiety, and collaborate on problem solving. Some of these strategies involve drawing metaphors such as "carrying your worries on your shoulders"; a thermometer to graph angry feelings; a sequence of events like a comic strip, with balloons for conversations about what happens; a chart to reflect changing moods throughout the day; and symbols to represent themselves. These strategies serve as starting points for sharing information in counseling sessions.

Several teachers in elementary schools use artistic strategies for assessment. A speech teacher tells a child a word and asks the child to draw it; the teacher draws it also and then compares her drawing to the child's drawing. All-day kindergartners learn to follow directions (e.g., "Place this over [under, etc.] there") by drawing a symbol for the letter of the day in various spaces of a matrix. For example, the directions for the letter *U* are to draw a red umbrella in the first space, a polka-dot-covered umbrella next to it, then a striped umbrella under the red one. This allows a quick visual check for comprehension. In helping students in a first-grade math class learn addition and subtraction, the teacher requests that a student "draw it out" in circles that he can see and count (Figure 6.2).

Associations can also be made for ESL students through artistic strategies. Learning a language that has adopted several, often inconsistent, rules for pronunciation and word formation requires various approaches to discovering meaning. An image can provide the connection between different languages whether it is collaged or drawn, such as the drawings first graders did to represent words in English and Spanish (Figure 6.3). Upper elementary ESL students can show their comprehension of content more completely in a visual retelling than if they write about it in English.

What about the academically gifted? These students are often so concerned with analytical reasoning that they lose their flexibility of thought. Opportunities to play with ideas are risky and challenging, but they're necessary in our complex world. Kantor, an authority on American business management practices, proposes that American business will need flexible thinkers to solve problems and compete in the global economy (in Kirby & Kuykendall, 1991). Problem solving requires flexibility and fluency. Using artistic strategies offers practice for academically gifted students in inventing, revising, and coordinating viewpoints.

My experiences and observations indicate that we all need the balance provided by artistic approaches to cognitive and affective problem solving. Just like a cross-training athletic program of running, biking, and swimming, teaching strategies need to embrace a number of experiential processes, including artistic strategies, if

Figure 6.2
A first grader draws circles to help learn addition.

Collection of the author.

Figure 6.3
Learning words in another language is easier when drawing a symbol for both words.
Collection of the author.

students are to become fluent thinkers. The processes of sketching, recording, clustering, mapping, and sequencing (individually and in collaboration) offer a wide variety of teaching opportunities.

 # How Might Artistic Strategies Be Applied?

Functions in the Art Curriculum

How do artistic strategies function in an art class? I propose five categories that overlap and blend: (1) *gathering ideas:* sketching, visual brainstorming, collaborating; (2) *planning:* goals, note taking, and note making; (3) *observing and recording:* memory and visual vocabulary building; (4) *connecting:* sequences, mandalas, maps, and analogies; and (5) *assessing and reflecting:* portfolios, charts, journals/sketchbooks, and personal learning. These strategies have been used in many art classes and have many variations.

Gathering ideas.   How does an artistic strategy assist learning and teaching in the first category? Many resources for ideas can be transferred into art media. These resources come most directly from students' lives and involve their cultures, histories, and environments.

Traditionally, artists and art students have put their ideas for artwork from other resources into sketchbooks and journals. Collections of collage material, interesting quotes, and references to experiences are all part of this research. These drawn notes are sketchy and are often termed "thumbnail sketches." McKim (1980) notes that this graphic ideation requires drawing skills to fully express good visual thinking. Would practice help students develop their drawing and idea-generation skills?

What happens when you do three, then fifteen, fifty, or hundreds of **sketches** quickly? Kent (Kent & Steward, 1992) was known for assigning sketches in quantity in her art classes. The results were more personally realized symbols of the required theme. In classes where I had students sketch 25 assigned "suns," the assignment was reported as difficult and exhausting for some but ultimately challenging for others, who started generating their own variations with color, scale, pattern, and other design elements. Figures 6.4a, 6.4b, and 6.5 show college- and elementary-level examples of this variety. These sketches could be considered concrete and visual brainstorming.

Clusters could also be used for visual brainstorming by an individual or a group. As a visual learning strategy, this format can become a whole-class technique providing practical information to share. The focus concept can be a word or a symbol that is central and often emphasized by size, color, or dimension, as all these qualities contribute to stronger mental abilities (Buzan & Buzan, 1996). Each additional idea radiates from this concept and may link to another to form a growing visual conversation. The act of encircling contains the thought and is another way to emphasize contributions to the whole (Rico, 1983) (see Figures 6.6–6.8).

Manipulating pieces of paper with symbols or words on them is another version of such free association. A pattern may form that discloses a pivotal idea to be used later in creating an artwork or writing perceptions of one that already exists. The details in an individual cluster are personally relevant visual or verbal information that can enhance the final product.

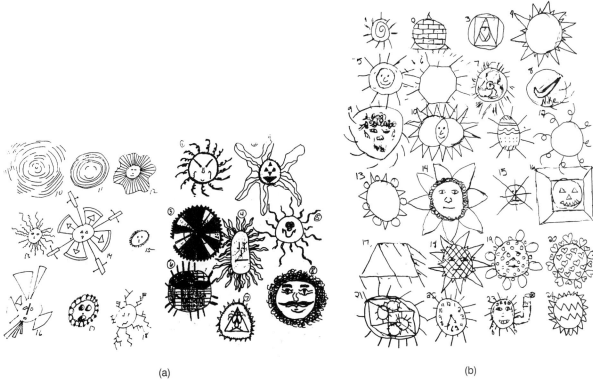

(a)　　　　　　　　　　　　　　　　　　(b)

Figures 6.4a, 6.4b
Wichita State University elementary education students developed 25 different sun symbols.

Collection of the author.

Figure 6.5
Elementary students (third through fifth grades) used their imaginations to create 12 different suns.

Collection of the author.

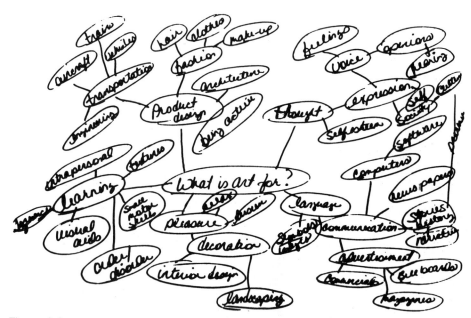

Figure 6.6
College students visually brainstormed answers for the functions of art.

Collection of the author.

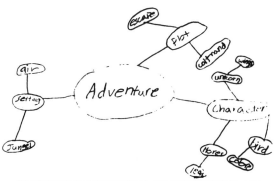

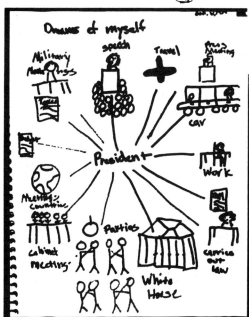

Figure 6.7
Elementary students organized their dreams of adventure and being president.

Courtesy of Dr. Lorraine Pflaumer. Collection of the author.

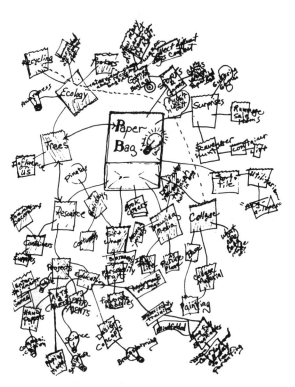

Figure 6.8
"What can be done with a paper bag?"

Courtesy of Terry Carson. Collection of the author.

221

To gain information when critically analyzing an artwork, I always require a sketch of the chosen painting or several sketched views of a sculpture (see Figures 6.9 and 6.10). My students find that this assignment leads them to concentrate on really seeing and recording as much information from the artwork as possible. This artistic strategy offers a close connection with the artwork. The student, as the perceiver of the artwork, and I, as the perceiver of the sketch, both feel a connection to the artwork. Even though the painting or sculpture might be moved to a different setting, it is linked to the individual who chose to draw, write about, and reflect on it.

Friendship with an artwork can be the result of a clustering or webbing process too. At a museum, one art teacher experienced a flood of memories in the associations he encountered by doing a cluster in front of a still life painting with a clock. Strong feelings about his father came up, and he cried. He was amazed that such a simple activity could be so profound and meaningful. His clustered words around the concept of time were *old, new, dated, forgotten, memories, sadness, dusty, organized.* This is his written statement:

> Time time time! Time for this and for that. No time for this or that, but time ticking-ticking, ticking away. Stop the Time? Can't do that—wish I could—turn it back. Good times—some bad times, but that's life. Times forgotten—for awhile, but remembered—with time. The old, once new, dusty and dated but not forgotten. A time to remember and reminisce—that precious TIME!

A student and I once chose the same artwork at a museum for our webs. Her response focused on the loneliness of the central figure in the courtyard. The act of associating words, images, and feelings in a web became so engrossing to me in my scenario about run-down row houses that I completely overlooked the little man. This process pointed out that viewers bring their own experiences and knowledge to analyzing and interpreting artwork. We both explored the painting together afterward, sharing our unique insights.

Figure 6.9

An informational sketch of a painting combines drawing and words to engage the learner.

Collection of the author.

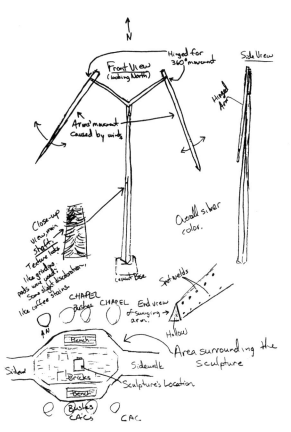

Figure 6.10
Sculptures are captured in many views and words.

Collection of the author.

Both sketches and clusters assist understanding and can act as resources for our own ideas. Visual brainstorming efforts through sketches and clusters are useful strategies for solving the problems of "what to do." Olson (1992) offers a number of strategies for increasing a student's visual vocabulary of ideas through sketches of many kinds of characters, places, and actions (see Figure 6.11). Other visual starting points for problem solving are readily available.

Students could begin with any "finish the drawing" formats—such as the *Anti-Coloring Book* series by Striker (1978–1982)—that already exist, or you could produce your own. These formats range from one line on a page to a fraction of a full picture. One third-grade teacher starts the classroom day with these "imagination transformations" to acclimate her students to school thinking (see Figure 6.12). Many art teachers generate these formats to expand upon an image or theme used by an artist or to inspire students who have extra time.

Collaborative work among students offers a variety of idea-generation options. These visual strategies include switching drawings or chairs at brief intervals and continuing the drawing process on the same paper. If each student uses a different color, each contribution could be discovered. Passing a sheet of paper folded into thirds allows three people to contribute to character formation (head, midsection, and legs, or forehead/eyes, nose/ears, and mouth/chin). The creatures in Figure 6.13 represent such compilations.

Working simultaneously on the same drawing or adding to another student's drawing allows for the inclusion of more visual clues and increases the resources available for incorporation in a final artwork. Structuring a tower of straws with tape

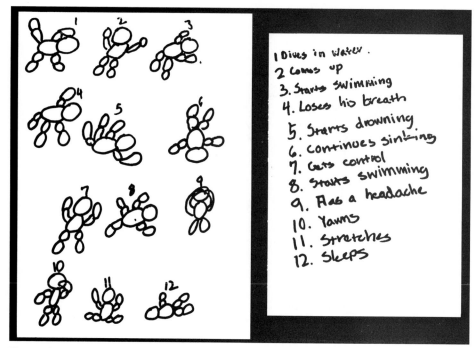

Figure 6.11
This child used circle figures to represent several poses for a mime sequence.

Courtesy of Dr. Lorraine Pflaumer. Collection of the author.

Figure 6.12
Beginning with one line on a page, these pictures represent "imagination transformations" by third graders.

Collection of the author.

Figure 6.13
Creatures adorn this elementary school hallway.

Collection of the author.

or combining collage elements into an assemblage as a group could lead to later individual or collaborative three-dimensional artworks. Gathering ideas is easier when using strategies such as sketching, clustering, and visually collaborating.

Planning.   The second category of strategy functions, planning, involves strategies similar to those used in gathering ideas to reach the goals of both learner and teacher. If students are to solve problems presented in their daily lives, visual ways of planning may assist their efforts to be involved. Our curricular goals can be realized through including artistic strategies in our planning. As a blueprint is made before a building is constructed and as a "sloppy copy" is drafted before a final written response is made, a visual rough draft may free many intermediate and secondary students from the drive for first-time perfection. In *Sketching School,* Martin (1991) describes a variety of sketching techniques for starting and developing artwork related to themes such as places, people, animals, and special events and applied in designing for fields such as theater, costume, and fashion.

Although students may independently sketch plans for their art projects, sketches are often required as part of the course unit objectives. Weaving, stitching, needleworking, and beadworking plans are often first charted on graph paper, while patterns are designed by hand or computer programs as plans for constructing in cloth or clay. Small-scale models can be developed for any large-scale three-dimensional project, from temporary stage sets to permanently installed ceramic walls. In planning for mural-size group projects, students place their observational drawings or magazine images on larger sheets. David Byrne, musician and filmmaker, describes his working process: "I covered a wall with drawings . . . then I reordered the drawings, again and again until they seemed to have some sort of flow" (Byrne, 1986, p. 9). Video segments are also planned as a visual script of interaction with an object (see Figures 6.14 and 6.15).

To stage her stories, one 10-year-old devised an artistic strategy using collage to assist in her characterizations and plots. She found pictures of people in magazines, cut them out, and constructed elaborate family networks of combined households

Figure 6.14
The story of Icarus is characterized in this visual script of a sculpture.

Courtesy of Jenny Clark. Collection of the author.

and multiple births (see Color Plate 6.1). Katie developed this strategy on her own and continues to use it because the photographs are in color and more lifelike than her drawings might be.

Visual planning by teachers may help chart curricular scheduling, design units, or create lesson handouts. Graphic representations of a contract can help students see the overall context of their learning (see Photo 6.1). Other visual plans might

Figure 6.15
Many views of this sculpture are shown in a visual plan.

Courtesy of Jan Bolick. Collection of the author.

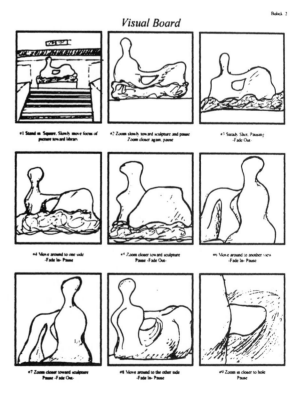

Photo 6.1
A teacher and student discuss an assignment contract using a circular map.

Collection of the author.

include a "back off" schedule, which can be charted from the future due date to the present by using lines or symbols with traditional media or computer database software. This visual record can assist in planning classwide and individual programs. Visual **note making** offers opportunities to individually code the steps of a process through color or symbols while a technique is demonstrated or a project is outlined (Tanner, 1984; Hanks & Belliston, 1992). **Note taking** may involve mapping information from a video, text, or document; it involves using design elements and principles to make the recording of the key ideas and branching details easier to understand and remember (see Color Plate 6.2).

Observing and recording.   Drawing from observation is a time-honored artistic strategy that can be used by elementary, secondary, and college students. What kinds of questions are answered by having the real thing to look at? Students consider the differences between what they remember and what they see and how they see it (see Color Plate 6.3).

In another lesson, all students are given the same objects, such as apples, rocks, popcorn, or leaves. A magnifying glass is available to allow for concentrated seeing. They are asked to observe their object closely, sketch it, and give it a personality (see the rock studies done by college students in Figure 6.16). After observing and recording, the real objects are gathered and then mixed together in a group. Each student approaches the pile and easily identifies her or his own. "It's like meeting an old friend," they declare. The process of observation and the strategy of sketching increase memory.

Other focusing strategies assist students in eliminating extraneous visual information (e.g., viewing through a rectangle cut out of the center of a card; viewing through a tube; or viewing through the thumb and first finger in an "OK" formation). My first

Figure 6.16
Observational drawings of rocks
with personality show different
viewpoints.

Collection of the author.

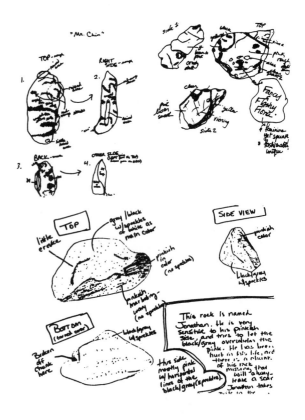

graders applied this process to paper cameras, with cut openings as their viewfinders, for pretend "far away" and "close up" shots that they drew later on paper "film."

In art classes, students learn through opportunities for visual vocabulary building. Drawing vocabulary related to art processes assists recall and understanding. Collected images are also useful for increasing visual information.

One art teacher discovered that collecting faces from magazines and then drawing on top of them assists her second graders in distinguishing the positions of facial features. "It looks like a mask" is a comment frequently made by her students when they are finished. This type of strategy could also record spatial placement, such as overlapping and foreground, middle-ground, and background relationships using tracing paper.

Edwards (1989) describes an upside-down drawing procedure that focuses on relationships and proportion while tricking the mind to sidestep habitual verbal interpretations. She also suggests concentrating on drawing the negative spaces formed by objects to observe them better.

Connecting.   A game of close observation can be timed to encourage the ability to record information quickly and build memory. Action poses can be drawn for one minute; mini still lifes can be drawn for three. A tray of small objects can be shown and then covered to see what will be recorded and remembered. Try a memory drawing game for yourself. What other connecting options are possible for art students?

Memory is one tool we use to make connections and learn to understand. Images are crucial to this process. Buzan and Buzan (1996) concur that our capacity to recognize images is almost limitless. "The more you educate people the more unique their vast and growing networks of associations become" (p. 66). Our associations are individual, cultural, and universal. Unsworth's *Connections: A Visual Game* (1995) provides photographic images to connect in a domino-like game. Players defend their associations as they link images. Art postcards, images cut from magazines, and drawings on cards could also be used to discover relationships collaboratively or individually.

Relationships are also shown through time and space. Sequences, time lines, and before/after storyboards are variations on time and space concepts that can be visual.

Sequences of change can portray hourly, daily, or weekly **transformations**. In *Mary Anne's Garden Drawings & Writings*, McLean (1987) presents this concept with many types of vegetables, flowers, wild plants, and animals. Contemporary artist Jennifer Bartlett displays her series of time-related paintings in her garden, while Monet showed several sequences of time relationships in his paintings of buildings and haystacks.

Time lines organize and display events from the past for a particular artist, society, or process. Students can connect their own imaginations to events to show "what happened next or what came before." Sequences of story connect beginning events to ending results in storyboards and books (see Figures 6.17 and 6.18) (for more on visual storytelling, see Chapter 5). Accordion books also allow students to explore their ideas of change.

Making connections visually might involve a **metamorphosis**. In this case, one object goes through a series of stages to become something else. Students can stretch their imaginations to draw the steps that occur during the metamorphosis, like a top becoming a ballerina (see Figures 6.19–6.23 for examples of the process of metamorphosis shown by college students). Morphing with computer images that blend faces, objects, or places is another form of this kind of visual connection. The result could be considered a Venn diagram of images.

Figure 6.17

One boy's adventures are shown in this storyboard as a plan for an accordion book.

Collection of the author.

Figure 6.18
Sequences of change or process are shown in these upper elementary students' notations.

Courtesy of Dr. Lorraine Pflaumer. Collection of the author.

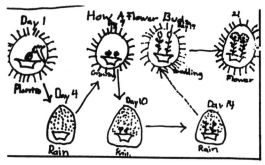

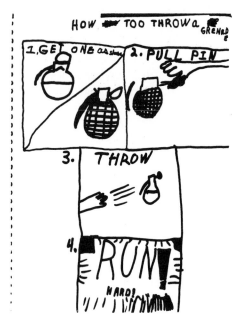

Figure 6.19
A top is transformed into a ballerina.

Courtesy of Dr. Judith Simpson. Collection of the author.

Figure 6.20
A light bulb is transformed into an energy source.

Courtesy of Dr. Judith Simpson. Collection of the author.

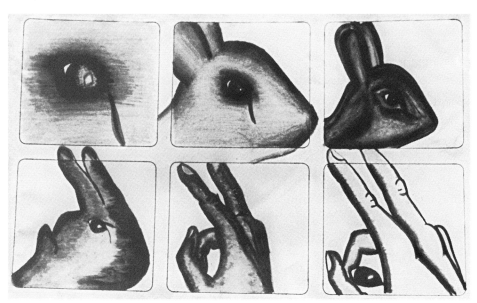

Figure 6.21
A rabbit's eye is transformed into one formed by a hand.

Courtesy of Dr. Judith Simpson. Collection of the author.

Figure 6.22
Shapes are transformed into a community.

Courtesy of Dr. Judith Simpson. Collection of the author.

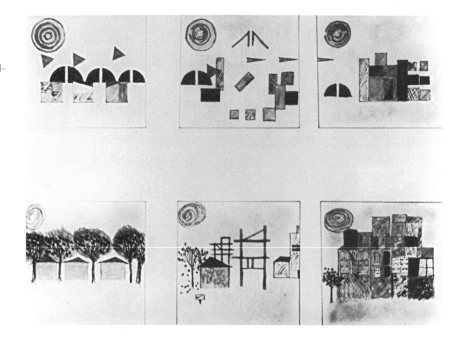

Associations may involve **metaphor** and **analogy** through visual images or symbols in mandala or other formats. Visual images are often equated with or stand for other concepts. **Mandalas,** usually presented as a bisected circle, have represented religious concepts for many societies in the Americas, Africa, Europe, Australia, and Asia. Like Jung, Fincher (1991) found that mandala designs assisted her self-understanding. She offers guidance by describing strategies like pretending to walk in the symbol and drawing what one encounters. She suggests that after completing the mandala one analyzes the colors, shapes, and images for associations. Examples of mandalas with luminous color are presented on a black surface by Cornell (1994) to connect the concepts of light and color.

Figure 6.23
A shoe's inside becomes a candle and holder.

Courtesy of Dr. Judith Simpson. Collection of the author.

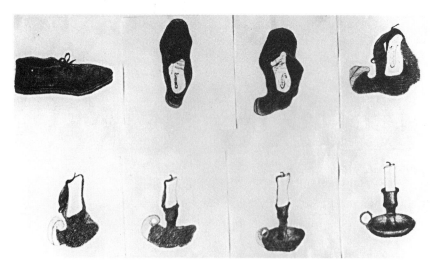

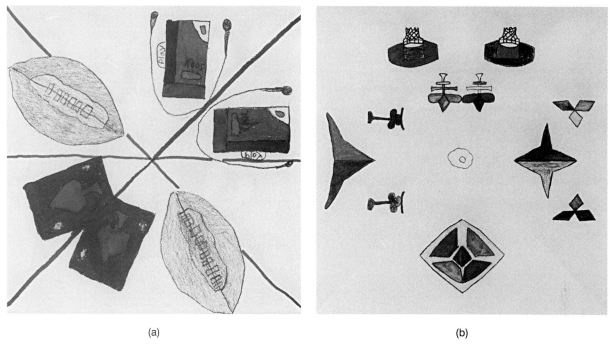

(a)   (b)

Figures 6.24a, 6.24b
Middle school students use symbols to express themselves in these mandalas.

Courtesy of Dr. Judith Simpson. Collection of the author.

Secondary students are interested in exploring self symbols. Seventh graders use folded squares to place their symbols in a mandala-like format (see Figures 6.24a and 6.24b). Your own mandala can express emotions and ideas through images and marks (see Color Plate 6.4 and Figures 6.25 and 6.26).

Marks have meaning. Analog mark-making exercises described by Edwards (1986) show the connection between language and marks. Often, looping lines

Figure 6.25
A college student explores thoughts and feelings through the mandala format. Artist: Lea Carmichael

Courtesy of Diane Thomas Lincoln. Collection of the author.

Figure 6.26
A college student explores thoughts and feelings through the mandala format. Artist: Jason Burley

Courtesy of Diane Thomas Lincoln. Collection of the author.

exclaim joy; pointed marks denote anger; and downward, dark shapes cry depression. My students found that their marks were very similar to each other and to the examples in Edwards's book. Through her research, one student found that upper elementary students were able to make these analogies as well.

Tanner (1984) proposes that teachers use analogies to assist students in understanding technical processes. He emphasizes that student recall is increased when their note making connects unfamiliar processes to known ones. Posters and handouts can show graphic relationships between familiar processes and art procedures, as in Color Plate 6.5, which equates papier-mâché and house construction.

Students can search their own memories for recalled scenes, people, events, and precious things. These connections are shared visually. The "memory maps" in Figures 6.27–6.29 and Color Plates 6.6 and 6.7 recall the past for these high school and college students.

Assessing and reflecting.   This section offers ways that the previously outlined artistic strategies could be used for curricular and personal evaluation. Pre-drawings, **KWL charts** (charts showing what is **K**nown, what the student **W**ants to know, and what was **L**earned), and maps can establish what is known about a process, subject, or theme before a unit begins. A continuous process portfolio most likely includes a number of early visual plans, collections of ideas, and recordings of objects and ideas. These options allow discussion of knowledge and progress between teacher and learner.

Assisting your students in discovering their preferred ways of approaching problems and making decisions could be proposed as part of the planning phase for a new project or as a reflection on a previous one. Buzan and Buzan (1996) propose

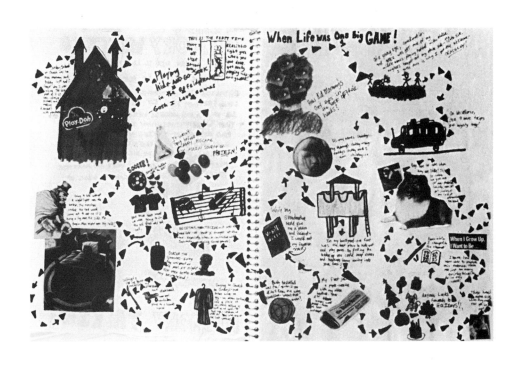

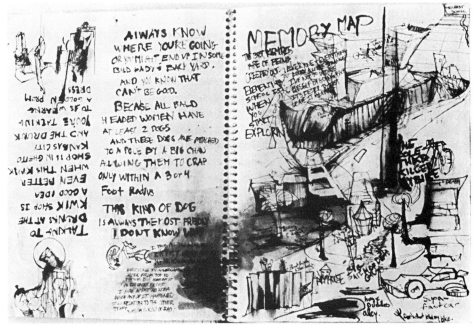

Figures 6.27, 6.28
High school students express their memories through mixed media and collaged images.
Artists: Ashley Brown (Figure 6.27); Will Blocker (Figure 6.28)

Courtesy of Pat Nemshock. Collection of the author.

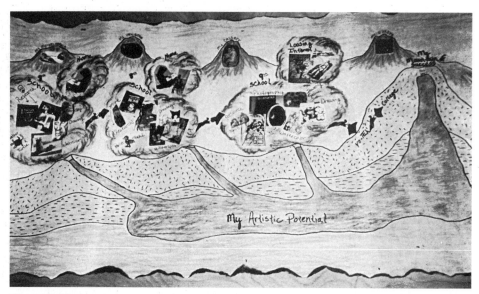

Figure 6.29
A college student refers to memories of secondary school art experiences through a layering diagram.

Courtesy of Teresa Hashbarger. Collection of the author.

a "yes or no" mind map to visualize options. Williams (1986) suggests sketching with colored pencils in a prescribed sequence of colors for a specified amount of time, with each color as another possibility. The resulting sketch conveys information regarding the individual's choice of starting point and the strategy she or he takes to complete the problem. As a visual record of time and decision making, this sketch may emphasize sections that need instructional assistance.

An individual project chart can help break down necessary steps and meet scheduled deadlines. This type of chart could be a personal effort, a contract with the instructor for a particular unit, a **rubric** of evaluation for a lesson, or a classroom display for collaborative projects. Just as sketchbooks and journals act as research and idea repositories, they also offer personal insight for further reflection. A map or personal time line that displays a student's graphic development could also be used for review.

In summary, artistic strategies offer options for personal exploration, classroom management, curriculum planning, and assessment. The five strategy categories discussed here use many of the same formats for the processing of information. These artistic strategies are very appropriate for art classrooms and individual learners. As such, they support National Visual Arts Standards 2, 3, and 5.

Many of the options explained for the art classroom can be integrated into other subject areas. Several have been discussed in this chapter in relation to diverse learners. Many authors support the use of artistic strategies in describing holistic ways of learning in their content areas. Integrating concepts that are important for learners will be outlined in the following section. This information relates directly to National Visual Arts Standard 6.

THEORY INTO PRACTICE

The research reviewed in this section is focused on connecting art to learning in the areas of language arts, science, social studies, and mathematics through visual thinking and learning strategies. Several studies imply that artistic strategies can be especially important and valuable as integrative methodology. Following the research discussion are examples that describe how these artistic strategies can be applied to practice in elementary through secondary schools. For instance, visuals such as KWL charts are practical presentations of student-centered learning in any area.

Language Arts, English, and Literature

As interest in developing literacy has grown, a visual–verbal connection has been indicated in language arts studies that encompass a philosophy of active involvement. Graves (1979) concludes that if drawing is important, children will not know what to write until they finish their drawings. He observes that for a beginning writer "drawing is one important means of maintaining child-initiated control" (p. 20). Researching elementary "process-writing" classrooms in Australia, Cambourne and Turbill (1991) describe drawing as a coping strategy that children "perceive as allowing them to use the tools of writing (pencil/paper) in ways which they have already learned to some degree and with which they feel confident" (p. 8). Goals for writing across the curriculum, according to Young (1992), include writing to learn and writing to communicate. Similarly, artistic strategies can be focused on immediate learning or on communicating in more finalized formats.

The relationship between organizing visual and verbal composition was explored by Caldwell and Moore (1991), who designed an empirical study of the use of drawing activities as planning for narrative writing. Rating 600 weekly writings over a 15-week period for 42 second and third graders resulted in statistically significant increases in writing quality scores. These researchers concluded that drawing is a viable and effective form of rehearsal and can be more successful than the traditional planning activity of discussion used by the control group. This empirical proof shows that artistic strategies allow for testing, revising, and synthesizing ideas before writing.

The potential of artistic strategies for solving problems, gaining control, and motivating learners is described by a first-grade teacher whose children enthusiastically construct compound words on tri-folded paper. For example: an image of fire on one side and a dog on the other opens to reveal a "hot-dog." Using their imaginations and their humor helps the children recall these words, as the visual catalog of "cup" words by a fifth grader demonstrates in Figure 6.30.

Olson's (1992) *Envisioning Writing* and Routman's (1991) *Invitations* offer innumerable practical suggestions for using drawing in conjunction with language arts. These often involve connecting and increasing language learning visually through using sketches as resources for writing, as well as writing associated words while drawing (Olson, 1992). Using such strategic tools as **picture mapping** in a circle (Routman, 1991), an event time line as a "quick map" of a chapter (Claggett & Brown, 1992), or a semantic map of character traits, themes, or cause-and-effect relationships (Figure 6.31) allows elementary and

Figure 6.30
Can you add more visual symbols to these "cup" puns by a fifth grader?

Courtesy of Dr. Lorraine Pflaumer. Collection of the author

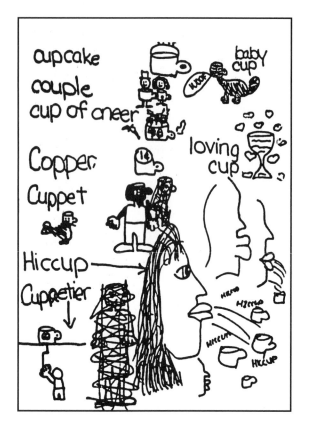

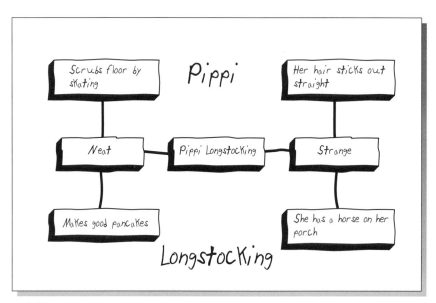

Figure 6.31
Characteristics of Pippi Longstocking are displayed in this map with dimensional boxes.

Collection of the author.

secondary students to interact with literature and teachers to assess comprehension at a glance.

Describing characters, plots, and settings by drawing them in a storyboard format makes for a more informative book report, according to one sixth-grade teacher. She notes that it is also more difficult to cheat on a drawn report.

Routine use of visual definitions helped one teacher assess a vocabulary problem for a first grader (see Figure 6.32). Was the story misunderstood? Was it a conceptual error or a spelling mistake? If corrected without the image, this confusion between *udder* and *under* might have gone unnoticed. The drawing alerted the teacher to check with the child. Others use visual definitions to evaluate letter sounds (see Figure 6.33).

Huber-Bowen (1993) defines a number of artistic strategies that can be used for pre-reading and pre-writing. These **graphic organizers** display relationships among concepts, topics, and themes visually and verbally. She differentiates between **sequence charts,** which show specific serial changes, and **flow charts,** which show more general, continual processes. Converging data meet in **stream charts**, while diverging data grow upward in a **tree chart**. Six sides of an issue are shown on cubes and described as **cubing**. These graphic strategies assist flexibility of thought and are important in all languages. (Refer to Figure 6.1 for visual representations of these approaches.)

London (1989) reminds us that "visual thinking and visual imagery is our *native language*" (p. 49), so it may be natural to consider the direct experience of drawing and writing in journals. "Shared notation" is the term that Pflaumer and Thomley (1989) use for their drawing and drama journals. Their elementary students use "the process of notation and the review of that notation as a means of

Figure 6.32
Story vocabulary is misunderstood by a first grader. Is it *udder* or *under*? Or is the udder under?

Collection of the author.

Figure 6.33
Sounds can be associated and assessed through visual images.

Collection of the author.

personal inventory" (p. 1). Writing and drawing are stressed as equally important and more powerful communication when interacting (see Figures 6.11, 6.18, 6.30, and 6.36, from students' journals).

Combining both visual and verbal formats cues recall and inspires solutions. One seventh grader created her own conversation cards with drawings of characters on one side and related verbal information on the other (Figure 6.34).

Figure 6.34
A middle school student draws her characters on one side and writes out their conversations on the other side of small cards.

Courtesy of Dr. Lorraine Pflaumer. Collection of the author.

Science, Social Studies, and Mathematics

The shared habits of observation and inquiry by artists, scientists, historians, and mathematicians offer additional uses for artistic strategies. Artistic strategy formats of diagramming and recording are useful in exploring and describing scientific processes. Charts categorize species and identify molecular structure. Gainer and Child (1986) use scientific illustration for encouraging systematic organization and emphasizing gradual drawing skills acquisition. A first-grade class looks at "Rotten Jack," their carved pumpkin, and observes clues of interrelated changes in time and color, such as "getting a white fuzz" and "looking like orange mashed potatoes," and they draw predictions of what might happen to the pumpkin as time goes on (Hubbard, 1989a). Louis, a third grader, details five steps for collecting insects through accurately rendered drawings (Thunder-McGuire, 1992). Pre- and post-paintings show what second graders learned in their ocean unit (see Color Plate 6.8).

Elementary students studying solids and liquids use drawings to describe both concepts, and middle school students studying molecular structures are assessed through their drawings of what they see through a microscope. The *Ultimate Visual Dictionary* (Binder, 1994) provides visual details from the cells of plants to the skeletal and muscular structures of our own bodies.

Although students might see a natural correlation between scientific observing and artistic strategies, teachers might not. One second-grade classroom had a magnifying stool that you could place over something to see it up close. Because the teacher did a lot of science experiments, I asked if the students ever drew while looking through this magnifier. She stared at me blankly, as if it would never have occurred to her.

Scientific concerns can be extended into the realm of social studies through the process of diagramming routes to and from places (Goodnow, 1977; London 1994); charts can be made of intended actions, like "a secret plan for snack recess" (Hubbard, 1989a, p. 85). Several routes of action and representations of space are indicated in the three diagrams in Figure 6.35. Geographic, geological, economic, and historical references to a region or time can be shown in maps and graphs.

Jorgensen (1993) describes a participatory immersion workshop that focuses on what students want to know. By using centers of primary resources, students observe, predict, and synthesize information in their history milieu drawings and writings. She defines these as environments of people, places, and events considered from the student's perspective. "Drawing lets them put their historical ideas into a visual form and lets me evaluate how their understandings are changing" (p. 42). Historical storytelling possibilities also involve illustrating passages that students have read. Even mythical figures can be compared in past and future visual descriptions (Figure 6.36).

Historical information can also be extracted from paintings, photographs, and artifacts through recording details or constructing models. Understanding context and relationships can be assisted by artistic strategies such as drawing a time line of pivotal life events, clustering predictions, or comparing data through charts (Figure 6.37). One upper elementary teacher uses a Venn diagram for comparing children in the past with her students. The intersecting center of the two circles assists her students in relating to the children of long ago.

Studying various communities and societies through concepts such as shelters, clothing, transportation, toys, and stories can be extended by individual or group graphic efforts. A third-grade class was studying Mong culture and decided to illustrate one story. Partners took sections of the story to sketch. Some worked on the drawings simultaneously, others had a chief artist. The sketch was dis-

Figure 6.35
First graders visually describe ways around and to various places.

Courtesy of Dr. Lorraine Pflaumer. Collection of the author.

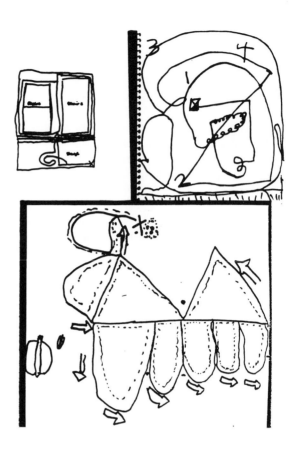

Figure 6.36
These Robin Hood depictions show an understanding of change in dress related to time.

Courtesy of Dr. Lorraine Pflaumer. Collection of the author.

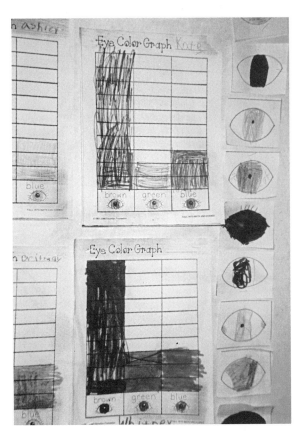

Figure 6.37
The color of eyes in an elementary classroom are compared using images and bar graphs.

Collection of the author.

cussed in front of the class for changes that would be necessary for the final book. Particular attention was paid to appropriate cultural details for the setting, sequence, and characters. These sketches allowed several responses to problems involving relationships to social studies concepts (see Figure 6.38).

Problem solving in math also relates to art and communities. *Designing Spaces: Visualizing, Planning, and Building* (Education Development Center, 1995) describes integrative approaches in middle school for art and math through architecture. This unit uses various visual strategies, from manipulating blocks to planning houses. Structures are drawn **isometrically** (in depth) and **orthogonally** (each side's face view) and then constructed in paper models. Students are encouraged to compare their sketches and improve the clarity of their plans. Figures 6.39 and 6.40 show third graders' architectural sketches and plans for houses, including bubble diagrams, inside and outside views, as well as collaged floor plans to scale.

In *Envisioning Information* (1994), Tufte states, "At the heart of quantitative reasoning is a single question: Compared to what?" (p. 6). He presents data in charts, time lines, and small multiples repeated in grid formats. He suggests that to gain clarity one should add detail and put layers of information into proper relationships by using differences in shape, value, size, and color. Many computer software programs allow data to be organized into various formats, such as horizontal and vertical bar graphs and two- and three-dimensional pie charts. The *MacMillan Visual Almanac* (Tesar, 1996) provides 2,000 examples of visual information about our world.

Figure 6.38
Collaborative sketches by third
graders interpret events in a
Mong folktale.

Collection of the author.

Kleiman (1991) proposes activities and student artwork related to size esti-
mates and scale factors through careful measurements of objects needed by
"Gulliver"-like people. Props like giant rulers and materials like colored pencils are
helpful in understanding mathematical concepts.

Fifty fifth-grade students were encouraged to generate drawings to assist their
solutions in interpreting mathematical word problems during intervention sessions focused on practicing drawing (Van Essen & Hamaker, 1990). In this empirical study, statistically significant improved solutions were indicated because a
large number of accurate drawings were generated. Artistic strategies became
useful for analysis and elaboration when students recorded relevant knowledge.

In Conclusion

Summarizing the use of artistic strategies in relation to general education requires
the recognition of these processes as **heuristic** tools useful to encourage individual discovery. Approaches to clustering, sketching, mapping, and graphing are
being developed and practiced in many schools. Commercial reading and writing
programs blackline sheets to reproduce a variety of graphic organizers. Strategies
for planning, comprehending, and assessing information in "tiny bites" (so-called
by one fifth-grade teacher), make their thoughts visible and concrete for students
just beginning their elementary schooling to those in higher education.

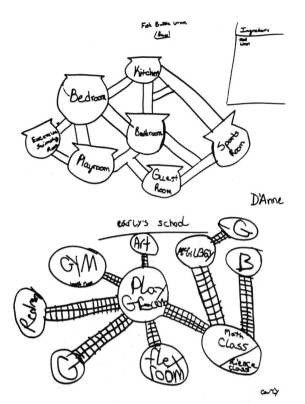

Figure 6.39
Bubble diagrams help students understand the needs of their "clients."

Collection of the author.

Figure 6.40
Architecture is explored through orthogonal and isometric drawings, as well as construction paper scale collages.

Collection of the author.

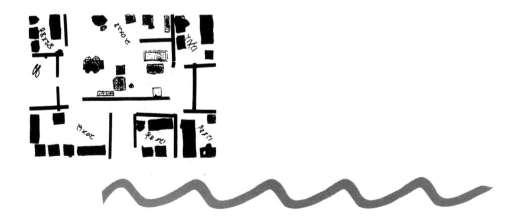

∿ What Are the Challenges to Using Artistic Strategies?

Many educators and researchers value teaching and learning strategies that assist their educational goals. One of McConnell's (1993) adult literacy students supported the use of "talking drawings" as a strategy for discovering what was known and assessing what was learned after a unit. However, she complained that using an artistic strategy was not often recognized: "You can't just learn anything at school, you have to write about everything as though that proves you've learnt something" (p. 269). This student implied that teaching strategies often reflect the teacher's learning style. We continue to teach in the way we learn best. Most academic teachers excelled in the language of words and numbers in school, yet using visual language may have been challenging for them. What challenges would a teacher of art face with these colleagues?

Three Perceived Limitations

In my interviews and discussions with classroom teachers and preservice education students, their rationales for not using artistic strategies involve their perceptions about visual learning and thinking. These limitations are often expressed in three areas: (1) drawing is not understood as valuable, (2) there doesn't seem to be enough time to be fully involved, and (3) not all students are considered talented. Many educators perceive that they are inadequate in demonstrating drawing strategies; some are ambivalent about such an approach; and others simply do not know about the possible contributions of artistic strategies. These rationales relate directly to our American cultural, educational, and economic training. In essence, what we perceive as worthy is expressed in our teaching.

Perceived value.   The perception of value or worth is often concealed by time or talent excuses. For example, drawing (or any art process) may not be encouraged or even allowed at home or in the classroom. These situations express clearly that art activities are not considered valuable enough. Other teachers report that their "bright ones (thought) coloring was babyish or immature . . . usually it's the poorer kids, some of the lower kids, they'll want to color" (Hamilton, 1993, p. 176).

Teacher expectations for student behavior also involve value perceptions and infer negative reactions to lessons. Drawing is sometimes explained as an act of boredom or inattention, displaying a lack of respect and involvement with lessons, or rebellious showing off. Unfortunately, some teachers are quite hostile to drawing behavior and tell their students that any drawings done during class will be cause for demerits. Students report that journals with drawings in them have been torn up publicly. These defensive actions affect the way the classroom functions and looks.

The lack of readily available materials to use for drawing and constructing shows a disregard for artistic strategies. Sometimes, marking materials are considered for writing only, even though crayons, markers, and pencils are equally useful for graphic work. One teacher observed: "I tell them to write the story first then draw the picture, but sometimes they do it the other way around." Other teachers might not even recognize the possibility of drawing first with writing tools. One uses slates for math work only and has not considered them for drawing at all.

The lack of displays of children's artwork or haphazard approaches to display are other indications of misunderstanding. Important work is emphasized by special presentations; therefore, artwork needs to be mounted and placed for an audience to view. This, of course, requires coordinating student efforts or using teacher preparation or presentation time.

Time requirements.   The second reason for not using visual strategies is often time. It may be expressed in excuses such as the following: the schedule of "real" work will not permit it; if children were allowed to draw, they would be "drawing all the time"; usually, "the kids who want to color find time," although they may rush through their work in order to draw. One teacher summarizes this view: drawing is "a secondary use of time . . . if they have an assignment that's due they're going to use that time to complete the work given . . . the time is so short I'm not maximizing the amount of time they should be spending on the text" (Hamilton, 1993, p. 177). Often, "free time" for drawing is purposefully gone before any drawing has a chance to begin. In *Invitations: Changing as Teachers and Learners K-12,* Routman (1991) advises teachers on illustrating:

> Young children often need to draw pictures before they attempt words. After children are writing easily, often by mid-first grade, they are gently encouraged to spend most of their time writing and to save their illustrations for their published books and projects as well as for independent work time. For children who are more comfortable just writing a story, we don't insist on pictures. (p. 224)

Teachers expect their students to be more creative, but often they do not provide time for practice in the area of visual creativity. Some do not recognize the connection between artistic strategies and their own history—"I'm not a real artist," although "I had to do it in order to remember when I was growing up."

Artistic strategies take time to plan and present. One teacher pointed out that "it gets boring. . . . I may not do it every day . . . it depends on what the lesson lends itself to." This remark is very accurate and compelling, yet it could be hiding a fear related to demonstrating an artistic strategy.

Assumptions of talent.   The third reason given for avoiding the use of artistic strategies concerns the issue of talent or ability. A teacher's own perceived artistic inadequacies might lead to apologies such as: "See, I'm not an artist. I would do better writing my story and then drawing. So a lot of kids reflect (what I do). . . . I'm horrible at drawing, it's a real challenge." As mentioned in Chapter 5, perhaps this teacher would be labeled "drawing disabled."

Even art teachers are often apprehensive about demonstration drawing. They might have accepted the responsibility as the class artist in elementary school, but they recognize that the problem now is to communicate information clearly and quickly. One solution is to develop drawing skills through practice and games like Pictionary®. Practicing artistic strategies like clustering and drawing part-to-whole and whole-to-part also helps when students request drawing assistance. The teacher can place tracing paper over a student's artwork to demonstrate a strategy or technique. Another solution would be to practice on areas like a chalkboard, projected overhead transparencies, and computer screens. Graphic artists use files of visual resources—your students could gather examples in visual research files of their own.

Students also have expectations. They often express a lack of confidence, and the "I can't draw, do it for me" situation occurs at all grade levels. An inappropriate solution that teachers often use is to remind their students that "not everybody is an artist"; they purposely do not "pressure the kids who do not want to draw." But what about the students who do not want to read, write, or cipher? Are they pressured not to do so?

Routman (1991) mentions the problem of inadequate drawing skills in a kindergarten class:

> As in other grades, I begin by discussing what I could write about. I start by drawing a picture and telling students that many of them probably draw better than I do. I am careful to refer to drawing as a form of writing and a way of telling my story. (p. 216)

Does Routman really draw at a kindergarten level? Does she write at that level? If so, the children might wonder why she is the teacher. Her explanation, however, was almost exactly like one from my interview of a third-grade teacher:

> I don't have an artist's ability . . . for me you have to, at least, recognize [my drawing as] better than the kids can draw. . . . When it comes to art I get totally turned off . . . art was never my favorite subject. I always had a hard time, I always got A's in it, but I never liked what I did, My standards were higher than what I produced. . . . I won't [get those skills], I'll go to another subject, another way [to avoid drawing]. (Hamilton, 1993, p. 179)

Luckily, the students in this classroom were allowed to use many artistic strategies that were integrated into the curriculum. Other teachers might deny these kinds of options if they express such strong feelings of anxiety and inadequacy.

Learned Helplessness

Sarason, a noted educational psychologist and researcher interested in educational reform, wonders why the universal experience and the predictable development of artistic activity is "ignored, blunted, devalued and extinguished" (1990, p. x) in our culture and by our schools. In his book *The Challenge of Art to Psychology,* he argues that the challenge is also one to our society's fundamental values and concerns "not only art or science education, but our conventional view of human nature and the ways that view suffuses the substance and organization of our schools." According to him, our own culture has "a narrow conception of artistic activity [that] prevents us from recognizing the presence of the artistic process . . . as a way of ordering self and media, an ordering that is developmentally intrinsic to the need for mastery and personal expression" (p. 6). Many negative elements—fear, paralysis, risk of ridicule in drawing and sharing, and the perception of being unworthy, incompetent, and unjustified to appreciate or evaluate artwork—are conveyed through our own myths and misconceptions. Sarason further contends the following:

> Artistic activity is extinguished relatively early in life in large part because of the individual's feeling of inadequacy in representing reality, the belief that artistry is a talent or gift that few possess, and intimidation by the perceived gulf between what the individual can do and what great artists have done. The result is a form of learned helplessness or inadequacy. (pp. 4–5)

Sarason goes so far in his indictment of a society that renders its members incapable of participating in artistic activities to consider it as " a form of human abuse" (p. 140). By defining the term *abuse* as "to use so as to injure or damage," he acknowledges that this artistic learned helplessness is not a conscious or visible practice in a society that elevates artists who sell their artwork, yet "denies that this activity is one that all people are capable of."

According to Healy (1990), the term **learned helplessness** is increasingly heard as a description of typical forms of behavior. One major theory even argues that learned helplessness and weakness in problem-solving strategies may be fundamental causes of learning disability (p. 187). Is it a cause, though, or a reaction to inappropriate teaching? Demonstrating their own learned helplessness in drawing further removes teachers from considering the value of using artistic strategies for learning.

The personal experiences that teachers and students acquire in our society shape their reactions to using artistic strategies. Many adults are still punishing themselves because their childhood "tree" was ridiculed by an insensitive older person. It is disheartening when teachers choose to relate an early art experience as an example of developmentally inappropriate practice. Their stories are still told with passion years later. These deep feelings are passed on to students unconsciously in these teachers' attitudes; some teachers decide to dismiss using artistic strategies consciously because of such experiences. Unfortunately, it was often the person with the responsibility for teaching art who caused such wounds.

SUMMARY

This chapter has defined artistic strategies as those that visually, spatially, or tactilely incorporate graphic images, symbols, and formats as the basis for communicating meaning instead of relying exclusively on words and numbers. Many examples of artistic strategies used as learning and teaching tools have been offered. The advantages of using these tools to serve diverse learners are in making their thinking concrete, encouraging connections, and allowing for easier evaluation. The challenges to this approach require reflection on the perceived limitations of value, time, and talent.

What would happen if everyone used artistic strategies as a matter of course? Would this dilute the importance of teaching art? It would do so only if we as teachers of art do not support these strategies as one of our contributions to education. Arnheim (1986) notes:

> Visual thinking is unavoidable. Even so, it will take time before it truly assumes its rightful place in our education. Visual thinking is indivisible: unless it is given its due in every field of teaching and learning, it cannot work well in any field. The best intentions of the biology teacher will be hampered by half-ready student minds if the mathematics teacher is not applying the same principles. We need nothing less than a change of basic attitude in all teaching. Until then, those who happen to see the light will do their best to get the ball rolling. Seeing the light and rolling the ball are good visual images. (p. 151)

It is important for the public to recognize that artistic strategies, introduced and elaborated upon in the art classroom, offer necessary training in thinking for all throughout the school curriculum. Providing these opportunities for learning will assist many of your students to achieve their best.

ACTION PLAN FOR INSTRUCTIONAL DECISION MAKING

～ *Practice* using artistic strategies for yourself.

～ *Use* artistic strategies when you construct curriculum units and lesson plans for integrative and collaborative learning.

~ *Consider* artistic strategies for classroom environments, as well as class- and unit-related information.

~ *Demonstrate* these strategies when you teach.

~ *Display* student-created charts, diagrams, and sketches as part of the artistic process.

~ *Discuss* their use of artistic strategies with students.

~ *Point out* the transference possibilities in note taking and note making and in planning and assessing projects for other subjects.

~ *Discover* colleagues who use artistic strategies with their students.

~ *Document* through photographs or *collect* examples of artistic strategy use in your community.

~ *Suggest* upgrading your school's computer technology services to include artistic-strategy-producing software.

~ *Search* the school library and the World Wide Web for additional examples.

~ *Conduct* your own research on the benefits and challenges of using artistic strategies.

DISCUSSION QUESTIONS

1. How would diverse learners benefit from using artistic strategies?
2. Should artistic strategy formats be student generated, teacher generated, or copied from commercial programs? What would be the advantages and disadvantages of each method?
3. Have you ever experienced learned helplessness? How might this behavior affect your teaching, your students, or your advocacy efforts?

SUGGESTED ACTIVITIES

Your Personal Plan

As a student aspiring to teach art, you need to acknowledge the importance of visual, spatial, and tactile learning for yourself and all students. You need to recognize that you can make the choice to validate these nonverbal learning opportunities by using the artistic strategies put forth in this chapter or piggybacking on these ideas and designing your own. You need to understand the benefits and challenges for choosing to use artistic strategies in your learning and teaching. You may become aware of other authors describing these methods and gather other ways to add to your artistic strategy options. Begin by trying the following in your journal/sketchbook:

~ Practice visual brainstorming with a cluster of words only, then symbols only, and then a combination of both. Consider associations with concepts or themes such as a color (red, favorite, ugly), a place (home, school, relaxing), or an emotion (happiness, fear, surprise). Create your own categories.

~ Map this chapter, this book, or another source, such as an artwork.

~ Describe a project by making a symbolic schedule or chart.

~ Try some observational or memory-building games.

~ Construct a resource file of images to sketch, map, or use for integrative lesson planning.

~ Make your note taking visual and memorable by using the elements and principles of design and your own symbols or codes. Add your own visual comments to this text.

~ Check the Annotated Resources for additional examples, research, and rationales.

~ Practice any of the suggested techniques until using artistic strategies becomes second nature.

Modeling Artistic Strategies

What can the teacher of art do to convince others that artistic strategies are useful? First, model the use of these strategies in your own curriculum. This modeling allows you to personally explore the possibilities for using visual thinking in entire classes or for specific students and situations. It also provides you with the opportunity to accept the role of defining and encouraging these strategies throughout the school program.

Demonstrations of artistic strategies by the art teacher during instruction, consistent use of these strategies, and feedback by students are all ways to model their use. Student-developed charts, maps, or sketches can be displayed in the classroom for easy checking by student or teacher. Art history time lines, as well as visual directions and rules, can be part of classroom decor.

It is especially important to discuss these strategies with students, consider their personal discoveries related to their own learning, and point out the transference opportunities to other subjects. Your students will be the best ambassadors for using artistic strategies that are relevant to them.

School-Based Research

After modeling the use of these strategies in your art program, discover the current use of artistic strategies in your colleagues' curricula. Observing classroom and hallway displays, talking to students about their assignments in other subjects, and discussing with your colleagues ways of involving students in learning are all steps to school-based research.

A classroom display can give both teaching and learning strategy information (see Figure 6.41). Writings accompanied by illustrations and projects displayed in conjunction with artwork may offer evidence that visual information processing is valued. In such cases, ask the teacher how the lesson was introduced (what did the students do? and how did they feel about the visual process?), while encouraging the continued use of artistic strategies. This may happen at any educational level, from preschool through adult education.

If no displays are available to research, uncovering the teachers' perceptions regarding the use of artistic strategies may be the next step. Interview-like discussions, though informal, may give clues to the receptivity of other faculty members. If

Figure 6.41
A poster that connects the concept of form visually and verbally was discovered in a music classroom.

Collection of the author.

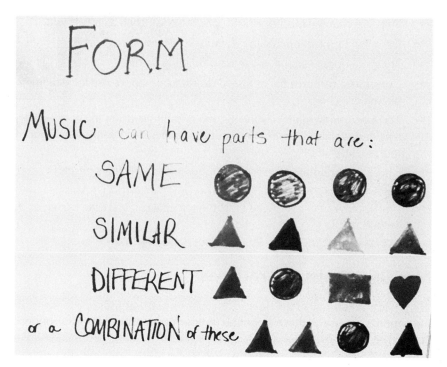

they are interested, you could show them student process portfolios and/or demonstrate an artistic strategy. They may already be using these strategies and not know it. You could offer informative rationales from research in art and other subject areas.

It is important to work with interested instructors. Those who aren't interested may be responding to some combination of the constraints of time, inadequacy, or their own values. Their beliefs may change over time, but they may be so deeply held that they aren't released easily. You may be working with some of their students directly, however, and students who find using artistic strategies beneficial may recognize their uses for other subjects and offer those connections. They may find evidence to support this use and share it with you, other students, family members, or the public.

Artistic Strategies in the Community

Building on their own successes with artistic strategies, students could be encouraged to share these techniques with younger siblings and their parents. A process that is successful for one child may be more readily considered by others in the family. Recognizing these strategies as vehicles for thinking for all ages might prevent some of the frustration encountered in traditional school instruction by visual, spatial, and tactile learners. If these strategies are successful for any family member, they are validated as important.

When parents become aware of these strategies as important contributions to learning, they increase their support for art in the schools. Art advocacy is more powerful when personally practiced and when connected to community life. In *Step Outside: Community Based Art Education* (London, 1994), the context of neighborhoods offers a number of inquiry options. Connecting to school themes, group projects, or public events through visual planning strategies allows for alternative choices to be seen and considered.

Research by teachers and students into the professions that use artistic strategies in the community might include a variety of local businesses and services. Urban planners, contractors, and landscape and building architects use visual planning and need to understand and communicate with artistic strategies. Hospital personnel chart patients' progress, while other charts display personnel reporting structures for all manner of organizations. Advertising relies on graphs, charts, and symbolic images to emphasize product performance. Local law enforcement officials diagram the placement of cars and people in a traffic accident. Witnesses manipulate putty to offer information about a probable suspect's face. Print and electronic media services and businesses would not exist without artistic strategies to convey information.

We are in the information age, with technology becoming increasingly visual. Icons are selected for browsing on the Internet and World Wide Web. Numerical and word data can be input into many software programs and represented as charts and diagrams in a very short time. Software can even create map formats with text files for individual branches that can be edited and enlarged. A scanned and manipulated image can be used as a learning tool, as well as a final product. Computer programs also offer opportunities for traditional sketching on a pen-pad. Images can be input for faxing and projected at teleconferences. A kinesthetic strategy of "tracing in the air" may be visually converted to actual drawings by technology that receives images done by pointing a finger at a screen. Technological advances make the improbable possible for visual communication every day.

ANNOTATED RESOURCES

Communication and Drawing Resources

Arnheim, R. (1969). *Visual thinking.* Berkeley, CA: University of California Press.
> *This seminal book defines visual thinking and offers rationales for its inclusion in education.*

Arnheim, R. (1986). *New essays on the psychology of art.* Berkeley, CA: University of California Press.
> *Various chapters in this book center on perceptual challenges, interdisciplinary focus, and the diversity of the arts' contributions to thinking and learning.*

Binder, J. (Ed.). (1994). *Ultimate visual dictionary.* London: Dorling Kindersley.
> *This reference tool offers visual information through photographs, drawings, and diagrams in sections from the universe to life on earth. Materials, processes, and equipment are shown in units on the visual arts, architecture, and music. An appendix lists words with page referents, but the images show a very compelling way to learn. (A series of individual "eyewitness visual dictionaries" are also offered by this publisher.)*

Buzan, T., & Buzan, B. (1996). *The mind map book: How to use radiant thinking to maximize your brain's untapped potential.* New York: Plume.
> *Based on learning-to-learn research, mind mapping is presented as the tool for engaging individuals and groups in thinking, making choices, and increasing memory and creativity. Practical procedures and rationales for studying, organizing, and presenting ideas are described, with easy steps and numerous examples from all age groups.*

Cornell, J. (1994). *Mandala: Luminous symbols for healing*. Wheaton, IL: Quest.
> *This is a wonderfully illustrated guide to creating illuminated mandalas. The connections among art, science, and healing are established, with exercises in light and color.*

Fincher, S. F. (1991). *Creating mandalas: For insight, healing and self-expression*. Boston: Shambhala.
> *Good background information on many cultural uses for mandalas is supplied. Associations for colors and symbols are suggested.*

Hanks, K., & Belliston, L. (1992). *Draw! A visual approach to thinking, learning and communication*. Los Altos, CA: Crisp.
> *This book is filled with visual information, techniques, and useful definitions of ideation, notation, and communication for all levels.*

Lazear, D. (1991). *Seven ways of knowing: Teaching for multiple intelligences*. Arlington Heights, IL: IRI Skylight.
> *Multiple intelligence theory is applied to student learning in text and visual formats. Chapter 3, "Seeing Is Believing ... and Knowing!" describes visualization activities as well as the use of mapping in a lesson plan for mathematics.*

Martin, J. (1991). *Sketching school*. Pleasantville, NY: Reader's Digest.
> *Focusing on techniques, themes, and uses of artistic strategies in careers such as fashion and textile and graphic design, this book offers information verbally and visually.*

Morgan, J., & Welton, P. (1992). *See what I mean? An introduction to visual communication*. London: Edward Arnold.
> *Visual models of communication are thoroughly described. Several artistic strategies are shown.*

Tesar, J. (1996). *The MacMillan visual almanac*. Woodbridge, CT: Blackbirch Press.
> *An outstanding collection of 2,000 charts, graphs, maps, and other visuals presents information relating to health, government, environment, business, and education.*

Tufte, E. R. (1994). *Envisioning information*. Cheshire, CT: Graphics.
> *This book provides excellent visuals from many civilizations, past and present, that display the use of design principles to clarify everyday information (e.g., train schedules, area maps, dance notations).*

Cross-Curriculum Education Resources

Claggett, F., & Brown, J. (1992). *Drawing your own conclusions: Graphic strategies for reading, writing and thinking*. Portsmouth, NH: Heinemann.
> *This is a program description of a high school literature course with extensive examples of mapping, sketching, and mandalas. This student work is very informative.*

Education Development Center (Ed.). (1995). *Designing spaces: Visualizing, planning and building*. Portsmouth, NH: Heinemann.
> *This workbook links architecture and mathematics. Exercises are provided along with examples of middle school students' use of artistic strategies.*

Educational Leadership.
> *This is a publication of the Association for Supervision and Curriculum Development. It offers theme issues related to learning and current educational prac-*

tices. Articles from two issues are presented in this chapter: one on the theme of "Learning Styles" (1990, [48]2) and one on the theme of "How Children Learn" (1997, [54]6). Future issues may also be pertinent to the application of artistic strategies across the school curriculum.

Johnson, P. (1993). *Literacy through the book arts.* Portsmouth, NH: Heinemann.
  Exciting options are shown for making books by elementary students, although they are applicable to other grade levels.

Jorgensen, K. L. (1993). *History workshop: Reconstructing the past with elementary students.* Portsmouth, NH: Heinemann.
  This book gives documentation of a program that uses artistic strategies to involve students in studying history. Student examples are easy to read, and concepts are easily replicated.

Olson, J. L. (1992). *Envisioning writing: Toward an integration of drawing and writing.* Portsmouth, NH: Heinemann.
  This book gives excellent strategies for increasing verbal and visual interaction. It includes many elementary student examples and benefit statements.

Robinson, G. (1995). *Sketchbooks: Explore and store.* London: Hadder & Stoughton.
  This book provides practical suggestions for incorporating sketchbooks into the entire elementary curriculum.

Routman, R. (1991). *Invitations: Changing as teachers and learners K-2.* Portsmouth, NH: Heinemann.
  Several artistic strategies are suggested through children's examples. Useful in many subject areas.

Artists' Resources

Byrne, D. (1986). *True stories.* NY: Penguin.
  This book gives a description of Byrne's movie with storyboard, costume, and characterization drawings. Very relevant for students who may know Byrne as a rock musician (Talking Heads).

Celant, C., Oldenburg, C., & van Bruggen, C. (1988). *A bottle of notes and some voyages.*
  Visual notes for large-scale sculptural projects, information on collaborative proposals, and exhibition photos are shared.

Kahlo, F. (1995). *The diary of Frida Kahlo: An intimate self portrait.* NY: Abrams.
  A facsimile of Kahlo's visual and verbal thoughts describing her life are presented in diary format.

Midda, S. (1990). *Sara Midda's south of France: A sketchbook.* NY: Workman.
  A painter's visual journey through the atmosphere and daily events of one year are richly shown in sketches of places and things discovered in the south of France.

McLean, M. A. (1987). *Mary Anne's garden drawings & writings.* NY: Abrams.
  This book of wonderful sequential drawings of daily and sometimes hourly observations of plants and animals in context connects art and the sciences.

Price, D. *Moonlight Chronicles.*
  This magazine chronicles one adventurer's daily experiences. It includes very positive comments on why drawing should be done every day and interesting contour sketches. Box 109, Joseph, OR 97646.

Taylor, J. (1986). *Beatrix Potter: Artist, storyteller and countrywoman*. NY: Frederick Warne.

Excerpts from Potter's journal (visual and verbal) and observational sketches provide the basis for the author's well-known characters.

Other artists' and adventurers' diaries/sketchbooks are available. Keep looking for examples of these types of journals while doing your own.

KEY TERMS

Analogy   A comparison showing similarity of features

Artistic strategy   Visual, spatial, or tactile incorporation of graphic images, symbols, or formats as the basis for communicating meaning concretely to yourself or others

Chart   A graphic representation of information

 ～ **Flow chart**   Continual, general process of information shown

 ～ **KWL chart**   Assessment of what is **K**nown, what is **W**anted, and what is **L**earned

 ～ **Organizational chart**   Displays reporting and responsibility structure of a group

 ～ **Pie chart**   Circular format with sections corresponding to various areas of information

 ～ **Sequence chart**   Specific serial changes of data shown in steps

 ～ **Stream chart**   Visual convergence of smaller sources into larger stream either vertically or horizontally

 ～ **Tree chart**   General information visually diverges into specifics (i.e., branching) either vertically or horizontally

Cluster (clustering)   A number of words or symbols growing out of a central symbol or word concept used in visual brainstorming (*see also Map and Web*)

Cubing   Activity that examines six sides of a subject three-dimensionally

Diagram   A drawing designed to explain how something works or to clarify parts of a whole

 ～ **Bubble diagram**   A diagram of connecting circles used by architects to show movement patterns

 ～ **Pictogram**   A diagram that represents quantity by comparing pictures of objects

 ～ **Venn diagram**   A diagram of two or more intersecting circles used to show the relationships among sets of information

Educational strategy   A directed way to reach a classroom or curriculum goal; a practical plan of action; a technique to solve an individual problem

Graph   A diagram representing a system of connections or information related in some way

 ～ **Bar graph**   Parallel bars of varying length and width used to illustrate comparisons horizontally or vertically

～ **Line graph**　A network of lines connecting various points

Graphic organizer　A summary of verbal and visual information indicating a relationship among ideas in chart, diagram, graph, map, or table format

Heuristic　Encouraging individual discovery or investigation

Isometric method　A method of projection showing an object in depth with angles of 30 degrees horizontally and 90 degrees vertically

Learned helplessness　Inadequacy as a result of cultural conditioning

Learning strategy　Any process that assists the learner in acquiring information or understanding

Mandala　A symbol representing the cosmos or self, usually organized in a bisected circular format

Map (mapping)　A drawing that represents the relationships between key topics and subtopics using symbols, words, color, and line quality to emphasize these connections; maps assist in recognizing, organizing, and recalling information (see also *Web*)

～ **Mind Map**　Registered trademark of The Buzan Centre, considered *the* tool for *externally* expressing thinking

～ **Picture map**　A map with symbols and arrows to show the sequence of events or important aspects of a story

Matrix　A rectangular arrangement of information into rows and columns (see also *Tables*)

Metamorphosis　A complete change of form

Metaphor　A word, a symbol, or an image that compares qualities not literally denoted

Note making　Process of organizing one's own thoughts

Note taking　Process of summarizing another's ideas

Orthogonal method　A method of projection showing each side's face view with all angles at 90 degrees

Rubric　A matrix used for evaluation

Sequence　A series; the following of one thing after another in succession

Sketch　A drawing done for planning and recording visual and verbal information

Table　The arrangement of words, numbers, or signs in parallel columns to exhibit a set of facts or relationships in a compact, comprehensive form (see also *Matrix*)

Teaching strategy　Any instructional effort that obtains a specific result

Time line　A visual sequence of events

Transformation　The act or process of changing form

Visual brainstorming　Individual or group activity to encourage associations without evaluating offerings, shown by clustering words or symbols around a central core concept

Visualizing　Recalling or forming mental images

Web (webbing)　A network of connecting data formed around a central idea (see also *Cluster* and *Map*)

CHAPTER 7

Shaping Elegant Problems for Visual Thinking

Sandra I. Kay
Teachers College, Columbia University

Guiding Questions

~ Who are the learners in my classroom?

~ What forms of thinking are meaningful in art?

~ How do I design the learning experience to fit my learners?

~ What are the characteristics of an elegant problem and how do they guide curriculum design?

You will always remember certain art studio assignments. If you are an artist, most likely the first assigned problem that comes to mind is one that presented you with a challenge and evoked a solution that pleased you. When some people are asked to recall an art lesson or experience, they quickly respond with the memory of a catastrophe that convinced them to go no further. Unfortunately, for many, this event occurs around fifth grade. Without confidence in their own art-making abilities, and with little opportunity to further their appreciation of art, many individuals think of art as a subject only for artists.

Who Are the Learners in My Classroom?

The role of appreciators of artistic creativity has received too little attention in art education practice. This lack of attention is found in all creative endeavors. According to Stein (1984), the creative process requires more than the individual. He describes this process as a transactional relationship between creative individuals and the public. He uses the term **contricipation** to describe the two major roles in the creative process: contribution and participation. Participators include intermediaries such as parents, teachers, or gallery owners that facilitate the success of the creative person. But there is also the audience:

> If the audience does not appreciate creativity and the creative person, then society's creativity will diminish markedly. . . . Composers could compose great music but no one would listen. Painters could paint magnificent paintings but no one would look at them, let alone buy them. Writers would write superb novels but no one would read them. (Stein, 1984, p. 31)

The participant in the creative process must be able to appreciate how a problem is selected and formed, how it is worked out and tested, and how the results and solution are communicated to others.

The concept of contricipation is important to the structure and design of the assignments you choose for your students. Shaping problems that provide effective memories for both the contributor and the participant requires careful consideration. An elegant problem provides an opportunity for many excellent responses or solutions from a variety of problem solvers.

Lesson Scenario

The following fourth-grade lesson scenario provides a context for the discussion on shaping *elegant* problems for visual thinking. A clay unit had been introduced weeks ago, with all three assignments and the agenda on the blackboard:

> Problem 1: Netsuke or miniatures; techniques: wedging and forming; A. demonstration: dinosaur/bird; B. work time
>
> Problem 2: ornament, jewelry, or glaze tile; techniques: slip and scoring (addition and subtraction); A. demonstration of each; B. work time
>
> Problem 3: container (other than ashtray); techniques: planning and patternmaking; A. demonstration: mug; B. work time

Never having experienced clay, these fourth graders had learned the basics of wedging, sculpting, and additive/subtractive surface decorations with the previous two assignments. We had worked up to the long-term lesson that we were about to begin.

Several of the 30 students brought in their sketches to preempt time spent on planning and increase time with clay. One young sculptor accompanied her sketches with the necessary pattern pieces cut from newspaper. Attentively quiet, the class anticipated the 5–10-minute discussion/demonstration that preceded individual work time. Building a slab-constructed mug using a rectangular pattern was demonstrated. Five precut patterns were available for interested students, but handles required individual designs. Options of slab and sculpted coil handles were displayed and demonstrated. Then, those with advanced preparation were asked to hold up their sketches for everyone to see. Designs ranged from candy jars with lids to a clay house.

One student pointed to John's sketch, exclaiming that his was not a container. Moving closer to the disagreement brewing, I noticed John's drawing was of an old man sitting by a tree with an engaged fishing pole. With pride in often being correct, Danny adamantly reminded the class that a container had to hold something. John's sketch was of a sculpture, not a container.

John rarely spoke and often appeared aloof during class discussions. Approaching gently, I queried him: "John, this does look like a drawing for a sculpture. Is it?" John nodded. With sincerity, I asked, "How is a sculpture a container?" This fourth grader explained, "If a sculpture contains a feeling or a memory, then it is also a container. Isn't it?" Everyone, including Danny, understood.

A shiver reached my spine as I realized that John had managed to expose his fourth-grade classmates to a level of thought embodied in advanced philosophical discourse (Langer, 1953a). Word of this interpretation spread throughout the grade levels. Discussions were overheard by classroom teachers in hallways throughout the school. Other sketches for sculptures appeared in subsequent classes. The topic even reached the teachers' room, where I was questioned regarding my teaching strategy for such a difficult concept. I credited John.

Several weeks later, during a visit from John's mother, I learned that his inspiration to stretch the problem definition came from his need to fill a void from the recent loss of his grandfather. Working through the grief of losing his soulmate, John spent every free moment at capturing the memories. John's mother had come in to personally thank me for being so flexible about altering or making an exception to the assignment. I explained that the problem was good enough to not require revision if exceptionally advanced thought was applied, as her son had demonstrated.

Modestly, her discussion continued around John's profoundly high IQ and his interest in advanced mathematics and science. Although capable as a young child, John had never held a particular interest for art. However, since the class discussion had occurred, he had accepted his parents' standing offer to go to art museums. Hours during the past two weekends had been spent looking at sculptures, particularly the funerary statues in the Egyptian wing. Believing that a scientist must be cultured, his parents were profoundly pleased with this change in attitude—thus the personal visit of thanks.

Although the lesson remained monumental for John through high school, his response had altered my perception of the potential range of capabilities at the fourth-grade level. Particularly for students at the high end of conceptual development, opportunities to discover abilities requisite to advanced understanding of art must be made available to students prior to Lowenfeld's recommendation of age 11.

Affective Dimension of Learning

Designing problems that provide meaningful encounters in art for all students must begin at a point just beyond the student's current level of ability and experience. However, the range of abilities and degrees of art experiences within a given class may be extreme. Naturally, most art teachers try to provide a challenge that is meaningful to the artistically creative child. Art education practice often mirrors the curriculum design that guides most studio coursework. The assumption that all children enjoy expressing themselves through visual art experiences may be questioned upon encountering a child with severe emotional difficulties or a child who excels in problems that require correct responses. These situations occur more frequently at the elementary levels, where students cannot opt out of art classes.

These potential appreciators and consumers of art, rather than the future producers, are the most challenging to reach. In developing creative, open-ended lessons for these students, teachers may find some of the lessons beyond the students' realm of understanding. The subsequent feelings of anxiety or alienation produce either disruptive behavior or disinterest (disengagement). No doubt, these negative feelings affect learning.

The affective dimension of learning is described in Csikszentmihalyi's "flow construct" of intrinsic motivation (1982). He suggests that when activity is at an appropriate level of difficulty for a child's current level of skill, learning and advancement are internally motivated (see Figure 7.1). Therefore, when a challenging task or understanding is mastered, a sense of pleasure as well as new knowledge is gained by the individual.

This flow state is that familiar experience of total absorption that occurs during creative activity when there is no sense of time and all that matters is before you. Csikszentmihalyi sees the flow construct as containing important implications for understanding the dynamics of growth. The level of challenge in a task must provide and maintain this flow state. To provide the intrinsic pleasure of learning in the flow channel, the challenge cannot be greater than the child's current skill level or the learner may feel too anxious about his or her ability to succeed. This feeling occurs when the task is too high on the task difficulty axis for the child. In contrast, if the learner's skill level has developed beyond the demands of the task, the child's motivation will drop below the flow channel into the realm of boredom. Either way, the benefits of the learning experience are lessened. Thus, the curriculum challenge is to provide the opportunity for each child to maintain the balance necessary to preserve the intrinsic pleasure of learning that occurs within his or her flow channel.

The clay container lesson exemplifies an appropriate width for the channel crossing. Designed to address the need for a low level of task difficulty by providing the mug pattern as an answer to the challenge of creating a container, the assignment forced a small step forward by requiring choices to be made regarding technique and design of

Figure 7.1
Flow Diagram of Motivational Theory

Adapted from Csikszentmihalyi, M., & Csikszentmihalyi, I. S. (Eds.). (1988). *Optimal experience: Psychological studies of flow in consciousness*. New York: Cambridge University Press.

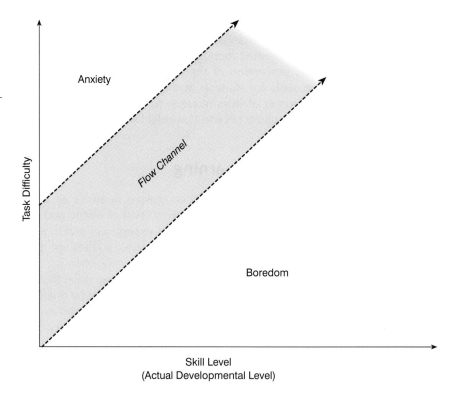

the mug handle. For some students, this was the optimal level of challenge at this time in their development. John took a very high road, making an unexpected leap. The adequacy of the design of the problem was demonstrated in this flexibility.

Social Dimensions of Learning

The developmental approach to learning in art, as described by Lowenfeld (1947), provides a ballpark in which to begin planning appropriate problems. But the huge variation in individual expressive capability within each stage, and apparent in any given classroom, requires further understanding. Vygotsky (1978) provided a theory of intellectual development that explains various mechanisms affecting individual approaches to problem solving. Abstract thought requires advanced intellectual development, or higher-level thinking skills. One way of developing abstract thought (whether verbal or visual) is by creating imaginary situations (Vygotsky, 1978). Children create imaginary situations through play and art. Therefore, learning in art occurs in relation to cognitive development.

Vygotsky believed that cognitive development originated from social interaction, which progressively led to the internalization of knowledge. He felt that all higher mental processes (such as visual thinking) begin as social processes whereby a particular behavior is first demonstrated and then requested by another individual (e.g., teacher) before it becomes internalized. Thus, cognitive development goes from other-regulation to self-regulation of behavior. This theoretical framework appears to support the value Lowenfeld (1947) originally placed on imitation. From this viewpoint, Vygotsky (1978) felt "that the only 'good learning' is that which is in advance of development" (p. 89).

As introduced earlier, based on this belief, assignments must be just beyond the child's current level of problem-solving skill. Research has demonstrated that the capability to learn under a teacher's guidance varies tremendously in children with equal levels of mental development. This area of fluctuation is described as the "zone of proximal development" (ZPD) and is defined as "the distance between the actual developmental level as determined by independent problem solving and the level of potential development as determined through problem solving under adult guidance or in collaboration with more capable peers" (Vygotsky, 1978, p. 86).

Theoretically, the zone of proximal development within each child varies in relationship to his or her intellectual ability (Csikszentmihalyi, 1982; Kanevsky, 1992). Supporting this theory, one can cite John's response to the clay container problem and his high IQ score. However, the static scores on IQ tests are not of interest in Vygotsky's dynamic assessment approach. Vygotsky was interested in presenting a set of tasks that were taught, then assessing how quickly the learner took ownership of the learning. In Vygotskian terms, it was John's behavior, when presented with the assignment, that demonstrated advanced intellectual ability. The zone of proximal development concept is clearly depicted by the contagious spread of the idea that a sculpture is a container because it holds feelings or memories.

This type of performance assessment is particularly relevant to classroom instruction. Presenting a problem and monitoring how quickly and conceptually advanced the students' solutions are informs student assessment procedures. If the shape of the problem is too complex or too simple for a particular student, as Csikszentmihalyi's "flow construct" indicates, the quality of the solution could be affected by reduced intrinsic motivation. Many context-specific factors must be considered when designing the elegant problem for your curriculum purposes. Knowing the various shapes that problems can take will help define the menu of choices to consider.

The cultural context.   A good comedian knows how to read an audience. A good art educator must do the same. An incident in one of my graduate classes exemplifies the importance of knowing your audience. In telling their teaching stories as an introduction to this course, my students provided a brief description of their encounters. One woman began by describing her first year in a very rural school district where logging is the major industry. The population was economically poor and interested only in sports, and she taught K–12 classes in a room with very few supplies. She said that had she not left for her current position as a middle school art teacher in a less rural area, she would have left teaching.

Another member of the class jumped in by stating that she had just finished her first year in a school district like the one just described. But this teacher had found the experience exhilarating. Although the community was poor, the people were industrious with their time, and their meager leisure activities involved outdoor events (e.g., hunting and fishing). She found the natural environment spectacular, a view shared by most other community members. Inspired by the surrounding beauty, the teacher began the year with a drawing unit on landscapes. The Hudson River School and other American painters (e.g., Remington, Sargent, Wyeth) were introduced. All of her classes spent September outside recording acute observations of seasonal changes in their world through drawing. This led to storytelling and narrative drawings (see Chapter 5, "Encouraging Visual Storytelling"). Enthralled by the ability to capture important events such as football games, log rolling competitions, and so on, this teacher found her students carrying sketchbooks to every community event. The community embraced her and art by providing donations of wood for carving sculptures, assisting her with a unit on papermaking, and demonstrating traditional crafts such as quilting and lacemaking.

The capstone of this story came when these two beginning teachers identified their school districts—both had taught in the same place! The successful teacher had designed her curriculum to match the audience. Few of us teach in such a homogeneous community, but the lesson is clear. Community-based art education is a concept worthy of attention (see London, 1994).

Cognitive Dimensions of Learning

Although the expressive qualities of art making are often discussed, attention to thinking skills in art education also has an extensive history (Dorn, 1994). Arnheim (1969) suggests that the imagination necessary to engage in artistic problem solving requires abstract thought. If we are to systematically develop abstract thought in our students, we must understand the cognitive processes associated with thinking in art. A theoretical framework that provides a more comprehensive understanding of the complexity of the learning process can be found in the research on individual differences in cognitive development.

The approach that a learner takes to an assignment involves the use of problem-solving strategies, which are integral to the study of thinking. Two main factors influence the problem-solving strategies used in any situation: the nature of the problem and the nature or experience of the problem solver. The dimensions of the learner's experience precede discussion of the nature or forms of problems.

The role of expertise.   Individuals respond to problems differently. The way individuals initially perceive a given situation or problem is affected by prior experience. This prior experience directs the response. In an art studio curriculum, we provide a problem or assignment and expect individual interpretations to emerge. Cognitive scientists, seeking to identify the necessary elements of critical and creative thought, focus on the level of **expertise** of the problem solver. Studies on expertise may prove quite valuable to art educators seeking explanations for the differences observed between the behaviors of the artistically talented and those of other learners in the classroom.

Newell and Simon (1972) use the term "problem space" to describe the internal response to a stimulus situation. The problem space defined by an individual in a particular situation affects the formulation of the problem. The initial perception of a problem or the problem space seems to differ depending on the level of expertise acquired. De Groot (1965) found that expert chess players perceived the board positions in terms of broad arrangements or patterns, whereas the novice players did not. Research in physics yielded a similar difference between expert and novice scientists, which was described as a difference between "deep and surface structures" to a problem (Chi, Feltovich, & Glaser, 1981). Experts in physics identify problems as similar if they perceive the principles used to solve the problems as similar. This is a similarity in "deep structure." Novices, on the other hand, perceive similarities that are related to "surface structure," such as comparing the same terms or objects used in two problems.

The age difference between expert and novice problem solvers in the previous studies led Schoenfeld and Herrmann (1982) to conduct a study in which students of the same age participated in a mathematical problem-solving experiment. The experimental group received training in problem solving, while the control group did not. The result from this analysis was compared with the responses from expert mathematicians. Students, after participating in the problem-solving training, had more responses of a deep structural nature that corresponded with the responses of experts. These results offer more direct evidence of a relationship between problem perception and expertise. Although as art educators in K–12 classrooms we will most likely not often encounter a student with highly developed expertise as an artist, it is important to know as much as possible about the destination if we are to help direct those aimed for such a goal.

Characteristics of a learning moment.   Whole classes can become absorbed in a moment of learning. Have you ever observed an entire class so totally absorbed that you could literally hear a pin drop? Have you ever watched a child play a computer game for hours? These symptoms describe the behavior of engagement during the flow experience described earlier. Spending time observing his own children hooked on Nintendo, a reflective educator proposed that the attraction was based on sound teaching theory put into practice (Moscati, 1993). His analysis of the activity highlights characteristics of any good learning moment:

⌁ Learning occurs in a personal and individual way, which includes options for personally controlled pace (accelerated or remedial), the amount of repetition, and degree of challenge.

⌁ Assessments are frequent, with a focus on progress without failure or cynicism. (Mistakes are opportunities to continue learning, and learning occurs without humiliation.)

⌁ Learning allows for the reinforcement of personal integrity.

⌁ Learning contains elements of surprise, adventure, excitement, and humor.

⌁ Learning is outcome based and assumes that everyone will register the highest levels of achievement.

- ~ A good learning moment generates its own enthusiasm for personal learning, instilling a sense of self-challenge, desire for greater challenges, and a sense of self-satisfaction (even triumph) upon completion.
- ~ The activity allows practice and cooperative learning in groups.
- ~ A good learning moment assumes that effort is all that is necessary to learn what is needed.

Empowering the learner to take ownership of his or her own learning requires attending to the affective and social dimensions of learning. An educator who has experienced the phenomenon of engaging an entire class at a level that reaches the silence necessary to hear that proverbial pin drop becomes hooked on the magic of teaching. More of us could capture memories of such moments through reflective writing and written self-evaluations. Recognizing the merit in such activities, one principal coaxed teachers into record keeping by asking them to keep reflective teaching journals and using the technique as an official evaluation tool (Goffman, 1995). Focusing on successful strategies, these journals add fuel to the fire necessary for the creative energies required in teaching.

As with any art form, the art of teaching is complex and multifaceted. With so much to learn, one can feel quite overwhelmed at times. In developing any new skill, this spiraling learning process toward the goal of developing expertise as a teacher involves practice and critique. Beyond the student teaching experience, most evaluations of your classroom practice will come from you. Too often, self-evaluation begins by addressing the disappointments. The one question that seems to surprise my student teachers and novices trying to analyze a less-than-successful lesson is "What went well?" or "What did you do right?" Yet, it is the answers to these questions that help one identify and define the necessary ingredients to repeat the formula for more successful teaching moments. As the ceramicist records the ingredients of an experimental glaze formula for later analysis, knowing what part of the lesson works well informs future directions.

~ What Forms of Thinking Are Meaningful in Art?

Many art educators view their role as one of introducing students to the way artists think—they present artistic problems and then cultivate artistic behaviors. Traditionally, the knowledge of how artists think has been gleaned from exposure to art history, criticism, and the teachers' personal experiences with making meaning in an art form. Although not extensive, research on the creative thought processes of artists offers further insight for the art educator (Carroll, 1994; Kay, n.d.; Pariser, 1985). Knowledge of the nature of expertise in the field can enhance the learning of a novice or assist the nonartist's appreciation of the complexity of thought involved in producing ideas in art. Although we accept the practice of studying studio techniques from experts, art educators do not necessarily study the expert thought processes of eminent artists.

Unlike children's engagement with art as they explore through trial and error, the visual language (Goodman, 1968) spoken by the artist must be mastered to eloquently guide the perception of its viewers. To achieve this mastery, the artist must have a working knowledge of the perceptual schema (pattern) in which information is transferred to the mind. A simple example would be using the knowledge that grayed colors recede to provide depth to a painted surface. With every decision, the artist selects information that the viewer attends (Arnheim, 1974; Goodman, 1968; Kaufman, 1966; Winner, 1982). This selection process becomes deliberate and calculated, with organizational rules used or discarded with meticulous care.

What Is Visual Thinking?

Most people would say that visual thinking is thinking in images, *seeing in the mind's eye.* Some people like to think with numbers; many like to think with words. Artists, it is believed, think with images. The word *imagination* is defined as "the act or power of forming a mental image of something not present to the senses or never before wholly perceived in reality" (*Webster's Ninth New Collegiate Dictionary*). One can form a mental image using pictures/figures, words, or numbers. As art educators, we seek to encourage and develop the imaginations of our students. So, if we are talking about visual thinking as thinking in images, the topic is important to prospective art educators. But this is only the simplified answer.

Arnheim (1969) coined the term **visual thinking,** defining it as visual perception (p. 14). Like visual perception, visual thinking is far more complex than the ability to think with images. As educators engaged with developing visual symbol systems and their role in an individual's imagination, it is important that you have a bit more than a cursory notion of visual thinking. In this chapter I will take a closer look at what has been said about visual thinking and perception, their roles in creative thought, and the potential role of the arts in developing productive and inventive thought. To do so will involve reviewing some of the ideas in art, psychology, communication, and science.

The Role of Perception in Thinking

Perception involves information obtained through the senses. The visual arts have informed the world of science on the nature of perception throughout history. Scientists acknowledge artists by using their work as exemplars to define or support perceptual theory (see Bateson, 1979; Gibson, 1960). Three different perceptual theories contribute to the description of visual perception (see Kay, 1990, for a review), but each offers various reasons for individual differences in the way information is perceived. A rose may be a rose, but your perception of that flower will be different from another viewer's perception, especially if the rose is red and the other viewer is color blind. In addition, more subtle differences occur: one viewer may note the velvety texture; another may be inspired by the form of the rose.

Beyond physical differences in perception, cultural and psychological factors affect perception. For example, in many African cultures size in pictorial representations is relative to importance, not distance. Contrarily, in an image of two people with one larger than the other, your perception would most likely be that one was farther away, not less important. It is critical to know that this is not the interpretation of all cultures, especially in a multicultural classroom. Another example can be found in perceived space as it significantly differs between Western and Eastern cultures. Hall (1966) describes one example: "In the West, man perceives the objects but not the spaces between. In Japan, the spaces are perceived, and revered as the *ma,* or intervening interval" (p. 70). Many cultural variations are documented in the literature of cultural anthropology.

Perception can be affected by both cognitive and affective characteristics of the learner. If one is taught to attend to the perception of textures, one will be aware of subtle variations (a necessary skill in microbiology). The tendency of an individual to select perceptual clues or make choices about what to attend to (such as the form rather than the color of the rose) brings affective characteristics into the picture (Kaufman, 1966). Personality, values, and interests are believed to play a part in the selective perception of each individual. This may be far more difficult for psychologists to prove scientifically than it is to accept as an anecdotal observation by a thoughtful art educator. As exemplified in a contour line drawing assignment of a shoe (see Figure 7.2), four variations depict different sensory emphases beyond capturing the form with line. Of these four upper elementary students, one noted the colors (Figure 7.2a), one emphasized textures (Figure 7.2b), another focused on form (Figure 7.2c), and the fourth indicated sensitivity to the light source (Figure 7.2d). Now look at two studies by a sixth-grade student (Figure 7.2e–f). Compare these with the integrated work of a study by an eleventh-grade student (Figure 7.2g).

Once perceived, memory, past experiences, and our thoughts and feelings begin to work on the mental images initially stored. Research has shown that the mental images we store in our minds are different from the idiosyncratic perception of information from the senses. Empirical evidence supports the belief that mental images reflect the way information is organized in long-term memory as analyzed representations. The organizational principles of long-term memory are now generally accepted as influencing perception and mental imagery. In other words, memory and thought act upon our perceptions to produce images in our minds. Three types of imagery theories offer different explanations for the apparent pictorial and spatial qualities of mental images (see Finke, 1985, for a comprehensive review). All three support the belief that mental imagery fundamentally resembles perception.

From this background knowledge, several major points are worthy of consideration when designing learning in art. First, the act of perceiving sensory information is a complex process. For most species, perception is a tool of survival. Yet the biological, cultural, and personal characteristics of an individual appear to affect his or her visual perception, creating the potential for large individual differences to occur at perhaps the most basic level—the reception of information obtained through the senses. This is important to the art educator seeking to develop visual perception. In fact, the art room is an excellent laboratory for observing perceptual difficulties that affect learning. Detecting perceptual difficulties, informing the special education staff, and providing compensation strategies are important contributions provided by the sensitive art educator.

Second, research has attempted to specify the relationship between sensory perception and the phenomenon of mental imagery. Although the exact nature of the relationship is not clear, imagery researchers agree that the relationship is strong. The notion that perception plays a role in intelligence was established less than a century ago (El Koussy, 1935; Spearman, 1927). Prior to the popularization of a theory of multiple intelligences (Gardner, 1983), the study of intelligence addressed thinking in images with descriptors such as spatial ability, visualization, figural information, and nonverbal thought.

In fact, the distinction between abstract reasoning using words and abstract reasoning involving figures was so clearly delineated that some intelligence tests were designed to measure them separately. IQ tests such as the Cognitive Abilities Test (COGAT) provide subscores for verbal (facility with words), quantitative (facility with numbers), and nonverbal (facility with figures or images) reasoning power. The differences among scores on the three subtests can be as great as 50 points. Proportionately higher scores on the nonverbal subtest appear to be characteristic of many artistically able students, although a formal study of this potential relationship would be an important contribution to the field.

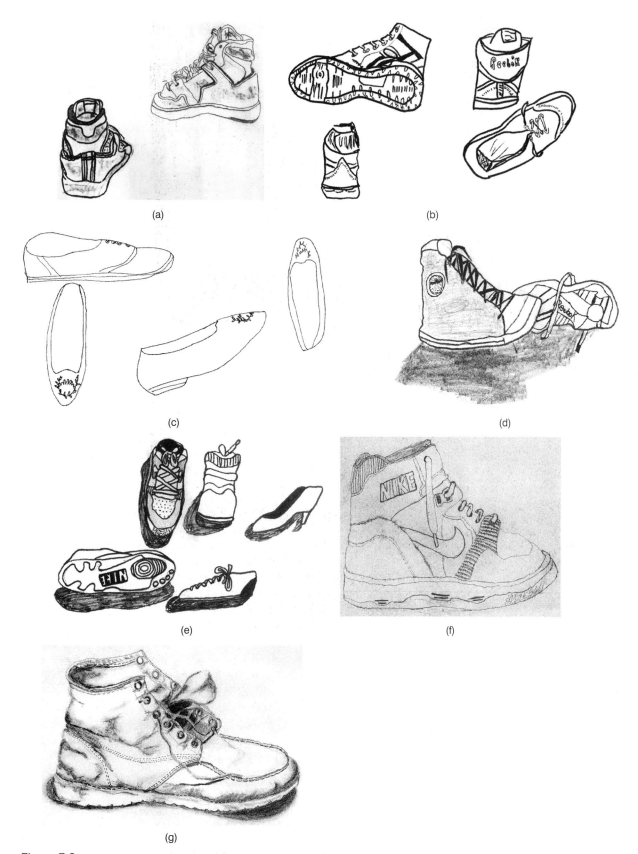

(a)

(b)

(c)

(d)

(e)

(f)

(g)

Figure 7.2
Samples of contour line drawings: shoe assignment. Upper elementary students (a–f; fourth through sixth grade) focused on different sensory emphases as compared with an eleventh grader's solution (g; in pencil).

269

Who Thinks Visually?

Several studies of the biographies of eminent scientists and mathematicians (e.g., Nobel laureates) reveal an intimate relationship with the arts (Root-Bernstein, 1989). The imaginative ability of these scientists occurs in artistic accomplishments as well as in their scientific endeavors. Note the following:

> Copernicus was a painter who also translated poetry. Galileo had intended to be an artist as a teenager, and wrote poetry throughout his life. Newton, too, painted and wrote poetry. . . . We've heard that Louis Pasteur was a gifted painter as a youth. (Root-Bernstein, 1989, p. 317)

Believing that there is a relationship between engaging in an art form and making creative contributions to a scientific field, Root-Bernstein (1989) is compiling a list that already includes several hundred eminent scientists with artistic proclivities.

A visual-spatial strategy (often referred to as nonverbal thought) may be necessary to capture the essence of the whole form to define a problem. Research (Ferguson, 1978) involved with the inventiveness of the scientific process has cited this type of strategy as necessary to creative endeavors in that field:

> As the scientific component of knowledge in technology has increased markedly in the 19th and 20th centuries, the tendency has been to lose sight of the crucial part played by nonverbal knowledge in making the "big" decisions of form, arrangement, and texture that determine the parameters within which a system will operate. (p. 46)
>
> This intellectual component of technology, which is nonliterary and nonscientific, has been generally unnoticed because its origins lie in art and not in science. (p. 64)

Art educators aware of the importance of nonverbal, or visual, thinking in scientific endeavors can make the kinds of connections necessary to engage scientifically oriented students in art by shaping the problems (assignments) to develop visual thinking strategies. More important, understanding the role of visual thinking outside the realm of art assists art educators in making real-life connections between the nonartist and the tools of thought developed through engagement in art.

Why Is Visual Thinking Important?

Cognitive psychologists describe three different ways we mentally represent and process information: linguistically, numerically, and visually, or spatially. Sternberg (1986) suggests that a thorough conceptual understanding is demonstrated when an idea can be represented in words, numbers, and images. The mental representation of information through images describes a major component of visual thinking (Arnheim, 1969), spatial ability (Smith, 1964), and spatial thinking (Dixon, 1983; Olson, 1992). Some empirical evidence supports the theory of a visual-spatial thinking strategy that is inherently different from the strategies used with verbal information (Kay, 1989).

Thinking with images has been cited as the most effective strategy for critical thinking skills associated with certain reasoning and insight problems (Sternberg, 1986). However, thinking with images is more often associated with the problem-solving strategies used in creative thought (Arnheim, 1969; Perkins, 1981). So, visual thinking can be used for both critical and creative thought.

Research in critical and creative thought has potential for influencing the perceived importance of an education in art. Information processing research began as an attempt to reproduce human thought processes in inanimate objects—namely, computer technology. In an attempt to reproduce thinking and **creativity**, scientists are seeking to identify the nature of human thought processes. The most important discovery in scientific research on seeking to develop creative thought in machines is that affective characteristics (personality, emotions, and other very human attributes) influence these thought processes. From the knowledge gained in the field of artificial intelligence, educators can learn more about facilitating the development of thought processes in their students.

Problem-Solving Theory: What Shapes Do Problems Take?

Some theories on problem solving concentrate on creative problem solving, while others address critical thought. Each theory categorizes problems into different types. Each type of problem requires a different problem-solving approach. For example, when shown a slide during an art history exam and asked to identify the artist acknowledged for that painting, the art history instructor is seeking one specific answer. This problem is called a closed, or well-defined, problem because it is clearly stated and requires a specific answer. On the other hand, if an art history instructor requires a final project that demonstrates thorough understanding of any pertinent topic of your choice, you are faced with an open-ended, or ill-defined, problem. Deciding what you will choose to study and what form the product will take (e.g., term paper, video, slide presentation) offers opportunities to formulate your own problem.

Theoretically, problems are often categorized in terms of placement on an imagined continuum. On one extreme of this continuum lie closed problems, with open problems located on the opposite end (Reitman, 1964; Sternberg, 1982). Closed problems are clearly formulated and require specific solutions (e.g., the task of copying a drawing). Open problems are structured to accommodate multiple perspectives, are not as clearly formulated as closed problems, and require working toward discovering the problem situation prior to pursuing a solution (e.g., an advanced independent study course in sculpture). The thought process (or cognitive skill) associated with the approach to an open problem is described as **problem finding.**

More specifically, problem finding involves the formulation of a problem prior to the actions taken to solve the problem (Kay, 1989). In this circumstance, the solution to the problem is directed by the choices made by the individual in his or her chosen definition of the problem. In their seminal work, Getzels and Csikszentmihalyi (1976) described the difference between **problem solving** and problem finding in creative thought as the difference between presented and discovered problems. A presented problem requires following routine steps using a particular method to arrive at a known solution. On the opposite end of the scale, discovered problems do not have specific requirements, so the problem solver must identify the problem and choose methods to arrive at solutions that satisfy the situation.

Wakefield (1992) has classified four different types of thinking skills involved in problem solving and problem finding by combining the types of problems with the types of solutions required. He presents a fourfold classification "based on the degree of constraint imposed on problems and their solutions" (p. 27). He explains that logical thinking is required when constraints are given to the problem and the solution. If asked to produce a value scale employing 10 gradations of grey, logical thinking is employed. Divergent thinking occurs when a closed problem (e.g., draw something in each of the 12 circles provided) has few rules or constraints on the solution. Creative thinking occurs when the freedom of the problem and the solution are not constrained. Optimal freedom of problem choice is the context in which an artist discovers and engages with ideas in the studio. When an open-ended problem is presented to an individual (e.g., a class assignment or commission), the position moves toward the closed end of the problem-solving continuum.

Problem finding or defining is a common element in most of the theories that propose steps to creative thought. Creativity is an interesting topic, with varying perspectives within and across disciplines. The three broad categories of creativity research (the three Ps of creativity) involve personality, product, and (thought) processes. The studies considered classic in this body of literature that directly relate to artists focus on the creative personality (Ghiselin, 1952; Koestler, 1964). Since a teacher cannot direct personality traits, it is the processes involved in creative action that hold the greatest potential for educational research and translation to classroom practice.

The Thought Processes of Artists

Most of the research on creativity that enlists the expertise of the artist takes the form of personal accounts and retrospective reports (Ghiselin, 1952; Koestler, 1964; Roe, 1975). Scientists argue that this type of data is subjective and inaccurate. Although some empirical research exists on the artistic productivity of children, only a few studies enlist the cooperation of artists as participants in research on the creative process, and of these few, most focused on personality rather than process. Here I give a brief review of studies less likely to be found in the art education literature.

Roe (1946, 1975) conducted a study on personality traits and the effects of alcohol on the creative process with 20 male artists. She categorized into four groups the descriptions given on the way a new painting was developed and noted a tendency for the creative process to differ among and within individuals, implying the lack of one consistent "process." Beittel and Burkhardt (1963) studied personality attributes of 47 college juniors majoring in art education and noted three approach strategies to drawing: academic, spontaneous, and divergent. These authors reported that their findings support a distinction between problem discovery and problem solving.

Possibly the first empirical study seeking to identify the process behind the creative thought rather than the creative personality of artists was done by Patrick (1937) when she observed 50 professional artists and 50 nonartists (as a control) sketch pictures based on a poem they were given. A detailed analysis of the process, enlisting verbal feedback, formed the core of the research procedure. This study reported two important results. First, she found no difference between the two groups in the amount of time they spent on the tasks (quantitative differences) but major differences in the quality of the results. Second, the problem-solving processes for both groups were described as periods of unorganized and organized thought (p. 67).

The thought processes described by Getzels and Csikszentmihalyi (1964, 1976) as problem finding and problem solving appear similar to those described by Patrick as unorganized and organized. In their original work (1964), the sample consisted of 179 sophomore and junior college art students with three fields of specialization: fine art, applied arts, and art education. Both male and female subjects were included in this core population. Because of the variations in performance among the groups, the problem-finding process was thoroughly examined in only male fine art students (N = 31).

Getzels and Csikszentmihalyi (1976) realized the potential in observing the discovered problem situation (open ended) in that it is closely related to the artistic process. A problem offering 27 objects for possible use in a still-life drawing was individually presented to 31 male art students. The instructions stated that the task was untimed, although the participants were encouraged to complete their work in "an hour or so" (p. 85). Although a discovered problem situation was presented, behavioral differences in the approach implied a crucial difference between those students seeking "to maximize the discovered nature of the task" and those who behaved as though they were in a "presented problem situation" (p. 90).

Questions arise when comparing the results of the Patrick study with this one. Although there were differences in qualities, Patrick did not find differences between the artists and the nonartists in the amount of time spent before engaging in the actual drawing or in the total amount of time spent on the entire task. Yet, in comparing creative and less creative college art students, Getzels and Csikszentmihalyi found major differences between the two in these problem-solving behaviors. Also, Patrick found that the artists did not change the essential structure of their work but only revised the surface structure. The art students identified as more creative in the Getzels and Csikszentmihalyi study were said to be more willing to change their entire product. Where Patrick found the nonartists to incorporate more objects into their sketches than the artists, the latter study found that those defined as more creative manipulated more of the still-life objects prior to initiating the drawing.

One possible reason for the discrepancy in the findings between these two studies is that the participants may be at different stages of their development. The thought processes of a second-year college art student are not likely to be at the most advanced level of expertise. The skills and behaviors of professional artists may differ considerably from those with less experience because their intense experience provides them with knowledge of what will fail, eliminating the need for extensive explorations.

The first possibility was examined in a study of the problem-solving and problem-finding behaviors of professional artists, semiprofessional artists, and nonartists (Kay, 1989). The purpose of the study was to explore the relationship between problem solving (the process of finding a solution to a stated problem) and problem finding (the process of formulating a problem prior to taking actions to solve the problem) in the manipulation of figural symbol systems by three groups of adults with varying degrees of expertise in art. (The possibility of qualitative differences in the approaches taken by these groups was supported in the literature on experts versus novices discussed earlier in this chapter.)

Sixty participants were selected, representing three independent groups. Of the 20 in each group, 10 were male and 10 were female. Twenty adult visual artists—10 sculptors and 10 painters—who regularly exhibit their work in museums or galleries and earn their living solely through the production of art made up the group of professional artists. The group of semiprofessionals consisted of individuals who had formal art training beyond high school, produced ideas in art, exhibited in galleries, but did not earn their living producing ideas in art. The nonartists were graduate students in education and psychology, had no formal art training since high school, and reported that they did not produce ideas in art under any circumstances.

These participants were given a series of tasks to complete. The entire process was videotaped and played back for the participants so their observations, thoughts, and responses could be audiotaped in an interview. The procedure, data analysis, and complete results are published elsewhere (Kay, 1989, 1991). The empirical study began with an examination of the proficiency variables highlighted in the earlier research by Patrick and/or Getzels and Csikszentmihalyi.

Like Getzels and Csikszentmihalyi's (1976) more creative art students, the professional artists were expected to take longer, pause more, and design more transformations than the semiprofessional artists, who would, in turn, outperform the nonartists in the same manner. This was not the case. The significant differences between the groups existed between the semiprofessional artists and the other two groups. The semiprofessionals behaved in the same manner as the art students involved in the Getzels and Csikszentmihalyi study. However, based on these initial variables, the professional artists did not differ from the nonartists. Patrick's (1937) study of creative thought in artists and nonartists supports the results of this study in that she found no quantitative differences between these two groups in the overall time spent on the drawing task.

The **qualitative** differences between Patrick's artists and nonartists were replicated through the process variables identified and analyzed using the videotaped recordings. In fact, the two-stage process of problem solving sketched by Patrick as unorganized and organized thought and later redrawn by Getzels and Csikszentmihalyi as the Problem Formulation Stage and Problem Solution Stage was found in these open-ended tasks that did not involve drawing.

The differences in the problem-finding behaviors of the three groups were analyzed. A strategy of considering many perspectives of various alternatives characterized the behavior patterns of the artists. For example, the artists would describe a decision that might involve the analysis of several variables (e.g., wrong color, right shape, good angle, "but then needs a contrasting form emerging from the right of the piece"). In contrast, the nonartist usually reported a focus on only one option, such as color, and ignored other dimensions. The nonartists were quite different from the other two groups in their approach to problem finding in that they employed fewer dimensions and viewed fewer perspectives. This implies a more narrow approach to problem defining. The strategy employed by the two groups of artists may be described as a visual-spatial thought process. Rather than directing a limited amount of information toward a goal that is sequentially determined or decided, a process of simultaneously addressing a large quantity of information is depicted.

The professional and semiprofessional artists differed because the semiprofessional artists handled many more game pieces, explored the materials, paused more, and made more changes in position or types of pieces than the professional artists. Like the expert chess masters studied by de Groot, greater depth and breadth of experience may provide a less likely chance for unsuccessful attempts or changes because of knowledge of what would fail. It is likely that the professional artists have more opportunities than semiprofessional artists to manipulate figural information and to make and learn from mistakes.

Another phenomenon not described in the expert/novice or creativity literature also appears to be reflected here. Based on the observations and interviews, the professional artists who participated in the study exhibited a behavior that I labeled a "personal aesthetic preference." The result of an artist's personal aesthetic preference forms the work or oeuvre that makes a Monet a Monet or a Dali a Dali. The artist's personal aesthetic framework seems to form an organizing principle for the professional artists' perceptual information gathering and consequent thought processes. This **aesthetic** appears to guide the search for specific information, providing a selective criterion within which one explores (Campbell, 1960). This personal aesthetic preference behaves like the engineering of a fine bridge, offering tensile strength to the pursuit of an idea. As in steel structures, this tensile strength supports the endeavor, yet it bends or flexes in response to the forces that act upon it. There are references in the literature to aesthetic characteristics of creative thought that help to shape a correct solution (Campbell, 1960; Meier, 1939; Perkins, 1981; Stein, 1974), but the idea of an aesthetic preference that guides the perception of new experiences has not been previously suggested. Obviously, more research is needed to understand the nature of expertise in the arts as well as generically.

But the results from the factor analyses of this study offer scientific evidence to support the idea that the thought processes involved in problem solving are different from those involved in problem finding. Although this may seem obvious to individuals more comfortable with directing their own learning than with figuring out the correct answer in a given situation, scientific verification of these perceptions is necessary for acceptance as a scientific truth. If the ability to ask questions or determine the problem to be solved is different from the ability to provide answers, major curricular revisions are necessary at every level of our educational system.

Developmental Issues Regarding Expertise

One cannot apply the research on adults to the behaviors of children. But as we learn more about the advanced levels of thought that an expert engages for his or her problem-solving processes, we may better understand the behaviors of children with advanced achievement in art. This talent may influence the approach an individual takes to your assignments. If the parameters of the assignment allow a student to pursue his or her own agenda (whether or not the student is aware of this agenda), the product is often more advanced than required. For example, given the homework problem of capturing a light source on a familiar object, a high school student chose a pencil sharpener—an object that metaphorically reflects light in addition to the concrete solution. With the student working solely in pencil, the pencil sharpener maintains his drawing tools and drawing illuminates his life. What he did not realize at the time was that the thematic underpinnings of all his work had to do with the way light responded to metal surfaces (Kay, n.d.).

I was particularly impressed by the efforts of one young lady's immersion in a landscape assignment. As an academically talented fifth grader, she managed her schedule to free extra time for the drawing during a span of several weeks. She spent several hours a day intensely recording her observation, and I watched as an image of the concrete stairs that led through the grass to the playground carefully emerged. When asked for the source of her inspiration, she said that the drawing was of her childhood—for her, the concrete stairs led either to the playground or back to the school. They led to freedom or to rules. The grass was always free. As each blade of grass was drawn, she could ponder the details of her life.

This ability to animate the physical environment with a perceptual metaphor is called physiognomic perception (Stein, 1984) and is found in creative individuals during the creative process. Metaphors and analogies are at the core of many creative thinking strategies (Gordon, 1961).

Some artistically talented artists are persistent in their need to address or "own" their own problems. At the high school level, the student may have learned how to negotiate the learning environment to suit personal needs (e.g., getting an extension on a due date). Young children with a serious attraction to art may have well-developed habits or work conditions prior to conforming to the timetable of school. It is an unforgettable experience to observe a 5-year-old prepare his work space at home by adjusting the light sources in the room, eliminating extraneous noises by closing windows, and searching for the correct fine-line marker to execute the task he set for himself and then spend several hours engaged in drawing without interruption.

Children with an aptitude or gift in art often demonstrate this ability before entering school. This precocity, a rapid developmental process, and high motivational levels are characteristics of the artistically talented (Hurwitz & Day, 1991). Some students are well on their way to defining and exploring their own problems prior to entering first grade (see Figure 7.3). In fact, a retrospective study of the talent development of sculptors reports the feeling that elementary art classes impeded their artistic development (Bloom, 1985). Although rare, examples of this high degree of precocity provide thoughtful art educators the additional challenge of designing problems that permit problem interpretation to encompass the young artist's personal agenda (also see Color Plates 7.1–7.4).

Figure 7.3
"Magnificent 7" contour sketch by Carson Rutter, age 5

Used with permission.

THEORY INTO PRACTICE

How Do I Design the Learning Experience to Fit My Learners?

Problem Exemplars

A look at some assignments that pose open-ended problem-solving situations with a record of appealing to or arousing enthusiasm from a wide audience of learners will ground the discussion on elegant problems.

Example 1

Real situations in an art class involve abbreviated periods, field trips, or assemblies that pose extra challenge to delivering meaningful art education to students. Utilizing a 20-minute period of time to create a teaching moment can be viewed as a frustration to a traditional curriculum or as a challenge to engage the students in a visual thinking exercise. The scissor "transformations" in Figure 7.4 are products of an assignment that asks the learners to examine a scissor with their imaginations. Transforming the ordinary into the extraordinary by elaborating on the contour of real scissors requires few tools or preparation but calls for visual thinking. Inspired by the challenge, many students will continue working on the idea at home and return the next day with the calibre of products exhibited here.

Example 2

Sometimes, the elementary art teacher finds that the day belongs to a field trip or special school performance and is assigned the role of chaperon. One way to engage students in artistic behaviors under these conditions is to provide training in aesthetic inquiry. The performance card shown in Figure 7.5 was originally

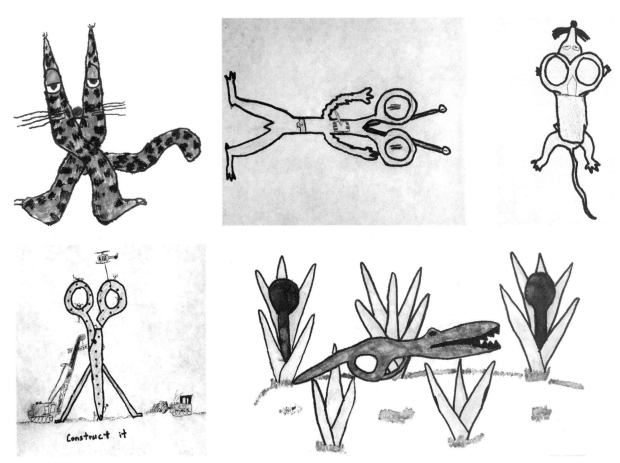

Figure 7.4
Scissor "transformations" (watercolor pencil) by upper elementary students

Collection of the author.

designed to engage the imagination of my students during performances attended during classtime with the students. Special programs in music, dance, and theater were often brought to the students by the parent organizations. But without some type of debriefing, discussion, or reaction, the students did not practice attending to (Greene, 1992) or did not develop language to describe their perceptions of these exposures. The usefulness of this tool to also broaden the viewing experience for visual artwork became apparent shortly after the first use. Subsequently, these cards have been used by high school and college undergraduate students as gesso (preparation) to the art criticism process.

Example 3

Drawing is a product of visual thinking. (So is sculpting, and too few art educators tackle the complexities of designing exposures with three-dimensional visual thinking. But drawing is a necessary skill and one deserving ample attention.) I would question any art curriculum that did not include a unit on drawing from observation. My preference at the elementary level was to begin the year with this unit starting with a still-life assignment. This provided a baseline (a perfor-

Performance Card: Never leave home without it.

Justin Paterno
Whistler's Mother

© 1983 Sandra Kay

1. • **Looks like:** an old grandma Knitting
6. • **Feels like:** a old woman drying to cover up
7. • **Sounds like:** crickety crack - crickety crack
4. • **Moves like:** a ~~short~~ slug
5. • **Tastes like:** The smell
2. • **Smells like:** cinnimon buns cookin in the oven
3. • **Reminds me of:** a gloomy day

Figure 7.5
Performance card sample completed on "Whistler's Mother"

Collection of the author.

mance assessment) to record the current level of achievement in observation, hand–eye coordination, and visual thinking/designing levels. By designing a still life with a large variety of complex and simple objects, and assigning the students the opportunity to choose what part they wanted to tackle and what lens they would put on their mind's eye (close-up, telephoto, panoramic, microscopic), an appropriate match between challenge and ability could be reached by all. This strategy is useful for all ages, from first grade to adults.

However, the objects employed in a still life deserve attention to attracting intrinsic motivation. Drawing the traditional still-life objects (glass bottles, fruit bowls, etc.) is an exercise for sophisticated and serious art students. To engage students in grades one to six, I found toys and play objects to be much more inspirational. Students with a fear of drawing could choose parts of a familiar object and concentrate on the skill of drawing. The close-ups of a bicycle shown in Figure 7.6 demonstrate the attempts by nonartists to address what they considered attemptable.

Example 4

Vygotsky's zone of proximal development is easily observed as third graders attend to the exhibited work of sixth graders. In fact, it was the pleading of young students that led to a building-block assignment that has engaged a range of students, from first graders to juniors in high school. Building a structure and then capturing it in a drawing is surprisingly enticing. Enough colored wooden building blocks can be inexpensively purchased to suit a class with five or six blocks per student. Other than the sound of a structure collapsing periodically,

Figure 7.6
These close-up drawings of bicycle parts are first attempts by nonartists, grades four to six.

Collection of the author.

Figure 7.7
Range of ability is depicted in samples of one third-grade class on building-block drawings.

Collection of the author.

this problem allowed one to hear the proverbial pin drop.* Third-grade students
challenged by the desire to reproduce three dimensions explored perspective
drawing, calling for assistance when required. The range of student capabilities
within a single class is evident in the third-grade samples in Figure 7.7.

---

* I am not a proponent of silent learning, but a principal I once knew couldn't decide whether the level of
noise was a good determinant of learning—especially when some assignments required more sound
than others. He often came into my room during these quiet moments to drop a pin, which disturbed
those who had not noticed him before.

 ## What Are the Characteristics of an Elegant Problem and How Do They Guide Curriculum Design?

From the examples presented in the "Theory into Practice" section and the discussion on thinking that precedes it, one can see a pattern or set of characteristics that distinguishes a problem as elegant. If a problem has the **flexibility** of problem space to engage audiences from elementary to postsecondary levels, there is an elegance to the design. Within those age ranges in the audience, the problem must also address varying abilities and engagement levels. Therefore, an elegant problem lends itself to many kinds of solutions by many types of problem solvers. In addition, the problem or assignment must provide the opportunity for **fluency** of responses. An elegant problem provides the opportunity for many choices of responses and solutions. With length and width variability, variations in depth are earmarked by the ability to **elaborate** or provide **original** solutions to the problem. Producing the environment for novel and inventive solutions characterizes a well-composed problem. If the assignment encourages flexibility, fluency, elaboration, and originality of responses, it has met the four characteristics often used to define **creative thought.** By designing a problem that encourages these behaviors, creative teaching elicits creative thought.

Another characteristic of elegant problems deserves highlighting: an elegant problem is worth solving. The issue of quality or value discriminates an elegant problem from others. Some problems are more important than others. The elegant problem allows for technical and intellectual growth as it elicits creative solutions from each individual. To do so, the problem must remain responsive to the various levels of expertise found in a student population. The growth necessary for a developing artist is different than the growth of a nonartist. Knowing more about the thoughts and behaviors of other artists broadens artists' and art educators' understanding of issues that engage artists' thought. (Although I have known a first-grade artist striving to capture movement or action in his own drawings to devour the techniques portrayed in Leonardo da Vinci's notebook, most first graders are interested in learning ways to show movement in their drawings and are willing to learn from "experts" in sixth grade.)

Some art educators feel that the issues and techniques presented to a first grader need not differ greatly from those presented to a twelfth grader except in amount and size of chunks. Whether this matches your personal philosophy of teaching, nonartists (those not interested in becoming artists) can grasp the challenge presented to develop visual thinking more easily than they can understand how the elements or principles of design will enhance their careers. The fact that these individuals may someday sit on town planning boards and make aesthetic decisions about our built environment may be too distant to come into clear focus, but it is a probability. Ownership of artistic knowing is important for everyone. Visual thinking is a skill that has universal application.

Finally, an elegant problem elicits elegant solutions. Knowing when an elegant solution has been reached is an interesting phenomenon. The criterion an individual uses to evaluate whether the novel solution is correct is an aesthetic criterion. According to Stein (1984), creative work in all fields employs this evaluation process:

> The experimental finding, the engineered apparatus, the portrait, the abstract painting, have a feeling about it that it "works." It is well designed. Everything fits just right. It is pleasing and satisfying. (p. 21)

Exposure to this qualitative type of decision-making process is an important contribution the arts have to offer both the expert and nonexpert. The transfer of this tool of thought to other situations or disciplines may be key to creative productivity.

SUMMARY

This chapter focused on four questions radiating from the choice to shape elegant problems for visual thinking. The major points are highlighted in the following list:

～   Who are the learners in my classroom?

The learners in your classroom are contributors and appreciators in the creative process. Both need to understand the process of making art—the former to continue developing expertise, the latter to develop skills as collectors, museum-goers, or supporters of the artistic process. To facilitate optimum growth in these learners, instruction is designed to address the affective, cognitive, and social (including cultural) dimensions of learning.

～   What forms of thinking are meaningful in art?

Visual thinking as a product of **cognition** is described as important to many creative individuals in scientific as well as artistic domains. Understanding the roles visual thinking may take in creative and critical thought provides educators with increased knowledge for guiding their learners to develop advanced thinking skills, when presented with any of the four types of problem situations.

～ How do I design the learning experience to fit my learners?

Meaningful learning experiences are made within the constraints of the conditions we face. The conditions of the learning environment include the physical qualities of time and space, as well as the psychological qualities of the learners you are addressing. Exercises in visual thinking (e.g., scissors transformations) or translating emotional response to verbal thought (e.g., performance card) provide guided instruction that can be used as references for deeper investigations in the future. Seizing the moment and tailoring lessons to fit the student variations that compose very different classes with the same course title are skills observed in excellent teachers.

～ What are the characteristics of an elegant problem and how do they guide curriculum design?

Creative teaching elicits creative thought. By designing problems that invite flexibility, fluency, elaboration, and originality of responses, you engage learners in the creative thought process. For a problem to be considered elegant, it also must be worth solving. The test for determining whether a problem is elegant is in the problem generated. If the problem elicits elegant solutions (aesthetically meaningful) to a large percentage of students and does so consistently over time, it merits the label "elegant."

ADVANTAGES AND CHALLENGES OF MAKING THIS CHOICE

There are many advantages to this approach for the educator as well as the learner. By changing the question from "What am I going to teach them tomorrow?" to "What do my students know and need to know to develop visual thinking strategies?" one alters the conversation about the art curriculum to language that other educators understand. Like the nonartists in the classroom, other teachers and administrators are not well enough acquainted with art to recognize the thought processes essential to all critical and creative thought. Most important, the dialogue in the classroom becomes more inclusive by acknowledging and valuing the role of the appreciator of art. Widening an understanding of what problem an artist tackled and possible reasons for the solution adds to the power of appreciation for some people.

Another advantage to this approach is in one's ability to reflect the higher-level thinking skills called for in this wave of educational reform. Focusing on shaping classroom problems or assignments to develop skills in visual thinking broadens the conceptual framework to include and address the skills necessary for creative thought. By developing problems that provide a "flow" experience for both the artist and the nonartist, all students are engaged in their optimal level of learning. Activities that incite personal meaning-making last as memories. Visual thinking is a skill necessary to the home decorator, doctor, lawyer, and plumber.

The challenges to this approach to creating meaning are plentiful. An understanding of cognitive psychology (especially perception), science, and special education becomes essential. Looking at learning in this way requires considerable thought and reflection before and after the experience. The educator interested in this pursuit must realize that the goal is far higher and will take longer—but the road to expertise as a teacher does not have many shortcuts.

ACTION PLAN FOR INSTRUCTIONAL DECISION MAKING

To go from arranging lesson plans and assignments to choosing problems that promote thinking alters one's frame of reference considerably. In any new task, making small steps toward the goal is better than making no steps. As the saying goes, the longest journey begins with the first step.

- ~ *Review* a lesson or unit that went fairly well.
- ~ *Analyze* why it went well. Were all the students engaged in their learning? If not, who wasn't? Was the lesson below or above the "flow" channel of that individual? If the lesson provided a choice of variations from closed to open problems (the cognitive dimension), did it also provide an appropriate width for the affective channel (allowing students to twist and distort the problem to meet their own personal agendas)?
- ~ Adding to the first run of a lesson design is often easier than beginning anew. After analyzing student responses, *take a new look* at your assignment. Does it meet all the characteristics of an elegant problem? Discussion with colleagues often invites new ideas and perspectives.
- ~ Once a degree of comfort is reached in designing lessons, *map out* your plans for the entire year (it's only 40 weeks at best). What thinking skills do your students have, and what do they need the most? These questions are congruent with the curriculum plan in hand (district, state, or cooperating teacher). Choosing to shape problems that promote visual thinking does not necessarily negate what was done before. It may, however, alter how one does what is done.
- ~ Once the year is mapped out (in units, exposure to materials and techniques, or design education), *imagine* a problem you could become excited about investigating that would address the former constraints. This procedure is called curriculum mapping and is often used to seek commonalities between subjects so that interdisciplinary units of study can be designed.
- ~ *Brainstorm* many problems for an assignment.
- ~ *Look* at the potential of each assignment by brainstorming possible solutions. Which is wider? longer? deeper than the rest? Choose the most exciting option, try it, and consider the results. (Good choices lead to good results. If the results are unsatisfactory, reanalyze your process.)

DISCUSSION QUESTIONS

1. In discussing the meaning of art with friends and family who are not involved in art, what are their perceptions of what you do?
2. What role does thinking play in the communication of feelings/emotions?
3. How is designing curriculum like designing a work?

SUGGESTED ACTIVITIES

1. If you do not already do so, write out your studio assignments (accurately and in detail, as they were delivered) in your sketchbook. Apply your thinking in the ways described for elegant problems and solutions.

2. When you observe teaching situations, take note (literally and figuratively) of the assignment/problem posed to the students. If necessary, rewrite it to better fit the elegant problem recommendations.

3. Look at your own work with a fresh eye. What problems inspired your preferred solutions? Keep a record of these potentially elegant problems.

ANNOTATED RESOURCES

Creativity and Imagination

Egan, K. (1992). *Imagination in teaching and learning: The middle school years.* Chicago, IL: University of Chicago Press.
  In this book, written in a user-friendly style, Egan discusses why imagination is important to education and the characteristics of students ages 8–15. A framework and examples are provided.

Greene, M. (1995). *Releasing the imagination: Essays on education, the arts, and social change.* San Francisco, CA: Jossey-Bass.
  This book provides the thoughtful educator with ideas for using our imaginations to construct our lives and the lives of our students toward a cultivated community. By the "mother of aesthetic education," it is a poignant piece to use in setting goals as a teacher.

Stein, M. I. (1984). *Making the point: Anecdotes, poems & illustrations for the creative process.* Amagansett, NY: Mews Press.
  Gleaning from his scholarly publications, the author has provided an entertaining and informative outline in this brief introduction to the creative process.

Curriculum Planning

Roukes, N. (1988). *Design synectics.* Worcester, MA: Davis Press.
  Written in lesson plan format, this book provides practical applications of the author's interpretation of synectic thinking skills. Well written and illustrated, it is a useful planning tool. (See also Art synectics *by same author.)*

Expertise

This is a relatively new area of research, so little is translated from educational research into plain language. The best way to learn more about expertise in art is to go to primary resources: any autobiography, or publications with quotes from artists such as those in retrospective exhibits.

Bloom, B. S. (Ed.). (1985). *Developing talent in young people.* New York: Ballantine.
  The findings of a study of talented sculptors, pianists, Olympic swimmers, tennis players, and mathematicians are described in a clear, easily readable manner. Based on interviews with family and talented individuals, the conclusions are dramatic.

John-Steiner, V. (1985). *Notebooks of the mind: Explorations of thinking.* Albuquerque, NM: University of New Mexico Press.
  This book provides a look into creative minds, with many quotes and reflections from these individuals.

Curriculum Planning

Rodari, F. (1991). *A weekend with Picasso*. New York: Rizzoli International.
  Excellent reproductions and insightful information accompany this children's book written in the first person.

Motivation

Csikszentmihalyi, M. (1990). *Flow: The psychology of optimal experience*. New York: Harper Collins.

Perception and the Senses

Ackerman, D. (1990). *A natural history of the senses*. New York: Random House.
  This is an enticing history and story about the senses and their fictional and nonfictional roles in society. It is filled with real-life applications of the perceptual skills developed in aesthetic education.

Bateson, G. (1979). *Mind in nature*. Glasgow, Great Britain: William Collins Sons.
  Received as a gift from one of the artists I interviewed for my research, this book provided a translation of much of the empirical research on perception in which I had been totally immersed. It is a gentle transition of meaning from science to art that enlightens the reader to the power of perception.

Curriculum Planning

London, P. (1994). *Step outside: Community-based art education*. Portsmouth, NH: Heinemann.
  Attending to the child's environment, London gracefully guides the reader through several elegant solutions to the problem posed of developing visual perceptual skills.

Ruef, K. (1992). *The private eye: Looking/thinking by analogy*. Seattle: The Private Eye Project.
  Directed at developing scientific observation skills in students, this curriculum guide provides invitations to develop artistic and creative skills in most of the lessons. Interesting art lessons can be derived as one also encounters concepts in the arts that transfer to other subject areas.

Thinking and Problem Solving

Eisner, E. W. (1994). *Cognition and curriculum reconsidered* (2nd ed.). New York: Teachers College Press.
  Looking at the relationships among sensation, cognition, and representation, Eisner discusses choices of art educators. This is a book I wish I had read early in my teaching (and research) career.

Sternberg, R. J. (1986). *Intelligence applied*. Orlando, FL: Harcourt Brace Jovanovich.

With practice problems and self-tests scattered throughout, this book presents and applies Sternberg's theory of intelligence in a comprehensible style. Although only one theory is covered in depth, it is a sound foundation for understanding all others. It has been well received by teachers seeking more information on the topic.

Curriculum Planning

Battin, M. P., Fisher, J., Moore, R., & Silvers, A. (1989). *Puzzles about art: An aesthetics casebook.* New York: St. Martin's Press.
The format of this book provides readers with open-ended problems dealing with aesthetic inquiry. It is useful as an advanced high school text but can be filtered to adapt some of the problems to elementary-level experiences.

Visual/Spatial Thinking

Dixon, J. P. (1983). *The spatial child.* Springfield, IL: Charles C. Thomas.
This is an excellent book on a learning style and thinking strategies that are underrepresented in educational research. Highly recommended for all art educators.

Curriculum Planning

McKim, R. H. (1980). *Experiences in visual thinking* (2nd ed.). Belmont, CA.: Wadsworth.
Complete with an index of strategies, this book provides options for a variety of experiences in visual thinking exercises. Designed for the teacher as choice maker.

KEY TERMS

Aesthetic   From the Greek word meaning "of sense perception, artistic"; appreciative of, responsive to, or zealous about the beautiful

Cognition   The act or process of knowing, including both awareness and judgment

Contricipation   A new word combining the activities of two major roles involved in the creative process—contribution and participation (Stein, 1984, p. 31)

Creative thought (creativity)   A process in which the individual finds, defines, or discovers an idea or problem not predetermined by the situation or task (Kay, 1989, p. 10)

Elaboration   Something planned or carried out with great care and worked out in detail. This is one of four major cognitive strategies often associated with creativity; it is a characteristic of the result of the creative process.

Expertise   The skill or knowledge representing mastery of a particular subject

Flexibility   Characterized by a readiness to adapt to new, different, or changing requirements. This is one of four major cognitive strategies often associated with creativity; it is a characteristic of the result of the creative process.

Fluency   Smooth and rapid effortlessness, flowing from one idea to another. This is one of four major cognitive strategies often associated with creativity; it is a characteristic of the result of the creative process.

Originality   Freshness of idea, design, or style; the result of independent thought or constructive imagination. This is one of four major cognitive strategies often associated with creativity; it is a characteristic of the result of the creative process.

Perception   Information obtained through the senses; observation; quick, acute, and intuitive cognition

Problem finding   Defining or formulating a problem by an individual prior to the actions taken to solve the problem (Kay, 1989, p. 10)

Problem solving   The process of finding a solution to a stated problem. Convergent problem-solving tasks require the identification of one correct response; divergent problem-solving tasks require the formation of a quantity of solutions to a problem (e.g., generating a list of uses for an object) (Kay, 1989, p. 10).

Qualitative   Of, relating to, or involving quality or kind; often contrasted with *quantitative,* which measures or expresses quantities or amount

Visual thinking   Perception; mental representation and ordering of information using images or figures

CHAPTER 8

Designing Units for Conceptual Thinking

Judith W. Simpson
Boston University

Guiding Questions

- ~ What is conceptual thinking?

- ~ What influences conceptual planning?

- ~ How do we design units for conceptual thinking?

- ~ How are metaphors used in the design of conceptual units?

- ~ How do we use thematic concepts in interdisciplinary curricula?

 ## What Is Conceptual Thinking?

Throughout this book, you have been exposed to many choices—ways to think about art, learners, and teaching. This chapter addresses how those choices may come together, in a variety of ways, to help you produce units of study that are concept based. Such units can help all learners to connect art to themselves and the world around them through connecting ideas.

The following is a vignette:

Children are taking turns crawling around on their hands and knees, under tables, around chairs, looking up and down. They are behaving as salamanders. They are trying to experience different points of view. Ms. M. urges them to think about what and how a lizard would see. She is linking compositional ideas with those in a story. Thinking about drawing things that run off the page, inferring space beyond the boundaries, and learning to see from many points of view are the purpose of the kinesthetic exploration. (Marsh, 1993)

Your journey just led you into the middle of a fourth-grade art lesson. It is the second in a sequence of four lessons that were designed to acquaint learners with illustration techniques and their connection, through the use of key concepts, to verbal meaning. Perhaps you would like to know what led up to this event. Before exploring this scenario in depth, however, it is best to define the term *conceptual thinking*.

Concepts are thoughts and notions that develop from a variety of inputs—our senses, feelings, and experiences. They are contextually based and often appear in isolated frameworks. People rely on what they know about things to form ideas and to understand them. Sometimes to connect concepts, we categorize objects, events, and beliefs. Each conceptual category has reference sets. For example, if we smell something sweet but cannot see the source, we think *sweet* whether we are smelling candy, cake, flowers, or perfume. Sensory inputs of taste and smell provide an idea of what sweet means.

Often, associations are made between ideas. Thoughts about art provoke thoughts of elements and principles, **canons, genres,** two- and three-dimensional work, galleries, and museums. On a parallel course, thoughts about science bring forth thoughts of formulas, rules, experiments, and laboratories. Artists may know more about the subject of art, through experiences and feelings, than they do about science. Thus, they can elaborate on art concepts perhaps more fully than they can about science concepts. The depth of individual experiences provides different levels of information that inform our thoughts. The deeper the understanding of a phenomenon, the more conceptual connections can be made.

Traditionally, each subject in a curriculum is studied in exclusion. Music, art, language, and math are usually studied without linking ideas among them in any way. The basic premises that may be common across disciplines remain isolated from each other. An example of a common connection among music, art, language, and math is the simple concept of pattern. Afforded the opportunity to study the meaning of pattern in all four of the mentioned subject areas, most students would gain significantly in their level of understanding about the idea.

Making conceptual connections is a sophisticated proposition that may not come easily even for people involved in the creative arts. Art is connected to *every* discipline and event in some manner, often through *everyday* events in and across cultures. Designing units for conceptual thinking involves more than having knowledge of the basic components and the structure of a unit plan. Successful designs depend initially on the teacher's ability to make connections between formal knowledge and everyday life. The next task is to find a way to connect that knowledge to learners.

The following is an example of one way an elementary art teacher helped her students to connect and use concepts. The vignette presented prior to the definition and discussion of conceptual thinking originated in this unit.

An Elementary Experience

Ms. M. thought that a storybook approach to the concepts of point of view and center of interest should enhance the prospect that art learners come to understand what both concepts mean (Marsh, 1993). She chose the book *The Salamander Room* (Mazur, 1991), with illustrations by Steve Johnson. One of her **goals** was that through discussion of specific qualities found in the illustrations learners would be able to understand and talk about their own and others' work in terms of point of view and center of interest. Other goals—such as familiarizing learners with illustrative techniques and media and enhancing connections between the visual and verbal notions of the two concepts—became the overarching concerns of the unit. Her goals were what she hoped the students would gain throughout the unit lessons. Since goals are teacher expectations, she worded them as follows:

> Learners should:
> become aware of the visual/verbal connections between the concepts of point of view and point of interest.
> become familiar with the techniques and media used in book illustrations.
> become comfortable talking about the aesthetic qualities of their own and others' work.

Once the goals were formulated, Ms. M. began the process of designing **objectives** that would help learners reach the goals.

First she talked to the fourth-grade classroom teachers. She wanted to know what the learners already knew about point of view and under what circumstances they learned to use and understand the words. She often took advantage of the knowledge that self-contained classroom teachers have about their students. Her learners had not formally studied *The Salamander Room* in their reading lessons, so she would be able to evaluate the impact of the verbal/visual unit based on the art room experience.

Ms. M. remembered having read some professional journal articles that addressed the idea of working with storybooks in the art room. She used material from the articles as support for her goals in the instructional concepts part of her unit. **Instructional concepts,** ideas that have been proven through either research or practice, provide rationales for making specific planning choices and illustrate to others that the plans are appropriately designed.

Objectives are assessable expectations about student behaviors and performance. They address three major domains of learning: cognitive (the information that students will learn), affective (the learners' personal responses), and psychomotor (skills that learners will develop). Before formulating her objectives, Ms. M. thought about what the learners could do. They were pretty sophisticated, lively, suburban 9-year-olds. She knew they could handle drawing materials, but could they use colored pencils to render images effectively? She knew they were at the age where a kinesthetic experience would be the cement needed to make the visual concept of point of view concrete in their minds. But would they get out of control? She knew they could be very cruel to one another when talking about their artwork, but could that be changed?

Through thinking about and answering these questions, her objectives became clear. Ms. M. decided that the major objectives for the unit would be that learners:

∿ learn the similarities and differences between point of view and center of interest in both verbal language and drawing.

∿ develop drawing skills with colored pencils.

∿ use different points of view and develop centers of interest in drawings.

∿ identify and discuss points of view, center of interest, and the effects of colored pencils in their own and others' drawings.

Once these decisions were made, lesson ideas came easily. Ms. M. had already decided to begin with the storybook. That idea would be fully developed for lesson one. Knowing that if she thought it through clearly, a kinesthetic activity for the second lesson would really work well, she planned on the "salamander crawl." The third lesson would introduce the drawing assignment, and a fourth would address the critical and aesthetic pieces she wanted students to experience. The lessons would be accomplished over a period of seven weeks, with three sessions allocated for drawing.

Staying with format found in the illustrations, Ms. M. decided to use a compositional device borrowed from the book. She provided the learners with 12-in.-x-18-in. white paper that had been ruled with black margin lines to create a border. The students could decide which of two border widths they wanted and how they wished to orient their paper—vertically or horizontally. Other necessary materials included colored pencils, drawing pencils, erasers, watercolor brushes, and a video camera for recording the unit. If she had used other reproductions, slides, or resources beyond the storybook, she would have listed these and the equipment needed to use them in the materials section of her unit plan.

The **evaluation** of this unit would be conducted during the fourth lesson. At that time, Ms. M. would engage the children in specific dialogue through carefully constructed questions. She would have the learners talk about their own and each others' work in terms of inferred space; she would check the drawings for detail, mixed and blended colors, and the control of dry or wet pencil technique. Drawings and discussion would reflect the learners' understanding of point of view and point of interest. A peer, teacher, and self-evaluation rubric would complete the production assessment of the unit (Figure 8.1). In other words, Ms. M.'s objectives, in the form of

RUBRIC FOR STUDENT ASSESSMENT
Self and peer evaluation form:
Check the box that most clearly describes the following criteria:

	Needs work	Can I.D.	Clearly	Strong	Excels
Has a center of interest					
Shows a definite point of view					
Uses colored pencils					
Tells a story					
Shows parts or pieces of objects					
Shows original thought					

TEACHER COMMENTS:

Figure 8.1

This is a sample rubric. Weights could be assigned to the individual cells for metric grading.

Judith Simpson.

questions, would be the evaluation criteria used for the multiple procedures for measuring the students' mastery levels. An example of a criterion question for the unit would be: Did students learn the similarities and differences between point of view and center of interest in both language and drawing (i.e., the first objective)?

Let us revisit the classroom to see how this unit turned out. The following is an overview taken from a videotape of the unit (Marsh, 1993):

> Ms. M. read *The Salamander Room* pointing out illustrations that demonstrated the techniques of inference, centers of interest, seeing from varied perspectives, images moving outside a frame. They closed the first lesson discussing the story and its illustrations. In the second lesson, the learners reviewed the story briefly and Ms. M. asked them to think about what it might be like to see through the salamander's eyes. She then told them they would take turns behaving like the salamander to experience his point of view. At the end of that session, children shared their notions of the "salamander crawl." The third lesson started with a discussion of the illustrations in the storybook and teacher examples of inferred objects and point of view. Ms. M. showed them various drawing techniques with colored pencils, gave the students the pre-bordered paper and told them to begin a narrative drawing, telling a story of their own. The drawing "must have" parts and pieces of things hidden behind the margins and parts and pieces of things going outside the border. She re-emphasized things close and things far away as being seen as larger or smaller, like the salamander crawls had revealed. Three sessions of drawing followed in which she demonstrated and the students used materials like the ones used by the book illustrator. They drew lizards, bugs, flowers, sailing ships, trees, animals and mountains sharing distanced spaces with parts of objects inferred and others growing outside the frames. Lively discussion about the drawings, what the various techniques and styles of using the materials conveyed, and how the space had been used confirmed, during the final lesson of the unit, that goals and objectives had been met.

Through a series of sequenced events that led up to creating the drawings, learners were guided through the steps of linking concrete concepts. The unit culminated in drawings and dialogue that reflected the depth of their understanding. (See Figures 8.2 and 8.3 and Color Plates 8.1 and 8.2.)

Figure 8.2
"Ready to Go," by Stephanie Hopkins, fourth grade. A figure appears outside the margin to convey a sense of space. The large dog appears closest to the viewer, indicating that it is the center of interest.

Courtesy of Mia Marsh.

Figure 8.3
"A Morning in the Forest," by Devon Burns, fourth grade. Animals and insects appear to share points of interest. Everything is very large from the ant's point of view.

Courtesy of Mia Marsh.

There are many ways to format a unit plan. The one used by Ms. M. is an example of a structure that includes goals, instructional concepts, and rationales that support the goals; objectives designed to help learners reach the goals; a sequence of lesson ideas or options; a list of materials and preparations for teaching that she would need; and evaluation criteria and procedures for assessment.

～ What Influences Conceptual Planning?

The previous elementary unit was influenced by the teacher's desire to teach and reinforce the meaning of two concrete ideas that are found in both language and art. In that particular circumstance, the art teacher could talk to the fourth-grade teachers to find out what material, relative to the concepts, students had been exposed to. A curriculum guide could also serve as a resource for finding the answers about what grade four is supposed to cover in a year. Elementary curriculum is designed toward the achievement of identical goals and outcomes for all students at each grade level. Pairing ideas between art and other areas of content is often more easily facilitated at the elementary level because of the homogenous nature of the curriculum.

In middle and secondary schools, however, courses of study are divided into disciplines. Subjects are traditionally taught independently of one another and may be elective. Linking concepts from other disciplines becomes a dedicated effort for art specialists in these settings. Again, curriculum guides may be a beginning, especially for new teachers. Although specific content may not be stated, goals and objectives found in the school's general curriculum may provide direction for planning. The primary learning concerns for each grade level in a district also reflect what the school community values.

Curriculum Guides

Curriculum guides represent hierarchical standards. National standards are the primary document; state boards of education generally adopt standards and write goals and objectives that reflect the national standards. Districts vary in the way they implement these standards. Some may have complete art curriculum guides; others rely on the individual schools within a district to weave art goals and objectives into their curricula. Periodically, the curriculum is revisited to reflect efforts toward change or reform in education.

Site-based teams of teachers from individual schools, parents from school districts, and administrators often provide input for the design of curricula in schools. In the case of site-based-management schools, although standards must be met, each school has the authority to meet them in the way deemed best for their learners. You need to know where the direction for designing yearly curricula is found in your school.

Most art teachers have personal responsibility for designing units that meet the goals and objectives of a curriculum document. Questions to guide your thinking should include the following:

What does the school community value?

What do my students know?

How do they know?

What is life like in the community outside the school?

How can I tap into the learners' experiences?

How can I use the information I have about students to take them through the "zone of proximal development"? (Vygotsky, 1978; see also Chapter 7, "Shaping Elegant Problems for Visual Thinking")

How can I help students to think conceptually?

Based on the curriculum guide, what choices can I make that will be the most meaningful for the learners?

Pedagogical Choices

Pedagogy is the art of teaching. Beyond conforming to standards and curricular guides, the teacher makes choices that affect pedagogy. Pedagogical choices are influenced by the ethos of the school, teachers' values and beliefs about the purpose of their mission, and educational trends. If the choice is made to use a variety of instructional strategies, a **constructivist** atmosphere may be provided (Brooks & Brooks, 1993). The teacher creates an environment in which meaning can be constructed by all students, including those with different learning styles, those who are said to have special needs, those who are gifted, those who are determined to be at risk, and all others enrolled in a class. As important as varying strategies may be to the desired learning outcome, the vehicle, or plan, that serves as the basis for teaching must be coherent in structure. The way the material is presented to students is related to coherence of the unit. Coherence is achieved when a clear concept grounds the unit content. In the next section I present several types of choices for coherent conceptual planning, beginning with themes.

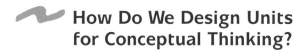 **How Do We Design Units for Conceptual Thinking?**

Connecting Concepts Through Themes

Thematic planning is reflective of a choice to cohere an art program that is not necessarily dependent on or integrated with other disciplines. A theme may be the basis for a unit, a 10-week term, a semester, or a yearly course. An example of a broad theme that provides endless curricular choices is community.

Learners bring something to school with them each day. Outside voices, places, colors, textures, movement, faces, spaces—all accompany the child into the classroom. Tapping into that storehouse of images makes sense at any level (London, 1994). Community is an actual and natural curriculum theme.

A middle school unit.   The following is an example of how a middle school art teacher planned a community-based unit. A prevalent sense of "placelessness" among his diverse students and an awareness that they knew little about the built environment that surrounded them led a middle school art teacher (Appler, 1995) to design a unit that addressed both of these issues. His primary unit goal was to acquaint students with the history of the architecture in the community. Other unit goals were that students should become more aware of (1) differences in architectural styles, (2) the influences that determined architectural changes, (3) the way architecture defines and gives identity to a community, and (4) the connections between people and the architecture in a community.

Objectives for each grade level in which the unit was to be taught varied within the lessons. Unit objectives were that students learn to (1) identify and name parts of buildings, (2) identify architectural features of their own homes or a home of their choice, (3) apply their knowledge in producing an artwork that included elements and/or stylistic renderings of architecture, and (4) describe how artists and other people relate to the built environment.

Grades six, seven, and eight participated in this unit. Each group of students was given a house style handbook; viewed tapes and slides illustrative of several architectural styles; and looked at the works of Grant Wood, Charles Burchfield, and Edward Hopper specifically for the artists' use of period buildings in their work. Walks through the community revealed many different types of stylistic features that characterized the architecture.

Each student used his or her own home or a neighborhood home of choice to develop a visual study (see Photo 8.1). Eighth graders did facade drawings that were later translated into slab vessels or reliefs in clay. Seventh graders, who had previously done self-portraits, used their house drawings as backgrounds to create "Amherst Gothic" paintings (see Color Plates 8.3 and 8.4). Sixth-grade students were asked to do line drawings that became the basis for filling in flat color areas to create a background for their previously drawn self-portraits.

Over a period of several weeks, students learned that buildings had stories to tell. They began to connect architectural styles they found in the community with availability of building materials, craftspeople, and money at different times of construction. Various elements were understood through this learning experience: the links among architecture, landscaping, and geographic constraints that establish the image of a community; the stories that buildings told in the students' and other artists' work; and the contribution that visual details like moldings and door handles make toward creating meaning.

Photo 8.1
*A middle school student works
on a drawing of his own home.*

Courtesy of Steven Appler.

A Teacher–Learner Collaborative Unit

Another way teachers might plan a thematic unit is by working with students to find centers of interest, or subthemes, to explore in visual statements. Teachers can either make all the decisions about unit/lesson design, or they can include the learner through directed decision making (Simpson, 1996).

What might be a scenario? Let us stay with our overarching theme of community and begin to narrow our definition to the neighborhood—a part of the community. Neighborhoods are made up of people, dwellings, commercial buildings, churches, schools, landscapes, ethnic markets, and unique characteristics that give them identity. They can provide strong substance for thematic plans. Productive themes have both differences and similarities. What makes neighborhoods different? What do people in neighborhoods do? How are the people in a neighborhood similar? A thematic unit could be designed for any grade level based on the culture of a neighborhood, the functions and purposes of the neighborhood, or the many kinds of people in the neighborhood.

Artists have consistently looked at people around them as subjects for their work. They have represented people working, celebrating, caring, and demonstrating concern, among other activities. Artifacts reveal how the people in the Paleolithic "neighborhoods" dined, hunted, and dressed. Door posts, masks, sculptures, musical instruments, and items of adornment illustrate what people in some African cultures value in their "neighborhoods." A plethora of art exists to support a curriculum about people in any neighborhood. In fact, so much visual material is available that it is necessary to choose the concepts within our broad theme with which we wish to work. A class could be involved in the choice making.

After a discussion about the community events, students might select a group of images like the ones in Faith Ringgold's *Tar Beach* (1991), Manet's *A Bar at the Folies-Bergère* (1882), Duane Hanson's *Janitor* (1973), and Sandro Botticelli's *Young Man with a Medal* (1470). Through discussion of the chosen works, learners could help decide the subtheme and concepts for the unit. Students could be asked what they see in the artworks. A critical analysis approach to the images would allow students to learn how the artists developed the works toward meaningful interpretation (for more on art criticism, see Chapter 4, "Engaging Learners with Art Images"). Since all the works focus on people in various settings, the subtheme might be neighborhood people. Dialogue about the pieces could lead to a discussion about whether the people in the two- or three-dimensional works would be seen in the local neighborhood. A list of neighborhood people similar to those in the artworks could be constructed. Further discussion, appropriate at the secondary level, about what the listed people do each day could produce a group of concepts such as struggles, anticipation, and freedom as the basis for lessons in either two- or three-dimensional media.

Certain themes in the units could personalize learning about the relationship between art and life: workers in a neighborhood and the effects of the environment on their jobs; the way seasons affect the neighborhood; faces of the future of both people and architecture in the neighborhood. Learners become more deeply involved in a process that begins with them (see Figure 8.4).

Social Issues Curriculum

At either the secondary or middle school level, a concept list could give rise to individual interpretations of a different nature. Social issues and attempts to make sense of the world are uppermost in the minds of contemporary adolescents. Often, students in urban areas need to rationalize their lives through visual expression. The following is a description of the use of the issues within a community as an art education curriculum.

In New York City's District 32, I discovered two Brooklyn art educators who use the world of their students as the conceptual base for their teaching. Mario Asaro and Meryl Meisler work with students considered to be high at-risk populations. Each teacher has documented successes with inner-city students, and their work is

Figure 8.4
On each black felt piece of this quilt, second graders used fabric crayons and collaged materials to produce their neighborhood scene.

Collection of the author.

Photo 8.2
Question Marks, *by Meryl Meisler and the "Drop Ins," installation at the Dia Art Foundation's "Education and Democrats" exhibit*

©Meryl Meisler.

reflected in exhibits produced by the group known as *Artists Teachers Concerned,* which supports art education in New York (Asaro, 1994). Examples of some of the concepts used by Meisler (1994) with her students (called the "Drop Ins") include gentrification, disease, nutrition, pride, freedom, concerns, and rights and responsibilities of citizens (*see* Photo 8.2). In each of the conceptual units, specific topics like AIDS, "my Brooklyn," food, and voting were discussed, written about, and visually researched. Students constructed group exhibits containing visual/verbal statements from each classroom member. Various forms of media—such as papier-mâché, photography, dektol (photo chemical), drawings, video, acrylic, watercolors, wood, and foam core—were used to express personal conceptual statements (*see* Figures 8.5 and 8.6 and Color Plate 8.5). Each student product reflected the synthesis of visual

Figure 8.5
Recycled Material, by students of Louise Greenberg and exhibited in "10 on 8 Windows" in midtown Manhattan

Artists Teachers Concerned, M. Asaro.

Figure 8.6
Stop the Violence in Our Homes, Schools, Churches, by students of John Bright and exhibited in "10 on 8 Windows" in midtown Manhattan

Artists Teachers Concerned, M. Asaro.

and verbal language. Calligraphy, word-processed reports, and handwritten comments were woven into the finished exhibits. Students learned to communicate their thoughts about their environment and its good and bad points. Positive reinforcement through public openings of their exhibitions made many of the students feel successful and proud of their own existence for the first time. The experience of participating in the social issues curriculum provided the students with an acceptable means of self-expression. Art became a reason to come to school, and the world of art became a reality.

Units such as these illustrate how community, neighborhood, and social issues utilize learner knowledge and experience that provide a basis for thematic curriculum design. Whether a teacher chooses to make the learner part of the conceptual planning team or not, a plan that is thematic has inherent coherence because it deals with many facets of the same subject. It follows a concept or set of ideas throughout an instructional unit and builds toward a conclusion that is reached through a series of sequential events that allow the learner to build understanding.

～ How Are Metaphors Used in the Design of Conceptual Units?

Another way of designing units for conceptual thinking is through the use of metaphor.

Defining Metaphor

Metaphor is a literary term that means the use of one term or phrase to mean another. In *Languages of Art* (1988), Goodman provides an example of the distinction between the literal and metaphorical meaning in language and in art:

COLOR PLATE 7.1

An example of unusual precocity in art is demonstrated by the work of Carson Rutter (age 6). Some of his more prized drawings are given titles. This one is titled "Hook." Note Tinkerbell on Peter Pan's hat.

Collection of the author.

COLOR PLATE 7.2

This unfinished sketch depicts the interaction between people—a major theme in Carson's work. The choreography of communication precedes details and background information.

Collection of the author.

COLOR PLATE 7.3

Movie scenes, such as this one of "Hook," are combined into thematic sketchbooks of memorable moments by Carson.

Collection of the author.

COLOR PLATE 7.4

As Tinkerbell advises Peter Pan, the sophistication of Carson's contour line quality is exemplified.

Collection of the author.

COLOR PLATE 8.1

"A Sunny Day," by fourth grader Adam Williams. This student clearly understood the concept of center of interest and the use of inferred space.

Courtesy of Mia Marsh.

COLOR PLATE 8.2

"Prehistoric Battle," by fourth grader Mike Christman. From the dragon's point of view, the world is small.

Courtesy of Mia Marsh.

COLOR PLATE 8.3

"Amherst Gothic" painting.

Courtesy of Steven Appler.

COLOR PLATE 8.4

"Amherst Gothic" painting.

Courtesy of Steven Appler.

COLOR PLATE 8.5

"To: Everyone who has ever lived, worked, and/or dreamed in Brooklyn."

©Meryl Meisler.

COLOR PLATE 8.6

"It doesn't really matter if there was already writing on this paper. This is a story about sun and rain and ducks, that's how they get born!" Drawing by Lyndsey French, age 4.

Collection of the author.

A picture literally possesses a gray color, really belongs to a class of gray things; but only metaphorically does it possess sadness or belong to the class of things that feels sad. (pp. 50–51)

Learners challenged by the use of metaphors are invited to think idiosyncratically about the use of images to imply ideas and about multiple meanings within artwork. This kind of thinking assists learners to develop individualized solutions to problems. Teachers can set up learning experiences that exploit metaphorical, imaginative thought.

Metaphorical Connections

Metaphor as a basis for unit design could be applied at any level. Young children can be introduced to it through story (as suggested in Chapter 5, "Encouraging Visual Storytelling"). As the cognitive ability to understand analogy (a comparison of one thing to another in some way) is established, the understanding of metaphor can be initiated using "What if . . . ?" and " . . . is like . . . " assignments. Gardner and Winner confirm that children between the ages of 4 and 6 are quick to realize that certain statements "cannot be interpreted literally" (Gardner, 1982, p. 159) and will come up with a "like," generally physical, comparison to construct metaphorical meaning. A cloud that looks like a fish is an example of this phenomenon. A small child might say, "Look, a fish in the sky!" or might relate birth to growth in a garden (see Color Plate 8.6).

Through the middle years, children often recognize the reason for figures of speech in prose and poetry but still find it difficult to equate metaphor to a less obvious visual source. The way metaphor is best understood at this level is in lessons that require students to look inside themselves for an "If I were . . . " comparison or a " . . . stands for . . . " idea. "If I were an elephant I could go anywhere I wanted" might lead to a self-portrait elephant.

The design of strong metaphorical units relies on our ability to make associations. Metaphor provides new ways of seeing familiar things—ways of making the strange familiar and the familiar strange. Imagery that contains metaphorical reference is often the best catalyst for meaningful, personal, visual expression for secondary students. Metaphorical imagery, as the container for one's innermost thoughts, protects the maker. Metaphor requires individual interpretation. Viewers arrive at conclusions that may or may not provide the true intent of the metaphorical image. For adolescents strongly influenced by peer pressure and a need for privacy, metaphors provide a vehicle through which they may make creative, meaningful statements.

Synectic thinking (making connections) can result in the making of new metaphors (Roukes, 1988). New metaphorical connections are the result of being able to understand "one kind of thing in terms of another" (Lakoff & Johnson, 1980, p. 5). As a matter of fact, the two authors express that perhaps all conceptual systems are metaphorically structured. Conceptual systems are constructed from our cultural values, attitudes, and experiences.

Metaphorical associations across cultures.   The idea that linguistic metaphors may not be understood between cultures is predicated on syntax and contextuality. Engel stresses that "the collective meanings of symbolic systems change over time and in different locations; they are contextual. The constructions of the mind, the concepts or meanings are contextual" (Engel, 1981, p. 5). There are, however, mythological and ritualistic visual metaphors that multiple cultures share. An example of this is the bird, which in many societies is metaphorical. Birds represent ancestral portraits and spiritual homes in a dualistic (good and evil) construct. Their visual forms imply meaning beyond literal associations. They are symbolic and part of a conceptual structure that is a set of ideas contextually grounded in the culture's belief systems.

A common metaphor such as the bird can be found in artwork from many lands. Birds represent the supernatural powers of witches in Benin sculpture; the American eagle embraces the symbols of war and peace simultaneously; the serpent/dove image is found in the Old Norse myth of the World Ash, Yggdrasil. In the Iatmul culture, huge carvings of birds as male ancestors serve as finial decorations on the double spires of the Men's House. Sea eagles are representative of the fighting spirit and symbolic of head hunting. Bird masks, birds incorporated into female power pieces, and birds as elements of totems represent ancestral spirit doubles for the members of Iatmul and Asmat New Guinea societies, as well as those of the Northwest Coast Native American cultures. The use of a shared visual metaphor provides the opportunity to incorporate contextual information during the study of objects from multiple societies. Learners can go beyond the surface qualities of an object to find its purpose. Metaphorical connections enable learners to understand the meaning of objects with which they are unfamiliar.

Many artists have also used birds metaphorically. The American painter Charles Burchfield often used the crow in his work to suggest "the feeling of spirits beyond the natural realm, of black angels who govern the mysterious woods beneath them" (Weekly, 1993, p. 92) (see Figure 8.7).

Figure 8.7
Crows in March, by Charles Burchfield, 1952, lithograph printed by George C. Miller, 13.5 x 9.75 in. (image).

Collection of the Burchfield-Penney Art Center, Buffalo State College. Gift of Mr. and Mrs. Sy Cohen.

From Metaphorical Images to a Secondary Plan

A unit of study for high school learners could be built around gaining personal power through metaphorical creatures. The unit could serve as a basis for thinking about the art of preliterate cultures as metaphorical communication and as evidence of the concept Dissanayake (1988) calls "making special." Embellishment of the animistic forms is a deliberate behavior that reinforces the notion of the importance of the object.

Students need various ways to use art as a "way of knowing about the world, as a way of making nonviolent statements about social and environmental problems . . . a means of validating one's personal ideas" (Simpson, 1995, p. 28). The use of metaphor in a secondary unit on personal power provides a way for students to make meaningful conceptual connections across cultures. The goals of this unit are as follows:

Learners should:

～ become aware of metaphorical imagery across cultures.

～ become familiar with the concept of power as expressed in art.

～ become aware of levels of meaning contained in an object.

～ become sensitive to the human need to "make special."

Anderson (1988) gives the following as an instructional concept:

Through cross-association and clusters of related meaning . . . metaphor . . . activates a higher level integration in the mind, related to humans' continuing need to harmonize our experiences and reconcile the dualities of our (psychospiritual and physical) selves. (p. 14)

Other support statements could supplement this section of the plan.

Objectives would evolve from answers to the following questions:

What can I expect my students to know?

Where did they learn what they know?

How will they respond to the concepts in the unit?

What will learners do?

How will they be involved? Why?

What criteria will be used for production?

What evaluation procedures will I use?

The objectives for this unit are as follows:

Learners will:

～ observe and discuss the similarities and differences of a variety of metaphorical images with a common theme.

～ research the use of animal imagery in a selected culture.

～ understand the nature of animals with symbolic power.

～ transform an existing metaphorical creature into another.

～ learn to use two-dimensional plans as a basis for the construction of a three-dimensional object.

～ write a narrative describing the meaning of the new object.

There are many other possible objectives. What would be your choices?

We know that the purpose of sequencing instruction is to build lessons toward a high point where information, observation, perception, imagination, and interpretation can come together. This approach is not simply linear or logical but rather a dynamic one that allows many intersections for clarification to occur. It also provides room for the learner to reflect upon the process of discovering new meaning.

Lesson options reflect the unit goals and objectives. The following is a sequence of possibilities.

The *first lesson* of the unit could involve discussing images of animistic objects across cultures that share a common metaphor. The concept of animals' symbolic power could be presented. Next, contemporary images familiar to learners could be compared and contrasted with those from other societies. Learners could be asked to research the purpose of objects from a culture of their choice.

The *second lesson* would involve sharing research findings with the class (images, understandings, differences, and similarities of the power of the symbolic objects). Learners would choose an image from their research to transform.

The *third lesson* might involve the beginning of a modification process—metamorphosis of the researched object, changing it gradually from one creature to another or changing it to reveal its symbolic role. Colors, shapes, lines, and patterns would be added, manipulated, or subtracted to help communicate the new visual message. A lesson of this type ideally would be executed on a computer, affording the learner multiple opportunities to revise changes and rethink them in a relatively short amount of time.

The *fourth lesson* may involve developing a three-dimensional model of the newly formed metaphorical creature. The result could be perhaps walking sticks with decorative tops, relief triptychs, or clay vessels for holding personal feelings.

Once a final product was completed, a narrative about the power contained within the piece would clarify its meaning for both the maker and the viewer. You could also add lessons that involve discussing the work through examining its metaphorical and aesthetic content.

The materials list would include reproductions or slides of 6–10 images that share a common metaphor. It may be necessary to make slides or color copies to get appropriate images. You might need various drawing materials, such as paper predivided into 10 frames for the metamorphosis drawings; sculpting materials; book lists for research; and decorative "junk." Access to computers would provide an option for a metamorphosis lesson that would make use of technology, allow the learners to try a wide variety of solutions, and mandate critical choice making.

As part of the evaluation, the student narrative provides a tool by which to measure their comprehension of the concepts of metaphor and symbolic power in art objects. The product criteria designed into the third and fourth lessons could be observed, discussed, and rated through peer and teacher assessment. This type of unit could also be evaluated through **portfolio assessment** techniques that document learner processes and procedures throughout the lessons (see Figure 8.8).

The preceding series of ideas for a secondary unit of study is a sequence of lessons that builds toward the creation of meaning. It defines a process that allows the learner to become involved with a concept, to gain personal insight about an idea, and to experience expressing the idea visually. The result is the construction of a learning situation that affords all learners an opportunity to make conceptual connections. The nature of lessons that encourage individuality and innovation allows students with special needs to experience the same personal successes as others in their classes.

PORTFOLIO ASSESSMENT FORM

NAME: _____   CLASS: _____   DATE: _____

TYPE OF ASSIGNMENT: _____   DATES REVIEWED: 1_____ 2_____ 3_____

REVIEWERS: TEACHER: 1____ 2____ 3____   PEERS: 1____ 2____ 3____   SELF: 1____ 2____ 3____

CRITERIA: Use criteria in individual assignment.

Scale: 1. Excellent   2. Very good   3. Good   4. Fair   5. Poor

Rate each area and comment in appropriate box.

	Teacher	Peer	Self
1. Artistic skills—careful use of media; effective handling of materials			
2. Aesthetic understanding—Are ideas effectively conveyed to the viewer?			
3. Use of an original technique or process of working—Is the idea unique?			
4. Level at which the work reflects careful planning			
5. Level at which the work satisfies the assignment criteria			

Further comments: Identify according to question and role.

Parent Review: Names _____   **Date:** _____

Comments:

Figure 8.8
Sample Portfolio Assessment Form

Judith Simpson.

Structuring Lessons

Lesson design is much like unit design, with the exception of exclusion of broad instructional concepts and addition of specific **instructional strategies** through which you will motivate and present material to students. Lesson plans are also more detailed.

Goals are generally drawn directly from the unit. Which goal(s) in the metaphorical unit is(are) targeted in the following lesson? Objectives are unit and lesson based. For example, in the lesson about transformation, the following objectives would be appropriate:

Students will:

~ choose an object to metamorphose from one creature to another.

~ understand the process involved in gradual modification.

~ use design elements of color, line, and texture to change the characteristics of the object.

~ learn the purpose of transformation.

Preparation needed before the lesson can be taught is sometimes included at this point of the plan. Further research may be needed, slides or copies of images must be gathered, a teacher product to test the idea should be completed, and possible materials for student production should be listed. Teaching posters and visual production displays help focus students on essential concepts and the criteria for successful completion of an assignment.

An instructional strategy section of the lesson plan must state the beginning, middle, and end of the presentation of material, and you must identify teacher participation in the lesson:

How are you intending to motivate your learners?

What will you do and say?

Will you do a materials demonstration?

How long will it take?

How long will students work independently?

How will you close the lesson?

There are several ways of writing out the instructional strategy section. Some teachers benefit by carefully scripting instructional plans; others work from plans that are clearly sequenced but very concise. Beginning teachers may find it helpful to write everything down to define what will be done and said. Supervisors, however, are seldom happy wading through paragraph after paragraph to get to the essence of an instructional presentation. An option for this section is to use a short sentence to explain each step of the presentation. Number each step and indicate at the end of the statement the amount of time the procedure is estimated to take.

Whatever method is chosen, the instructional part of a lesson plan serves several purposes. It is an outline to organize instruction, to prevent omissions, and to provide teachers with a quick review between classes. A supervisor will look at it to see what the level of organization is, how appropriately the instructional methods and strategies match the developmental needs of the learners, how well learners are made aware of stated goals and objectives, and how clearly the **criteria** are defined for achieving success in meeting the goals and objectives.

Materials are listed precisely in lesson plans (e.g., 10 pairs of scissors, two dozen sets of crayons, 12 watercolor brushes). The reason for this is to avoid last-minute preparations for an entering class and to assist in the orderly distribution and collection of materials.

The evaluation procedure of lessons will be determined by the day's activity and a choice of observation, discussion, critique, peer, and self-assessment methods. To shape your criteria, turn your objectives into the form of a question by mirroring your statements.

⌁ How Do We Use Thematic Concepts in Interdisciplinary Curricula?

Thematic planning has become a central idea in many curriculum reform models. Schools that practice interdisciplinary teaching develop programs based on broad topics that can support a semester or year of exploration. One rationale for thematic courses of study is that they require teams of teachers from varied grade levels or disciplines to work together to create a coherent curriculum. Also, well-chosen themes have relevance to the population of students and can become vehicles for the use of multiple instructional strategies.

A thematic planning team is sometimes made up of volunteers; at other times it includes a group of curriculum committee members compensated for extra assignments. Art teachers are usually included on planning committees in schools where art is considered a subject equal to other disciplines and integral to the education of the child. Art teachers should volunteer to be on planning teams where there is no mandate to do so. Being part of a curriculum team informs colleagues of the importance of art in the cognitive and affective development of children. Personal involvement with thematic planning helps the art educator to make strong conceptual connections to the rest of the curriculum. The effectiveness of an art educator on an interdisciplinary planning team is directly proportionate to his or her ability to articulate the ways art can be a vehicle for thought and expression.

The use of a carefully chosen conceptual theme establishes a connection for the learner that provides a basis for paralleling concepts among art, other disciplines, and life. Art is about more than products and processes, it is about ideas.

Choosing a Theme for Integrated/ Interdisciplinary Curricula

Themes that are broadly based—like neighborhoods, heroes, war, and peace—can be developed meaningfully. Choices that lack content and scope tend to encourage a "potpourri" approach to planning and cause fragmentation rather than coherence (Jacobs, 1989). Choices that favor the content of any one discipline are, according to Jacobs, apt to encourage polarity.

A potpourri curriculum results when the theme lacks a thread that weaves through each discipline. Choosing topics like England and classifications or categories like plants, animals, and bugs rather than thematic concepts can prevent an indepth exploration of content in all subject areas involved. Although it is tempting to spend a great deal of time studying a single country from all its perspectives, individual disciplines may still be taught the same way as they are traditionally. Common ideas being addressed at different times in every content area fail to accomplish the conceptual connection; art or any other subject is not related to anything other than its role in the studied country.

Polarity occurs when one discipline is favored as the guiding structure through which all others will be taught. An example of this would be an insistence that every other subject studied be looked at through the lens of biology and plants. Although it would be possible to make connections between most disciplines and plants, scientific limits could preclude innovative connections and associations from taking place. The result of polarity is a dilution of the content within each discipline.

How can you learn to work with others in planning courses of study? One way is to practice team planning before entering the teaching profession.

Practicing Team Planning

The opportunity to do some team teaching during preservice often occurs during fieldwork or campus programs. Although it is a great opportunity to experience working with a colleague, it is not the usual situation an artist/teacher encounters. Therefore, art education students can experience difficulty in primary attempts to collaborate. Several strategies can be productive preparation for team choice making.

Let us establish a scenario. Two to four people are given the task of finding a theme that will connect the real world of the learner to art and other disciplines. The major instructional goal of the curriculum is to provide learners with opportunities to experiment with, invent, and understand basic concepts and make connections *through* the subject—not just learn about it. Collectively, the team must find a theme and support the choice through making connections between it and other subject areas in the curriculum.

A good way to begin is by brainstorming and making a list of several themes. Find reasons to accept or reject certain ones, based on the criterion that a **metacurriculum** must provide substance in each content area. Metacurriculum designs include all areas of study integrated in one curriculum structure. Problems occur when a thematic choice lacks meaningful conceptual connections in each discipline. For example, the choice of empathy as a theme may be fine for visual art, literature, performing art, and social sciences, but would the connection be as apparent in mathematics? The test of a well-chosen theme involves whether it can be examined broadly, it provides a venue for examining similarities and contrasts, common patterns exist in one or more of the disciplines involved, and it is interesting enough to sustain exploration through many lenses over a period of time.

Once the team has accepted an idea, devise some task sheets that assign each member specific questions to research:

Does the topic require field studies?

What are the objectives?

Should existing models be looked at?

What will each team member look for?

How will findings be shared?

Look at models of other curricula. Studying applications of the theme in other settings will allow you to construct some concept questions that may begin to link the theme across the curricula. Listing concepts (such as observations) and events (such as commemorations) provides a basis for making another list:

What do we know about the theme?

What do we need to know?

How do we want to expand our findings to develop connections among discipline content?

Use a process called webbing (see Chapter 6) to connect concept questions and tie the pieces together. Establish a diagram that illustrates the process the team took. Generally, consensus is the result of everyone being able to see the validity in an idea. Making a visual model helps to reveal unanswered questions and to provide a basis for further discussion or explanation for presentation.

A model using community as the overarching theme and creating an interdisciplinary subtheme called "Faces of the Community" illustrates how four quarters of a curriculum could be designed around the following concepts: aging faces in the community, concealing/revealing faces, the face of the future, and society's changing face within the community (see Figure 8.9).

Parallel concepts about aging faces are being studied in visual art, sciences, social studies, math, performing arts, and language arts. While learners in the art room are studying people in their community through portraits, photographs, and transformation with theatrical techniques, they are also calculating ages of buildings and charting dates, learning about faces in community history, examining the notion of genetics in facial anatomy, and writing family biographies and reading plays about people of different ages. The concept of aging faces explored, examined, and expressed in many disciplines allows learners to experience a deeper understanding through meaningful connections.

An Example of an Interdisciplinary Elementary Experience

Following is a description of a community collaborative project that represents a truly interdisciplinary curriculum. The project began with a researched idea that was developed by Catherine Gilpin, an instructional support teacher at the Boyd-Berry Elementary School in Springfield, Missouri. It ended with songs and stories that songteller Bob Dyer helped the learners from grades two to four develop. The students per-

MODEL OF CURRICULUM
Submitted by: Ann Bauer, Elizabeth Harrison, Diana Lieker, John Runca, Jr.

COMMUNITY

FACES
OF THE COMMUNITY
(PEOPLE, ARCHITECTURE, NATURE, LAND, AND OBJECTS)

| AGING FACES OF THE COMMUNITY | CONCEALING REVEALING FACES | FUTURE FACE OF THE ... | SOCIETY CHANGING FACE OF ... |

Figure 8.9
Model of the structural base for an interdisciplinary curriculum based on a community theme

Submitted by Ann Bauer, Elizabeth Harrison, Diana Lieker, and John Runca Jr. (1994). Collection of the author.

formed their compositions in front of a mosaic mural created by themselves and community members under the direction of visual artist Christine Kreamer-Schilling. They created legends, tall tales, ghost stories, and songs that verbally translated what they had learned, and they wrote about their own lives in their community.

Kreamer-Schilling (1995) describes the impact of visually translating the learning through creation of a mosaic mural called "The Mid-Town Map" (see Color Plate 8.7):

> A mosaic mural is a lot like a community . . . small colorful pieces are pulled together to create one grand design . . . and I believe that the act of creating a mosaic mural can actually strengthen a community. The mural project . . . was an attempt to do just that. Having the city's highest "mobility" rate (120% turnover in student population in one year) these transient students felt little sense of community, of belonging. . . . Interviews, field trips to study native plants, treasure hunts to discover and catalogue local landmarks, and walking tours to learn about and draw local architecture, all produced a lot of personal experience and data. The mural became a visual storehouse for all the information students gathered, as well as a way to demonstrate to the children that they were a vital part of the picture.
>
> The wonder of any collaborative project is that the whole is greater than the parts. The mosaic mural has the added bonus of gathering all the parts and pieces up into one very rich and tactile teaching tool. Daily, it glistens in the hallway, a tantalizing reminder of all the facts and stories that are preserved in it. The hundreds of colorfully glazed clay shapes are packed with tales that tie the children to their community.

Beyond creating an integration of verbal/visual narrative, students participating in a project such as the Boyd-Berry mosaic experience working with geometric shapes, learn the history of the community, gain kinesthetic dexterity, find out about the scientific bonding of material to material, and get to exercise a host of interpersonal and intrapersonal skills in a cooperative endeavor. The most obvious benefit of such a learning experience is that it provides the student with many memories and avenues to travel back through to retrieve significant information. Retention is increased and understanding is enhanced when many single events coalesce in common meaning.

THEORY INTO PRACTICE
An Exercise in Making Conceptual Connections

Greene (1988) tells us that "being *able* to accomplish what one chooses to do" (p. 3) is dependent on more than our choices. Teachers need to develop the skills to put ideas into practice. Few of us can look at our own education and see consistent opportunities for conceptual thinking. Thinking in a synectic way is exciting. Certain activities can help activate conceptual thinking and apply it to curriculum design. The following is a step-by-step process you may wish to try.

The first step is to think about art as a body of knowledge—not a collection of things. Thinking contextually allows one to think conceptually. Art does not just happen. It tells human stories. Art does not exist only in galleries and museums.

The second step is to begin a resource collection of anything and everything that sparks your interest. Borrow ideas from other sources. Gather newspaper clippings, gallery announcements with images, pages from old art magazines, great photographs, advertisements, and any other visuals you think could provide lesson material. Put all these things in separate plastic sleeves in a loose-leaf notebook. Collect for several weeks.

The next step is to make a list of or to group **disparate** visuals that seem to have some connection. Find themes that could help you to classify or categorize what you have already collected. Push toward the less-than-obvious connections. For example, go beyond the idea that all things red, all fruits and vegetables, all buildings, or all vehicles must be grouped together. Look for strange ways to connect seemingly unrelated things. Maybe you have a reproduction of a painting, an ad for a new car, a newspaper article reporting a disaster, and a child's drawing. What do they have in common? How could you connect them? Do this for about four weeks. Connect things, leave them alone, go back the next week and see if you can make more exciting associations, and repeat this until the connections reflect creative, original thought.

Once you have classified your visuals, you have a theme. Now find concepts that reside in that theme. For example, you have a group of things in pieces: a chomped-on carrot, a toy doll with one leg missing, a dog with one eye, a house with no roof, a plane with one wing. Maybe the concept is destruction, maybe the concept is picking up the pieces, maybe the concept is the relationship of parts to the whole.

Find artwork that reflects your concept. Could we find artwork that reflects destruction, picking up the pieces, or the relationship of part to whole? Are we held within a time line or stylistic period or any one culture to find our works? Can we bridge worlds, ages, places, and spaces within our concepts?

Begin listing artworks that you know deal with your concepts. Look further to discover work that you may have forgotten or not known about. Assemble a **tabletop gallery** from your resource file. If your school does not have reproductions, make some slides or color copies.

Theme, concept, and visual exemplars chosen, now think about what your art content, techniques, and concepts will be. In other words, will your content be portraits painted in watercolor, using balanced shapes with one piece missing? Will your content be sculptures of chairs hand built in clay that have to function with fewer than four legs?

For the next four weeks, use your resource material to come up with three to five unit themes, applicable concepts, and lesson designs appropriate for elementary level children. Do the same for a middle school art program.

In the last four weeks of the semester, devise units and lessons from the same materials that would reflect concepts and art content and techniques for secondary students.

When you finish this exercise, you will have a set of unit design ideas that reflect a desire to teach toward the development of conceptual thinking.

A Student Model of a Secondary Conceptual Unit

The following unit was designed by Jill Hessinger, an art education major who, throughout a semester, completed the previously described exercise in conceptual connection making. Her comment about her unit was (paraphrased), "I never thought I could get to this point, every plan I had ever done was so technique based. I worked hard to understand the conceptual thing, but now it makes so much sense, I'm really excited about it." As a beginning teacher, Jill carefully scripted her first lesson since it was the foundation upon which students could build understanding. She prefaced the unit with this statement:

> Throughout history, artists have been fueled by their own feelings of vulnerability. Many artists have portrayed a sense of humankind's vulnerability with respect to an ever-changing society. But what about subject matter that appears vulnerable, but is otherwise? The artist may be sending a mixed message. Is the artist toying with our preconceived notions of our own vulnerability? (Hessinger, 1995)

Displaced Vulnerability

Grade Level: Secondary
Descriptive Title: A Metaphoric View of Displaced Vulnerability
Unit Goals: Adapted from the Visual Arts Standard-Commencement General Education-New York State

Art Standard 1
Create artworks in which students use and evaluate different kinds of media, subjects, themes, symbols, metaphors, and images.

Art Standard 2
Select and use media and processes that communicate intended meaning in their artworks, and exhibit competence in at least two media.

Art Standard 3
Analyze and interpret the ways in which political, cultural, social, religious, and psychological concepts and themes have been explored in visual art.

Art Standard 4
Analyze works of art from diverse world cultures and discuss the ideas, issues, and events of the culture that they convey.

Instructional Concepts
According to Manuel Barkan, designer of the "troika" model of art production, art criticism, and art history:

> When I design something or paint something . . . I start from . . . an idea, a purpose. . . . There is a transformation. . . . The idea doesn't come out the same way I conceived it. The material never takes . . . a preconceived form. The material forces me to do something. Well, it doesn't force me. I lend myself to the material. The idea comes out differently. . . . I feel differently and I see anew. (Zahnor, 1989, pp.170–174)

Every art communicates because it expresses. It enables us to share vividly and deeply in meanings to which we had been dumb, or for which we had but the ear that permits what is said to pass through in transit to overt action. . . . Communication is the process of creating participations, of making common what had been isolated and singular. (Dewey, 1934, p. 244)

Critics come to a work of art with a history—a world view—and these do, should and must affect how they see a work of art (Barrett, 1994, p. 10)

Students should learn that each art form has its own characteristics and makes its distinctive contributions, that each has its own history and heroes. . . . Students also need to understand that art is a powerful force in the everyday life of people around the world, who design and make many of the objects they use and enjoy. (Barrett, 1994, pp. 13–14)

Relation to Life

Many students may feel vulnerable in this ever-changing society. Sometimes students may be swept up in the fast pace and believe that things are out of control. It may seem as if outside influences are manipulating them. In order for students to gain control of insecurities and begin to perceive their vulnerability as something they can deal with, they first have to identify it. Then, they can contemplate various ways to literally displace it, and relate the literate with metaphor. When students do this, they are utilizing diversified problem-solving techniques which are beneficial to them in other studies and in life. (National Art Education Standards. *Discovering who we are*.)

Objectives

Students will create a sculpture which expresses their ideas of vulnerability and displacement.

Students will use various media, symbols, and metaphors in their work.

Students will exhibit competency in the handling of their chosen media.

Students will complete a *Metaphoric View of Displaced Vulnerability* worksheet and a *Self-Evaluation* worksheet.

Students will identify and analyze social, political, cultural, religious, and/or psychological influences in exemplary artwork and in class productions.

Lesson Options

Throughout the ages, the artist has lived in two worlds—the visible and the invisible. (Fearing, Beard, & Martin, 1979, p. 75)

Lesson 1

Introduce unit with art talk from exemplars. Explain the terms vulnerability (unprotected from danger, susceptible to injury) and displaced (moved from the usual or proper place, or in psychiatry, to transfer an emotion to a logical, yet inappropriate object). Define metaphor (a figure of speech or visual presentation in which a word, phrase or image is likened to another) and literal (real, not going beyond actual facts; accurate; as, the literal truth). How do the defined terms apply to the exemplars?

Rubens' work visualizes the myth of Achilles' heel. Thetis, immortal mother of Achilles, attempts to provide immortality to her son by dipping him into the River Styx. But this left a vulnerable spot, the heel with which he was held. Like Superman, Achilles was invincible. And like Superman, whose vulnerability was kryptonite, Achilles was struck down when his tendon was severed. The Achilles myth is a literary metaphor for man's vulnerability. Just as we all desire security through strength, everyone has an Achilles' heal.

Barlach's work portrays man's aspirations and vulnerability through World War I terms. This theme is relative to the world of today since many countries are embattled in wars and civil conflicts. Upon close examination of the sculptural piece, one notices that the figure contradicts itself; it appears to be gliding through the air yet one foot is rooted to the ground. (There are always conflicts between a country's ideals and its military vulnerability.) This sculpture is a visual metaphor for all military conflicts.

Bourgeois' work traps vulnerable body parts, such as the eyes, with heavy marble. According to Bourgeois, eye communication is totally separate from body language; they speak on their own. Eyes are not only themselves vulnerable, but are the Achilles' heel to one's inner sanctions since they can reveal the wearer to others. The eyes are a metaphor for human emotions; they take on the responsibility of making something (emotions) intangible, tangible.

Magritte uses what appears to be vulnerable subject matter and transforms it into a vision of the unexpected and disturbing. As viewers, we become suspicious of his painted world and begin to question his (and our) reality. Is Magritte using metaphor in *The Tomb of the Wrestlers*? Does he see things in his world that we do not? A rose is a delicate and fragile product of nature. When it is portrayed as big as a room it takes on the proportions of something out of *Little Shop of Horrors*. Or is the room small? What is the scale of our vulnerability?

The work from the unknown American artist preys on the vulnerability of man's inner fears. The totem is so powerful that it must be hidden in a box. But then how is something this potent created, and for what reason? When can it be brought out of the box? What political, cultural, social, religious and psychological concepts must be present to need to bring the totem out and what meanings should be attached to it? Could the box be a metaphor for censorship, and the totem, social issues? What else could the *Boxed Totem* stand for? If we tie this work with the Achilles myth, how might we do it? Is the totem the heel, or is the box? Why?

Students will be given a journal worksheet entitled *A Metaphoric View of Displaced Vulnerability*. The worksheet will include an overview of the class discussion and will ask students to list their Achilles' heel(s) and the outside influences that make them feel vulnerable (see Materials for sample worksheet).

Students will be asked to bring an old shoe to the next class. It is suggested to look at home (students should ask first if they can take it since it might be unwearable after they are done with it); suggest thrift shops, rummage sales, house and garage sales as a source. Students could split the cost with another student. NO GOOD SHOES, PLEASE!

Lesson 2

Using their worksheets, students will begin to think about what type of assemblage, shoe sculpture they can create representing their Achilles' heel, and ways to displace their vulnerabilities in order to better control them. Students are to represent, metaphorically, their ideas and they are to continually refer to their worksheets as they are working. Exemplars will be displayed while students begin sketch work. Various materials will be available. Tag board will be available for bases. Students will submit their concept ideas, sketches, and chosen materials for teacher approval.

Lesson 3 through completion

Students work on the sculpture. If there are to be changes in their work, students are to document the revisions.

Final Lesson

Students will participate in class critiques, and hand in their worksheets, documentation, written work and self-evaluation sheets.

Materials

Exemplars: Peter Paul Rubens, *Achilles Dipped into the River Styx* (1630–5); Ernst Barlach, *The Avenger* (1914); Louise Bourgeois, *Nature Study: Eyes* (1984); Rene Magritte, *The Tomb of the Wrestlers* (1960); Artist unknown, *Boxed Totem* from the book *A Fish That's a Box*, by M. M. Esterman, 1990, *A Fish That's a Box*, Arlington, VA: Great Ocean Publishers.

Varied art materials applicable to sculptural techniques. Students may supplement available art room materials.

Evaluation Criteria

Did the student create an assemblage which expresses his or her idea of personal vulnerability and displacement?

Did the student use varied media, symbols, and metaphors?

Did the student exhibit competency in the chosen media?

Did the student document the work? Did the student complete two worksheets?

Did the student participate in class discussions and critiques?

Worksheet Example

A Metaphoric View of Displaced Vulnerability

Name   Date

Definitions according to **Webster** (displaced, vulnerability, literal, metaphor)

1. Write a brief statement of the significance of the works discussed in class (list works, provide space for answers).
2. Define the term Achilles' heel. List your own Achilles' heel(s).
3. What political, cultural, social, religious, and psychological concepts influence your feelings of vulnerability?
4. List ways that you could displace your vulnerability? (literally and metaphorically paralleled)

Connecting Ideas to Other Disciplines

Take any of your written unit ideas, and make a list of other subject areas to which your chosen concepts relate. Use a schema such as a wheel, with your theme and concepts at the center. Between the spokes of the wheel, place subjects like language, history, science, math, reading, art, music, and dance and fill in the missing connections. An example may be the concept of destruction: in language, stories or poems could be written that deal with plagues and pestilence; in history and science, students could study the history of the plague in Europe, the scientific quest to find cures, and the effects of famine on the body; in math, you could study ratios of people affected versus the unaffected and economic impacts in terms of trade goods; art, music, and dance that reflect the effects of disease could fill in the wheel.

SUMMARY

Throughout this chapter I have examined conceptual thinking as a basis for curriculum design. Beginning with a definition of conceptual thinking, examples such as the elementary unit helped to illustrate the interplay between ideas and actions.

Certain influences must be considered in designing a curriculum. Existing documents such as national and state standards, as well as systemwide plans, must be a primary consideration in designing units and lessons. Our own pedagogical choices influence the ways we choose to implement a curriculum.

Conceptual design choices include themes, social issues, and metaphors. All these notions afford developmentally appropriate unit choices at any level.

The concept of interdisciplinary curriculum was also explored in this chapter. Again, the use of a theme provides unity and cohesion in a curriculum that spans disciplines. If we choose to become involved in writing an interdisciplinary curriculum, we must feel comfortable working with a team.

The role of the art teacher is powerful. The greater our ability to design situations that provoke students into exploring, selecting, organizing, perceiving, and experiencing the world from a visual perspective, the more we are teachers of meaning and the more we provide the context for learners to construct personal meaning through art.

ADVANTAGES AND CHALLENGES OF MAKING THIS CHOICE

Advantages

Whether you are planning alone or with a team, thematic, metaphorical, conceptual approaches help to connect the teacher and the subject to the learner. Opportunities for more authentic education are provided by a learning environment that reflects an understanding of who the student is, what influences or shapes learner thinking outside of school, and how student experiences and developmental levels affect learning.

Studies indicate that visual learners are apt to be low achievers, adolescent dropouts, and behavioral problems. Learners confronted with the challenge of English as a Second Language and urban learners with **field-dependent** tendencies have difficulty succeeding in traditional, verbally dominated classrooms. Concept-based, thematic, and metaphorical designs in art provide a foundation for interaction between verbal and visual ideas. The holistic nature of this combination affords a way of knowing that improves the chances of success for the "at risk" child. Passow (1991), Payne (1984), Rodriguez (1984), and others remind us of the power of holistic curriculum in the education of urban adolescents. Others benefit from cohesive curriculum as well. Experiences in the art room, utilizing the approaches discussed throughout the book, ensure a higher level of student involvement in the process of finding new ways to make conceptual connections and to find personal meaning in art.

The problem of choosing content that is relevant to the learner is nonexistent when student-centered lessons are designed. Tap into learner experiences to find appropriate concepts. Lessons that have meaning include processes to connect ideas, challenge learner perceptions of content, and provide an impetus to formulate new metaphors through art media (Simpson, 1996).

As students gain understanding of any subject, their interest in that subject increases. Increased participation results in fewer behavior problems and higher rates of on-task participation during classes. Learners value knowledge that empowers them. Expressing and communicating ideas through art is a form of empowerment. A graduate student related the following:

> Most of the students in the room admit they are taking art because they needed another course. Most also say they are going to elect to take it again. They come to school most days because they are working on their "art" books. They make paper, choose images, draw and paint, write, design covers and special containers for their thematic books.

The students in this class represent a diverse ethnic and academically skilled population. Neither gender is favored in the design of the production problem. Personal ownership, pride, and craftsmanship can be evidenced in their work. They make creative decisions, decide how to best convey their ideas, and communicate a message through a visual process. Working through the critical thought process makes art meaningful to learners.

Panofsky (1972) recognizes the importance of self in the acquisition of meaning. He speaks of intrinsic focus having the greatest influence on how humans interpret the signs and symbols of the world. Art experiences like the preceding examples utilize both the intrinsic and extrinsic knowledge bases of the learner and intensify meaning.

Integrated Curriculum

Making use of the **synergistic** relationship between art and other subjects creates a learning climate that maximizes the odds of students truly understanding a shared concept. Enormous amounts of information can be connected in a way that makes sense to learners. Information can be synchronized, allowing concepts to be synthesized and learners to think, "Where does this fit, rather than why do I need to know this" (Jacobs, 1989, p. 43).

Art becomes part of the real world and understood as an integral piece of the human condition. Students learn through art rather than about it. The need to find creative, personal statements regarding ideas is satisfied through the expressive modes of performance, writing, and art making. Concepts experienced across disciplines are strongly connected for the learner.

Challenges

The main challenge in thematic, conceptually connected planning is that assumptions may exist as to the role of an art program. Art classes are sometimes viewed as places where "stuff" is made, where holiday decorations for the school and scenery for plays are fabricated, and where learners go to get a break from learning. One has to be sure to articulate the role of art in developing thinking processes in the learner when opting to change that perception. Teachers must be proactive, not reactive, in dealing with misconceptions about the role of art education in schools.

A prevalent view of art history is that it is best studied on a time line. Planning a curriculum based on ideas rather than dates is sometimes misunderstood. It is important to choose images that bridge cultures and time periods and to reinforce the conceptual plan. Articulating reasons for approaching art content this way can be supported by good unit design.

Students who participate in inquiry-based, exploratory learning are often reticent to return to traditional classes. Parents can misunderstand the purpose of a learner-centered curriculum and fear an **integrated curriculum.** The nature of interdisciplinary and integrated courses of study differs from that of traditional programs. Parents often think their children are not learning the necessary skills or basic content of any discipline if the structure is nonlinear. A thoughtful choice of evaluative procedures and assessment tools can substantiate the value of learner-centered practice.

Time constraints created by schedules that allow elementary art teachers one 45-minute period per week with a class make continuity and coherence difficult. A schedule like this may mean that each class begins with a brief review but need not preclude sequencing an idea or the continuance of the same lesson over several weeks. If instruction is conducted in regular classrooms, work storage should be discussed with the classroom teacher previous to teaching the unit.

Overwhelming numbers of students seen each week can cause organizational problems if one becomes involved in too many different unit designs. Selecting an all-school theme, a grade-by-grade conceptual set, or a course-by-course conceptual structure helps to avoid logistic and preparation problems (see Figures 8.10–8.12 and Color Plates 8.8 and 8.9). Getting too ambitious could cause dilution of content and create a potpourri curriculum situation.

Figure 8.10

A first grader's crayon drawing of "Things That Live Under My Bed," part of a "Celebration of Ourselves" theme for grades one through eight

Collection of the author.

319

ACTION PLAN FOR INSTRUCTIONAL DECISION MAKING

~ *Identify* the goals and objectives of your school's curriculum.

~ *Identify* the needs of your learners.

~ *Create* a list of key concepts appropriate for each grade level.

~ *Relate* your concepts to major themes.

~ *Choose* artwork that reflects the themes across cultures.

~ *Develop* conceptual units that address the curriculum structure.

~ *Sequence* lessons within your unit to build toward meaning.

~ *Choose* production activities that build learner skills and reinforce the chosen concept.

~ *Create* exciting instructional strategies that will engage the learner.

~ *Share* conceptual units with colleagues in other disciplines.

DISCUSSION QUESTIONS

1. Can I take the same theme and develop units that are appropriate at the elementary, middle, and secondary levels?

2. How does conceptual planning help students to connect art to life and to themselves?

3. Why are units and lessons based on concepts more meaningful to learners?

4. Is it possible to plan interdisciplinary units without having the art activity become a supplement to other subjects?

5. How do I plan interdisciplinary or integrated arts lessons that are based on the content in visual art and that reinforce the thematic concept?

6. What form of assessment is most applicable to learner-centered planning?

SUGGESTED ACTIVITIES

1. Using the semester assignment discussed in the text can be the most productive way to begin to make conceptual connections.

2. In your journal, keep a list of ideas independent of those in your conceptual resource notebook. Write down why those ideas could be important to students of different ages. List artists whose work supports the ideas.

3. Visit a classroom as an observer, and document what you see and hear. Are the lessons about ideas? Do students know why they are doing what they are doing? Can the students relate the activity to ideas beyond the making?

ANNOTATED RESOURCES

Dissanayake, E. (1988). *What is art for?* Seattle, WA: University of Washington Press.
Dissanayake presents a case for art as a distinctly human form of expression. The author has said that she takes an "anthro, bio, physio, psycho, sociological" point of view of art as "making special."

Goldberg, M. R., & Phillips, A. (Eds.). (1992). *Arts as education* (Reprint Series No. 24). Cambridge, MA: Harvard Educational Review.
This is a collection of articles that support the arts as an "essential aspect of development" and "central" to education.

Gardner, H. (1982). *Art, mind, and brain.* New York: Basic Books.
This book investigates creative growth and development.

Goodman, N. (1988). *Languages of art* (6th ed.). Indianapolis, IN: Hackett.
Goodman investigates how ideas and symbol systems that represent them in various disciplines are combined in a quest for "true" meaning.

Greene, M. (1988). *The dialectic of freedom.* New York: Teachers College Press.
In her argument for the pursuit of freedom in education, Greene emphasizes the role of the arts in personal expression and empowerment.

Jacobs, H. H. (1989). *Interdisciplinary curriculum: Design and implementation.* Alexandria, VA: Association for Supervision and Curriculum Development.
This guide presents a comprehensive view of the design and purpose of integrated, interdisciplinary curriculum.

Lakoff, G., & Johnson, M. (1980). *Metaphors we live by.* Chicago: University of Chicago Press.
The authors present the concept that metaphor is part of everyday perception, thought, and action.

London, P. (1994). *Step outside: Community based art education.* Portsmouth, NH: Heinemann.
London presents the community and its resources as the structure for an art education curriculum.

Manning, M., Manning, G., & Long, R. (1994). *Theme immersion: Inquiry-based curriculum in elementary and middle schools.* Portsmouth, NH: Heinemann.
This book discusses how themes are selected and implemented in curricula.

Moody, W. J. (Ed.). (1990). *Artistic intelligences: Implications for education.* New York: Teachers College Press.
This is a collection of writings that emphasize the integrative nature of the arts in education, as well as the importance of the development of the child's intelligence through the arts.

Paley, N. (1995). *Finding art's place.* New York: Routledge.
Three art education "experiments" that take place outside of the school are highlighted in this book. The role of art education and the struggles of urban youth to find their place in our culture are the subjects.

Panofsky, E. (1972). *Studies in iconology: Humanistic themes in the art of the Renaissance.* New York: Harper & Row.
This book is a study of the levels of symbolic meaning in art.

Payne, C. M. (1984). *Getting what we ask for: The ambiguity of success and failure in urban education.* Westport, CT: Greenwood.
The author provides a rationale for high teacher expectations for all learners.

KEY TERMS

Canon   A standard for judgment; criterion

Constructivist   Educational environment that allows the student to construct personal meaning that is essential to learning

Criteria   Established conditions that must be met within any assignment

Disparate   Having no apparent connection; clearly different

Evaluation   Measures and documentation of student progress

Field-dependent learning   Learning that is nonlinear and dependent on understanding the whole concept before examining its parts

Genre   A particular sort, kind, or category of art characterized by a certain form or style (such as still life, portrait, etc.)

Goals   Teacher expectations for student learning

Instructional concepts   Ideas supported through published research that give educational validity to your unit ideas

Instructional strategies   Methods of motivating students, delivering information, and ensuring that learners are clear about what is expected of them

Integrated curriculum   A course of study that connects subjects with the skills and content that are interrelated within them

Metacurriculum   A curriculum in which the same skills are taught across subjects (higher-order thinking would be an example of the type of skill that could be taught throughout a curriculum)

Objectives   Assessable expectations for student behaviors and performance

Pedagogy   The art of teaching

Portfolio assessment   An organized body of student work that is reviewed by the student, teacher, and others to monitor growth in knowledge, skills, attitudes, efforts, and achievements throughout a course of study; students select material based on clear criteria for selection and judgment; a portfolio encourages a student to reflect on past work, see progress, and chart a course for improvement

Synergism   The combination of two or more things that create an effect greater than the individual parts

Tabletop gallery   An accordion-fold display made from matboard scraps taped together and small reproductions

PART **3**

Artful Teaching

CHAPTER **9**   **Teaching as an Art Form:**
Creating Meaning Through Art

CHAPTER 9

Teaching as an Art Form: Creating Meaning Through Art

Judith W. Simpson
Boston University

with contributing statements from all authors

Guiding Questions

~ What is your role as a teacher of art?

~ How do the choices you make help you to become an artful teacher?

~ How do art teachers create a context for meaning?

In 1956, Herbert Read wrote:

> ... the purpose of art education, which should be identical with the purpose of education itself, is to develop in the child the integrated mode of experience with its corresponding "syntonic" physical disposition, in which thought always has its correlate in concrete visualization. (p. 105)

The word *syntonic* means responsive and adaptive to the social and personal environment. Concern about the purpose of art education remains the same as in Read's day—it is critical to the holistic development of the child. As both Read (1956) and Dewey (1934) stressed, the central notions of a child's experience are key to meaning, and visual expression is critical to the growth of one's creativity and divergent thinking abilities.

Concern for the learner provides a rationale for making informed choices in teaching. Art teaching is about fostering the artistic behaviors in all of us. It provides opportunities for learners to develop visual thinking patterns that allow alternative ways to communicate in and understand more fully the nature of the global society.

 ## What Is Your Role as a Teacher of Art?

Perhaps now that you have read and responded to the questions posed in the preceding chapters, your reasons for choosing to become a teacher of art have been strengthened. The role of the art teacher is complex and charged with the primary responsibility for the visual education of children. This responsibility includes and expands upon the making of things. As Arnheim (1969) pointed out, we are responsible for developing the "tools for abstract thinking" by teaching learners how to think visually. Art classes are the ground where the seeds of imagination are cultivated.

The importance of art in the curriculum is often predicated on the ability of teachers to articulate its worth. As O'Fallon (1995) cautions, "The battle is ultimately about what we 'the arts' do in the shaping of the human as actor in and upon the world" (p. 23). Knowing how visual art benefits the learner becomes your responsibility. Teaching that reflects substance is evidenced in learners' understanding. Art concepts integrated with other subject areas for the purpose of enhancing cognition reveal the power of visual learning. Participatory learning through visual communication enables children for whom a predominantly verbal system of education is not working to be successful.

Photo 9.1
Teacher Aletha Race captures the attention of a class working on African dashikis.

Judith Simpson.

Art as a socially acceptable means of expression can provide learners with a vehicle through which to respond to a less than perfect world (Simpson, 1995). Understanding other cultures is facilitated by studying art objects that have supported various belief systems over time. By choosing to become a teacher of art you have also chosen to teach something about humanity.

～ How Do the Choices You Make Help You to Become an Artful Teacher?

Through synthesizing ideas presented in this text and connecting them with learners, you can assess your own learning. You might want to think about how the information in each chapter could be applied at the elementary, middle, and secondary levels. How do the pieces fit together? What additional experiences might expand your knowledge base about how teachers teach and how learners learn?

Following is a brief review of the subject matter in the book, including questions that address becoming an artful teacher. Thoughts about artful teaching, as seen through the lenses of the authors of each chapter, are included.

Knowing about the development of our students and about the factors that influence their cognitive and affective growth is key to our understanding how to teach them. Sarason (1990) tells us that "the conceptual task of the teacher in regard to any subject matter or activity is to have a clear picture of how it arises, unfolds, and gets transformed as the child develops" (p. 16). We must know not only how the child develops but also how the subject matter relates to the child's world. The diversity in classrooms goes beyond ethnicity—it includes socioeconomic ranges, vast differences in early childhood preparation for school, high transiency, and fluctuating attendance rates. Real children in real classrooms bring a set of learning conditions to school with them each day. How will your understanding of the artistic growth and development of learners influence how you make appropriate instructional choices?

Marianne Kerlavage states how knowing something about child development helps you to become an artful teacher:

> A good teacher, by my definition, is one who understands what her or his student knows and is able to do and then proceeds to aid the student in moving to the next level of understanding, creative thought, and technical competence. For teachers to be able to do this, they need to understand the general holistic development of children and young adults. There needs to be a total understanding of the ways individuals grow and develop artistically, aesthetically, physically, cognitively, socially, and emotionally. Equally as important is a need to define community, cultural, ethnic, religious, economic, and family variables, which also influence and perhaps even redefine growth, development, and artistic behavior.
>
> Artful teaching, then, requires one to create learning activities that will (1) help the students to define and recognize their own learning, ability, and developmental place; (2) create avenues for all students to push themselves to new levels of learning and technical skill; and (3) be flexible enough for all students to grow at their own pace. Artful teaching in a developmental framework does not mean that we have unstructured free time. It means that we have clear-cut learning expectations for all students. It means that our goal involves learning and growth in and through the visual arts, not just playing with materials. Artful teachers must develop research skills to use in creating a portrait of their students. They also must become masters at assessment—not only assessment of student understanding and program effectiveness but, even more valuable, assessment that aids students in understanding their own growth.

Photo 9.2
Working with individual students is often the art teacher's role. Jeff Fair helps a high school student with his painting.

Marianne Kerlavage.

When you were studying art, you may have been more aware of, or identified more with, certain artistic behaviors than others. Practicing artists seldom document their own processes from beginning to end. Therefore, we are not always cognizant of the best ways to bring about artistic behavior in students. Classroom teachers of art who do not have a history of personal art making often understand this phenomenon from a more logical perspective. Choosing to vary your strategies in the classroom, to expand your knowledge of art and art making, and to build a solid set of studio competencies yourself could maximize the artistic development for all your learners. Karen Carroll says:

> In my thinking, good teachers of art have expertise in the making of art. They have a broad base of skills related to various media and different ways of working. They also have a good grounding in American art, world art, anthropology, history, science, and literature. They have finessed some special skills and forged a body of their own work so that they know the difference between engaging with a highly teacher-directed assignment and forming one's own visual problems. They then take this expertise and think about how it might serve the needs and readiness of their learners, which may vary tremendously from class to class and student to student. They ask themselves: What do I know of art that would be useful to my students? I also hope classroom teachers know to call upon art teachers, where they can, for help in thinking about the ways they can make the processes of teaching and learning more visual and artful.
>
> Part of making "the making of art" useful to students rests upon the development of skills, processes, and knowledge about art. Learners cannot process interdisciplinary ideas, themes, or concepts if their skills in art are limited. Learners also need information about art, ways of talking critically about both product and process, and conversations that explore the reasons people make and respond to art.

How might expanding your own experience and expertise with different artistic behaviors benefit your students? What artistic behaviors would you like to develop in your learners, and why?

Photo 9.3
Teacher Holly Patterson works with a student making an artistic decision.

Marianne Kerlavage.

Through images, learners begin to connect art to themselves, to life, and to the world. Context and content come alive through making art based on art. Knowing about art content is an ongoing process. We can decide to make discoveries with learners to help us develop a strong knowledge base. Selecting objects and images that explain ideas across cultures assists students in understanding the similarities and differences between peoples. Objects and images stimulate the imagination and create a sense of curiosity, providing a format for discourse about art as well as for art making. How might expanding the range and depth of your own knowledge of art objects and images benefit your learners? What ways of engaging learners with art objects and images can you imagine using with your learners?

In Chapter 4, Jean Delaney dealt with the use of images and objects in the classroom. The following comments define how she views the artful teacher:

> I've always thought of teaching as an art form. Good teaching involves many of the same processes that are involved in creating images and objects. An artist experiments, and shapes textures, lines, and colors to create a work of art, but it requires a lot of hard work, a great deal of reflection, and many false starts before the feelings and ideas crystallize.
>
> The process of shaping a unit or lesson plan is similar. It also requires hard work; builds on personal experiences; involves inspiration, contemplation, experimentation, and reflection; and may require many false starts before ideas and feelings crystallize. In addition, a teacher needs to know what learners bring to the encounter with an art image or object.
>
> As with an artist's inspiration, an idea for a unit or lesson plan can come from a variety of sources. An exhibition of folding screens at the National Gallery of Art inspired me to create a plan that would engage middle school learners. Both intuitive and practical knowledge are involved in shaping experiences with art images and objects, and the process is not a sequential one any more than creating an art image or object follows a

specific, predetermined sequence. Just as an artist may revisit ideas and rework a painting, an artful teacher reflects upon the responses of students to the learning strategies he or she has designed and may reshape them to work better.

The power of the visual narrative goes beyond the literal stories on cave walls and graffiti in subways. All narratives are not about survival, but it might be said that all artists are storytellers. Even the New York painters in the 1950s and 1960s conveyed the story of a frenetically paced society with the energy of their marks and strokes upon the canvas. Hopper and others often invite us to finish their stories. Young children tell elaborate tales about mysterious lines and linear shapes that defy identification. Clearly, stories are a major part of the visual art of learners from very early on. Janet Olson sees artful teaching as being mindful of the power of story:

> In my chapter, I suggested that stories are a natural vehicle for understanding and appreciating the lives of others. I presented some of the research found in the field of language arts to enable further understanding of how the concept of story develops in children. I view this information as especially helpful to art teachers, to ensure the developmental appropriateness of lessons that relate to story. It is essential that teachers who choose to relate an art curriculum to the concept of story be good listeners, develop good dialoguing skills with their students, and also teach their students a variety of translation skills. Artful teachers who use story must help students to translate meaning from the verbal to visual forms of expression.
>
> I have attempted to make a commanding case for constructing an art curriculum under the all-consuming umbrella of story. All other curriculum issues can be addressed successfully within this overall framework. I hope that my chapter offered the artful teacher a relevant and viable educational choice that provides a more natural and human understanding for the role that art plays in the lives of all people.

Now that you have been introduced to the uses of story as more than illustration of a passage, how can you think about effectively using the concept of story in your teaching?

Photo 9.4
A student receives a suggestion from teacher Tara Breslin.

Karen Carroll.

As research affirms, the complex nature of teaching makes it impossible to prepare for the classroom by mastering only one instructional strategy (Bartolome, 1994). We have no assurance that what works with one group of students will work with another. Visual strategies help learners to develop what Arnheim (1986) says are the cognitive procedures known as "intuitive perception and intellectual analysis" (p. 29). Both of the procedures are necessary for the mind to function at its fullest. The visual supplements the written word in a way that affords learners the opportunity to comprehend a phenomenon, an object, an image, or an event in a more complete way. Chapter 6 addressed how and why you might incorporate artistic strategies into your teaching. The author, Cheryl Hamilton, defines an artful teacher in this way:

> To me, a good teacher of art is enthusiastic, knowledgeable, skilled, and caring about art as content and about children as artistic learners. However, without the ability to communicate well, these characteristics cannot be fully shared with students. Classroom communication includes speaking, listening, writing, drawing, painting, forming, constructing, demonstrating, reading, observing, organizing, and presenting. All these communication skills can be learned, practiced, and improved.
>
> I believe an artful teacher is like an amazing juggler who incorporates a bowling ball, a birthday cake with lit candles, a filled water balloon, and perhaps a few sharp blades into the act. This performance requires the smooth handling of these dissimilar elements so that the effect is seen as effortless. Just like the juggler works with all the elements in the act, the artful teacher communicates with the changing elements of students, course content, colleagues, administrators, and communities. An artful teacher grows in understanding throughout life. During this process, an artful teacher offers these gains in skills, knowledge, and passion for art to all through a variety of communication formats.
>
> Begin your teaching performance by asking yourself the following: What forms of communication do I prefer? What forms am I willing to try? What forms do I need to improve? Allow yourself plenty of time to become an artful teacher, but start now by learning to communicate well.

How might the way you shape a problem affect what and how students learn? Have you ever been in a situation where you knew what the teacher wanted but you didn't believe in the answer? Visual problems that are challenging and can be solved successfully by diverse learners have more than one answer. Teaching for creative development necessitates designing lessons that allow learners to perceive, select, and explore, through their own lenses, all the possible visual solutions to the problem. This takes practice on the part of a teacher and a willingness to establish criteria and parameters that allow for individualism. Sandra Kay shares her definition of an artful teacher:

> For me an artful teacher, like a piece of art, is one who touches the souls of others. This individual asks questions like: What do my students know, what do they need to know, and in what ways will I channel or guide their learning or thinking toward that end? Then ask, How do I make the journey worth taking?
>
> Designing elegant problems takes thoughtful practice. Think back on the assignments or problems posed to you in your learning career. Which aroused your imaginal sensibilities? These are the assignments that most likely impressed your classmates to the degree that you remember some of their solutions too. Ask yourself whether the problem is suitable for all the students in your classes now. If not, how can you alter it (reduce, expand, elaborate on it) to be meaningful to a broader audience? Does that audience include the would-be scientist, engineer, or editor?
>
> Once you have refined one problem to its elegant state, you will find all others easier to design. You do not have to reinvent the wheel. The work and autobiographical writings of great artists contain great inspiration. Sharing the words of an artist with your

students (of any age) will help many of them see one elegant solution to the stated problem. You will know when the problem is elegant, for it will be simple and profound, which is appealing to all audiences, more often than one would expect.

Teaching from ideas and concepts helps to expand the range of possibilities for problem design. Providing situations where learners can connect diverse art images and objects, through exploring a concept common to them all, does several other things as well. For example, everyone has their own view of the concept of personal freedom. Adolescent learners may also have a preference for a medium through which they can best express the notion. Middle school learners may think about freedom as being able to stay out until a certain hour or working to earn their own money, whereas elementary students might consider freedom as having the ability to fly. Art images and objects exist to support each of these levels of thinking—from the simple to complex and from concrete to abstract. The openness of designing units based on ideas rather than topics provides a teacher with rich possibilities for the encouragement of divergent thinking.

I truly believe that people can learn to think about diverse subject areas as congruent and confluent. In other words, although most of us are educated in isolated disciplines, we can teach ourselves how ideas from multiple subjects may overlap or come together sensibly. Since art relates to every area in the average curriculum, we can learn to find ways to integrate art and art concepts into any set of notions we choose.

The word *relevance*, although overused in terms of learners' needs, does have credence. If we can find the pathway into the learner's mind, we can parade an unending cast of characters down that pathway and they will be well received. If, on the other hand, there seems no reason for any of the characters to even be on the path, the mind will remain closed to them. The artful teacher can find openings through which to peak and sustain the level of interest in art and provoke interaction within the classroom.

Photo 9.5
A high school printmaker works with teacher Celeste Ingraffia.

Eli Vonnegut.

Designing curricula that encourage original thought and help learners to break conventional boundaries and engage in creative processes moves beyond the surface understandings often relied upon in unit design. This is artful teaching. To engage in artful teaching, an educator must become facile at thinking about levels of knowing. How deep can we go? What provokes true interest? What tools do students need to want to engage in a more in-depth exploration?

What kind of process do you see yourself using to develop ideas for teaching? How can you learn to go beyond the obvious to find exciting challenges for students?

The teaching process is continuous—we grow each time we encounter and solve a new problem. We learn with and from our students. Whether it is giving a thorough materials demonstration, providing a format for critical discussion, or sharing a search for information about art, artful teachers are in a mode of ongoing personal development.

How Do Art Teachers Create a Context for Meaning?

Meaning is never singular. It is derived from understanding the interrelatedness of actions, ideas, beliefs, perceptions, information, symbols, and a variety of other stimuli. Fowler (1994) addressed the need for a variety of ways to "represent, interpret, and convey our world" because no one subject can do all this. Humans have a need for many symbol systems to help them sort through all the information encountered from various sources. Fowler goes on to say that the purpose of the arts is "not to convey data but to supply insight and wisdom—in a word, *meaning*" (p. 7).

Making connections between visual statements and verbal information increases perceptual understanding. "Seeing" becomes a synthesis between mental and physical images, a way of personalizing and directly relating information to the learner. A curriculum that provides only one way of seeing and favors the use of the linguistic, logical/mathematical intelligences ignores the formation of varied symbol systems and precludes visual ways of knowing. Chomsky (1972) talked about "surface structures" and "deep structures" of language. According to him, a surface structure of language can be defined as that which we can see and hear whether we understand the language or not. The deep structure is where the meaning resides in the minds of language users. Visual symbols help us to interpret the meaning that resides in the deep structure of communities and cultures whose words we may not understand.

Making art is a way of organizing, reorganizing, constructing, and reconstructing, searching, and researching ideas. Finding meaning in a complex world is something all children struggle with. Symbolic meanings shape our thoughts and perceptions and structure knowing. Art symbolization is personal and global, interpretive and straightforward—a way of making meaning that is relevant to all students. We are constantly exposed to videos, billboards, graphic advertisements, and contrived costuming and makeup—layers of meaning are embedded in the visual messages that surround us. People who have keenly developed the ability to determine the difference between the appeal of appearance and true substance are less susceptible to making faulty judgments about what they see. We can teach learners to find and discern the quality of meaning in commercial visual messages (Simpson, 1991).

As artful teachers, we can "improve balances between cognitive studies and affective experiences in ways that make a child's school contacts with the arts coher-

Photo 9.6
Organizing and reorganizing is part of working with collage. Samantha Minor is engaged in helping her students through this process.

Jonna Meyler.

ent, enabling and consistent with community values" (Baker, 1991b). We can help learners to find meaning in a very complex visual world as well as a mode with which to express and communicate their own worldly messages.

Forming a Personal Agenda Toward the Creation of Meaning

Creating meaningful experiences in the classroom will require further preparation, continual and ongoing professional involvement, and growth. We cannot overstate the importance of continually observing and examining events in the classroom, collecting and analyzing children's artwork for programmatic assessment, visiting other schools, and joining professional associations. Keeping a journal, from the first day you enter the classroom as a teacher, provides you with a base of experiences on which to reflect. One student completing the preservice professional sequence in art education stated, "To be a good teacher or good in any field of work, you need to be constantly learning and using what you learn."

In addition to being a researcher, you must be a continual learner. A series of art education students' thoughts on this subject exhibit the commitment to becoming an artful teacher who constructs meaningful learning situations for learners:

> I don't feel that my education is finished at this point. Life is a learning experience but will not be enough (in school, on the job, training). It is important to keep up with the times,

Photo 9.7
Teacher Bridget Warner inter-acts with elementary learners.

Marianne Kerlavage.

and always try new and different things. That means I'm going to have to take more classes, workshops, etc., to continue to be a good teacher and well informed. (student #1)

In other words, developing as a teacher and artist is a lifelong task, if one is to achieve true artistry. (student #2)

How can you expand your base of experiences with children and young people? Observations are generally required as part of your coursework. Beyond simply observing, the most beneficial training you can have involves practical, hands-on experience that requires you to interact with learners and to make decisions while working with them. Comments made by students corroborate this statement:

Another area which I regret I did not seek further knowledge of is secondary education. I only observed a high school situation for six hours. I do not feel that I know nearly enough about secondary schools and students in them. I have been seeking readings on my own, just so I can get a better idea of what to expect. (student #1)

I wish I had more experience in dealing with students at the high school level. It has been a few years since I was in high school and it is easy to forget what is important to students at this age. (student #2)

It took me a while to get into saying things in the manner that a young child could understand [in reference to an eight-week prepracticum in a second-grade classroom]. I need to make lessons more age appropriate. I may be going to a high school for my first placement. I'm going to practice by talking with high schoolers. I need practice presenting materials and ideas to spark interest in an older crowd. (student #3)

You can gain experience working with children in community settings other than schools. Most organizations welcome volunteers who can engage people in learning experiences. Familiarizing yourself with children's behavior, their primary interests, and their levels of ability helps you to be less apprehensive about following through with your teaching plans. Having confidence about your learners' needs provides a basis for the construction of meaningful units and lessons.

Joining and participating in professional organizations is a way of gaining additional experiences about how teachers teach and learners learn. Learning styles vary. There are many ways of approaching learning problems. Presentations by other professionals often provide a fresh view of an old problem. Reading professional journals and doing some of your research in the classroom may also increase your knowledge base about teaching. Researching requires specific observations and practical interaction with learners. Directing research questions to a population that you feel you have had a little experience with will benefit you greatly. Such action goes beyond the passive observation and requires your participation for meaning. What additional experiences about how teachers teach and learners learn might you need?

Most undergraduate programs are structured to provide art education majors with a variety of two- and three-dimensional studio courses. It can be difficult for someone who is not an art major to take studios during the academic year. During the summer and in lifelong learning programs, drawing, painting, and sculpting classes are often available. If you are a classroom teacher, you may wish to take advantage of nontraditional programs that do not require graduate status to increase your knowledge of art-making techniques. Using your studio strengths and developing areas that will enhance your ability to be a well-informed teacher will help you to design meaningful, elegant problems for learners. What do you consider the strengths of a good teacher? What characteristics of a good teacher would you like to develop?

Photo 9.8
A student works on a self-portrait under the direction of teacher Glen Weisberger.

Karen Carroll.

When asked "What, if anything, do you wish you had done before you begin to student teach?" many art education majors voiced concerns about their studio backgrounds:

> I plan on taking ceramics in the summer after student teaching in hopes that I can build . . . experience to teach my students ceramics and sculpture. (student #1)
>
> I wish I had taken another photography class to increase my knowledge in that area. . . . I would [also] like to know more about the [art software] computer programs. (student #2)
>
> I wish I had ceramics and more painting, drawing, and weaving. (student #3)

The building of studio skills is an ongoing process and need not be accomplished only in formal graduate programs. You might work out, in a variety of media, the same problems you design for your students. If the assignment is a fertile one, it can be accomplished at any grade level or level of expertise. How many ways can you find to solve your assigned visual problems? How can doing this help both you and your students?

The Meaning of *Teacher*

The following is a philosophical statement from M. Siefert, an art education student teacher:

> I remember being a student, sitting in the same seats that I look upon now. The feeling of anxiousness crept into every bone in my little body as I wondered what each day would bring. Would I travel to a distant land or search for a far away star? It didn't really matter where I ended up because I knew that I had the most special of all teachers to take me there. In that teacher, I placed my thoughts, questions and problems. As I was challenged to think, answer and solve on my own, I realized I was becoming an individual. I was growing up.
>
> Education is not only what we learn in class. It is about what we do with our knowledge after we leave those little desks and journey on to the next grade. Education is not only about the knowledge we've gained, but also the source from which this knowledge emerged . . . the TEACHER.

Teacher as Artist

Teacher as artist is an appropriate metaphor. Each time we encounter a new class, we must approach it much the same as we would a blank canvas. We need to select and organize our thoughts. An artist makes the decision where to place the first line or dot of color or add the first piece of clay to a maquette. Teachers must think about all the possibilities in, all the ramifications of, all the pitfalls in making decisions about planning for the first meeting with new learners.

The teaching and artistic processes continue to be similar. Each confrontation with the canvas and meeting with the learner requires decision making, reflection, organization, flexibility, openness to new information, singular dedication, and the desire to communicate effectively. Just as artists have shared information through visual expression, teachers share through a synthesis of verbal and visual languages. Just as artists leave their mark upon society, teachers make theirs on their students. Both artists and teachers make deliberate choices to become makers of meaning.

Throughout this book you have been challenged to interact with the information presented in a personal, reflective manner. The questions posed have given you much to think about and can continue to be asked as you become a teacher of art.

Photo 9.9
Demonstrating the process of sculpting with wire is teacher Linda Kies.

Marianne Kerlavage.

Time and experience always change our ideas. The purpose of this book is to provide you with a source you can revisit frequently to find new meaning that is pertinent to current situations. An artist often builds on past images to create new meaning—an artful teacher must do the same.

ANNOTATED RESOURCES

Arnheim, R. (1969). *Visual thinking.* Berkeley, CA: University of California Press.
  The importance of perception and perceptual processes in how people think is viewed from the perspectives of art, science, and psychology.

Arnheim, R. (1986). *New essays on the psychology of art.* Berkeley, CA: University of California Press.
  This is a series of essays that explore the role of perception in the cognitive construction of the real world.

Chomsky, N. (1972). *Language and mind.* New York: Harcourt.
  In this book, Chomsky examines linguistic structures and meaning.

Dewey, J. (1934). *Art as experience.* New York: Perigree.
  This is a seminal work on the impact of the relationship between the formal structures of the visual arts and humanity.

Sarason, S. (1990). *The challenge of art to psychology.* New Haven, CT: Yale University Press.
  Seymour Sarason makes a strong case for art education by providing reasons why all people should have opportunities to develop their natural artistic abilities.

APPENDIX A

*National Visual Arts Standards**

1. **Content Standard: Understanding and applying media, techniques, and processes**

Achievement Standards Grades K–4:

Students

a. know the difference between materials, techniques, and processes

b. describe how different materials, techniques, and processes cause different responses

c. use different media, techniques, and processes to communicate ideas, experiences, and stories

d. use art materials and tools in a safe and responsible manner

Achievement Standards Grades 5–8:

Students

a. select media, techniques, and processes; analyze what makes them effective or not effective in communicating ideas; and reflect upon the effectiveness of their choices

b. intentionally take advantage of the qualities and characteristics of art media, techniques, and processes to enhance communication of their experiences and ideas

c. use art materials and tools in a safe and responsible manner

Achievement Standards, Proficient, Grades 9–12:

Students

a. apply media, techniques, and processes with sufficient skill, confidence, and sensitivity that their intentions are carried out in their artwork

b. conceive and create works of visual art that demonstrate an understanding of how the communication of their ideas relates to the media, techniques, and processes they use

c. use art materials and tools in a safe and responsible manner

Achievement Standards, Advanced, Grades 9–12:

Students

d. communicate ideas regularly at a high level of effectiveness in at least one visual arts medium

e. initiate, define, and solve challenging visual arts problems independently using intellectual skills such as analysis, synthesis, and evaluation

f. use art materials and tools in a safe and responsible manner

2. Content Standard: Using knowledge of structures and functions

Achievement Standards Grades K–4:

Students

a. know the differences among visual characteristics and purposes of art in order to convey ideas

b. describe how different expressive features and organizational principles cause different responses

c. use visual structures and functions of art to communicate ideas

Achievement Standards Grades 5–8:

Students

a. generalize about the effects of visual structures and functions and reflect upon these efforts in their own work

b. employ organizational structures and analyze what makes them effective or not effective in the communication of ideas

c. select and use the qualities of structures and functions of art to improve communication of their ideas

Achievement Standards, Proficient, Grades 9–12:

Students

a. demonstrate the ability to form and defend judgments about the characteristics and structures to accomplish commercial, personal, communal, or other purposes of art

b. evaluate the effectiveness of artworks in terms of organizational structures and functions

c. create artworks that use organizational principles and functions to solve specific visual arts problems

Achievement Standards, Advanced, Grades 9–12:

Students

d. demonstrate the ability to compare two or more perspectives about the use of organizational principles and functions in artwork and to defend personal evaluations of these perspectives

e. create multiple solutions to specific visual arts problems that demonstrate competence in producing effective relationships between structural choices and artistic functions

f. create artworks that use organizational principles and functions to solve specific visual arts problems

3. **Content Standard: Choosing and evaluating a range of subject matter, symbols, and ideas**

Achievement Standards Grades K–4:

Students

a. explore and understand prospective content for works of art

b. select and use subject matter, symbols, and ideas to communicate meaning

Achievement Standards Grades 5–8:

Students

a. integrate visual, spatial, and temporal concepts with content to communicate intended meaning in their artwork

b. use subjects, themes, and symbols that demonstrate knowledge of contexts, values, and aesthetics that communicate intended meaning in artworks

Achievement Standards, Proficient, Grades 9–12:

Students

a. reflect on how artworks differ visually, spatially, temporally, and functionally, and describe how these are related to history and culture

b. apply subjects, symbols, and ideas in their artworks and use the skills gained to solve problems in daily life

Achievement Standards, Advanced, Grades 9–12:

Students

c. describe the origins of specific images and ideas and explain why they are of value in their artwork and in the work of others

d. evaluate and defend the validity of sources for content and the manner in which subject matter, symbols, and images are used in the students' works and in significant work by others

4. **Content Standard: Understanding the visual arts in relation to history and culture**

Achievement Standards Grades K–4:

Students

a. know that the visual arts have both a history and specific relationships to various cultures

b. identify specific works of art as belonging to particular cultures, time, and places

c. demonstrate how history, culture, and the visual arts can influence each other in making and studying works of art

Achievement Standards Grades 5–8:

Students

a. know and compare the characteristics of artworks in various eras and cultures

b. describe and place a variety of art objects in historical and cultural contexts

c. analyze, describe, and demonstrate how factors of time and place (such as climate, resources, ideas, and technology) influence visual characteristics that give meaning and value to a work of art

Achievement Standards, Proficient, Grades 9–12:

Students

a. differentiate among a variety of historical and cultural contexts in terms of characteristics and purposes of works of art

b. describe the function and explore the meaning of specific art objects within varied cultures, times, and places

c. analyze relationships of works of art to one another in terms of history, aesthetics, and culture, justifying conclusions made in the analysis and using such conclusions to inform their own art making

Achievement Standards, Advanced, Grades 9–12:

Students

d. analyze and interpret artworks for relationships among form, context, purposes, and critical models, showing understanding of the work of critics, historians, aestheticians, and artists

e. analyze common characteristics of visual art evident across time and among cultural/ethnic groups to formulate analyses, evaluations, and interpretations of meaning

f. analyze relationships of works of art to one another in terms of history, aesthetics and culture, justifying conclusions made in the analysis, and using such conclusions to inform their own art making

5. **Content Standard: Reflecting upon and assessing the characteristics and merits of their work and the work of others**

Achievement Standards Grades K–4

Students

a. understand there are various purposes for creating works of visual art

b. describe how people's experiences influence the development of specific artworks

c. understand there are different responses to specific artworks

Achievement Standards Grades 5–8:

Students

a. compare multiple purposes for creating works of art

b. analyze contemporary and historic meanings in specific artworks through cultural and aesthetic inquiry

c. describe and compare a variety of individual responses to their own artworks and to artworks from various eras and cultures

Achievement Standards, Proficient, Grades 9–12:

Students

a. identify intentions of those creating artworks, explore the implications of various purposes, and justify their analyses of purposes in particular works

b. describe meanings of artworks by analyzing how specific works are created and how they relate to historical and cultural contexts

c. reflect analytically on various interpretations as a means for understanding and evaluating works of visual art

Achievement Standards, Advanced, Grades 9–12:

Students

d. correlate responses to works of art with various techniques for communicating meanings, ideas, attitudes, views, and intentions

e. describe meanings of artworks by analyzing how specific works are created and how they relate to historical and cultural contexts

f. reflect analytically on various interpretations as a means for understanding and evaluating works of visual art

6. **Content Standard: Making connections between visual arts and other disciplines**

Achievement Standards Grades K–4:

Students

a. understand and use similarities and differences between characteristics of the visual arts and other arts disciplines

b. identify connections between the visual arts and other disciplines in the curriculum

Achievement Standards Grades 5–8:

Students

a. compare the characteristics of works in two or more art forms that share similar subject matter, historical periods, or cultural context

b. describe ways in which the principles and subject matter of other disciplines taught in the school are interrelated with the visual arts

Achievement Standards, Proficient, Grades 9–12:

Students

a. compare the materials, technology, media, and processes of the visual arts with those of other arts disciplines as they are used in creation and types of analysis

b. compare characteristics of visual arts within a particular period or style with ideas, issues, or themes in the humanities or sciences

Achievement Standards, Advanced, Grades 9–12:

Students

c. synthesize the creative and analytical principles and techniques of the visual arts and selected other arts disciplines, the humanities, or the sciences

d. compare the materials, technology, media, and processes of the visual arts with those of other art disciplines as they are used in creation and types of analysis

References

Abbott, J. (1997). To be intelligent. *Educational Leadership, 54*(6), 6–10.

Ackerman, D. (1991). *A natural history of the senses.* New York: Vintage Books.

Anderson, R. (1989). *Art in small scale societies* (2nd ed.). Englewood Cliffs, NJ: Prentice Hall.

Anderson, T. (1988). Interpreting works of art as social metaphors. *Visual Arts Research, 5*(2), 42–51.

Applebee, A. N. (1978). *The child's concept of story.* Chicago: University of Chicago Press.

Appler, S. A. (1995). The need for heritage education: A case study (unpublished master's project, State University of New York College at Buffalo, Buffalo, NY).

Arieti, S. (1976). *Creativity: The magic synthesis.* New York: Basic Books.

Armstrong, T. (1994). *Multiple intelligences in the classroom.* Alexandria, VA: Association for Supervision and Curriculum Development.

Arnheim, R. (1962). *The genesis of a painting: Picasso's Guernica.* Berkeley, CA: University of California Press.

Arnheim, R. (1969). *Visual thinking.* Berkeley, CA: University of California Press.

Arnheim, R. (1974). *Art and visual perception.* Berkeley, CA: University of California Press.

Arnheim, R. (1986). *New essays on the psychology of art.* Berkeley, CA: University of California Press.

Arnheim, R. (1989). *Thoughts on art education.* Los Angeles: The Getty Foundation.

Arnheim, R. (1992). *To the rescue of art: Twenty-six essays.* Berkeley, CA: University of California Press.

Asaro, M. (1994, April). *Artists teachers concerned.* Paper presented at the State University of New York College at Buffalo, Buffalo, NY.

Aukerman, R. (1991, April). Turned on by Turner. *School Arts,* pp. 28–29.

Aukerman, R. (1992, April). Children's art from fine art. *School Arts,* pp. 30–32.

Aukerman, R. (1993, October). Learning from della Robbia. *School Arts,* pp. 18–19.

Aukerman, R. (1994). *Move over Picasso.* New Windsor, MD: Pat Depke Books.

Baker, D. W. (1989). Personal communication. Milwaukee: University of Wisconsin.

Baker, D. W. (1991a). *An inquiry into the role of the visual arts in early childhood.* Milwaukee: University of Wisconsin Press.

Baker, D. W. (1991b). What is an art education for? In K. L. Carroll (Ed.), *What Is Art For? Keynote Addresses, 1991 NAEA Convention* (pp. 5–13). Reston, VA: National Art Education Association.

Baker, D. W. (1994). Toward a sensible art education: Inquiring into the role of the visual arts in early childhood education. *Visual Arts Research, 20*(2), 92–104.

Baker, D. W. (1995). Art and cognitive development. *Visual Arts Research, 21*(2), 37–42.

Baker, D., & Kerlavage, M. (1989). *Children's preferences in art images.* Unpublished research. Milwaukee: University of Wisconsin.

Ballard, K. (1995). Life tellers: An excursion into contemporary Aboriginal art. Unpublished unit and lesson plans. Southwest Missouri State University.

Banks, J. A. (1994). Transforming the mainstream curriculum. *Educational Leadership, 51*(8), 4–8.

Barker, E. (1995). Artifacts. Unpublished unit and lesson plan. Lebanon, MO: Lebanon High School.

Barrett, T. (1994). Principles for interpreting art. *Art Education, 47*(8), 13.

Barth, Britt-Mari. (1991). From practice to theory: Improving the thinking process. In S. Maclure & P. Davies (Eds.), *Learning to Think, Thinking to Learn* (pp. 147–170). New York: Pergamon Press.

Barth, J. (1995, March). Stories of our lives. *The Atlantic Monthly,* pp. 96–110.

Bartolome, L. I. (1994). Beyond the methods fetish: Towards a humanizing pedagogy. *Harvard Educational Review, 64,* 173–194.

Bateson, G. (1979). *Mind and nature.* London: Fontana.

Battin, M. P. (1994). Cases for kids: Using puzzles to teach aesthetics to children. In R. Moore (Ed.), *Aesthetics for Young People* (pp. 89–104). Reston, VA: American Society for Aesthetics, *Journal of Aesthetic Education,* and the National Art Education Association.

Battin, M. P., Fisher, J., Moore, R., & Silvers, A. (1989). *Puzzles about art: An aesthetics casebook.* New York: St. Martin's Press.

Beittel, K. R., & Burkhardt, R. C. (1963). Strategies of spontaneous, divergent, and academic art students. *Studies in Art Education, 5*(1), 20–41.

Bennett, W. J. (Ed.). (1993). *The book of virtues.* New York: Simon & Schuster.

Berk, L. (1994). *Child development* (3rd ed.). Boston: Allyn and Bacon.

Bettelheim, B. (1977). *The uses of enchantment.* New York: Vintage.

Binder, J. (Ed.). (1994). *Ultimate visual dictionary.* London: Dorling Kindersley.

Bloom, B. (1985). *Developing talent in young people.* New York: Ballantine Books.

Boas, F. (1955). *Primitive art.* New York: Dover.

Brandt, R. (1990). On learning styles: A conversation with Pat Guild. *Educational Leadership, 48*(2), 10–15.

Brooks, J. G., & Brooks, M. G. (1993). *The case for constructivist classrooms.* Reston, VA: Association for Supervision and Curriculum Development.

Broudy, H. (1987). *The role of imagery in learning.* Los Angeles: The Getty Center for Education in the Arts.

Brown, M., & Korzenik, D. (1993). *Art making and education.* Chicago: University of Chicago Press.

Bruner, J. (1986). *Actual minds, possible worlds.* Cambridge, MA: Harvard University Press.

Burton, J. (1980a, September). Beginnings of artistic language. *School Arts,* pp. 6–12.

Burton, J. (1980b, October). The first visual symbols. *School Arts,* pp. 60–65.

Burton, J. (1980c, November). Visual events. *School Arts,* pp. 58–64.

Burton, J. (1980d, December). Representing experience from imagination and observation. *School Arts,* pp. 26–30.

Burton, J. (1992). Art education and the plight of the culture: A status report. *Art Education, 45*(1), 7–18.

Buser, T. (1995). *Experiencing art around us.* St. Paul, MN: West Publishing.

Buzan, T., & Buzan, B. (1996). *The mind map book: How to use radiant thinking to maximize your brain's untapped potential.* New York: Plume.

Byrne, D. (1986). *True stories.* New York: Penguin.

Caine, R. N., & Caine, G. (1991). *Making connections: Teaching and the human brain.* Alexandria, VA: Association for Supervision and Curriculum Development.

Cairney, T. (1997). New avenues to literacy. *Educational Leadership, 54*(6), 76–77.

Caldwell, H., & Moore, B. (1991). The art of writing: Drawing as preparation for narrative writing in the primary grades. *Studies in Art Education, 32*(4), 207–219.

Cambourne, B., & Turbill, J. (1991). *Coping with chaos.* Portsmouth, NH: Heinemann.

Campbell, D. T. (1960). Blind variation and selective retention in creative thought as in other knowledge processes. *Psychological Review, 67,* 380–400.

Cardellichio, T., & Field, W. (1997). Seven strategies that encourage neural branching. *Educational Leadership, 54*(6), 33–36.

Carroll, K. (1987). Towards a fuller conception of giftedness: Art in gifted education and the gifted in art education. *Dissertations Abstracts International,* 4807A. (University Microfilms No. 8721089).

Carroll, K. (1994). Artistic beginnings: The work of young Edvard Munch. *Studies in Art Education, 36*(1), 7–17.

Case, R. (1985). *The mind's staircase.* Hillsdale, NJ: Erlbaum.

Cassirer, E. (1972). *An essay on man.* New York: Harper and Brothers.

Chi, M., Feltovich, P., & Glaser, R. (1981). Categorization and representation of physics problems by experts and novices. *Cognitive Science, 5,* 121–152.

Chomsky, N. (1969). *The acquisition of syntax in children from five to ten.* Cambridge, MA: MIT Press.

Chomsky, N. (1972). *Language and mind.* New York: Harcourt.

Chomsky, N. (1976). *Reflections of language.* London: Temple Smith.

Claggett, F., & Brown, J. (1992). *Drawing your own conclusions: Graphic strategies for reading, writing and thinking.* Portsmouth, NH: Heinemann.

Coles, R. (1989). *The call of stories.* Boston: Houghton Mifflin.

College Board. (1994). The College Board profile of SAT and achievement test takers for 1990, 1991, 1992, 1993. Princeton, NJ: Author.

Collins, G. (1987). Feminist approaches to art education. *Journal of Aesthetic Education, 42*(1), 83–94.

Collins, G., & Sandell, R. (1988). Informing the promise of DBAE: Remember the women, children, and other folk. *Journal of Multicultural and Cross-Cultural Research in Education, 6*(1), 55–63.

Cooney, W., Cross, C., & Trunk, B. (1993). *From Plato to Piaget.* New York: University Press of America.

Cornell, J. (1994). *Mandala: Luminous symbols for healing.* Wheaton, IL: Quest.

Corrin, L. (1992). Information sheet for Mining the Museum Exhibition. Baltimore, MD: The Museum for Contemporary Art and the Maryland Historical Society.

Cremin, L. (1988). *American education: The metropolitan experience 1846–1980.* New York: Harper & Row.

Csikszentmihalyi, M. (1982). Learning, "flow," and happiness. In R. Gross (Ed.), *Invitation to Lifelong Learning* (pp. 167–187). Chicago: Follett.

de Groot, A. (1965). *Thought and choice in chess.* New York: Basic Books.

Delaney, J. M. (1992). Images and experiences: Issues, theories, and methods concerning the curricular use of the art object (unpublished doctoral dissertation, University of Wisconsin, Milwaukee).

Dewey, J. (1910/1991). *How we think.* Buffalo, NY: Prometheus Books.

Dewey, J. (1934). *Art as experience.* New York: Perigree.

Dickie, G., Sclafani, R., & Roblin, E. (Eds.). (1989). *Aesthetics: A critical anthology.* New York: St. Martin's Press.

Dissanayake, E. (1988). *What is art for?* Seattle, WA: University of Washington Press.

Dissanayake, E. (1992). *Homo aestheticus: Where art comes from and why.* New York: Free Press.

Dissanayake, E. (1995, January). *Heart, mind, and hand.* Paper presented for the Getty Foundation, Washington, DC.

Dixon, J. P. (1983). *The spatial child.* Springfield, IL: Charles C. Thomas.

Dodson, B. (1985). *Keys to drawing.* Cincinnati, OH: North Light.

Donaldson, A. (1996). Exploring current issues with 19th and 20th century media. Unpublished unit and lesson plans. Southwest Missouri State University.

Dorn, C. (1994). *Thinking in art.* Reston, VA: National Art Education Association.

Dow, A. W. (1899). *Composition.* Boston: J. M. Bowles.

Duckworth, E. (1996). *"The having of wonderful ideas" and other essays on teaching and learning* (2nd ed.). New York: Teachers College Press.

Duncum, P. (1984). How 35 children born between 1724 and 1900 learned to draw. *Studies in Art Education, 26*(2), 93–102.

Dyson, A. H. (1990). Symbol makers, symbol weavers: How children link play, pictures and print. *Young Children, 42*(2), 50–57.

Dyson, A. H., & Genishi, C. (Eds.). (1990). *The need for story: Cultural diversity in classroom and community.* Urbana, IL: National Council of Teachers of English.

Education Development Center (Eds.). (1995). *Designing spaces: Visualizing, planning and building.* Portsmouth, NH: Heinemann.

Edwards, B. (1986). *Drawing on the artist within.* New York: Simon & Schuster.

Edwards, B. (1989). *Drawing on the right side of the brain.* Los Angeles: Tarcher.

Efland, A. (1987). Curriculum antecedents of DBAE. *Journal of Aesthetic Education, 21*(2), 57–94.

Efland, A. D. (1990). *A history of art education.* New York: Teachers College Press.

Eisner, E. (1972). *Educating artistic vision.* New York: Macmillan.

Eisner, E. (1985). *The educational imagination* (2nd ed.). New York: Macmillan.

Eisner, E. (1991). Address to the Secondary Division of the National Art Education Association, Atlanta, GA.

El Koussy, A. A. H. (1935). The visual perception of space. *British Journal of Psychology,* Monograph Supplement, *20,* 1–80.

Engel, M. (1981). The mind, art, and history. *Visual Arts Research, 14,* 4–17.

Engel, S. (1995). *The stories children tell.* Salt Lake City, UT: W. H. Freeman & Company.

Erikson, E. H. (1950). *Childhood and society.* New York: Norton.

Erikson, E. H. (1968). *Identity, youth and crisis.* New York: Norton.

Fearing, K., Beard, E., & Martin, C. I. (1979). *The creative eye* (Vol. 2). Austin, TX: W. S. Benson.

Feinstein, H. (1989). The art response guide: How to read art for meaning, a primer for art criticism. *Art Education, 42*(3), 43–53.

Feldman, E. (1992). *Varieties of visual experience.* Englewood Cliffs, NJ: Prentice Hall.

Feldman, E. (1994). *Practical art criticism.* Englewood Cliffs, NJ: Prentice Hall.

Ferguson, E. S. (1978). The mind's eye: Nonverbal thought in technology. *Educational Horizons, 57*(1), 42–46.

Fincher, S. F. (1991). *Creating mandalas: For insight, healing and self-expression.* Boston: Shambhala.

Finke, R. A. (1985). Theories relating mental imagery to perception. *Psychological Bulletin, 98*(2), 236–259.

Fischer, K. W. (1987). Commentary: Relations between brain and cognitive development. *Child Development, 58,* 623–632.

Fountas, I. C., & Olson, J. L. (1996). Reading the image and viewing the words: languages intertwined. In R. S. Hubbard & K. Earnst (Eds.), *New entries: Learning by writing and drawing* (pp. 84–96). Portsmouth, NH: Heinemann.

Fowler, C. (1994). Strong arts, strong schools. *Educational Leadership, 52*(3), 4–9.

Freud, S. (1974). *The ego and the id.* London: Hogarth. (Originally published 1923)

Gablik, S. (1984). *Has modernism failed?* New York: Thames and Hudson.

Gablik, S. (1991). *The reenchantment of art.* New York: Thames and Hudson.

Gainer, R., & Child, J. (1986). Scientific illustration for the elementary school. *Art Education* (11), 19–22.

Ganson, T. (1996). Comment in museum information sheet. New York: Burchfield-Penney Art Center, Buffalo State University.

Gardner, H. (1980). *Artful scribbles: The significance of children's drawings.* New York: Basic Books.

Gardner, H. (1982). *Art, mind, and brain*. New York: Basic Books.

Gardner, H. (1983). *Frames of mind*. New York: Basic Books.

Gardner, H. (1990). *Art education and human development*. Los Angeles: The Getty Center for Education in the Arts.

Gardner, H. (1991). *The unschooled mind: How children think and how schools should teach*. New York: Basic Books.

Gesell, A. (1933). Maturation and patterning of behavior. In C. Murchison (Ed.), *A Handbook of Child Psychology*. Worcester, MA: Clark University Press.

Getzels, J. W., & Csikszentmihalyi, M. (1964). *Creative thinking in art students: An exploratory study* (Cooperative Research Project No. E-008). Chicago: University of Chicago Press.

Getzels, J. W., & Csikszentmihalyi, M. (1976). *The creative vision: A longitudinal study of problem finding in art*. New York: Wiley.

Ghiselin, B. (1952). *The creative process*. Berkeley, CA: University of California Press.

Gibson, J. J. (1960). Pictures, perspective, and perception. *Daedalus, 89,* 216–227.

Glazer, S. M. (1989). Oral language and literacy development. In D. S. Strickland & L. M. Morrow (Eds.), *Emerging Literacy: Young Children Learn to Read and Write* (pp. 16–26). Newark, DE: International Reading Association.

Goffman, D. (1995). Personal communication.

Goldstein, E. (1986a). Personal communication.

Goldstein, R. (Ed.) (1986b). *Guide to the permanent collection*. Milwaukee, WI: Milwaukee Art Museum.

Goleman, D. (1994). *Emotional intelligence*. New York: Bantam Books.

Golomb, C. (1974). *Young children's sculpture and drawing: A study in representational development*. Cambridge, MA: Harvard University Press.

Golomb, C. (1992). *The child's creation of a pictorial world*. Berkeley, CA: University of California Press.

Gombrich, E. H. (1969). *Art and illusion*. Princeton, NJ: Princeton University Press.

Goodman, N. (1968). *Languages of art: An approach to a theory of symbols*. Indianapolis, IN: Bobbs-Merrill.

Goodman, N. (1988). *Ways of worldmaking*. Indianapolis, IN: Hackett.

Goodnow, J. (1977). *Children drawing*. Cambridge, MA: Harvard University Press.

Gordon, W. J. (1961). *Synectics*. New York: Harper.

Grant, C., & Sleeter, C. (1988). *Making choices for multicultural education: Five approaches to race, class, and gender*. Columbus, OH: Merrill Publishing Company.

Graves, D. H. (1979). Let children show us how to help them write. *Visible Language, 13*(1), 16–28.

Greene, M. (1988). *The dialectic of freedom*. New York: Teachers College Press.

Greene, M. (1992). Texts and margins. In M. R. Goldberg & A. Phillips (Eds.), *Arts as Education* (pp. 1–17), Cambridge, MA: Harvard Educational Review.

Gruber, H. E. (1978). Emotion and cognition: "Aesthetics and science." In S. S. Madeja (Ed.), *The Arts, Cognition, and Basic Skills* (pp. 134–145). St. Louis, MO: CEMREL.

Guild, P. (1994). The culture/learning style connection. *Educational Leadership, 51*(8), 16–21.

Guilford, J. P. (1967). *The nature of human intelligence*. New York: McGraw-Hill Book Company.

Hale-Benson, J. (1986). *Black children: Their roots, cultures, and learning styles*. Baltimore, MD: Johns Hopkins University.

Hall, E. T. (1966). *The hidden dimension*. Garden City, NY: Doubleday.

Hamilton, C. M. (1993). Drawing across the curriculum: A study of the uses of drawing in an elementary school (unpublished doctoral dissertation, University of Wisconsin, Milwaukee).

Hanks, K., & Belliston, L. (1992). *Draw! A visual approach to thinking, learning and communication*. Los Altos, CA: Crisp.

Hart, L. M. (1991). Aesthetic pluralism and multicultural art education. *Studies in Art Education, 32*(3), 145–159.

Hatch, T. (1997). Getting specific about multiple intelligence. *Educational Leadership, 54*(6), 26–29.

Healy, J. M. (1990). *Endangered minds: Why our children don't think*. New York: Touchstone.

Henley, D. (1992). *Exceptional children, exceptional art: Teaching art to special needs*. Worcester, MA: Davis Publications.

Herman, G. N., & Hollingsworth, P. (1992). *Kinetic kaleidoscope: Exploring movement and energy in the visual arts*. Tucson, AZ: Zephyr.

Hessinger, J. (1995). Displaced vulnerability: A unit for secondary learners. Paper written at State University of New York, Buffalo, New York.

Hjerter, K. G. (1986). *Doubly gifted: The author as visual artist*. New York: Harry N. Abrams.

Hobbs, J., & Salome, R. (1991). *The visual experience*. Worcester, MA: Davis Publications.

Hood, G. A. (1995). *Keeping our stories alive: An exhibition of the arts and crafts from Dene and Inuit of Canada*. Santa Fe, NM: Institute of American Indian Arts Museum.

Hooker, J. (1996). Putt Art. Unpublished unit and lesson plans, Southwest Missouri State University.

Housen, A. (1983). The eye of the beholder: Measuring aesthetic development (unpublished doctoral dissertation, Harvard University Graduate School of Education).

Hubbard, R. (1989a). *Authors of pictures, draughtsmen of words*. Portsmouth, NH: Heinemann.

Hubbard, R. (1989b). Inner designs. *Language Arts,* *66*(2), 119–136.

Huber-Bowen, T. (1993). *Teaching in the diverse classroom: Learner centered activities that work.* Bloomington, IN: National Educational Service.

Hurwitz, A. (1993). *Collaboration in art education.* Reston VA: National Art Education Association.

Hurwitz, A., & Day, M. (1991). *Children and their art.* San Diego, CA: Harcourt Brace Jovanovich.

Hurwitz, A., & El-Bassiouny, M. (1993). *Memory and experience: Thematic drawings by Taiwanese, Oatari and American children.* Cairo: Dar Al-Maaref.

Itten, J. (1963). *Design and form: The basic course at the Bauhaus* (J. Maass, Trans.). New York: Reinhold.

Jacobs, H. H. (1989). *Interdisciplinary curriculum: Design and implementation.* Alexandria, VA: Association for Supervision and Curriculum Development.

Johnson, N. R. (1988). DBAE in cultural relationships. *Journal of Multicultural and Cross-Cultural Research in Art Education, 6*(1), 15–23.

John-Steiner, V. (1985). *Notebooks of the mind: Explorations of thinking.* Albuquerque, NM: University of New Mexico Press.

John-Steiner, V. (1987). *Notebooks of the mind: Explorations of thinking.* New York: Perennial.

Jorgensen, K. L. (1993). *History workshop: Reconstructing the past with elementary students.* Portsmouth, NH: Heinemann.

Kandinsky, W. (1981). *Sounds* (Elizabeth R. Napier, Trans.) New Haven, CT: Yale University Press. (Original work published 1912 by Piper Verlag of Munich)

Kane, F. (1982). Thinking, drawing—Writing, reading. *Childhood Education, 58*(5), 292–297.

Kanevsky, L. S. (1992). The learning game. In P. Klein & A. J. Tannenbaum (Eds.), *To Be Young and Gifted.* Norwood, NJ: Ablex.

Kaufmann, I. (1966). *Art and education in American culture.* New York: Macmillan.

Kay, S. (1989). Differences in figural problem-solving and problem-finding behavior among professional, semi-professional, and non-artists (Doctoral dissertation, Columbia University, 1989). *Dissertation Abstracts International, 50,* 9002552.

Kay, S. (1990). Cognitive theory—An element of design for art education. *Design for Arts Education, 92*(2), 10–20.

Kay, S. (1991). The figural problem solving and problem finding of professional and semiprofessional artists and nonartists. *Creativity Research Journal, 4,* 233–252.

Kay, S. (1994). A method for investigating the creative thought process. In M. A. Runco (Ed.), *Problem Finding, Problem Solving, and Creativity* (pp. 116–129). Norwood, NJ: Ablex.

Kay, S. (n.d.). *Assessing qualities of artistic talent.* Unpublished manuscript.

Keefe, J. W., & Ferrell, B. G. (1990). Developing a defensible learning style paradigm. *Educational Leadership, 48*(2), 57–61.

Kellogg, R. (1967). *The psychology of children's art.* New York: Avon Books.

Kellogg, R. (1969). *Children's drawings/children's minds.* New York: Avon Books.

Kellogg, R. (1970). *Analyzing children's art.* Palo Alto, CA: Mayfield Publishing Company.

Kent, C., & Steward, J. (1992). *Learning by heart.* New York: Bantam.

Kerlavage, M. (1995a). A bunch of naked ladies and a tiger: Children's responses to adult works of art. In C. Thompson (Ed.), *The Visual Arts and Early Childhood Learning.* Reston, VA: National Art Education Association.

Kerlavage, M. (1995b). *Art development and cultural constraint.* Reston, VA: National Art Education Association.

Kirby, D., & Kuykendall, C. (1991). *Mind matters: Teaching for thinking.* Portsmouth, NH: Heinemann.

Kissick, J. (1993). *Art: Context and criticism.* New York: Brown & Benchmark.

Kleiman, G. M. (1991). Mathematics across the curriculum. *Educational Leadership, 49*(2), 48–51.

Knapp, M. S. (1995). *Teaching for meaning in high poverty classrooms.* New York: Teachers College Press.

Koestler, A. (1964). *The act of creation.* New York: Macmillan.

Kohlberg, L. (1984). *Essays on moral development: Vol. 2. The psychology of moral development.* San Francisco: Harper & Row.

Kornhabe, M., & Gardner, H. (1991). Critical thinking across multiple intelligences. In S. Maclure & P. Davies (Eds.), *Learning to Think, Thinking to Learn,* pp. 147–170. New York: Pergamon Press.

Kreamer-Schilling, Christine. (1995). Unpublished correspondence.

Krukowski, L. (1990). Contextualism and autonomy in aesthetics. *Journal of Aesthetic Education, 24*(1), 123–134.

Lakoff, G. (1988). Cognitive semantics. In M. Santambrocco & P. Violi (Eds.), *Meaning and Mental Representation,* pp. 119–154. Bloomington IN: Indiana University Press.

Lakoff, G., & Johnson, M. (1980). *Metaphors we live by.* Chicago: University of Chicago Press.

Langer, S. K. (1953a). *Feeling and form.* New York: Charles Scribner's Sons.

Langer, S. K. (1953b). *Philosophy in a new key.* New York: Mentor Books.

Lanier, V. (1981). Popularization without curriculum content for aesthetic literacy. *Art Education, 34*(6), 5–12.

Lanier, V. (1987). A*R*T*, A friendly alternative to DBAE. *Art Education, 40*(9).

Lankford, E. L. (1984). A phenomenological methodology for art criticism. *Studies in Art Education, 25*(3), 151–158.

Lankford, E. L. (1992). *Aesthetics: Issues and inquiry.* Reston, VA: National Art Education Association.

Lazear, D. (1991). *Seven ways of knowing: Teaching for multiple intelligences.* Arlington Heights, IL: IRI Skylight.

Lin, Z. (1996). Personal communication.

Lippard, L. (1990). *Mixed blessings: New art in a multicultural America.* New York: Pantheon Books.

London, P. (1989). *No more secondhand art: Awakening the artist within.* Boston: Shambhala.

London, P. (1994). *Step outside: Community-based art education.* Portsmouth, NH: Heinemann.

Lowenfeld, V. (1947). *Creative and mental growth.* New York: Macmillan.

Lowenfeld, V. (1952). *Creative and mental growth* (2nd ed.). New York: Macmillan.

Lowenfeld, V. (1957). *Creative and mental growth* (3rd ed.). New York: Macmillan.

Marsh, M. M. (1993). The use of picture books in the art room: A means of establishing aesthetic awareness as proposed by discipline-based art education (unpublished master's project, State University of New York College at Buffalo, Buffalo, New York).

Martin, J. (1991). *Sketching school.* Pleasantville, NY: Reader's Digest.

Mazur, A. (1991). *The Salamander Room.* New York: Knopf.

McCarthy, B. (1981). *The 4 MAT system: Teaching to learning styles with right and left mode techniques.* Barrington, IL: Excel.

McConnell, S. (1993). Talking drawings: A strategy for assisting learners. *Journal of Reading, 36*(4), 260–269.

McKim, R. J. (1980). *Thinking visually.* Belmont, CA: Wadsworth.

McLean, M. A. (1987). *Mary Anne's garden drawings & writings.* New York: Abrams.

Meier, N. C. (1939). Factors in artistic aptitude: Final summary of a ten-year study of special ability. *Psychological Monographs, 5*, pp. 140–158.

Meisler, M. (1994, April). *The drop-ins.* Paper presented at State University of New York at Buffalo, Buffalo, NY.

Mitchell, W. J. T. (1986). *Iconology: Image, text, ideology.* Chicago: University of Chicago Press.

Moscati, F. (1993). Is Nintendo's "addiction" based on learning theory? *Education Week, 12*(39), 1.

Murray, D. (1984). *Write to learn.* New York: Holt, Rinehart & Winston.

Nadaner, D. (1985). Responding to the image world: A proposal for art curricula. *Art Education, 37*(1), 9–12.

National Art Education Association. (1994). *The national visual arts standards.* Reston, VA: Author.

National Art Education Association. (1995). *Visual arts education reform handbook: Suggested policy perspectives on art content and student learning in art education.* Reston, VA: Author.

Newell, A., & Simon, H. (1972). *Human problem solving.* Englewood Cliffs, NJ: Prentice Hall.

Nunn, K. (1995). Art in your environment. Unpublished unit and lesson plans, Southwest Missouri State University.

Oddleifson, E. (1994). *Seeking quality in our public schools: Helping our children and teachers excel.* Washington, DC: The Center for Arts in the Basic Curriculum, Inc.

O'Fallon, D. (1995). Choices at the intersection of arts and education. *Arts Education Policy Review, 96*(3), 21–27.

Olson, J. (1992). *Envisioning writing: Toward an integration of drawing and writing.* Portsmouth, NH: Heinemann.

OMG, Inc. (with C. Fowler & B. J. McMullan). (1991). *Understanding how the arts contribute to excellent education.* Prepared for the National Endowment for the Arts. Philadelphia: OMG, Inc.

O'Neil, J. (1990). Making sense of style. *Educational Leadership, 48*(2), 4–9.

Panofsky, E. (1972). *Studies in iconology: Humanistic themes in the art of the Renaissance.* New York: Harper & Row, Icon Edition.

Pariser, D. (1985). The juvenelia of Klee, Toulouse-Lautrec and Picasso: A report on the initial stages of research into the development of exceptional graphic artistry. In B. Wilson & H. Hoffa (Eds.), *The History of Art Education.* State College, PA: Pennsylvania State University.

Parsons, M. (1987). *How we understand art: A cognitive account of aesthetic experience.* New York: Cambridge University Press.

Passow, A. H. (1979). A look around and a look ahead. In A. H. Passow (Ed.), *The Gifted and the Talented: Their Education and Development* (pp. 439–456). The Seventy-eighth Yearbook of the National Society for the Study of Education, Part 1. Chicago: University of Chicago Press.

Passow, A. H. (1991). Urban schools a second? or third? time around: Priorities for curricular and instructional reform. *Education and Urban Society, 23*(3), 243–255.

Paston, H. S. (1973). *Learning to teach art.* Lincoln, NE: Professional Educators Publications, Inc.

Patrick, C. (1937). Creative thought in artists. *Journal of Psychology, 4*, 35–73.

Payne, C. M. (1984). *Getting what we ask for: The ambiguity of success and failure in urban education.* Westport, CT: Greenwood.

Perkins, D. N. (1981). *The mind's best work.* Cambridge: Harvard University Press.

Perkins, D. N. (1988). The possibility of invention. In R. J. Sternberg (Ed.), *The Nature of Creativity* (pp. 362–385). Cambridge: Cambridge University Press.

Pflaumer, L., & Thomley, J. (1989). *Journal keeping—Shared.* NAEA presentation handout.

Piaget, J. (1926). *The language and thought of the child.* New York: Harcourt, Brace, and World.

Piaget, J. (1951). *Play, dreams, and imitation in childhood.* New York: Norton.

Piaget, J., & Inhelder, B. (1967). *The child's conception of space.* New York: Norton.

Piaget, J., & Inhelder, B. (1969). *The psychology of the child.* New York: Basic Books.

Preble, D., & Preble, S. (1994). *Artforms* (5th ed.). New York: HarperCollins College Publishers.

Read, H. (1956). *Education through art* (rev. ed.). New York: Pantheon.

Reitman, W. R. (1964). Heuristic decision procedures, open constraints, and the structure of ill-defined problems. In M. W. Shelley & G. L. Bryan (Eds.), *Human Judgements and Optimality* (pp. 282–315). New York: Wiley & Sons.

Rico, G. L. (1983). *Writing the natural way: Using right brain techniques to release your expressive powers.* New York: Thatcher/Perigee.

Risatti, H. (1990). *Postmodern perspectives: Issues in contemporary art.* Englewood Cliffs, NJ: Prentice Hall.

Rodriguiz, C. V. (1984). Impact of the arts on the adolescent of the twentieth century. *Journal of Art Education, 37*(3), 28–30.

Roe, A. (1946). Artists and their work. *Journal of Personality, 15,* 1–40.

Roe, A. (1975). Painters and painting. In I. A. Taylor & J. W. Getzels (Eds.), *Perspectives in creativity* (pp. 157–172). Chicago: Aldine.

Root-Bernstein, R. S. (1985). Visual thinking: The art of imagining reality. *Trans-American Philosophy Society, 75*(6), 50–67.

Root-Bernstein, R. S. (1989). *Discovering.* Cambridge, MA: Harvard University Press.

Roukes, N. (1988). *Design synectics.* Worcester, MA: Davis.

Routman, R. (1991). *Invitations: Changing as teachers and learners K–12.* Portsmouth, NH: Heinemann.

Ruopp, A. (1996, April). Narrative drawing with middle schoolers: A study in personal histories. *School Arts,* 20–21.

Sakatani, K. (1996). *In the box: Designing virtual environments through the arts.* San Mateo, CA, Foster City School. Presentation handout at National Art Education Association Conference.

Samples, B. (1987). *Open mind, whole mind: Parenting and teaching tomorrow's children today.* Rolling Hills Estates, CA: Jalmar Press.

Sarason, S. (1990). *The challenge of art to psychology.* New Haven, CT: Yale University Press.

Scheffler, I. (1977). In praise of the cognitive emotions. *Teachers College Record, 79*(2), 171–186.

Schickedanz, J. (1986). *More than the ABCs: The early stages of reading and writing.* Washington, DC: National Association for the Education of Young Children.

Schiele, E. (1985). *I, eternal child.* (Anselm Hollo, Trans.). New York: Grove Press.

Schiff, B. (1995, June). For Mondrian, art was a path to the universal. *Smithsonian,* 98—107.

Schoenfeld, A. H., & Herrmann, D. J. (1982). Problem perception and knowledge structure in expert and novice mathematical problem solvers. *Journal of Experimental Psychology: Learning, Memory, and Cognition, 8,* 484–492.

Selman, R. (1980). *The growth of interpersonal understanding.* New York: Academic Press.

Simpson, J. W. (1991). Is time a circle or a straight line? *Journal of Art Education, 44*(4), 42–46.

Simpson, J. W. (1995). Choices for urban art education. *Arts Education Policy Review, 96*(6), 27–30. Washington, DC: Helfret Publications.

Simpson, J. W. (1996). Constructivism and connection making. *Journal of Art Education, 49*(1), 53–59.

Sizer, T. (1992). *Horace's school: Redesigning the American high school.* Boston: Houghton Mifflin.

Skinner, B. F. (1957). *Verbal behavior.* New York: Appleton-Century Crofts.

Smith, I. M. (1964). *Spatial ability.* San Diego, CA: Robert R. Knapp.

Spearman, C. (1927). *The abilities of man.* New York: Macmillan.

Stake, R., & Kerr, D. (1995). Rene Magritte, constructivism, and the researcher as interpretor. *Educational Theory, 45*(1), 55–61.

Steiger, J. (1995). *Vincent van Gogh's "Three Pair of Shoes."* Unpublished research paper, Southwest Missouri State University.

Stein, J. (1993, October). Sins of omission. *Art in America,* 110–113.

Stein, M. I. (1974). *Stimulating creativity: Individual procedures.* New York: Academic Press.

Stein, M. I. (1984). *Making the point: Anecdotes, poems, & illustrations for the creative process.* Buffalo, NY: Bearly Limited.

Sternberg, R. J. (1982). *Handbook of human intelligence.* Cambridge: Cambridge University Press.

Sternberg, R. J. (1986). *Intelligence applied.* Orlando, FL: Harcourt Brace Jovanovich.

Sternberg, R. J. (1988). *The nature of creativity.* Cambridge: Cambridge University Press.

Sternberg, R. (1997). What does it mean to be smart? *Educational Leadership*, *54*(6), 20–24.

Stolnitz, J. (1960). *Aesthetics and philosophy of art criticism: A critical introduction*. Boston: Houghton Mifflin.

Stoops, J., & Samuelson, J. (1983). *Design dialogue*. Worcester, MA: Davis.

Striker, S. (1978–1982). *The anti-coloring book* (series). New York: Holt, Rinehart & Winston.

Sylwester, R. (1995). *A celebration of neurons: An educator's guide to the human brain*. Alexandria, VA: Association for Supervision and Curriculum Development.

Szekely, G. (1988). *Encouraging creativity in art lessons*. New York: Teachers College Press.

Tannenbaum, A. J. (1983). *Gifted people*. New York: Macmillan.

Tanner, M. (1984). Artistic reading: Comprehension with a flair. *Art Education*, *37*(1), 17–23.

Taylor, J. H., & Ryan, J. (1995). Museums and galleries on the Internet. *Internet Research: Electronic Networking Applications and Policy*, *5*(1), 80–88.

Tesar, J. (1996). *The Macmillan visual almanac*. Woodbridge, CT: Blackbirch Press.

Thistlewood, D. (Ed.). (1991). *Critical studies in art and design education*. Portsmouth, NH: Heinemann.

Thunder-McGuire, S. (1992). Becoming a field biologist: Louis' artist's bookmaking. *Art Education*, *45*(4), 52–58.

Tolstoy, L. (1960). *What is art?* (Almyer Maude, Trans.). Indianapolis, IN: Bobbs-Merrill. (Original work published 1898)

Torjusen, B. (1986). *Words and images of Edvard Munch*. Chelsea, VT: Chelsea Green Publishing Company.

Townley, M. R. (1978). *Another look* (Teacher's ed.). Reading, MA: Addison-Wesley.

Tufte, E. R. (1994). *Envisioning information*. Cheshire, CT: Graphics.

Uitert, E. (1978). *Van Gogh drawings*. Woodstock, NY: Overlook Press.

Unsworth, J. M. (1995). *Connections: A visual game*. Palo Alto, CA: Dale Seymour.

U.S. Department of Labor, SCANS/The Secretary's Commission on Achieving Necessary Skills. (1991). *What work requires of schools: A SCANS report for America 2000*. Washington, DC: U.S. Government Printing Office.

Van Essen, G., & Hamaker. C. (1990). Using self-generated drawings to solve arithmetic word problems. *Journal of Educational Research*, *83*(6), 301–312.

Volk, T. (1995). *Metapatterns: Across space, time and mind*. New York: Columbia University Press.

Vygotsky, L. S. (1978). *Mind and society: The development of higher order psychological processes*. Cambridge, MA: Harvard University Press.

Vygotsky, L. S. (1986). *Thought and language* (A. Kozulin, Trans.). Cambridge, MA: MIT Press.

Wakefield, J. F. (1992). *Creative thinking: Problem-solving skills and the arts orientation*. Norwood, NJ: Ablex.

Weekly, N. (1993). *Charles E. Burchfield: The sacred woods*. Albany, NY: SUNY Press.

Weimer, M. (Ed.). (1993). Learning styles. *The Teaching Professor*, *7*(4), 4.

Weir, R. H. (1962). *Language in the crib*. Janua Linguarum Series Maior 14. The Hague: Mouton and Co.

Williams, L. V. (1986). *Teaching for the two-sided mind*. New York: Touchstone.

Wilson, B., Hurwitz, A., & Wilson, M. (1987). *Teaching drawing from art*. Worcester, MA: Davis.

Wilson, B., & Olson, J. (1979, September). A visual narrative program—Grades 1–8. *School Arts*, pp. 26–33.

Wilson, B., & Wilson, M. (1982). *Teaching children to draw: A guide for teachers and parents*. Englewood Cliffs, NJ: Prentice Hall.

Winner, E. (1982). *Invented worlds: The psychology of the arts*. Cambridge, MA: Harvard University Press.

Young, A. (1992). The writing/thinking connection. Notes from April lecture and workshop at University of Wisconsin-Milwaukee.

Zahnor, M. (1989). Manuel Barkan: Twentieth-century art educator. In P. M. Amburgy, D. Soucy, M. A. Stankiewicz, B. Wilson, & M. Wilson (Eds.), *The History of Art Education: Proceedings from the Second Penn State Conference, 1989*. Reston, VA: National Art Education Association.

Zeller, T. (1984). Encountering art through study sheets. *School Arts*, *83*(7), 29–33.

Index

Processes, in structuring experiences, 136–138
Prochownik, Walter, 127
Professional organizations, 336
Projects, shaping of, 15. *See also* Problem, elegant
Proportion
  and artistic challenges stage, 54
  in emerging expertise stage, 51
Psychomotor domain, 291
Puns, in visual symbols, 238
"Putt Art," 140–141

Qualitative questions, 110, 114, 274, 288
Quick time movie, 20, 21

Race, Aletha, 326
Rastegar, Monica, 9
Rauschenberg, Robert, 127
Reading/writing learners, 213, 215
Realism, Dawning, 50
Reality, child's comprehension of
  vs. fiction, 180–181
  internal vs. external, 41
Reasoning
  and language, 209
  and words vs. figures, 268
Recording, as strategy function, 227–228
Reflection, 20
  as strategy function, 234, 236
Relativism, cultural, 117, 161
Relevance, 332
Rembrandt, 172
Remington, Frederic, 264
Renaissance art, 126
Representation
  metaphorical, 101, 113
  motivation for, 91
  principles guiding, 91–92
Representational accuracy, 99, 114
Research
  and artful teaching, 336
  school-based, 251–252
Retable of St. Michael and Gargano, 164
Ringgold, Faith, 154, 172, 178, 297
Ritual
  art works in, 117, 119, 120
  and "making special," 120–121
  in our culture, 120
Rivera, Diego, 172, 177
Rubens, Peter Paul, 313, 315
Rubric, 210, 236, 257
  for student assessment, 292

Ruopp, Amy, 14, 81, 82
Rupp, Christy, 128
Rushdie, Salman, 178
Russell, Charles, 212

Salle, 127
Sargent, John Singer, 264
Schedules, time constraints from, 318
Schema, 37, 72, 91, 114
Schiele, Egon, 173
Schnabel, 127
Scholder, Fritz, 178
School-based research, 251–252
School context, 64–66
Science, and artistic strategies, 241–244
Scientists, artistic endeavors of, 270
Scott, Joyce, 128, 178
"Scream, The", 172
Sculpture, 277
  Achilles-heel representation, 314
  and self-portrait assignment, 184, 185, 186, 187
  visual script of, 226
Self-portrait
  by e.e. cummings, 175
  by eighth-grader, 101
  by first grader, 45
  as goal, 63, 64
  monoprint lesson, 64
  by 17-year-old, 25, 27, 28
  by Anne Sexton, 175
  symbolic, 184, 185, 186, 187, 188
  by third-grader, 46
Self-symbols, 233
Semiotic theory, 123, 162
Sensuous materials, 77–78, 114
Sequence, 210, 257
Sequence charts, 210, 211, 239, 256
Sexton, Anne, 174, 175
Shahn, Ben, 172
Shakespeare, William, 165, 172
Shapiro, Miriam, 151
Shared notation, 239–240
Shoe(s)
  Achilles-heel sculpture of, 314
  contour line drawings of, 268, 269
  student's design for, 106
  transformation of, 232
  as van Gogh symbol, 139
Shorthand images, 50
Sight, 102, 104
Sighting techniques, 99, 114
Significant form, 77–78, 114
Silent learning, 279n
Sketch, 210, 219, 222, 236, 257

Slide lecture, 138
Small-scale societies, art in, 117, 120
  and art teacher's learning, 18
Smith, Juane Quick-to-See, 178
Smithson, 154
Social development, 29
  in artistic challenges stage, 57
  and artistic thinking stage, 61
  and early symbol making, 41–42
  and emerging expertise stage, 53
  and mark making, 36
  and symbol making stage, 49
Social dimensions of learning, 263–264
Social issues curriculum, 298–300
Social studies, and artistic strategies, 241–244
Society-centered position, 129
Sociocultural theory, 29
Socioeconomic influences, 67–68
Software. *See also* Computer-based methods
  for data organization, 243
  for quick time movies, 21
Space
  and artistic challenges stage, 54
  and artistic thinking stage, 59
  development of understanding of, 40
  perceived, 267
  and symbol making stage, 44, 46, 47, 48, 49
Special-needs learners, 65, 136
Spreadsheets, 211
Stabnick, Jennifer, 19
Stages of development. *See* Developmental stages
Stage theory, 29
Standards, 6–7
  and artistic challenges stage, 54
  National Visual Arts Standards, 6, 7, 195, 198, 339–343
Starry Night (van Gogh), 95, 138
Steiger, Jamie, 10
Stella, Joseph, 127
Still Life in the Studio (Matisse), 137
Still lifes, as meaningful to students, 193
Story(ies), 163, 205, 330. *See also* Narrative
  by artist-writers, 172–176
  arts as preserving, 165
  and cultural diversity, 178–179
  of friends and classmates, 178
  from other cultures, 172, 176–178
  personal, 11–13, 168
  visual and verbal expression linked in, 179

About the Authors

Judith W. Simpson
An assistant professor of visual arts in the School for the Arts at Boston University, Dr. Simpson holds a B.S. in art education from the University of Hampshire at Durham, an M.S. from Massachusetts College of Art, and a Ph.D. in urban education/art education from the University of Wisconsin-Milwaukee. She has published in *Art Education, Arts Education Policy Review,* and in proceedings from the First National Conference on Urban Issues, *Crossing boundaries: Collaborative solutions to urban problems.* Her main research interests are on making connections between art and the learner's world, between ideas in art and other academic subjects, and their impact on students particularly in urban settings.

Jean M. Delaney
An associate professor in the Department of Art and Design at Southwest Missouri State University, she received her Ph.D. in urban education/art education from the University of Wisconsin-Milwaukee, M.A. in clinical psychology from Loyola College, MD, and B.A. in art education from Fairmont State College, WV. Among her numerous teaching awards, Dr. Delaney was awarded a grant to coordinate the Central Region Crayola Dream-Makers Program, and served as editor of *Art Scholarships* for NAEA and *An Art Program for Students in the Middle School Years* for Baltimore County, MD. Her research interests include using the arts across the curriculum, mentoring at-risk students through art, and engaging learners with art.

Karen Lee Carroll
Currently the graduate director of art education at the Maryland Institute College of Art in Baltimore, Dr. Carroll holds an Ed.D. in art education from Teachers College, Columbia University, an M.Ed. in art education from Pennsylvania State University, and a B.S. in art education from the State University College at Buffalo. Her work has appeared in *Studies in Art Education, Art Education, School Arts,* and in NAEA anthologies on preservice art education and research methodologies. Dr. Carroll has received numerous teaching awards and her research includes the work of Edvard Munch.

Cheryl M. Hamilton
An assistant professor in art education in the School of Art and Design at Wichita State University, she received her B.F.A. in education at the University of Nebraska, M.S. from the University of Tennessee-Knoxville, and Ph.D. in urban education/art education from the University of Wisconsin-Milwaukee. From 1985 to 1990, she directed the Crayola Dream-Makers Program and edited the teachers guide. Dr. Hamilton is responsible for the graphic development of the Kansas visual arts curriculum standard publication. Her research is on the areas of visual communication in grade school classrooms and on the interrelationship between art and other academic disciplines.

Sandra I. Kay
A visiting scholar at Teachers College, Columbia University and the district coordinator of gifted programs at Monroe-Woodbury Central School District, Dr. Kay has an Ed.D. and masters degree in special education from Teachers College, Columbia University, and B.S. and M.S. degrees from the State University of New York at New Paltz. She has published in *School Arts, The Journal of Aesthetic Education, Design for Arts Education, and Teaching Exceptional Children,* and other journals. Her research focuses on developing talent/expertise and the problem-finding aspects of creative thought, visual thinking, and other habits of mind that engage the imagination and promote self-directed inquiry in children and adults.

Marianne S. Kerlavage
Currently the director of art education programs at Millersville University, PA, she received her Ph.D. in urban education/art education from the University of Wisconsin-Milwaukee, masters from Marywood College, and M.Ed. and B.S. from Kutztown University. Dr. Kerlavage has published in *NAEA Anthology on Early Childhood, Visual Arts, Research,* and *Young Children,* and is project director of three Pennsylvania state grants for curriculum development at the public school K-12 and university levels. Her research interests are on extending knowledge in the profession about the growth and development of children and its influence on pedagogical and methodological understanding.

Janet L. Olson
Currently the chair of the Department of Art Education at Boston University School of Art, Dr. Olson received her bachelors degree from St. Olaf College, masters in art education from Boston University, and Ed.D. from Teachers College, Columbia University. She is the author of *Envisioning Writing: Toward an Integration of Drawing and Writing* (Heinemann Press, 1992), and recently co-authored chapters in *New Entries: Learning by Writing and Drawing* (Heinemann Press, 1996) and *A Handbook for Literacy Educators: Research on Teaching the Communicative and Visual Arts* (NCTE, 1997).